ecpr PRESS

practices of interparliamentary coordination in international politics

the European Union and beyond

Edited by
Ben Crum and John Erik Fossum

ecprPRESS

First published by the ECPR Press in 2013

Paperback Edition published by the ECPR Press in 2014

The ECPR Press is the publishing imprint of the European Consortium for Political Research (ECPR), a scholarly association, which supports and encourages the training, research and cross-national cooperation of political scientists in institutions throughout Europe and beyond.

ECPR Press
University of Essex
Wivenhoe Park
Colchester
CO4 3SQ
UK

Typeset by Anvi

Printed and bound by Lightning Source

British Library Cataloguing in Publication Data

A catalogue record for this book is available from the British Library

Paperback ISBN: 978-1-9102593-0-6

Hardback ISBN: 978-1-907301-3-8

www.ecpr.eu/ecprpress

ECPR – *Studies in European Political Science*
Series Editors:
Dario Castiglione (University of Exeter)
Peter Kennealy (European University Institute)
Alexandra Segerberg (Stockholm University)
Peter Triantafillou (Roskilde University)

ECPR – *Studies in European Political Science* is a series of high-quality edited volumes on topics at the cutting edge of current political science and political thought. All volumes are research-based offering new perspectives in the study of politics with contributions from leading scholars working in the relevant fields. Most of the volumes originate from ECPR events including the Joint Sessions of Workshops, the Research Sessions, and the General Conferences.

A Political Sociology of Transnational Europe
ISBN: 9781907301346
Edited by Niilo Kauppi
Europeanisation and Party Politics
ISBN: 9781907301223
Edited by Erol Külahci
Interactive Policy Making, Metagovernance and Democracy
ISBN: 9781907301131
Edited by Jacob Torfing and Peter Triantafillou
Perceptions of Europe
ISBN: 9781907301155
Edited by Daniel Gaxie, Jay Rowell and Nicolas Hubé
Personal Representation: The Neglected Dimension of Electoral Systems
ISBN: 9781907301162
Edited by Josep Colomer
Political Participation in France and Germany
ISBN: 9781907301315
Oscar Gabriel, Silke Keil and Eric Kerrouche
Political Trust: Why Context Matters
ISBN: 9781907301230
Edited by Sonja Zmerli and Marc Hooghe
New Nation-States and National Minorities
ISBN: 9781907301360
Edited by Julian Danero Iglegias, Nenad Stojanović and Sharon Weinblum
The Political Ecology of the Metropolis
ISBN: 9781907301377
Edited by Jefferey Sellers, Daniel Kübler, Alan Walks and Melanie Walter-Rogg

Please visit www.ecpr.eu/ecprpress for up-to-date information about new publications.

| contents

| list of figures and tables

| list of abbreviations

ACP	African, Caribbean and Pacific Group of States
AFSJ	Area of Freedom, Security and Justice
ALDE	Alliance of Liberals and Democrats for Europe
AMISOM	African Union's Mission to Somalia
CCCTB	Common Consolidated Corporate Tax Base
CDA	Dutch Christian-Democratic People's Party (Christen-Democratisch Appél)
CDU	Christian Democratic Union (Christlich Demokratischen Union Deutschlands)
CMC	Crises Management Concept
CONOPS	Concept of Operations
CoOP	Country of Origin Principle
CoR	Committee of the Regions
COSAC	Conference of Parliamentary Committees for Union Affairs (Conférence des Organes Spécialisés dans les Affaires Communautaires)
CPA	Commonwealth Parliamentary Association
CRCT	Crises Response Coordination Team
CSDP	Common Security and Defence Policy (of the EU)
CSU	Christian Social Union of Bavaria (Christlich-Soziale Union)
CU	Dutch Christian Union (ChristenUnie)
DQI	Discourse Quarterly Index
EAC	European Affairs Committee
EC	European Commission
ECB	European Central Bank
ECPRD	European Centre for Parliamentary Research and Documentation
EDC	European Defence Community
EEAS	European External Action Service
EELV	French Europe Ecology - The Greens (Europe Ecologie - Les Verts)
EESC	European Economic and Social Committee

EFSF	European Financial Stability Facility
EFTA	European Free Trade Agreement
EGP	European Green Party
EMPL	EP Committee on Employment and Social Affairs
EP	European Parliament
EPP	European People's Party
EPP-ED	European People's Party-European Democrats
ESM	European Stability Mechanism
EU	European Union
EUMC	EU Military Committee
EUMS	EU Military Staff
EUTM Somalia	EU military Training Mission of Somali security forces in Uganda
EWM	Early Warning Mechanism
FDP	German Free Democratic Party (Freie Demokratische Partei)
FEMM	EP Committee on Women's Rights and Gender Equality
FN	French National Front (Front National)
FNE	France Nature Environment (France Nature Environnement)
FST	Treaty on Stability, Coordination and Governance (Fiscal Stability Treaty)
GATS	General Agreement on Trade in Services
GMO	Genetically Modified Organisms
Greens/EFA	Greens/European Free Alliance
GUE/NGL	European United Left/Nordic Green Left
ID	Independence/Democracy
IMCO	EP Committee for Internal Market and Consumer Protection
IMF	International Monetary Fund
IMO	International Maritime Organization
IPEX	Interparliamentary EU information eXchange
IPU	InterParliamentary Union
JHA	Justice and Home Affairs
JURI	EP Committee on Legal Affairs
LIBE	EP Committee on Civil Liberties, Justice and Home Affairs
MEI	French Independent Ecological Movement (Mouvement Ecologique Indépendant)

MLPF	Multilevel Parliamentary Field
MP	Member of Parliament
MEP	Member of the European Parliament
MoDem	French Democratic Movement (Mouvement Démocratique)
MSOs	Military Strategic Options
NATO	North Atlantic Treaty Organization
NATO-PA	NATO Parliamentary Assembly
NAVCO	EU Naval Coordination Cell
NGO	Non-Governmental Organisation
NP	National Parliament
NPA	French New Anti-Capitalist Party (Nouveau Parti Anti-capitaliste)
OPLAN	Operational Plan
OSCE	Organization for Security and Co-operation in Europe
PA	Parliamentary Assembly
PARLOPOL	Joint committee of members of the European Parliament and national parliaments to oversee Europol
PASD	Progressive Alliance of Socialists and Democrats
PCF	The French Communist Party (Parti Communiste Français)
PES	Party of European Socialists
PPE	Peoples Party of Spain (Partido Popular)
PS	French Socialist Party (Parti Socialiste)
PSC	Political and Security Committee
PvdA	Dutch Labour Party (Partij van de Arbeid)
PVV	Dutch Party for Freedom (Partij Voor de Vrijheid)
RECON	Reconstituting Democracy in Europe
SEDE	EP subcommittee on Security and Defence
SER	Dutch Social and Economic Council (Sociaal-Economische Raad)
SHAPE	Supreme Headquarters Allied Powers Europe (NATO)
SPD	German Social Democratic Party (Sozialdemokratische Partei Deutschlands)
SPÖ	Austrian Social Democratic Party (Sozialdemokratische Partei Österreichs)
SWD	Seasonal Workers Directive
TEU	Treaty on European Union

TRIPS	Trade-Related aspects of Intellectual Property rights
UEN	Union for Europe of the Nations
UMP	French Union for the Presidential Majority (Union pour la Majorité Présidentielle)
UN	United Nations
UNCTAD	United Nations Conference on Trade and Development
VVD	Dutch People's Party for Freedom and Democracy (Volkspartij voor Vrijheid en Democratie)
WEU	Western European Union
WEU-PA	WEU Parliamentary Assembly
WFP	World Food Programme
ÖVP	Austrian People's Party (Österreichische Volkspartei)

| contributors

WILLY BEAUVALLET is a post-doctoral fellow in Political Science, associate member of SAGE laboratory (Societies, Actors and Government in Europe) at the University of Strasbourg. He teaches at the University of Paris I, Panthéon-Sorbonne. Among his recent publications: 'The European Parliament and the politicisation of the European space – the case of the two port packages' (Rowell and Mangenot, 2010); 'Professionalization and socialization of the members of the European Parliament' (*French Politics* 2012, with Sebastien Michon).

ARTHUR BENZ is Professor of Political Science at the Technische Universität Darmstadt, Germany. His recent publications include *Der moderne Staat. Grundlagen der politologischen Analyse* (2008), *Governance and Democracy - Comparing National, European and Transnational Experiences* (2006, ed. with Yannis Papadopoulos), and *Federal Dynamics: Continuity, Change and the Varieties of Federalism* (2013, ed. with Jörg Broschek).

ARON BUZOGÁNY is a post-doctoral fellow at the German Public Administration Research Institute in Speyer. He holds a doctorate in political science from the Freie Universität Berlin. His recent publications on national parliaments in the European Union were published in *Politische Vierteljahresschrift, Zeitschrift für Parlamentsfragen, Zeitschrift für Politikberatung* and *Der moderne Staat*.

IAN COOPER is Senior Researcher at ARENA, Centre for European Studies at the University of Oslo. Currently, his research is focused on the collective role of national parliaments in the European Union. His recent work has appeared in the *Journal of Common Market Studies, West European Politics*, and the *Journal of European Integration.*

BEN CRUM is Associate Professor at the Department of Political Science of the Vrije Universiteit Amsterdam. He works on the political theory of European integration. Among his recent publications are: *Learning from the EU Constitutional Treaty* (Routledge 2012), 'Saving the Euro at the Cost of Democracy' (*Journal of Common Market Studies* 2013) and 'The Multilevel Parliamentary Field - A Framework for Theorising Representative Democracy in the EU' (*European Political Science Review* 2009, with John Erik Fossum).

JOHN ERIK FOSSUM is Professor in Political Science at ARENA, Centre for European Studies at the University of Oslo. He is chair of ECSA Norway, was substitute coordinator of the FP6 project RECON and the FP5 project CIDEL, and is co-director of NORCONE (The Norwegian Constitution in a Changing European Context). Recent publications include: *Rethinking Democracy and the European Union* (2012, co-edited with Erik O. Eriksen); *The Constitution's Gift* (2011, with Agustín Menéndez); and 'The Multilevel Parliamentary Field - A Framework for Theorising Representative Democracy in the EU' (*European Political Science Review* 2009, with Ben Crum).

COSIMA GLAHN currently works as a Junior Policy Advisor for the Strategic Alliances and Partnerships group at the Deutsche Gesellschaft für internationale Zusammenarbeit (GIZ). She holds a BA from the University of Mannheim and an MA in 'International Studies/Peace and Conflict Studies' from the TU Darmstadt and the Johann Wolfgang Goethe University Frankfurt/Main. She was a student research assistant at the Peace Research Institute Frankfurt (PRIF).

VIERA KNUTELSKÁ is Assistant Professor at Charles University in Prague, Faculty of Social Sciences, Institute of Political Studies. She has published various papers on national parliaments, including 'National Parliaments in the Council: Parliamentary Scrutiny Reserves' (*Central European Journal of International & Security Studies* 2013); 'Working Practices Winning Out over Formal Rules: Parliamentary Scrutiny of EU Matters in the Czech Republic, Poland and Slovakia' (*Perspectives on European Politics and Society* 2011); and on EU decision-making, including 'Role of Political Affiliation across the European Institutions in the Dynamics of the EU Legislative Process' (*AUCO Czech Economic Review* 2012, with Radko Hokovský).

CHRISTOPHER LORD is Professor at ARENA, Centre for European Studies at the University of Oslo. He has published extensively on Democracy, Legitimacy and the European Union. His books include *A Democratic Audit of the European Union* (2004).

SÉBASTIEN MICHON is a Senior Researcher at the CNRS (National Centre for Scientific Research) and member of the SAGE laboratory (Societies, Actors and Government in Europe). He teaches at the Institute of Political Sciences in Strasbourg. Recently, he published: 'When Europe Mobilises' (in Gaxie and Hubé (eds), Rowell 2011, with Hubé and Méon) and 'European Parliament: the emergence of specialists of European political work' (in Georgakakis (ed), Rowell 2013, with Willy Beauvallet).

ERIC MIKLIN is Assistant Professor in the Department of Political Science at the University of Salzburg and a fellow at the Salzburg Centre of European Union Studies (SCEUS). Among his publications are 'Government Positions on the EU Services Directive in the Council: National Interests or Individual Ideological Preferences?' (*West European Politics* 2009); 'Inter-parliamentary cooperation in EU affairs and the Austrian Parliament: Empowering the Opposition?' (*Journal of Legislative Studies* 2013); 'EU Politicisation and National Parliaments: Visibility of Choices and Better Aligned Ministers?' (*Journal of Legislative Studies* 2014).

DIRK PETERS is Senior Research Fellow at the Peace Research Institute Frankfurt. He is the author of *Constrained Balancing: The EU's Security Policy* (2010) and co-editor of *The Parliamentary Control of European Security Policy* (with Wolfgang Wagner and Nicole Deitelhoff, 2008).

JOHANNES POLLAK is Professor of Political Science at Webster University Vienna and Head of the Political Science Department at the Institute for Advanced Studies (IHS) in Vienna. Among his recent publications are 'The pitfalls of representation as claims-making' (*Journal of European Integration* 2013); 'Unequal but Democratic? Equality according to Karlsruhe' (*Journal of European Public Policy* 2013). He is also the editor of the WUV/UTB series 'Europa kompakt'.

HILMAR ROMMETVEDT is Head of Research in political science at the International Research Institute of Stavanger (IRIS) and Adjunct Professor at the University of Stavanger, Norway. He is Program Chair of the IPSA Research Committee of Legislative Specialists. His publications include *The Rise of the Norwegian Parliament* (2003), *Politikkens allmenngjøring og den nypluralistiske parlamentarismen* (2nd ed., 2011), and articles in journals such as *Comparative Political Studies, Journal of Legislative Studies, Government and Opposition, Public Management Review, Scandinavian Political Studies, West European Politics* and *World Trade Review*.

DANIEL RUIZ DE GARIBAY is assistant programme specialist at the Social and Human Sciences Unit of UNESCO office in Jakarta, Indonesia. He has been Basque Government Research scholar based at the University of Reading, UK (2008 – 2011) and Schuman Scholar at the European Parliament (2006 – 2007). He has published the following articles on the field of interparliamentary relations: 'Relations between national parliaments and the European Parliament: opportunities and challenges' (Elcano Royal Institute, ARI 153/2011, Madrid); 'El papel de los parlamentos nacionales en la EU y la función de sus oficinas de representación en Bruselas' (Elcano Royal Institute, ARI 53/2010, Madrid); and 'Citizens' Representation in the EU after the 2009 elections to the European Parliament: The Role of National Parliaments' (Elcano Royal Institute, ARI 114/2009, Madrid).

YOAV SHEMER-KUNZ is a PhD candidate in political science at the University of Strasbourg (SAGE laboratory – Societies, Actors and Government in Europe, UMR 7363) and at the Department of Political Science of the Vrije Universiteit Amsterdam. His current research is in interparliamentary and intra-party coordination in Europe as a political opportunity for small political parties.

PETER SLOMINSKI is Assistant Professor at the University of Vienna/ Institute for European Integration Research. Among his recent publications: 'The Ambiguities of Legalization and the EU's Strategy of Extra-Territorial Border Control' (*European Foreign Affairs Review* 2012); 'Agree Now – Pay Later: Escaping the Joint Decision Trap in the Evolution of the EU Emission Trading System' (*Journal of European Public Policy* 2013, with P. Müller); 'The Silence of the Shepherds - How the Austrian Parliament Informs its Citizens on European Issues' (*Journal of Legislative Studies* forthcoming 2014, with J. Pollak).

WOLFGANG WAGNER is Professor of International Security at the Vrije Universiteit Amsterdam. Recently he published *Die demokratische Kontrolle internationalisierter Sicherheitspolitik* (Baden-Baden 2011). His work on the parliamentary control of military missions also appeared in *Parliamentary Affairs, Journal of European Public Policy (*European integration online papers) and *Armed Forces and Society.*

| acknowledgements

Interparliamentary coordination has taken on added importance in today's Europe and the broader international context. This book is based on the workshop, 'Interparliamentary Relations in Europe' that formed part of the 2010 ECPR Joint Sessions in Münster, Germany. The papers that were presented at the workshop have since then been significantly revised and updated. In addition, the book has greatly benefited from the addition of several important and topical chapters that help us to provide a more complete picture of this important phenomenon.

We are grateful to the ECPR for the workshop; to our respective institutions (Political Science, VUA and ARENA Centre for European Studies at the University of Oslo) for infrastructural support. In addition, we would like to thank the Democracy Programme at the University of Oslo for financial support in editing and formatting the manuscript. We are also grateful to Solveig Strand and to Helga Rognstad for the editing and formatting they have done, and for the help of Tracey Lofti, Laura Pugh and the rest of the ECPR Press team in turning this volume into its final shape.

Ben Crum and John Erik Fossum
August 2013

chapter one | practices of interparliamentary coordination in international politics: the European Union and beyond

Ben Crum and John Erik Fossum

Introduction

Parliaments risk becoming the main losers in internationalisation. Today, an ever-greater number of political decisions are being taken at the international level, many with profound national political implications. As part of this process of internationalisation we see a marked shift in executive-legislative relations as the main actors that occupy the international stage are executives and experts. In this picture, parliaments, in contrast, appear more as outsiders or even as passive bystanders. What is clear is that they have been slow to reassert control of decisions that are taken beyond the confines of the nation-state and whatever access they have to international politics is mostly filtered through their executives. The result of this is a growing gap between the actual decisions that affect a state, on the one hand, and those decisions that the state's parliament is able to shape, on the other.

The international financial crisis has exacerbated this problem, a mismatch that has become particularly visible in the European Union (EU). As the European Parliament (EP) (2011) recently noted: 'the democratic credibility of European integration has suffered enormously from the manner in which the euro crisis has been dealt with to date [...]'. Indeed, with the introduction of the so-called 'European semester', national budgets are now first scrutinised by the European Commission (EC) before they become the object of debate for national parliaments. Even more intrusive is the fact that, under European pressure, technocratic governments were temporarily installed in Greece and Italy. Added to that is how the populace, especially in crisis-struck countries, vent their anger at the political representatives for failing to come up with adequate crisis responses and for having become co-opted by foreign powers. These developments might end up placing representative institutions in a double squeeze: from executives and experts who seek to avoid parliamentary oversight and control, and from populists who mobilise and seek to capitalise on declining public confidence in parliaments as the central democratic institutions.

The financial crisis thus provides a particularly striking illustration of how parliamentary institutions' failure to become adequately involved in international decision-making has fundamental implications for the democratic legitimacy that these arrangements can enjoy. While this was recognised well before the crisis struck, the situation is becoming ever more urgent. It prompts a reconsideration of the role and mode of parliaments' operations.

Taking a step back to consider possible rectificatory measures, we may discern two tracks for how parliamentary democracy may be (re-)aligned with international decision-making. The first track is the development of international parliamentary institutions that are not only directly attached to international organisations but are also directly elected by the citizens.[1] The EP is the most notable example of a directly elected supranational parliament that has a direct say in (most) decision making at EU level. But then, the EU is not an ordinary international organisation; it has prominent supranational features. Thus, the first track is really about the setting up of a supranational or a transnational parliament proper.

The more common alternative which gives rise to the second track is to reinforce the ability of national parliaments to address international politics through the development of closer relations across borders (cf. Slaughter 2004). Such relations may initially take the form of *ad hoc* contacts and exchanges of information and best practices but they may also become more institutionalised and eventually even lead to an integrated system of closely interacting parliaments. This track then includes efforts to attach a parliamentary assembly to an international organisation; such an assembly is typically composed of delegates from the national parliaments of the member states. This approach is adopted by many international organisations such as NATO, the OSCE and the African Union. In fact, by 2011 Kissling (2011) counts twenty-six 'parliamentary organs' that are actually structurally incorporated in an international organisation and another thirteen 'international parliamentary agencies' that are dedicated to a particular international organisation. Ultimately, one could envisage the proliferation of international parliamentary institutions to constitute a globe-spanning network with a United Nations Parliamentary Assembly at its pinnacle (cf. Falk and Strauss 2001). The development of international parliamentary institutions that are made up of delegates of national parliaments is therefore one aspect of the second track that parliaments can use to catch up with the internationalisation of politics. This track may involve the establishment of new representative bodies but, in contrast to the first track, they will not consist of parliamentarians who have been directly elected by citizens.

The relevance of this second track of interparliamentary coordination is rendered apparent by the fact that most international politics remain essentially intergovernmental in character; national governments remain the key actors and are essentially in control of whatever decisions are adopted. In such a context, interparliamentary coordination is a means for national parliaments to compensate for the information advantage that the executives enjoy because of their direct involvement in international politics. As Robert Putnam (1988) has famously pointed out, executives may well want to exploit this information advantage by misrepresenting the negotiation situation they face at the international level.

---

1. For overviews of different forms of parliamentary institutions, *see* Kraft Kasack (2008) and Kissling (2011).

Interparliamentary coordination provides national parliaments with a means to cross-check the information they get from their executives.[2]

Another merit of interparliamentary coordination is that it remains closely wedded to the distinctive sources of democratic legitimacy that national politics enjoys. National parliaments operate in well-established contexts of integrated national public spheres, familiar political cleavages, and sentiments of national allegiance and trust in the national constitutions. Thus, their public visibility is high and the same applies to the perceived legitimacy of the decision-making processes that they are engaged in. Even though we may see some traces of an emerging transnational society, such as public deliberation and identities across borders, the political advantages of the national context are impossible to replicate at the international level without very substantial additional efforts. Indeed, this is borne out by the limited public visibility and legitimacy enjoyed by international parliamentary institutions, a point that also applies to the supranational EP.

Interparliamentary coordination suffers from the major limitation that it remains inherently fragmented. However much parliaments coordinate, they are unlikely to add up to a single coherent voice that can control the actual decisions adopted by the collective of governments that they scrutinise. What is more, effective coordination requires the dedicated effort of the parliamentarians involved and such dedication cannot always be guaranteed, given the limited time and resources available. Indeed, parliamentarians' short-term interests in individual gains in national politics are likely to outweigh more long-term, collective interests in interparliamentary coordination.

Parliaments thus face a major challenge in keeping up with the internationalisation of political decision-making, and there is no reason to believe that they will easily find an effective way of doing so. Still, to the extent that parliaments are, and remain, central to our understanding of modern democracy, it is of great importance to track their responses to internationalisation, the various forms these take and the various effects they have. Such knowledge is vital to establishing whether and, if so, under what specific conditions, parliamentary democracy is in fact sustainable under conditions of internationalisation.

Interparliamentary coordination: what should we focus on?

This book focuses on what parliamentarians do to adjust their behaviour in response to the internationalisation of political decision-making. With this behavioural focus, the book is more concerned with interparliamentary coordination in the sense of the second track (outlined above) than with the explicit process of

---

2. One way of thinking about the ensuing system is as a form of 'audit democracy' – a notion initially developed to make sense of the democratic dimension in the intergovernmental conception of the EU (*see* Eriksen and Fossum 2002; 2012). In such a system, parliaments will not be directly elected by the citizens because there is no uniform body of rights-bearing citizens to elect them in the first place. Such a parliamentary assembly will mainly serve to: supervise and control the international organisation's actions through providing forums for bringing forth relevant information on its actions; launch commissions of inquiry and include other bodies to undertake critical scrutiny of aspects of the organisation's activities; and engage civil society actors.

institution building (establishing supranational parliamentary institutions) that is a key aspect of the first track. Most of the literature on interparliamentary relations looks comparatively at the institutional set-up of different parliaments and the means they have at their disposal to scrutinise international and European politics (e.g. Maurer and Wessels 2001; Raunio 2005; Auel and Benz 2006; Kiiver 2006a; O'Brennan and Raunio 2007). This book supplements that body of literature by placing the focus on how parliamentarians operate within the broader institutional set-up, including the choices they make in engaging themselves (or not) with actors outside of their own parliament and constituency.

More specifically, the purpose of the book is twofold. The first aim is to examine empirically how an internationalising context drives parliamentarians to coordinate their work with colleagues in other parliaments; what benefits they derive from such coordination; and how this coordination affects their power positions *vis-à-vis* executive actors, among themselves, and in society in general. Second, drawing on these empirical insights, the book aims to clarify the broader implications of these developments for the practice and theory of democracy. This implies establishing whether or the extent to which the largely informal means of interparliamentary interaction might make up for, or counterbalance, the oft-noted executive dominance of international politics. Further, it brings up the broader question of whether new forms of interparliamentary coordination allow for the sustainability of parliamentary democracy under conditions of internationalisation, the fragmentation of political sovereignty, and the proliferation of multilevel politics.

The empirical questions – about parliamentarians' engagement in interparliamentary coordination, what motivates this, and what benefits the engagement produces – are approached here from a range of complementary angles. One relatively straightforward way to look at them is to analyse the ways that different parliaments respond to a shared challenge, such as scrutinising their government's engagement in EU affairs, or institutional provisions such as the EU IPEX-database and the Early Warning Mechanism (EWM) established by the EU Treaty of Lisbon. A second way is to look for variations in parliamentary engagement across policy spheres, which may reflect differences in the nature of the issues involved or differences in the (international) policy instruments employed. Parliaments may adopt a different strategy when their government adopts an international regulation (on, for instance, a standard for mobile telephony) than when it engages in a joint military mission. Yet again, a third perspective is to focus less on different parliaments and more on the networks that link parliaments together in terms of party groups or other ascriptive features by which parliamentarians may identify and organise themselves.

As to the wider theoretical question about the sustainability of parliamentary democracy under conditions of internationalisation, it is important to note beforehand that we are under no illusions as to the intrinsic merits of these new arrangements. Our point of departure is that parliaments are under pressure in an age of globalisation, and we are well aware of the fact that most of the evidence available so far – and much of what is included in this volume – indicates that parliamentarians' efforts are likely not to make up for this. We do not expect interparliamentary coordination to be a holy grail, a panacea that can readily deliver viable democracy in the interstate context.

Instead, our theoretical ambition is far more modest and rather preliminary in character. We start from the empirical observation that there is a growing trend of interparliamentary coordination and that this is often referred to as a possible democratic remedy. Whereas there are obvious grounds for taking this trend seriously from a democratic perspective, this is only possible if we reconsider established orthodoxy. We need to look more closely at the kind of representative relationship that this structure of parliamentary coordination may spawn. The lack of real-life precedents makes this an important intellectual undertaking. It also triggers important questions: can parliaments exercise effective control in such a context? For whom and to whom do they speak? How can the actual decision makers be held accountable? Such questions cannot be properly addressed unless we consult the theoretical literature. To that effect, we will draw on recent advances in the thinking on representation and deliberation (Castiglione and Warren 2006; Eriksen and Fossum 2012; Mansbridge 2003, 2009; Rehfeld 2005, 2009; Saward 2006, 2010; Urbinati and Warren 2008). These examinations will shed light on the important question of whether interparliamentary coordination has democratic potential, or is largely a dead-end and mainly a symbolic gesture.

The European Union as a vanguard

In many respects, the EU constitutes a vanguard, a particular case for reviewing the ability of parliamentary democracy to keep up with the internationalisation of politics. Importantly, within the Union both tracks of realigning parliaments with international decision-making have been taken up in a far-ranging and quite distinctive manner. On the one hand, as noted, the EU has given rise to the world's most fully-fledged supranational parliament, the EP, which is directly elected by the citizens of the member states and holds full co-decision powers in basically all important spheres in which the Union legislates. Thus, the powers of national parliaments over EU affairs have been complemented by a supranational parliamentary body that operates at the level of the Union as a whole.

In connection with this, it should be noted that the EP also could be said to have emerged out of the second track that we identified above. Even though the initial Assembly was established as a supranational body, the EP was composed of national parliamentarians until the introduction of direct elections in 1979. This shows that it is possible for a parliamentary arrangement to move up the ladder, from the second to the first track.

But what is also important to note with regard to the EU is that, in parallel with the EP consolidating its parliamentary role under the first track, from the early 1990s onwards, the Union also established a range of measures to facilitate the coordination among national parliaments on EU decision-making. These included the establishment of the Conference of Parliamentary Committees for Union Affairs (of Parliaments in the European Union) (COSAC) and the introduction of the EWM on infringements of the subsidiarity principle in the EU Treaty of Lisbon. Also, many national parliaments have reformed their organisational structures to facilitate closer scrutiny of EU affairs and to improve coordination with other parliaments in the EU (at EU level, at Member State level and even at sub-Member State level such as, for instance, the German *Länder*) (Neunreither 1994).

The outcome is that the EU at present pursues *both tracks simultaneously* (cf. Winzen *et al.* 2012). This suggests that, at least in principle, EU decision-making relies on an extensive and highly institutionalised system of parliamentary powers. Article 10 of the Treaty on European Union nicely sums up the premises on which this system is based:

1. The functioning of the Union shall be founded on representative democracy.

2. Citizens are directly represented at Union level in the European Parliament. Member states are represented in the European Council by their Heads of State or Government and in the Council by their governments, themselves democratically accountable either to their national Parliaments, or to their citizens.

The fact that the EU pursues both tracks simultaneously also suggests the actual configuration to be quite complex. Given that the EU pursues both EP parliamentarisation and interparliamentary coordination (encompassing in turn both horizontal and vertical patterns of interaction), we may question whether EU decision-making really can be said to be organised along two distinct nexus of representation (EU citizens-EP and national citizens-their NP, respectively), as Article 10 implies. It should hardly come as a surprise that the multilevel EU system is highly complex, contains overlapping or imbricated constituencies and unclear lines of representation and accountability.

In connection with this, it is important to underline the sheer complexity of the system of parliamentary rule that marks EU decision-making. Indeed, compared to all political systems (although India is to some extent excepted, notably in cultural but not in institutional terms), the EU is marked by an almost unprecedented cultural pluralism and institutional heterogeneity. This institutional heterogeneity shows up in huge discrepancies in the size of the member states and in significant institutional variations through federal, quasi-federal and unitary arrangements at the member-state level. This lack of institutional symmetry has important implications for interparliamentary coordination. In particular it means that executive-representative relations will differ considerably across the system.

Thus, in the EU context, interparliamentary coordination takes on great complexity given the sheer diversity of the EU. Importantly the EU system of government is quite distinct from any federal-state government. In fact, most executive responsibility for EU policies goes back to the national governments. At the EU level, executive powers have traditionally been delegated to the European Commission. However, besides the Commission, the secretariat of the Council of the EU, as well as a number of independent European agencies, have come to administer substantial executive tasks.[3] In the absence of an EU-level government at its apex, the EU has far less coherence as a political system than any federal state. The implication of this is that the EP lacks a proper governmental counterpart or at least finds it dispersed across different institutions and levels. There is then, essentially, no single institution and not even a single level within the EU that can be seen as the centre where sovereignty is embodied. Indeed, in many respects the national governments operate as distinct political sub-centres for their citizens, even if they have come to pool and delegate important powers at the European level.

All in all then, the EU has clearly moved beyond being an ordinary international organisation in that it has turned into a deeply institutionalised, continuous decision-making apparatus. At the same time, as its functioning remains fundamentally premised on its member states, the EU is properly regarded as a tightly imbricated system of multilevel governance. The question that we pose in this book is whether and how parliaments accommodate such a context.

This question has become more urgent in light of the financial crisis and the EU's response to it, which serves to underline that it is also an institutional – even constitutional – crisis. The fact that the EU's response has to a large extent been directed by national governments underlines the continued salience of the EU's polycentric and intergovernmental features. And even if the eventual result has been an increased European oversight of national budgetary and economic policies, these measures were brought in at the insistence of member state governments (not least, Germany). This process involves close coordination between the European Commission at EU-level and member governments, largely excluding the EP, and appears to involve national parliaments only at the end of the process.[4]

Notably, the prescribed solution to the sidelining of parliaments from this process is further interparliamentary coordination. Indeed, the one provision in the Treaty on Stability, Coordination and Governance in the Economic and Monetary Union that regards democratic control (Article 13), calls upon the EP and national parliaments to convene a conference of members of their budgetary and financial committees to discuss and monitor the policy developments. Similarly, the EP has stressed not only the need for a more prominent role for it and for national parliaments in this system, it has also underlined the need for coordinated action. The EP '[t]akes the view that the European Parliament is the appropriate venue for economic dialogue and cooperation between national parliaments and the European Institutions [...]' (European Parliament 2011). *The Economist*'s Charlemagne (2012) underlines that, in order to address the EU's democratic deficit, reforms are needed at both European and national levels. A critical component is that 'national

---

3. For excellent accounts of how this structure has emerged and what its distinctive traits are, see Curtin and Egeberg (2008) and Curtin (2009). The latter uses the label 'composite executive power' to depict this system (2009:65).

4. The experience from the first round of the 'European Semester' showed that the national parliaments' role was delimited by very short deadlines (European Parliament 2011).

parliaments need to be more involved in the EU's work, starting with closer scrutiny of its policies'. Because of the way the EU is configured such greater involvement will in turn also require greater interparliamentary coordination.

The EU thus presents us with a crucial test case for parliaments to adapt to a context in which a new international political layer is inserted on top of the established national political systems. While it benefits from the establishment of a supranational, EP, it is clear that the ability of parliamentary democracy to reassert itself also hinges on the rising trend of interparliamentary coordination; this also figures centrally in the reform proposals that practitioners and observers bandy about.

Finally, the EU developments raise the question of whether what is happening in the EU is unique to it, or whether it is part of a broader pattern of internationalisation of parliamentary relations. We examine this through investigating whether there are also parallel interparliamentary developments within more standard international organisations, such as the WTO and NATO. In that sense, the achievements and pitfalls of interparliamentary relations in the EU, as they have been developing so far, may contain important lessons for the evolution of global politics, at least in terms of the broader prospects for extending representative democracy beyond the state.

How to analyse interparliamentary coordination?

This book is designed to deal with important gaps in the existing literature. One such is the limited attention that analysts have paid to actual *practices* of interparliamentary relations in comparison to the formal, institutional structures that have been established to facilitate them. In fact, as many of the reforms anticipated in the earlier literature have only come into full effect with the Treaty of Lisbon (2009), this book presents a first opportunity to assess their actual, empirical implications. Most of the chapters were written before the EU developed its response to the crisis, with the exception of Chapter Eight by Arthur Benz who provides an overview of the crisis and an assessment of the effects it has thus far had on parliaments and patterns of interparliamentary coordination. The crisis is dynamic and the EU's responses are so recent that it is too early to tell what they will do to the specifics of interparliamentary coordination, including whether they will end up in more coordination or not. Yet, barring dramatic changes, many of the patterns exhibited here will likely subsist through the crisis.

The questions that are guiding the empirical chapters are:

(a) Which interparliamentary contacts are actually maintained, and which form do they take?

(b) What motivates these contacts? Which incentives make parliamentarian actors interact (or not)?

(c) What effects do these interparliamentary contacts bring about? Do the parliamentarian actors achieve their aims? Are there any relevant unexpected effects? How do the actions of the different actors sum up?

Our starting assumption is that many of the formal arrangements for interparliamentary coordination that have been established in the EU are of limited effect. Yet, the studies in this book will show that there is more coordination than we can glean from the formal arrangements because much of the actual interparliamentary coordination proceeds informally, through non-institutionalised channels, such as informal party contacts. In that light the internationalisation of politics actually gives rise to far more interparliamentary coordination in Europe than is captured when looking only at formal arrangements. Furthermore, we assume that there will be significant variation in the form, intensity and effects of these interparliamentary contacts in different spheres of decision making and along different actor dimensions. That, in turn, underlines the need to combine the study of formal parliamentary arrangements with detailed examinations of informal practices within a broader actor configuration.

The second point that sets this volume apart from the existing literature is the way it thematises important theoretical issues that the development of interparliamentary arrangements raise, notably pertaining to representation and democratic accountability. The predominant literature on parliamentary engagement in European and international politics tends to be comparative, taken up with a country-by-country analysis of how parliamentary scrutiny is conducted in individual member states. However, given its focus on individual parliaments as units of analysis, such a comparative strategy yields little of an aggregate perspective on the parliamentary character of the multilevel political system of the EU overall. In contrast, in order to be in a position to address the wider-ranging questions of democratic theory, this book proposes to adopt a more holistic perspective that seeks to assess the overall effect of interparliamentary interactions in the international systems of governance in which they are embedded.

For this purpose, we adopt the notion of a 'multilevel parliamentary field' (Crum and Fossum 2009, 2012). The multilevel parliamentary field essentially envelopes all – national and supranational – parliamentary institutions involved in EU decision-making. It is a heuristic device that helps us to establish how the two tracks (that we identified above for how parliaments may be aligned with international decision-making) are employed together to form a distinct configuration. We find the notion of 'field' as developed in the sociology of organisations (cf. Powell and DiMaggio 1991) to be the most suitable metaphor for capturing the traits of this system. It suggests that the totality of parliamentary institutions in the EU can be seen as a set of 'institutions that, in the aggregate, constitute a recognized area of institutional life', with some element of connectedness and structural equivalence (Powell and DiMaggio 1991). Notably, however, rather than assuming these parliamentary institutions to be organised in a single hierarchical structure, the institutions in the field are connected by their shared function of representing people's interests in EU decision-making and the role perceptions and interactions that come with that.[5]

---

5. Our conception of the organisational field therefore differs somewhat from that of Powell and

Essentially, the notion of a 'multilevel parliamentary field' serves as a conceptual container to capture the totality of interparliamentary relations in multilevel, international political systems, such as the EU. As such, it serves a double heuristic function that corresponds to the double objective of this volume: it opens up both empirical, descriptive perspectives, as well as theoretical, normative ones.

From an empirical standpoint, the holistic perspective provided by the notion of a multilevel parliamentary field renders apparent the 'systemic' character of interparliamentary patterns and the implications this has for the EU as a whole. An important concern in this book is precisely to shed light on the actual workings of the field, with particular emphasis on the nature, scope and density of interaction.

Thus, in building on this theoretical framework, our contributors reveal hitherto unexplored aspects of interparliamentary relations that show that contacts between parliaments and parliamentarians do not necessarily operate along the interinstitutional nexus but also – and in some cases even more so – run through other channels, such as political parties, expertise groups, interest groups, and civil society organisations.[6] Looking at the behavioural patterns across the totality of these channels, we can examine whether they serve to develop and diffuse specific practices and norms. These may include practices of coordination, shared understandings of what standards of parliamentary control should apply to Union matters, divisions of labour and expertise across parliaments, partisan interactions, links to civil society, etc. Investigating such practices can shed more light on the actual factors – actors, patterns of interaction and structural elements – that help to sustain and carry such interaction. Uncovering this is essential to understanding the sustainability of a field over time. It is also essential to the question of the transferability of the field notion from the EU-context to other less integrated settings.

In what sense such criss-crossing contacts eventually amount to 'a field' will be reviewed in the chapters. Thus, the studies in the chapters contribute to the empirical testing of the veracity of this notion, as well as to its further theoretical clarification and refinement. A complete assessment of the field would have required attention to the structures of representation that link state institutions and civil society in each member state, as well as at the EU-level. Such an enormous undertaking is clearly well beyond the scope of this book. Nevertheless, the investigations conducted here will help to explore the usefulness of the notion of the multilevel parliamentary field as a heuristic device to shed light on the democratic character and merits (as well as demerits) of interparliamentary cooperation.

On the theoretical side, therefore, the framework of the 'multilevel parliamentary field' is a means to consider the implications that interparliamentary

---

DiMaggio. To them a 'recognized area of life' has generally been defined in sectoral terms, often understood as a (professional) sector.

6. This is entirely in line with how scholars of a more deliberative bent think of representation. Consider in particular Mansbridge's (2003) notion of 'anticipatory representation', which precisely captures the systemic nature of representation.

interaction has for how we understand and conceptualise representative democracy in an international context and, indeed, for how we understand democratic *representation*, as such. For instance, the most fundamental revision that the multilevel parliamentary field suggests for established, national conceptions of parliamentary democracy is to give up on the idea of vesting parliamentary sovereignty in a single institution or, as is the case in federations, dividing it according to a constitutionally specified division of powers and competencies (which renders the central parliament the most senior body in the system because of the competencies that are conferred on the federal level).

In the international domain, no single overarching parliamentary power is constituted in such a manner as to be able to claim ultimate authority over national parliaments or according to a federal-type specification of powers and competencies. Given the historical and normative precedence of national parliaments in Europe, international politics cannot force them into a single, hierarchical mould. Even if a supranational parliament such as the EP is established, it has some of its roots in, and has to operate side by side with, national parliaments. It must complement the controls that national parliaments exert through their national governments. Thus, if parliamentary sovereignty, as an extension of popular sovereignty, is to be secured, parliaments need to find a way of coordinating their activities (in today's Europe there is little to suggest that they can be integrated).

Once we move to the more theoretical and normative terrain, it is important to underline that we understand the multilevel parliamentary field foremost as a heuristic device. There is little in the field's notion that predisposes us in a normative sense. Even *if* we find that interparliamentary relations in the EU qualify as a multilevel parliamentary field, the task remains to establish its democratic merits. Indeed, as Lord argues in his chapter, there are good grounds for being sceptical about the field, at least from the perspective of standard conceptions of political equality and accountability.

The recognition that, in international politics, parliamentary sovereignty becomes dispersed over multiple parliamentary institutions is a particularly important stepping stone in rethinking *representation* and *accountability*. As regards representation, the interweaving of parliamentary institutions raises fundamental questions with regard to the relevant constituency (Rehfeld 2005): who should parliamentarians speak for and to? Should they only speak for the constituency that has elected them or should they address the totality of citizens involved in the international system? Indeed, arguably, the condition of internationalisation raises the expectation that political representatives ultimately have to speak to world citizenry as a whole. In general, the very ambiguity of the constituency question under the conditions of internationalisation raises further questions pertaining to the territorial principles by which constituencies have traditionally been delineated. In international politics, the line between who needs to be included and who can be excluded from the decision-making process is far from self-evident (Fraser 2008). By implication, an open question is how different interests have to be weighed against one another, and what political equality requires: does it require all positions to be weighed by the exact number of individual citizens they represent, or does it, rather, require the equal treatment of different communities or categories of interest?

As the book will show, a characteristic feature of the EU's multilevel parliamentary field is that of overlapping constituencies with representatives facing multiple audiences and having to make strategic choices regarding who they address and in what way. These questions of constituency and representation should be considered in light of new insights into the way in which representatives and the represented relate (Castiglione and Warren 2006; Urbinati and Warren 2008). The classical opposition between the delegate and the trustee model (Pitkin 1967) has been superseded by new models of representation in which the relationship between representatives and the represented is much more dynamic and interactive (Manin 1997; Mansbridge 2003). In turn, recent research has also highlighted the active role of representatives themselves in constructing the constituency that they claim to represent (Saward 2006; 2010).

Another problem that the internationalisation of politics accentuates relates to the question of democratic accountability. Representative democracy generally requires parliaments to be able to exercise effective control over those making collectively binding political decisions. However, in international politics there is often a question of where exactly the final authority and responsibility for decision making can be located. As Peters and Pierre (2004) note, politics in a multilevel setting faces a particularly vexing challenge if it is to meet with the standards of democratic government because of 'the fuzzy instruments of accountability and political control' on which it relies. Specifically, multilevel governance tends to 'dilute responsibility among a large number of actors: this is "'the problem of many hands" or the "paradox of shared responsibility"'' (Papadopoulos 2007, referring to Bovens 1998).

The perspective of the multilevel parliamentary field brings to light the fact that the object of accountability is likely to be diffuse in multilevel politics and that this may equally apply to the subject, the relevant parliaments. Even if executive actors can be identified as being politically responsible, they are likely to be accountable to a plurality of representative forums. Importantly, as parliaments have different interests and operate at different levels, these accountability relationships may well push in different directions. Effective parliamentary control thus also requires a certain level of coherence between the different representative institutions involved in overseeing the decision makers. Otherwise, they risk being played off against one another, with their interventions cancelling each other out.

Ultimately, these theoretical concerns point to the question of whether representative democracy as we know it can be reconfigured in an internationalising, multilevel political system. And, if so, what are the possible merits and demerits associated with such a reconfiguration? Does it increase or reduce the quality of democracy? Our holistic and empirically grounded perspective suggests that there may be ingenious ways in which parliamentarians can (re-)claim power in a multilevel political system. At the same time, our perspective also cautions against drawing overly facile conclusions: a proper assessment of the resulting quality of representative democracy in the multilevel configuration that makes up the EU cannot confine itself to the balance sheet of the individual parliament, or even a simple summation of these, but requires an approach that properly captures the systemic features.

Outline of the book

The rest of this volume is made up of five parts that explore interparliamentary interactions from different, albeit complementary, angles. In Part I we provide an overview and assessment of the measures that have been developed in order to engage national parliaments in EU decision-making. The focus is on their actual operation and the extent to which the stated objectives are met in practice. In Chapter Two, Aron Buzogány reviews the variety of arrangements through which national parliaments scrutinise EU decision-making and, particularly, the way in which they have used various interparliamentary networks to exchange (and to learn from one another's) experiences. In Chapter Three, Viera Knutelská examines the effectiveness of supranational measures to elicit interparliamentary coordination, in particular, drawing on the evidence provided by the Interparliamentary EU Information eXchange (IPEX). Part I concludes with Chapter Four by Ian Cooper which provides a first empirical review of the EWM, the main new measure provided by the Treaty of Lisbon to strengthen national parliaments' powers in the EU, on the basis of the most notable case so far: the Seasonal Workers Directive.

Part II presents more case studies as it examines the variation in interparliamentary relations in the EU across different policy domains. The first three chapters of this section roughly correspond to the three pillars that, pre-Lisbon, formally divided the EU policy structure (although, it should be added that important vestiges of the pillars still exist, a fact that is duly commented upon). Chapter Five by Ben Crum and Eric Miklin examines interparliamentary coordination on one of the most politically contested dossiers of the last decade in the regulation of the European single market: The EU Services Directive. This chapter traces the similarities and differences in how this Directive was processed by the different national and European, parliaments, and how the different concerns came to be accommodated in the eventual decision. In Chapter Six, Daniel Ruiz de Garibay addresses the area of Justice and Home Affairs (the former 'third pillar' of EU decision-making). Specifically, this chapter reviews the various channels that European parliaments have used to coordinate their efforts to scrutinise Europol, the European Law Enforcement Agency. This review is particularly topical given the requirement to update the relevant regulation since the EU Treaty of Lisbon came into force. In Chapter Seven, Dirk Peters, Wolfgang Wagner and Cosima Glahn examine parliaments' involvement in the scrutiny of EU military missions on the basis of the case of the anti-piracy mission, Atalanta, off the Somali coast. These three chapters show that interparliamentary coordination takes different forms and faces different challenges depending on the mode of decision making and the stakes that are involved in each policy sphere. Part II is concluded by Chapter Eight, in which Arthur Benz examines how the Euro crisis has affected relations among parliaments and the system of interparliamentary interaction.

The chapters in Part III query interactions in the EU parliamentary field from different actor perspectives. In Chapter Nine, Johannes Pollak and Peter Slominski review parliamentary powers and practices in the trusted terms of interinstitutional relations between parliaments. In Chapter Ten, Yoav Shemer-Kunz pays particular attention to an important component that helps to sustain the multilevel parliamentary field, namely the political party. In his chapter he focuses on intra-party linkages across parliamentary levels, focussing on the case of the French Greens and the manner in which the party used the 2009 EP elections to reinforce its position on the national political scene. Chapter Eleven by Willy Beauvallet and Sébastien Michon highlights yet another dimension of the EU multilevel parliamentary field by examining the systematic differences in the role conceptions and networks of female members of the EP compared to their male colleagues.

In contrast to Parts I through III that are based on within-EU studies and comparisons, Part IV introduces three international organisations – the former Western European Union (WEU), NATO and the WTO – to explore what kinds of interparliamentary relations have developed and to what extent there are parallels with the EU experience there. In Chapter Twelve, Wolfgang Wagner examines the sessions of the parliamentary assemblies of the WEU and NATO to establish that these tend to be more frequently attended by representatives from parliaments with relatively limited powers over military affairs than by their colleagues from strong parliaments, because the former have more to gain from the exchange of information provided by these assemblies. This suggests that such assemblies are best understood as instruments that national parliaments use to compensate for information deficits at the national level, rather than operating as international actors in their own right. In Chapter Thirteen, Hilmar Rommetvedt turns to the World Trade Organization to examine how it has obtained a parliamentary dimension. Observing that international trade contributes to the crumbling of the border between domestic and international politics, Rommetvedt seeks to identify the drivers of the parliamentarisation of the WTO and to characterise the nature of the parliamentary dimension that is emerging.

The last part, Part V, contains two chapters that analyse interparliamentary coordination in a wider theoretical context and also raise some critical issues. Chapter Fourteen by Christopher Lord reviews the academic etymology of the Bourdieuian notion of a political field and highlights the risks in adopting this notion. At the same time, Lord relates the analysis of parliaments in Europe to the debate about the democratic deficit of the EU and proposes a specific standard of legitimacy against which their performance is to be assessed: a) public control, on the basis of b) political equality, and with c) individual rights to justification. In the concluding chapter, Chapter Fifteen, we sum up the main findings from the different parts and discuss what these findings imply for the prospects of extending representative democracy to an internationalised world, across state borders, and at the supranational level.

part i. national scrutiny mechanisms in the EU

chapter two | learning from the best? interparliamentary networks and the parliamentary scrutiny of EU decision-making

Aron Buzogány

Introduction

European integration has led to constitutional and political developments which traded national sovereignty for attaining the potentially higher benefits of increased integration. As a result, a substantial part of domestic legislation goes back to community law. Rather than active co-legislation, national parliaments have a major task in the *ex ante* and *ex post* control of community policy-making. In carrying out the scrutiny of EU policies, national parliaments' European Affairs Committees (EACs) traditionally play the central role. Consequently, institutional choice and the design of such parliamentary scrutiny procedures have been among the main points of interest for scholars focusing on the adaptation of domestic legislatures to EU integration. Explanations for the differential 'oversight powers' of parliaments among EU member states put forward predominantly domestic explanatory variables. Thus, the development of such oversight procedures has been described as a variable of political-administrative relations, coalition types, political culture, party-based or popular euroscepticism or the strength of parliaments or parliamentary committees prior to establishing oversight in EU matters (Raunio 2005).

Incorporating this domestic-centred view, this chapter extends the perspective on processes of institutional choice in EU scrutiny design and argues that, in addition to domestic factors, interaction and learning processes triggered by interparliamentary networks have played an increasingly important role during the last decades. Explanations for institutional choice need therefore to take into account the complexities of the 'multilevel parliamentary field' that has emerged in the EU (Crum and Fossum 2009). This perspective helps us to explain the choice of scrutiny instruments in EU member states by showing that national parliaments can emulate existing examples from other national models, choosing from a 'menu' of possible solutions available in the 'parliamentary field' when designing their own scrutiny mechanisms. Institutional entrepreneurs, such as single parliaments, their bureaucracies and interparliamentary fora have played a substantial role in promoting the institutionalisation of specific models of scrutiny.

This chapter proceeds as follows. The next section sketches a theoretical framework informed by organisation theory. It adapts institutional learning to the concept of the 'multilevel parliamentary field'. The following section introduces interparliamentary networks and institutional entrepreneurs. It describes how different, bilateral and multilateral, formal and informal interparliamentary networks that help to tie the field together have developed historically among parliamentary actors at multiple levels of the European multilevel system. The fourth section presents the two main models of parliamentary scrutiny established by national parliaments of the member states to control EU-related policy-making and shows that over time there has been a development towards choosing the mandating-based scrutiny model over the document based one. The fifth section complements this analysis by reviewing crucial moments of institutional choice when establishing EACs in different member states and illustrates that such choices also partially go back to the role played by interparliamentary networks. The chapter closes with an evaluation of the future potential of representative democracy in the EU and the role interparliamentary networks can play there.

Institutional learning in the multilevel parliamentary field

New institutions, such as new EACs, emerge more often through bricolage than exact planning on the drawing-board. Actors build upon and reinterpret models that are familiar and function elsewhere. Such adaptation processes take place in 'organisational fields' which are characterised by increased interaction, inter-organisational structures and the mutual awareness among participating organisations that they are involved in a common endeavor (DiMaggio and Powell 1983). In the case of the national parliaments of the EU member states, such learning processes can be located in the tightly networked space of a multilevel parliamentary field. Organisational analysis, and particularly the work of the Stanford School, offers a theoretical lens that helps us to understand these processes by focusing on the flow of practices within large social systems and by explaining why organisations dealing with similar questions become increasingly similar to one another (DiMaggio and Powell 1983). Solutions perceived as successful, legitimate and appropriate are adopted through organisational isomorphism. Institutional uncertainty and the lack of clear causal relations leading to organisational goals increase organisational isomorphism and the adaptation of potentially successful models (DiMaggio and Powell 1983). The institutionalisation of innovations in organisational fields is marked by 'interpretative struggles' over the meaning of institutional solutions (Zilber 2002). Institutional entrepreneurs with relevant resources play a central role here by 'creat[ing] a whole new system of meaning that ties the functioning of disparate sets of institutions together' (DiMaggio 1988). Their preferences and interactions are crucial for institutionalisation processes. At the same time, local actors are also able to contextualise, translate and theorise the available 'master ideas' which are taken for granted but remain rather vague in their details and are thus open for 'editing' (Sahlin-Andersson 1996) and adjustment for domestic use.

Drawing on DiMaggio and Powell's conceptionalisation of the organisational field, Crum and Fossum (2009) have introduced the idea of a 'multilevel parliamentary field', which is constituted by parliaments and shaped by the character and density of interparliamentary interactions between them. Such interactions are both formal and informal; they comprise 'divisions of labour and expertise across parliaments, partisan interactions, links to civil society, etc.' (Crum and Fossum, this volume). The multilevel parliamentary field perspective lends itself as a helpful theoretical device for analysing national parliaments' institutional choices of scrutiny mechanism. The organisational field perspective conveniently complements the rather positivistic bias in the literature on institutional transfer (Benson and Jordan 2011) by adding a constructivist twist. It reminds us of the importance of international socialisation and deliberation processes, which hitherto have been mostly analysed from a political theory (Eriksen and Fossum 2000; Joerges and Neyer 1997) or an international relations perspective (Checkel 2005; Flockhart 2004).

When focusing on the institutional choice of oversight mechanisms of national parliaments in European Affairs, such a constructivist perspective is particularly welcome. In contrast to domains of public policy, where the European Commission has developed directives (hard law) or at least recommendations (soft law), no such Commission-initiated template is available in the case of scrutiny. In responding to the treaty changes that consecutively provided more rights to national parliaments (Buzogány and Stuchlík 2012), the parliaments themselves have created a (multilevel) organisational field to assess and learn from one another's practices.

At the same time, it is important to stress the socially constructed nature of the chosen institutional solutions. Little secure knowledge about the effectiveness of the different scrutiny models exists; their merits and pitfalls are contextually tied to the complexities of each political system and are practically impossible to fully incorporate into comparative benchmarks and rankings. We can consider the very process of deliberative pondering of different characteristics of institutional solutions as an 'interpretative struggle' carried out with the participation of politicians, parliamentary staff and independent experts that accompanies the institutionalisation of parliamentary control of EU affairs in the member states. Thus, while in parallel with the debate about the EU's democratic deficit, the 'master idea' of the necessity of (some form of) domestic parliamentary control of European policy-making has led to the isomorphic creation of EACs in all member states, the conceptionalisation of exactly what this should look like has remained rather vague and adjustable to each national parliament's needs.

Choosing an institutional scrutiny model is a complex procedure in which actors in the 'multilevel parliamentary field' evaluate the solutions already available. Such institutional choices often rely on the 'logic of appropriateness' (March and Olsen 1989). This perspective underlines that actors are driven by their perceptions of what is appropriate or exemplary behaviour. At the same time, institutional choices are also determined by perceptions of the 'adaptability' of the scrutiny model to domestic circumstances. In most of the cases, scrutiny in European Affairs builds on previously existing instruments of parliamentary control. Therefore, institutional choice in EU matters starts with an internal evaluation of which parts of the model to be adopted would work and which would overburden the existing system. This points to an issue that is central to the design of the scrutiny systems: the delicate balance between efficiency and accountability provisions. Simply put, an overly strong parliamentary scrutiny system would significantly constrain the governments' room for manoeuvre and would therefore obstruct the delegation of decision making at the EU level (Auel and Benz 2005). One obvious way to deal with this dilemma is to choose á la carte from existing scrutiny solutions and build institutional 'hybrids' which can balance efficiency and accountability demands.

Interparliamentary networks

The multilevel parliamentary field is populated by various formal and informal intraparliamentary networks. Interparliamentary cooperation has become more intensive during the past three decades. While the impact of such meetings has often remained beyond the networks' control and is often criticised as mere 'cheap talk' by both participants and academic observers (Bengtson 2007; Raunio 2011), the more important issue in this context is that these highly secluded and often symbolic fora have contributed to the establishment of a common discursive field of representative democracy in a multilevel setting. The discussions taking place in these networks can be seen as constituting the very nucleus of an 'intermediary public sphere' which promises to contribute to the institutionalisation of heterogeneous norms (Habermas 1998). Using the distinction between 'weak' and 'strong' publics introduced by Fraser, interparliamentary networks can be considered as 'weak' publics as their deliberations focus on opinion formation but not on outright decision making (Fraser 1992).

For analytical purposes, we can distinguish between bilateral and multilateral interparliamentary networks. Both can involve formal and informal avenues of communication (Table 2.1). While the emphasis in these networks is certainly on politically elected actors (MPs), networks forged among parliamentary and party staff working on EU-related issues in different domestic parliaments are at least as important on the informal level. Bilateral intraparliamentary networks have been established between various parliaments, often based on historical, regional or cultural proximity. Parallel to this development, political parties have strengthened their cooperation both within the party families of the EP and bilaterally (EPP 2009). According to data from the European Commission's General Secretariat, from the late 1980s to the early 2000s, the intensity of interparliamentary cooperation has grown steeply regarding formalised meetings, joint committee meetings, bilateral meetings and meetings of parliamentary staff (Maurer and Wessels 2001). Also, the number of contacts between the European and national parliaments has increased, including those at the level of Sectoral Committees (Neunreither 2005). Such fora include the EU Speaker's Conference, which brings together the Chairs of EACs of national parliaments and the President of the EP, and interparliamentary sittings of Sectoral Committees of the European parliaments with their peers from national parliaments. Added to this, the parliaments of the countries holding the rotating presidency of the

EU Council regularly organise sittings between the Sectoral Committees of the national parliaments.

However, probably the most important venue regarding European scrutiny has been the founding of COSAC, which became the strongest interparliamentary forum for coordinating national parliament activities following its creation in 1989. Its historical antecedents go back to the European assizes launched by French President, Mitterrand, in 1989 which resulted from a compromise about the establishment of a Second Chamber of the EU composed of representatives of national parliaments and complementing the EP. While the idea of the second parliamentary chamber could not capture the minds of the executives, they agreed instead on establishing COSAC, which remains a strictly consultative body and has no powers whatsoever to bind national parliaments or determine their position (Eriksen and Fossum 2002). At least theoretically, this is exactly what gives it the potential of becoming, in a Habermassian-sense, a truly open space for transnational deliberation (Blichner 2000). In the meantime, COSAC has become increasingly institutionalised; it commands bureaucratic structures (albeit rather weak ones) and organises biannual conferences together with the parliament of the country holding the rotating presidency. COSAC also produces biannual reports on different issues related to the scrutiny of EU policies which have contributed to the diffusion of best practices among parliaments.

The increasing density of interparliamentary networks dealing with the domestic dimension of EU policies has been paralleled by ongoing discussions on the democratic legitimacy of the Union. During the European Convention, the role of parliaments has been hotly debated in Working Group IV, which brought together practitioners and academics. While the immediate results were assessed rather sceptically (Fraga 2005), such venues provided a momentum for restructuring interparliamentary cooperation at the level of parliamentary committees and civil service. During the preparation of the Rules of Procedure for the newly established EACs in Eastern Europe (2003–2005), the frequency of such meetings was particularly high as the question of national parliaments

Table 2.1: A typology of interparliamentary networks

	Bilateral	**Multilateral**
Formal	Joint meetings between national parliaments Joint meetings between national parliaments and the EP	COSAC EU Speaker's Conference Regional parliamentary networks European Convention
Informal	Contacts between MPs and MPs/MPs and MEPs via their European party families Information exchange between parliamentary staff	Brussels offices of national parliaments (Monday Morning Meetings) Information exchange e.g. ECPRD

emerged as a hotly debated topic in the European Convention. COSAC has been particularly active in this regard; it organised several conferences as well as published a series of comparative studies on the EACs of the member states (COSAC 2004a). Another influential network formed on the informal level brings together the representatives of the national parliaments in Brussels who share floors in the EP's 'Banana' building and regularly deliberate on issues concerning interparliamentary cooperation.

Finally, another actor in this parliamentary field is the European Centre for Parliamentary Research and Documentation (ECPRD) which functions within the EP and promotes exchanges of information, ideas and experience on subjects of common interest to the EP and national parliaments, including the exchange of studies carried out by the parliaments' research departments. During the early 2000s, the ECPRD functioned as a hub for parliamentarians from different member states, which also included the translation into national languages of the Eastern European accession states studies on scrutiny methods. This enabled newer member states' parliaments to copy the 'best practices' available in other EU member states by using the blueprints which were transmitted through bilateral and multilateral interparliamentary networks. Interparliamentary networks bringing together both decision makers from parliaments and parliamentary staff working in the EACs played an important role in designing the details of scrutiny systems. The next section provides an overview of the development of parliamentary scrutiny over the last decades.

Models of parliamentary scrutiny of EU affairs

Comparisons of parliamentary scrutiny in EU affairs usually rely on three variables: the involvement of specialised committees, access to information (scope and timing) and voting instructions (Raunio 2005). These variables depend largely on constitutional powers, even if their practical application may differ. Involvement of specialised committees is important as this allows for more expertise in scrutinising government. Bringing specialised standing committees into play means that all MPs and not just a small minority in the EAC become routinely involved in EU matters. As a result, parliaments make better use of their own policy expertise and are able to monitor the government's behaviour more effectively. Access to information relates to the timing and scope of information provided to the parliaments by the government (Maurer and Wessels 2001). In general, we can expect that the earlier (and the more) information is provided by governments, the better chances the EAC has to scrutinise. Finally, some parliaments issue voting instructions to their Brussels-bound negotiators. There are, however, substantial differences regarding how binding these instructions are and whether the government has to report on its voting in the Council of Ministers to the EAC. Other parliaments do not focus on the Council's work but try to get involved at a rather early stage in the decision-making process.

Table 2.2 gives an overview of EACs in the EU member states, including the year of membership, the year of founding, a characterisation of the scrutiny rights and the choice of the overall scrutiny model.[2] The national scrutiny models differ in respect of their structural attributes such as the timing and scope of information made available by governments, the bindingness of parliamentary opinion for the governments and the inclusion of other sectoral parliamentary committees into formulating the opinion of the parliament. While clustering the scrutiny models into two distinct groups is rather ideal-typical due to the eclectic and hybridic characteristics of the chosen models, we use here the categorisation employed by several COSAC surveys and much of the literature which differentiates between a mandating system and a document based model (COSAC 2007).

The mandating model focuses on the position of the government in decision making at the European level. EAC meetings take place before EU Council meetings and MPs give ministers recommendations (i.e. a mandate) to endorse legislation at the European level. The archetypal mandating system was established by Denmark in 1972, where the 'Market Committee' of the Folketing formulates politically binding positions for the government, which acts on its behalf. The development of this model can be explained by special features of the Danish Party Government which is characterised by frequent minority governments and high levels of popular scepticism towards EU membership. This resulted in rather weak governments that encountered a strong parliament seeking to bind the government's hands. Eventually, the mandating system has come to be adopted by a large number of countries, even if national models in regulating scrutiny, scope, timing, and frequency of systematic mandating and the bindingness of parliamentary positions differed considerably. Some parliaments have installed 'systematic mandating requirements' and may force governments to change their positions. Other parliaments, while having the power to issue politically binding mandates, use them rather infrequently. For example, the Austrian Government

---

2. The three sub-variables that make up the independent variable ('scrutiny strength') were first presented by Raunio (2005) for the EU 15. For the EU members joining in 2004, these scores were gathered from the legal texts collected in Szalay (2005) and cross-checked with country specific information such as scholarly articles and homepages of the EACs. In the case of involvement of specialised committees, its intensity was coded based on the explicit references in Rules of Procedures or Statutes of National Parliaments. Estonia and Slovenia are the clearest cases in this regard: in both countries standing committees are automatically involved. Most other parliaments have the right to include more specialised committees. Here, the classification was made based on the bindingness of the corresponding legislation. The second sub-variable was assessed based on scope and timing of access to information. Szalay provides comparative data on the elements of government position and explanatory memoranda. Timing was defined on the basis of any legal requirement towards the government to deliver its opinion to the parliament and on the actual timing of the parliamentary opinion. There is a high variance among the parliaments in how explicit these requirements are. The third variable regarding voting instructions is based on the dichotomic categorisation; 'consultative' and 'politically binding' found in the legal texts. In a next step, the three sub-variables were computed to a single score. This was rescaled to a seven-digit scale in order to make them comparable to Raunio's scores of the EU 15 parliaments. The chapter does not deal with Second Chambers in the EU, which are established mostly in federal or regionalising states and often hold different functions.

Table 2.2: The strength of parliamentary scrutiny in the EU (2005)

Country	Year of EU membership	Year of EAC Founding	Involvement of Specialised Committees	Access to Information	Voting Instructions	Average	Scrutiny model
Denmark	1973	1972	Moderate	Strong	Strong	Strong	Mandating
UK	1973	1974	Weak	Moderate	Weak	Weak	Document
France	1952	1979	Weak	Moderate	Weak	Weak	Document
Netherlands	1952	1986	Moderate	Moderate	Moderate	Moderate	Document/Mixed
Luxembourg	1952	1989	Weak	Moderate	Weak	Weak	Document
Belgium	1952	1990	Weak	Moderate	Weak	Weak	Document
Greece	1981	1990	Weak	Weak	Weak	Weak	Document
Germany	1952	1991	Strong	Strong	Moderate	Moderate	Document
Finland	1995	1994	Strong	Strong	Moderate	Strong	Mandating
Portugal	1986	1994	Moderate	Moderate	Weak	Weak	Document
Spain	1986	1994	Weak	Moderate	Weak	Weak	Document
Sweden	1995	1994	Moderate	Strong	Moderate	Medium Strong	Mandating
Ireland	1973	1995	Weak	Strong	Weak	Weak	Document
Italy	1952	1996	Weak	Moderate	Weak	Weak	Document
Austria	1995	2000	Weak	Strong	Moderate	Medium Strong	Mandating
Latvia	2004	2003	Weak	Strong	Strong	Medium Strong	Mandating
Malta	2004	2003	Moderate	Moderate	Weak	Weak	Document
Czech Rep	2004	2004	Weak	Strong	Weak	Weak	Document

(Cont'd.)

Table 2.2: (Cont'd.)

Country	Year of EU membership	Year of EAC Founding	Involvement of Specialised Committees	Access to Information	Voting Instructions	Average	Scrutiny model
Estonia	2004	2004	Strong	Moderate	Strong	Medium Strong	Mandating
Hungary	2004	2004	Moderate	Moderate	Strong	Medium Strong	Mandating/Mixed
Lithuania	2004	2004	Strong	Strong	Strong	Strong	Mandating
Slovenia	2004	2004	Strong	Strong	Strong	Strong	Mandating
Slovakia	2004	2004	Moderate	Strong	Strong	Medium Strong	Mandating

Sources: for the EU 15: Raunio 2005; for EU 10, own calculation based on Szalay 2005[2].

---

2. Specifically, pp. 126–127 (Specialised Committees), pp. 131–141 (Access to Information) and p. 142 (Voting Instructions)

can in certain cases override the mandate given by the *Nationalrat* but has to provide reasons for doing so.

By contrast, the document based model, of which the UK is the primary example, focuses on the scrutiny of EU documents at relatively early stages of decision making. EACs select and prioritise certain EU documents for closer debate, which are deliberated upon in a relatively detailed manner. Parliaments using the document based scrutiny model cannot exert direct control over their government's bargaining, as is the case with the mandating model. The emergence of this model is best explained by specific features of the British political system. The 'first past the post' electoral system regularly produces large majorities for the governing party which can rely on the support of the parliament which makes the strict control of government in European affairs less acute. Parliamentary influence here is, rather, based on persuasion through deliberation in parliamentary hearings or issuing well-founded expert opinions; as a last instance, they use so-called 'scrutiny reserves' that require government consultations with parliament before taking decisions at the EU Council. If such a scrutiny reserve is overridden by the government, the minister in charge has to provide immediate written explanations on the case.

Comparing the scrutiny procedures chosen in the member states reveals that the more recent waves of EU enlargement have resulted in a trend towards adopting the mandating-based model, which is often described as 'stronger' in formal terms (Raunio 2005).[3] This holds even for countries whose national parliaments have relatively weak positions and relatively high levels of support for the EU, both among political parties and the population. The scrutiny models developed in the Eastern European member states come close to the Nordic or the Austrian versions of EU oversight, which are generally regarded as the strongest in the EU. Lithuania and Slovenia can even be considered to be among the strongest scrutinisers, on a par with the Finnish or the Danish systems. Countries like Hungary, Poland, Slovakia, Estonia and Latvia have opted for quite strong scrutiny procedures, being similar to countries such as Austria or Sweden. While about two thirds of the old member states have document based scrutiny systems, this was followed only by one third of the new member states: the Czech Republic, together with the two Mediterranean states, Cyprus and Malta. All three states preferred a document based scrutiny system. The next section illustrates that while the domestic setting was crucial until the 1990s, as the interparliamentary field became denser, international influence on institutional choice became gradually more important.

---

3. Note, however, that many studies point out that formal strength of scrutiny does not necessarily lead to strong scrutiny (see e.g. Pollak and Slominski 2003, for Austria).

Adapting scrutiny systems: From domestic constraints to best practices

Denmark's *Marketudvalget* and the United Kingdom's *Committee on European Secondary Legislation* provide two diametrically opposed answers to the question of parliamentary control of EU affairs. Here, as in most EU founding member states, institutional choice was largely driven by domestic constraints. In the Danish case, the main triggers behind the establishment of the very strict scrutiny system were frequent minority governments. The scrutiny system had to make sure that no Danish Government could decide in Brussels against the will of the majority of the Folketing. By contrast, the British usually enjoy strong parliamentary majorities due to the electoral system. Thus, controlling the decisions of Brussels-bound bureaucrats was not a major necessity here. As a result, the UK parliaments adopted a more selective scrutiny method, which at the same time allowed for more in-depth deliberations. In France, the weak position of the *Assemblée Nationale* in the political system was reflected in the rather restricted legal competences of the *Délégation pour les Communautés Européennes* in controlling the Government in EU affairs. Its role was regarded more as an alternative venue to provide information about the EU to civil society than to exercise outright oversight (Rizzuto 2004). Similarly, the German *Bundestag* failed to establish a fully-fledged standing committee during the 1970s and 1980s due to the resistance from other standing committees and eventually became a subcommittee to the Foreign Affairs Committee, rendering it even more toothless. Later, the *Bundestag's Europa-Kommission* acted as a special committee and became an informal forum of interparliamentary cooperation among German MEPs and MPs (Hrbek 2011). Both the French and the German parliaments managed to strengthen their positions during the early 2000s, paralleling the increased emphasis on the role of national legislatures in the EU after the accession of Sweden, Finland and Austria and the preparations for the ratification of the Maastricht Treaty.

Also the Benelux states are usually considered late awakeners regarding the capacity of their national parliaments to control their governments' activities in EU affairs. For a long time, political parties in the Benelux states were united by a pro-European attitude. Combined with other shared characteristics of consociationalism and frequent rule by oversized majority coalitions, this left very little reason for checking their governments' activities in Brussels. In addition, whereas the plenary and the party groups played a central role in legislative activities (Janowski 2005), the Benelux parliaments had rather underdeveloped committee structures. This led to the creation of relatively weak EACs during the late 1980s. Some strengthening of parliamentary involvement rights in this field took place at the end of the nineties when, for example, the Dutch *Tweede Kamer* followed the British model by adding *ex post* mechanisms of scrutinising government in plenary debates following European Council summits, while explicitly warning of 'Danish circumstances' (Hoetjes 2001) which would overburden the Dutch system.

Southern European parliaments, for their part, emulated the French version of scrutiny, characterised by executive superiority and a rather weak position of EACs (Magone 2007). Common cultural and constitutional references to the French statist model were particularly important in the Spanish, Portuguese and partially also the Greek case, where parliaments struggled to define their new role after emerging from dictatorships only a few years before their EU accession. European integration provided an important anchor for stabilising democratic development. In the meantime, this was also accompanied by the consolidation of weak legislatures, dominated by pro-integrationist parties. The development of EU affairs committees has largely been a reactive adaptation to the consequences of the Maastricht Treaty. All southern parliaments shared low levels of legislative professionalisation and weak administrative capacities. In contrast to the democratising Southern European states, in Italy, a founding member of the European Coal and Steel Community, it was the blatant failure to comply with EU legislation that eventually led to rationalising EU coordination through the 'La Pergola' Law which established a parliamentary timetable for implementing the community legislation by the national parliament. While La Pergola strengthened executive coordination by providing a parliamentary fast track procedure, a side-effect of the adoption of Legge No. 11/2005 on European affairs and the increasing political dialogue with the European Commission was that the *Camera dei deputati* became increasingly active in EU affairs (Matarazzo and Leone 2011).

In 1995, with the accession of the two Nordic states, Sweden and Finland, as well as Austria, three parliaments were keen to preserve their strong domestic positions after they entered the EU (Fitzmaurice 1996). The *Riksdag* and the *Eduskunta* adapted the Danish mandate-oriented model, while Austria followed the Danish example with some specific adaptations. In the case of the Nordic countries, this choice was triggered not only by perceptions of cultural closeness, but also of 'institutional fit' as they shared with Denmark the tradition of minority governments and a secluded party system (Damgaard and Jensen 2005). In Austria, accession negotiations toward EU membership were accompanied by cautions about the Union's democratic deficit and this made the stronger Danish system seem desirable, particularly for the opposition parties. The formally rather strong position of the *Nationalrat* in EU affairs was a result of a bargain as the Government needed the opposition's vote when passing the Constitutional Acts on Austria's accession to the EU (Hegeland and Neuhold 2002). Thus, domestic factors and the internationally available 'best practice' of the Danish *Folketing* both played a role in determining institutional choice during the fourth accession wave in 1995.

While the sturdy formal scrutiny rights given to the Swedish, Finnish and Austrian legislatures were hardly unexpected due to the strong positions they already held within the political system, the strength of European parliamentary scrutiny systems in the Central and Eastern European states which were part of the fifth accession wave in 2004, was quite unexpected. Comparative literature focusing on the region has often underlined the weaknesses of parliaments in Central and Eastern European transition states since the late-nineties (Olson and Ilonszki 2011). This development was reinforced by EU accession, which gave powers to the core executives, often at the expense of parliaments. Fast-track harmonisation of the EU *acquis* turned parliaments into 'law-factories' that often lacked time to deliberate over the quality of their output (Goetz and Meyer-Sahling 2008). As EU-related questions had a low salience both for the public and in domestic political debate, the question that emerges is why and how did these Central and Eastern European parliaments manage to gather strong scrutiny positions regarding European policies? While domestic level explanations play a central role in understanding the choice of institutional solutions in the 'older' EU member states, the advanced institutionalisation of the debate on parliamentary control until the early 2000s has made international factors more important. In terms of organisation theory, the 'travelling idea' of parliamentary scrutiny, together with the vocal backing of institutional entrepreneurs such as the Nordic parliament's activist EACs and the COSAC network led to the diffusion and sedimentation of certain concepts. At the same time, local translating and editing made them adaptable within their domestic context.

Seven out of the ten parliaments that became EU member states in 2004 adopted scrutiny models which strongly relied on the so-called Nordic version of the mandating model (Table 2.2). As (particularly) the Danish EAC, as an institutional entrepreneur, had an activist strategy towards the accession states' parliaments, this choice does not seem coincidental (Jungar 2010). When studying the 'state of the art' on EU 15 EACs, public officials and MPs from the EU 10 tasked with establishing or reforming European committees were confronted with the seemingly common knowledge within the interparliamentary field that the scrutiny models of the Nordic countries were especially worth looking at (Jungar 2010). The frequency of the meetings in various fora allowed for the development of an 'advocacy coalition' in this clearly delimited field of expertise which increasingly shared perceptions of the problem and of the adequate answers to the questions of EACs. Armed with knowledge and insights gathered through interactions with other parliaments, members of this coalition could actively shape the domestic institutional structure. While multilateral fora were important at the stage of deciding the general direction of which scrutiny method to take, bilateral relations played a more important role in deciding upon the details of the institutional set-up. Obviously, when choosing 'role models' cultural and political ties played an important role. As the Baltic States had strong ties with their northern neighbours, an obvious choice was for them to turn towards the countries on the Northern edge of the Baltic Rim. But it was not only the Baltic States that looked towards the shining northern examples. Also, the Polish, Hungarian, Slovak and Slovenian parliaments adapted these scrutiny models that were regarded as most successful. For example, Hungary took a close look at the Finnish model and used the personal contact of the former Hungarian ambassador to Helsinki with the Secretariat of the *Eduskunta* in order to assess the comparative benefits and potential pitfalls of the model (Ágh 2006). At the same time, the Hungarian model was also informed by neighbouring Austria (Kurtán 2002).

When looking at the example of the Danish *Folketing* in detail, MPs and parliamentary staff in charge of designing new scrutiny mechanisms became aware that the Danish version of scrutiny was quite demanding for their relatively weak and unskilled parliaments. They saw that the tight scrutiny model which characterises the Danish version of the mandating model could become problematic as it could slow down the work of the Government and hinder it in representing the national interest in Brussels. Conflicts over EU policies, which had triggered the strong Danish scrutiny systems, were not present in the ten new EU member states. On the contrary, experts from the Hungarian EAC highlighted that it was an eminent national interest that party politics should be kept out of EU affairs (Buzogány 2012). Thus, most parliaments from Central and Eastern Europe chose to weaken the Danish version by dampening its impact through making binding mandates optional. Here, they relied on the Austrian, Swedish and Finnish adaptations of the Danish version of the mandating model, which were regarded as the most advanced and comprehensive ones and fitted well into the institutional structures of relatively small member states. An added benefit was that the Finnish and Swedish versions were to a certain extent already institutional hybrids as they took references not only from Denmark but combined these with characteristics of the British-inspired document based model.

In the case of the three parliaments who did not follow the Nordic model (Czech Republic, Cyprus and Malta), bilateral contacts with the UK and French legislatures (in the case of the Czech Parliament) played an important role in institutional choice. For the two Mediterranean states, this choice was determined by their close ties to the UK which heavily influenced their parliamentary culture. More important, however, were the limited resources the two parliaments possessed, which would make exercising an exhaustive scrutiny quite difficult. Rather than emphasising the strength of parliamentary scrutiny, the Czech solution focused on the division of labour between its two Houses (Zehnpfund and Rhomberg 2009). According to Zralá (2005), the two Houses could not agree on the conduct of relations among themselves, and the Czech Senate tried gaining additional powers, both *vis-à-vis* the Government and the Lower House, the *Poslanecká sněmovna*. As a result, the Czech Republic eventually opted for a solution where each House would hold – even if they were weak – EU scrutiny powers instead of one unified scrutiny committee, while the Government would only be responsible to the Lower House. While domestic considerations (and blockades) played an important role in determining this scrutiny model, the choice of the institutional solution was far from being a *tabula rasa*. Faced with the constraints mentioned, the designers of the Czech scrutiny system looked to established scrutiny models which promised to function well in a bicameral system, such as the British and the French models (Pítrova and Coxová 2007).

Beyond the institutionalised collaboration of parliaments, additional channels also fostered the diffusion of expertise related to the involvement of parliamentary actors in EU affairs. These brought together experts from the parliaments and the parliamentary administration, politicians, and academic researchers dealing with the control of European affairs by national parliaments. Such workshops were cross-financed by parliaments and research institutions or in some cases could use funds made available from different EU sources. In most cases, smaller groups with a functional or a regional perspective would gather. The Polish Senate, for example, organised meetings with the Czech and the Slovenian Upper Houses in order to evaluate their role, also *vis-à-vis* their Lower Houses in scrutinising EU affairs. In other cases, think tanks such as the European Policy Centre organised a venue together with the European Integration Committee of the Polish *Sejm*, which brought together MPs and MEPs from Denmark, the United Kingdom and Italy, allowing for debating with Polish MPs about the strengths and weaknesses of different scrutiny methods. Besides contacts with the parliaments of the 'old' member states, the EACs of the Central and Eastern European countries were traditionally engaged in close regional collaboration. Thus, Poland and the three Baltic states held regular meetings, as did the four Visegrád states (Czech Republic, Slovakia, Hungary and Poland) prior to the COSAC meetings (Lazowski 2006).

Conclusion

This chapter has focused on learning in bi- and multilateral interparliamentary networks within the broader ambit of the multilevel parliamentary field. It has focused on the development of national parliaments' domestic scrutiny procedures regarding the control of EU-level policy making. Institutional choice for a particular scrutiny system was based on the perceived success of the model; existing contacts to the 'donor' model; and the perceived 'fit' with the national context. In contrast to the 1970s and 1980s, when mostly domestic-level variables determined institutional choice, in more recent years, newcomer parliaments, when making their institutional choices, could emulate the 'best practices' of those member states that were regarded as particularly successful. This perception was nurtured in a complex multilevel 'learning field' that brought together diverse actors working on different aspects of EU scrutiny issues. Learning processes did not occur in a vacuum but had to bridge contradicting expectations regarding the efficiency of the scrutiny and accountability of the respective government, a dilemma that often resulted in hybrid institutional solutions.

From what has been discussed here, two points emerge regarding the future of a parliamentary dimension of European integration. The first point concerns the gap between formal scrutiny rights and the practical usage thereof in national parliaments. There is empirical evidence to show that, in fact, strong scrutiny mechanisms do not automatically translate into increased parliamentary activity. For example, the Austrian parliament, which is considered to be one of the parliaments with the strongest scrutiny rights, hardly ever makes use of them (Pollak and Slominski 2003). It seems, rather, that the practical usage of scrutiny rights is moderated by the effects of policy fields (Neuhold and de Ruiter 2010; Sprungk 2010), coalition types (Holzhacker 2005) or MP role perceptions (Kropp 2010). This also carries some obvious consequences for learning in interparliamentary networks. Without taking these effects into account, the mechanical adaptation of externally conceived institutions can easily thwart their original content and lead to suboptimal solutions.

In fact, theories of institutional transfer point not only to success stories but also to (at least three) typical cases of failed transfer (Dolowitz and Marsh 1996). In the first case the borrower might not hold enough information about how the borrowed institution functions (uninformed transfer). Second, if only parts of the borrowed institutions are transferred, this may lead to problems of implementation (incomplete transfer). Finally, the borrower might also be unaware of the complexity of how the borrowed institution is embedded into its own domestic context (inappropriate transfer). While it is certainly too early to assess the practical usage of scrutiny rights in the last wave of institutional adapters, the first in-depth analyses seem to point to serious gaps between promises and practices (Knutelská 2011b; Buzogány 2012).

A second point concerns the possible effects of the Lisbon Treaty and shifts our attention to the EU level. Already, before the Lisbon Treaty entered into force, the Commission sought to institutionalise a political dialogue (the 'Barroso Initiative') with national parliaments in order to improve the process of policy formulation and to bring the EU closer to its citizens. As part of this dialogue the European Commission now sends its new proposals and consultation papers to national parliaments for them to provide input. The Lisbon Treaty introduced several changes relating to the role of the EP and national parliaments in EU policy making (for details, see Crum 2005). This seems to have strengthened the position of the supranational parliament which increasingly acts as an outright scrutiniser at the European level. The Treaty has also given significant rights to national parliaments in the area of subsidiarity and has extended the period within which they can object to draft legislation by submitting a reasoned opinion, from an original six to the current eight weeks. This can result in a review of the proposal based on the 'yellow' and 'orange' card mechanisms. The yellow card mechanism starts after objections of non-compliance are received from at least one-third of the parliaments. The orange card mechanism starts if a majority of the national parliaments object to the Commission's proposal. However, the question that remains here is whether national parliaments are indeed empowered by the Lisbon Treaty and begin using their powers in such circumstances. At first sight, the treaty provisions regarding the rights granted to parliaments are so complex and the required quorums for having a say in the ordinary legislative procedure are so prohibitively high that reaching them may easily prove too difficult for national parliaments. The only viable parliamentary path is to pool forces to forge the majorities necessary for an effective use of the EWM (see Cooper, this volume). To do so, national parliaments need to foster and enhance cross-country exchanges of information and cooperation. The interparliamentary networks discussed in this chapter and their new technical tools (such as IPEX database, collaboration within COSAC and interaction among national parliaments' liaison offices in Brussels) can facilitate horizontal cooperation, including but not limited to, establishing commonly shared 'best practices' for interaction between governments and legislatures. Increasingly, national parliaments and the EP can act as connected vessels in organising and coordinating scrutiny procedures. At the same time, the main added value of the new Treaty provisions might be of a rather indirect nature. The new procedures can empower domestic parliamentary actors by making them more aware of the European dimension of their activities and lead to legitimacy gains through the increased politicisation of EU politics within their respective national public spheres.

chapter three | cooperation among national parliaments: an effective contribution to EU legitimation?

*Viera Knutelská**

Introduction

In recent years, various new tools of interparliamentary information exchange and cooperation have been developed. The aim of these tools is to improve the ability of national parliaments to scrutinise the European decision-making process, both at national and European levels, and for them to form and voice their opinions at both these levels. This chapter describes the development and use of these channels in the context of the democratic legitimacy of the EU and in the framework of the European multilevel parliamentary field.

The fact that national parliaments have a role in legitimising European integration has been gradually acknowledged since at least the early 1990s and the role of national parliaments has been both promoted and studied, as will be shown in the first section of this chapter. This acknowledgement has led to various developments, both formal and practical. Successive treaties have increasingly come to refer to national parliaments, and both European institutions and national parliaments themselves have reacted to this development by fostering mutual cooperation. The European Commission has opened a dialogue with national parliaments and encouraged them to use the Commission as a channel to voice their positions directly at the European level. National parliaments themselves have used the already existing fora, COSAC and the Conference of Speakers of EU Parliaments (the Conference of Speakers), to promote more interparliamentary cooperation and to create new tools of information exchange, such as IPEX.

The second section of this chapter is devoted to the potential role of national parliaments in ensuring European democratic legitimacy and concludes with a conceptualisation of the criteria to assess the extent to which they have emerged as a collective actor in EU affairs. The third section describes the incentives and mechanisms for interparliamentary cooperation. As national parliaments now have regular but not very frequent contacts in such fora as COSAC and the Conference of Speakers, they have been able to develop new instruments of cooperation and even test them in specific cases. The coordinated tests of subsidiarity checks organised by COSAC in anticipation of the introduction of the EWM are a good example of first attempts at acting collectively. The cooperation among national

---

* The author would like to acknowledge the support of the Czech Science Foundation (Grant No. 407/09/1747).

parliaments in these cases is analysed in the fourth section. Moreover, national parliaments now have at their disposal some newly developed tools, particularly IPEX, that offer them an opportunity to communicate and exchange information on a daily basis on everyday issues. The use of IPEX, its scope as well as its limits, and the challenges national parliaments face, are analysed in the fifth section. All these aspects of interparliamentary cooperation are bound together within the concept of the European multilevel parliamentary field. The sixth section then briefly analyses the achievements and prospects of national parliaments at the European level.

National parliaments and the EU's democratic legitimacy

For a long time it has been claimed that the European integration process has strengthened executives at the expense of legislatures (Moravcsik 1994) and that national parliaments have been the main losers in this process (Maurer and Wessels 2001). Although national parliaments have reacted to this process and learned 'to fight back' (Hix and Raunio 2000), most of their reactions have happened at the national level. National parliaments have developed systems of national scrutiny of European affairs primarily in order to scrutinise, influence and control their governments and their activities in the Council. Many of these systems have been extensively studied and are well described in the literature, either in separate studies (*see* e.g. Pahre 1997; Hegeland and Neuhold 2002; Pollak and Slominski 2003; Hansen and Scholl 2002; Slagter 2009; Sprungk 2010) or in edited volumes through comparative studies (Maurer and Wessels 2001; Cygan 2001; Auel and Benz 2006; O'Brennan and Raunio 2007; Tans *et al.* 2007; Barrett 2008). However, these developments have approached the deparliamentarisation problem almost exclusively from a national perspective. By attempting to have better oversight of their governments' activities in the EU, national parliaments only really influence the national legitimacy of European policies in their respective member states. Simply put, the strong position of, for example, the Danish Parliament in scrutinising the Danish Government's position on European policies may improve the legitimacy of the EU in Denmark but not in other member states, and not in the EU as a whole. The fact that national parliaments may emulate the best practices used by other national parliaments and learn from one another (*see* Buzogány in this volume) does not affect the limited impact of national routes to legitimising the EU.

This does not, however, mean that the European route to legitimisation is open only to the EP, although the EP is of course an important institution in legitimising the EU as a new type of political system (Wessels and Diedrichs 1997). What is notable is that national parliaments as a collective can also affect the legitimacy of the European level by entering directly into the European legislative process and interacting with other European institutions.

Of course, in practice, this distinction does not preclude individual national parliaments from combining both routes, or doing so in cooperation with, not in opposition to, their governments (Dimitrakopoulos 2001). It does, however, elicit new questions regarding the possibilities of national parliaments' cooperation or even coordination at the European level.

This chapter uses the concept of the 'multilevel parliamentary field' in the European Union (Crum and Fossum 2009; *see also* the introductory chapter in this volume) to understand the nature, relevance and possible cooperation of national parliaments for the EU's legitimacy. While the concept of a network could be sufficient for studying interparliamentary information exchange and cooperation as factors influencing the performance of individual national parliaments within their national political systems, the MLPF concept allows us to integrate into our analysis such factors as European-level incentives (treaties, the Commission's activities, etc.) and perceive national parliaments as a collective.

For the national channel of democratic legitimisation of European integration to work at the European level, the activities of national parliaments at this level should meet some criteria of collective actorness. Unlike legitimisation at the national level, where each national parliament individually controls its respective governments, legitimisation at the European level requires that the activities of national parliaments are carried out collectively. While this does not necessarily mean that every single parliament or parliamentary chamber must actively participate every time any European-level tool of parliamentary involvement is used, isolated activities of individual national parliaments towards European institutions cannot contribute to European-level legitimisation on their own. (Although these could contribute to a national-level legitimisation of European issues in a given member state.)

These criteria of collective actorness can be derived from the notion of the MLPF that stresses the relevance of shared function, the structural character of the field and the fact that the field is more than the sum of its constitutive parts (Crum and Fossum 2009; *see also* Cooper in this volume).

I define these criteria of collective actorness as follows:

(a) National parliaments perceive one another as sharing the same function within the integration process. The shared perception of their role as representing peoples' interests in EU decision-making keeps the components of the parliamentary field together (Crum and Fossum 2009) and allows for the interpretation of the activities of national parliaments at the European level within the context of legitimisation (and is not just a simple attempt to acquire more power for the sake of power itself);

(b) National parliaments are aware of the scrutiny processes and positions held by other members of the multilevel parliamentary collective, a precondition that makes it possible for national parliaments to act collectively by conscious effort (and not just act at the same time by simple coincidence). This leads directly to the third criterion;

(c) National parliaments are able to execute coordinated efforts to influence the European decision-making process.

In the following I will consider to what extent these criteria are fulfilled in the present-day EU.

Incentives and mechanisms for interparliamentary cooperation

In the last twenty years, national parliaments' involvement in European affairs and interparliamentary cooperation has been encouraged by multiple formal and practical developments.

The idea that national parliaments should have some role in the EU has been recognised in treaties since the Maastricht Treaty which included a Declaration on the Role of National Parliaments in the EU. The Declaration was devoted especially to the encouragement of the exchange of information and contacts between national parliaments and the EP.[1] Five years later, in the Amsterdam Treaty, the Declaration was 'upgraded' to a Protocol, namely the Protocol on the Role of National Parliaments in the EU. The Protocol distinguished between an individual parliament's scrutiny of its own government and the involvement of national parliaments in the activities of the EU. It included the, historically speaking, first obligations for European institutions towards national parliaments; the Protocol requires that the Commission forwards its consultation documents to national parliaments. It also refers to COSAC and acknowledges its right to address the European institutions in relation to their legislative activities.[2]

The role of national parliaments has also been debated by the Convention on the Future of Europe and came to be reflected in the proposed texts of the Constitutional Treaty and the Treaty of Lisbon. Working group IV of the European Convention, discussing the role of national parliaments, has specifically distinguished between three different roles of national parliaments: scrutinising governments, monitoring the application of the principle of subsidiarity, and involving national parliaments at the European level through multilateral networks or mechanisms. It also called for a clarification and a strengthening of the role of COSAC (European Convention 2002). The Lisbon Treaty contains numerous references to national parliaments; it gives national parliaments the right to receive information and documents from the EU and charges them with ensuring the compliance of Union law with the principle of subsidiarity.[3] Moreover, the Treaty on the EU now contains a specific article on the national parliaments' role in the EU (Article 12 of the Treaty on European Union) and two related protocols (the Protocol on the Role of National Parliaments in the EU and the Protocol on the Application of the Principles of Subsidiarity and Proportionality). The first protocol (Article 9) states that the 'European Parliament and national parliaments shall together determine the organisation and promotion of effective and regular interparliamentary cooperation within the Union'. The second protocol introduced

---

1. Declaration on the role of national parliaments in the European Union, Treaty on European Union, Official Journal C 191, 29 July 1992.

2. Protocol on the role of national parliaments in the European Union, Treaty of Amsterdam amending the Treaty on European Union, the Treaties establishing the European Communities and related Acts, Official Journal C 340, 10 November 1997.

3. Treaty of Lisbon amending the Treaty on European Union and the Treaty establishing the European Community, Official Journal C 306 of 17 December 2007.

the Early Warning Mechanism allowing national parliaments to interfere in the European legislative process directly (see Cooper in this volume).

The European institutions have also reacted to these developments, sometimes going further than the Treaties formally prescribed. The Commission, in anticipation of the ratification of the Constitutional Treaty, introduced the so-called Barroso Initiative in 2006, and, among other measures, started forwarding the legislative proposals and other documents to national parliaments before it was under any legal obligation to do so. The Commission has begun developing other channels of relations with national parliaments, such as visits to national parliaments, participation at the COSAC meetings, openness to communication with national parliaments, etc. (COSAC 2005). It also started monitoring its relations with national parliaments more closely and, since 2005, has published annual reports on its relations with them.[4]

The national parliaments have responded to these developments by creating various channels and instruments of interparliamentary cooperation that, in turn, were expected to boost this cooperation. The most relevant instruments are COSAC, permanent representatives of national parliaments in Brussels and the IPEX database.

COSAC was established in 1989 by a decision of the Conference of Speakers. It meets twice a year and serves as a venue for the exchange of information and teaching best practices. COSAC and the Conference of Speakers have since then launched various other initiatives to facilitate interparliamentary cooperation, such as the creation of IPEX and the organisation of the coordinated test of subsidiarity checks, in anticipation of the introduction of the Early Warning Mechanism. The role of these fora in organising these cooperation tools (see the specific sections below) indicates that national parliaments share some perception of their common function in the European integration process. This can be further illustrated by specific declarations of such a role that can be found in their documents, such as: 'national parliaments contribute actively to the good functioning and to increase the democratic legitimacy of the European Union' (Conference of Speakers of the European Union Parliaments 2008) or 'the Conference of Speakers [...] aims at safeguarding and promoting the role of parliaments' (Conference of Speakers of the European Union Parliaments 2010).

Another network facilitating the cooperation among national parliaments is formed by the permanent representatives of national parliaments in Brussels. At the moment, all national parliaments have created an office of a permanent representative in Brussels (sometimes there are two representatives for individual chambers in bicameral parliaments).[5] The titles of these permanent representatives

---

4.   Annual reports on relations between the Commission and national parliaments are online and available at: http://ec.europa.eu/dgs/secretariat_general/relations/relations_other/npo/index_en.htm (accessed 3 July 2012).

5.   A list of these representatives is online and available at http://www.cosac.eu/permreps/ (accessed 3 July 2012).

vary – they may be either permanent representatives to the EP or to the European institutions. Some are affiliated to the respective Permanent Representations of their governments, others are more institutionally independent. However, all permanent representatives of national parliaments have offices at the EP's premises in Brussels which facilitates not only the cooperation between their parliaments and the EP/European institutions, but also the mutual cooperation among national parliaments.

The permanent representatives mostly facilitate informal, day-to-day cooperation. It is usually the Conference of Speakers and COSAC that launch new initiatives and prepare the framework for interparliamentary cooperation. For example, the Conference of Speakers has adopted the guidelines of interparliamentary cooperation. The first version, known as The Hague Guidelines (Conference of Speakers of the European Union Parliaments 2004), was adopted in 2004 in response to the draft Constitutional Treaty and the Protocols appended to it. The Guidelines determine the main objectives of interparliamentary cooperation in Europe, which are:

(a) to provide information and strengthen parliamentary scrutiny in all areas of competence of the EU; and

(b) to ensure the efficient exercise of parliamentary competencies in EU matters, in particular in the area of subsidiarity control by national parliaments.

The Guidelines list eight possible occasions or venues for interparliamentary cooperation: the Conference of EU Speakers; meetings of sectoral committees organised by national parliaments or by the EP; COSAC; simultaneous debates in interested parliaments; secretaries general; IPEX; representatives of national parliaments in Brussels; and the ECPRD. Moreover, they list four fields of cooperation. First, in the field of subsidiarity control, the parliaments are recommended to inform others of their activities concerning the subsidiarity checks. Second, parliaments are encouraged to exchange information and documents at all levels. The use of IPEX is promoted in both these fields. Third, the Guidelines support the organisation of conferences or other events, and fourth, they suggest that the Conference of EU Speakers could select priority policy areas. The Guidelines were slightly amended at the Conference of Speakers in Lisbon in June 2006 (Conference of Speakers of the European Union Parliaments 2008).

All these developments have created an environment that is conducive to interaction among national parliaments and within the European decision-making process, as well as between other institutions that are active within this process. National parliaments have been prompted to consider possibilities for collective activities through various incentives. These include, first, formal treaty changes, ranging from the mere mentioning of national parliaments in the Maastricht Treaty to the new rights and competences of national parliaments pertaining to the European level under the Lisbon Treaty. Second, they also include reactions of the European Commission, the institution that (under these new provisions) has the greatest obligations towards national parliaments. Such reactions also represent an additional set of incentives for national parliaments to work out ways of ensuring mutual communication and cooperation.

National parliaments have also undertaken some practical steps to improve their cooperation, especially in response to the drafting of the Early Warning Mechanism in the Constitutional Treaty. These include especially the launch of the IPEX database and the organisation of the coordinated tests of subsidiarity checks.

Coordinated tests of subsidiarity checks

In preparation for the Early Warning Mechanism, COSAC, in 2004, decided to 'carry out an experiment' and test the subsidiarity checks on a legislative proposal from the European Commission (COSAC 2004). This first test concerned the Third Railway package in 2005 and was followed by seven others;[6] the last one was concluded just after the Lisbon Treaty came into force. The idea behind the tests was to (a) try out the mechanisms of subsidiarity checks adopted in individual member states; (b) find out whether national parliaments can comply with the requirements of the Early Warning Mechanism (such as the time limits imposed); and (c) see if national parliaments can reasonably be expected to reach the required number of votes (one third or a simple majority) to raise the yellow or orange cards.

The tests revealed several problematic aspects of the subsidiarity checks and the potential cooperation of national parliaments.[7] The main challenge for national parliaments pertained to the short time limits as many parliaments found it difficult to finish the check in time even without disseminating information on their opinion to other national parliaments or attempting further cooperation.

---

6. Legislative proposals on which the coordinated test of subsidiarity checks were organised are: (1) Third Railway package - test running from 1 March 2005 until 12 April 2005; (2) Regulation on the applicable law and jurisdiction in divorce matters – test running from 17 July until 27 September 2006; (3) Proposal for the full accomplishment on the Internal Market for Postal Services – test running from 31 October until 11 December 2006; (4) Proposal for the Framework Decision on Combating Terrorism – test running from 26 November 2007 until 21 January 2008, (the first time it ran for eight weeks, according to the provisions of the Lisbon Treaty); (5) The Council Directive on Implementing the Principle of Equal Treatment between Persons Irrespective of Religion or Belief, Disability, Age or Sexual Orientation – from 9 July 2008 until 4 September 2008; (6) Proposal for the Directive on standards of quality and safety of human organs intended for transplantation – from 10 December 2008 until 6 February 2009; (7) Proposal for the Council Framework Decision on the right to interpretation and to translation in criminal proceedings – from 20 July 2009 until 14 September 2009; (8) Proposal for a Regulation of the European Parliament and of the Council on jurisdiction, applicable law, recognition and enforcement of decisions and authentic instruments in matters of succession and the creation of a European Certificate of Succession - from 21 October until 17 December 2009.

7. All data in this section are based on the COSAC reports. Online. Available at: http://www.cosac. eu/subsidiarity-tests/ (accessed 3 July 2012). More detailed analysis of the tests can be found in Knutelská (2011a).

During the first three tests, national parliaments had major problems with completing the checks within the six-week deadline. This resulted in altering the Protocol in its Lisbon Treaty version that extended the time limit to eight weeks. Parliaments also repeatedly complained about the late availability of legislative proposals in all-language versions. However, as the Treaty specifically states that the eight-week period begins after the transmission of a draft legislative act in the official languages of the Union, this should not be a major problem, although national parliaments capable of processing legislative proposals in the working languages of the Commission sometimes have the advantage of more than just eight weeks to check the proposal. Moreover, the number of parliaments finishing the subsidiarity check in time has risen with the extension of the deadline between the third and the fourth test, as shown in Table 3.1.

The time concerns proved to be especially relevant in cases where the six/eight-week period overlapped with parliamentary recess, especially during summer, but also during Christmas holidays. The Commission took these tests, and the arrangements national parliaments had made, into account when preparing its practical arrangements for the operation of the Early Warning Mechanism after the Lisbon Treaty came into force. For example, it promised to use IPEX to post copies of legislative proposals as well as reasons for its decisions made in response to any alleged breaches of subsidiarity by national parliaments. Perhaps the most significant result was the Commission's promise that 'in order to take account of national [p]arliaments' summer recesses, the Commission considers that the month of August should not be taken into account when determining the deadline referred to in Protocol No. 2' (European Commission 2009b).

Moreover, despite the limitations of the Treaty, the Commission has invited national parliaments to comment not only on subsidiarity issues, but also on the substance of a proposal, although it asked them to distinguish between the two (European Commission 2009b).

The coordinated tests of subsidiarity checks were also the first opportunity for national parliaments to exchange information and to try to cooperate in a real case of scrutiny that was subject to the actual legislative process in the EU. It is thus the first example in which the second (mutual awareness of activity) and third (coordinated effort) criteria of collective actorness can be evaluated. Table 3.2 summarises the interparliamentary cooperation in tests four to eight (as the questionnaires and reports on the first three tests do not offer specific information in this regard). In this case, 'cooperation' is understood as any communication and/or information exchange (passive or active) on the subject of the coordinated

Table 3.1: Timely completion of the coordinated tests of subsidiarity checks

	ST1	ST2	ST3	ST4	ST5	ST6	ST7	ST8
No. of parl. chambers completing the check in time	NA	11	10	25	17	27	21	11
Collision with summer recess	N	Y	N	N	Y	N	Y	N

Source: COSAC reports on coordinated tests

Table 3.2: Interparliamentary cooperation in the coordinated test of subsidiarity checks

	Any attempt at cooperation with other national parliaments	Cooperation through permanent representatives	Cooperation with individual parliaments	IPEX used to search for information on scrutiny in other national parliaments
ST No. 4	9	0	5	6
ST No. 5	18	6	2	10
ST No. 6	17	8	4	12
ST No. 7	14	6	2	12
ST No. 8	19	6	2	14

Source: COSAC reports on coordinated tests

test. The data show that roughly half of the parliaments/parliamentary chambers attempted some cooperation. There is also a clear preference for using the newly established channels of cooperation – the permanent representatives and IPEX – to individual bilateral relations. While it would be premature to claim that national parliaments were aware of proceedings in other parliaments *during* the scrutiny process, the indicated effort of national parliaments to offer and/or obtain this information clearly shows that many national parliaments perceived the information exchange as an important part of the process.

Moreover, the fact that the COSAC Secretariat has begun to emphasise the cooperation (by using questionnaires to ascertain levels of cooperation with other national parliaments since the fourth coordinated tests also points to an increasing awareness of the importance of the collective activities of national parliaments at the European level, particularly under the provisions of the Early Warning Mechanism.

Use of IPEX

In order to be able to exchange information more regularly and effectively, the Conference of Speakers started to consider the creation of an information exchange website as early as the year 2000. National parliaments have created various functions and fora to support the functioning of IPEX: the IPEX Steering Group, the IPEX Board and the IPEX correspondents. The first website was created in 2004, fully launched in 2006 and substantially revised in 2011. It contains dossiers on all European legislative proposals and allows national parliaments and the European Commission to upload information on the scrutiny process, subsidiarity checks – including all documents parliaments have drafted or adopted in the process – and the Commission's reactions. The Hague Guidelines (Conference of Speakers of the European Union Parliaments 2004) summarise the expected role of IPEX:

The objective of IPEX (Interparliamentary EU information eXchange) is to support interparliamentary cooperation in the European Union by providing a platform for the electronic exchange of EU-related information between parliaments in the Union including a calendar of meetings and forums for exchange of views on subsidiarity control. Each parliament/chamber has an IPEX correspondent to represent the parliament.

The assets of the IPEX database can best be evaluated by examining its overall use and its application in some relevant examples.

There are various types of information each parliamentary chamber can post on IPEX. On each dossier each parliamentary chamber can use simple icons to indicate:

(a) the progress of scrutiny, i.e. whether the scrutiny has started and is in progress or is already finished;

(b) if a subsidiarity check is in progress and possible subsidiarity concerns;

(c) important information to exchange;

(d) a reasoned opinion in accordance with Protocol No. 2, stating why the national parliament considers the draft not to be in compliance with the principle of subsidiarity.

Moreover, there is an icon to indicate the European Commission's response. The data on the use of IPEX by national parliaments/parliamentary chambers to date (3 July 2012) is summarised in Table 3.3. The amount of information posted on the IPEX website has increased over the years, especially with the Lisbon Treaty's entry into force, when national parliaments started posting information on possible subsidiarity issues and reasoned opinions. However, the usefulness of the database in terms of finding specific information on proceedings and opinions of multiple or even the majority of national parliaments on any issue of interest is still very limited and faces several challenges.

First, in many cases parliaments limit themselves to the use of icons. Even the icon indicating that the national parliament has important information to exchange does not guarantee that IPEX contains any substantial document (opinion, position etc.). Only the indication of a reasoned opinion is almost always accompanied by a corresponding document, the reasoned opinion itself. However, with the exception of Sweden which has twenty-seven reasoned opinions, no national parliament has had more than eleven reasoned opinions.

Second, there is often some delay between the national parliament's proceedings and posting the respective information on IPEX. Especially substantial information often appears with considerable delay. This can pose problems, especially if national parliaments want to use IPEX as an input source within the eight-week time limit of the Early Warning Mechanism.

Third, the language problem may be an issue. Even if substantial information is posted directly on IPEX, it often appears only in the official language of the parliament in question. As already mentioned, this was also the case with the coordinated tests of subsidiarity, when many national parliaments posted information only in their national languages, i.e. used only original versions of documents. On the other hand, the number of courtesy translations has increased. For example, most of the reasoned opinions (used since the Lisbon Treaty came into force) now available in IPEX[1] are translated into English, with the exceptions of a couple of opinions by Spanish, Slovak and Bulgarian parliaments and those originally in French - which is also, of course, a working language of European institutions (and includes all the reasoned opinions by the French and Belgian Parliamentary Chambers and some of the reasoned opinions of the Luxembourg Parliament). The only parliament that neither uses a language that is also a working language of the European institutions, nor has ever offered a translation of a reasoned opinion is the Bulgarian Parliament (which has so far issued only two reasoned opinions). The Spanish Parliament offered English translations on only two reasoned opinions out of a total of eight, but these are the latest opinions from 2012, which may suggest that the approach of the Spanish Parliament in this regard has also changed. Moreover, some parliaments, namely the German Bundesrat, the Irish, Portuguese and Swedish, sometimes post French translations alongside the English ones. However, time is again an issue and translations are sometimes posted later than original documents.

All these past or ongoing shortcomings of IPEX raise questions about how often it is used by national parliaments to look up information on proceedings in other parliaments and thus used for more than just posting information. This is not possible to evaluate from the IPEX database itself, but the responses from national parliaments on the coordinated tests of subsidiarity checks indicate that national parliaments were especially interested in proceedings in countries that have national parliaments known for their active involvement in European affairs, such as the United Kingdom, Denmark and France (Knutelská 2011a). However, at the same time, these parliaments, with the exception of the French Senate, were not especially active in posting information on IPEX during subsidiarity tests or afterwards. This may mean that the key information that national parliaments mostly look for is only rarely to be found.

On the other hand, the efforts that national parliaments have put into building this system cannot be dismissed as non-effective. The amount and availability of information has been increasing over time. Moreover, even if the specific information is not available on IPEX, the network of IPEX correspondents can be used to obtain it. IPEX contains contacts on IPEX correspondents from every parliament or parliamentary chamber so the information can be requested quickly and easily.

---

1. On 3 July 2012, with the exception of seven reasoned opinions that are only indicated but not available at all.

Table 3.3: Use of IPEX by national parliamentary chambers

	Indicated use of IPEX in subsidiarity checks	Subsidiarity issue	Important information to exchange	Reasoned opinion	Response by the European Commission
Austrian National Council	0	13	46	6	14
Austrian Federal Council	4	19	53	4	14
Belgian Senate	2	4	10	1	1
Belgian Chamber of Representatives	0	5	23	3	2
Bulgarian National Assembly	2	0	47	2	1
Cyprus House of Representatives	3	2	1	1	4
Czech Senate	4	8	131	1	41
Czech Chamber of Deputies	0	8	12	1	2
German Bundestag	1	5	62	2	10
German Bundesrat	5	47	122	7	29
Danish Parliament	0	14	22	5	15
Estonian Parliament	2	3	3	0	0
Spanish Cortes Generales	0	3	13	8	1
Finnish Parliament	0	0	0	2	2
French Senate	1	43	91	10	8
French National Assembly	3	5	7	1	1
Hellenic Parliament	4	7	28	0	12
Hungarian National Assembly	1	7	7	0	1
Irish Houses of Oireachtas	2	2	0	0	5
Italian Senate	1	37	97	3	41

(Cont'd.)

Table 3.3: (Cont'd.)

	Indicated use of IPEX in subsidiarity checks	Subsidiarity issue	Important information to exchange	Reasoned opinion	Response by the European Commission
Italian Chamber of Deputies	3	35	82	4	25
Lithuanian Parliament	3	8	43	3	3
Luxembourg Chamber of Deputies	0	9	16	10	9
Saeima Parliament of Latvia	4	5	8	1	0
Maltese House of Representatives	1	1	2	2	1
Dutch Senate	1*	13	54	7	9
Dutch House of Representatives	1*	17	49	7	7
Polish Senate	0	22	25	10	7
Polish Sejm	0	3	76	11	5
Portugese Assembleia da Republica	4	10	49	2	12
Romanian Senate	3*	2	3	1	2
Romanian Chamber of Deputies	3*	2	0	2	4
Swedish Parliament	3	45	157	27	66
Slovenian National Assembly	0	2	2	0	0
Slovenian National Council	0	0	0	0	0
Slovak National Council	1	8	24	4	1
UK House of Lords	0	8	14	2	17
UK House of Commons	0	3	14	7	1

*Both parliamentary chambers exercised the subsidiarity tests in common procedure.
Source: IPEX. Online. Available at: http://www.ipex.eu/IPEXL-WEB/home/home.do (accessed 3 July 2012).

Achievements and prospects

The data on the coordinated tests of subsidiarity checks and on IPEX are useful both in order to assess national parliaments' fulfilment of the criteria for collective actorness at EU level as well as to evaluate the relevance of the different incentives described in Section Two of this chapter.

Firstly, the way these initiatives were launched suggests an emerging shared role perception among national parliaments. Although both COSAC and the Conference of Speakers are basically interparliamentary meetings, it is important to note that the decisions on IPEX or the coordinated tests were both made in the name of these respective institutions ('COSAC decided to carry out an experiment' (COSAC 2004)), not in the name of national parliaments, which shows that national parliaments meet with the first of the three criteria of collective actorness.

Secondly, IPEX, including both the database itself and the network of IPEX correspondents (and other channels, such as the permanent representatives), gives national parliaments an excellent opportunity to be aware and informed of the scrutiny process or positions of other national parliaments. National parliaments thus fulfil the first two criteria of operating as a collective actor at the European level.

The data, however, do not offer much information on the third criterion: execution of coordinated efforts to influence the European decision-making process. Nonetheless, the development of interparliamentary cooperation can offer some insight into national parliaments' and other institutions' attitudes towards such a possibility.

As already shown, various references in the treaties since the early 1990s have acknowledged the role of national parliaments and COSAC in European integration. Despite this, cooperation among national parliaments evolved little in response to these developments as long as they were restricted to a declaratory nature. National parliaments reacted only when the Draft Constitutional Treaty promised them some actual, albeit very limited, powers in the European legislative process rather than merely recognition. As a reaction to the fact that the new rules can be effective only if a sufficient number of national parliaments participate, national parliaments immediately started devising means to enable such cooperation. The very development of IPEX and the coordinated tests of subsidiarity checks are proof of that.

Other European-level incentives also seem not to be as strong as the formal powers granted by the Treaty. For example, as shown in Table 3.4, even though

Table 3.4: Number of opinions received by the Commission from national parliaments

Year	2005	2006	2007	2008	2009	2010
Number of opinions	124	112	149	136	250	387

Sources: European Commission 2009a, 2010 and 2011.

the Commission has encouraged dialogue with national parliaments (at least since the Draft Constitutional Treaty), the number of opinions sent to the Commission by national parliaments every year remained roughly the same between 2005 and 2008 but almost doubled in 2009, when the Lisbon Treaty's entry into force became likely, and again increased considerably in 2010. Once more, this demonstrated that the best incentive for interparliamentary cooperation is the introduction of actual competencies at the European level.

Although country-specific incentives are not the main interest of this chapter, it is also interesting to note that the amount of information national parliaments post on IPEX does not correspond to the formal strength of the national scrutiny system. The parliaments that currently post most information on IPEX are those of Austria, Germany, Italy, the Netherlands, Sweden, the Czech and French Senates and the Polish Sejm, i.e. both stronger and weaker parliaments (see Buzogány in this volume). Moreover, informal or factual influence does not seem to correspond to the use of IPEX, as demonstrated, for example, by the House of Lords, an institution that is among the most influential in the EU (Cygan 2001). Even if the responses to questionnaires on coordinated tests showed that information on proceedings in the strongest parliaments is probably the most sought after, it is not entirely clear what makes a national parliament/parliamentary chamber more active on IPEX. New member states are somewhat less active, with the exception of the Czech Senate and both Polish Chambers.

Even if European-level incentives have clearly been crucial for increasing interparliamentary cooperation, national parliaments cannot simply rely on the European institutions to encourage their cooperation. Although the role of national parliaments and the need for interparliamentary cooperation has been acknowledged by other institutions for quite some time, this acknowledgement has been clearly reinforced by increased cooperation. This can be illustrated by the behaviour of both the European Commission and EP.

The Commission's first report on its relations with national parliaments in 2005 refers to the need to adjust to the new situation. It states that

> the Commission cannot remain indifferent to the representation of the national assemblies [...] in Brussels [,] it cannot ignore the extension of the paradigms of prior parliamentary examination since enlargement, nor can it afford not to exchange views with the national parliaments.

(European Commission 2006)

Moreover, it emphasises its wish 'to ensure that this new national parliaments approach fully respects the institutional balance' (European Commission 2006). This report was drafted after the Constitutional Treaty failed to be ratified and the future of the formal powers of national parliaments was unclear. However, because COSAC continued with the subsidiarity tests and the launch of IPEX, the Commission's approach changed the following year. The Barroso Initiative was launched and the report on relations in 2006 already claimed that 'the Barroso Commission has made its relations with the national parliaments a top priority'

(European Commission 2007). The accommodating approach of the Commission when devising practical arrangements for the application of the Lisbon Treaty (e.g. respecting the summer recess) was also a reaction to the activities of national parliaments themselves.

The EP has also developed multiple communications channels and tools of cooperation with national parliaments. It participates both in COSAC and the Conference of Speakers, and it organises various types of occasional common activities such as joint parliamentary meetings, joint committee meetings, interparliamentary committee meetings and parliamentary seminars or visits. However, the EP has always preferred to emphasise national parliaments' role in scrutinising and controlling their own governments. The EP's resolution on relations with national parliaments from 2002 defines national parliaments' role in regard to (a) their power *vis-à-vis* their respective governments; (b) the exercise of responsibilities in constitutional matters; and (c) closer, more effective cooperation with the EP (European Parliament 2002). Moreover, while the resolution claims that 'the European Parliament does not see itself as the exclusive representative of the citizens' and that 'the role of national parliaments is very important', it stresses that

> the peoples of the Union are represented to the full by the European Parliament and the national parliaments, each in its own realm, [...] [the parliamentarisation of the Union must involve] the broadening of the European Parliament's powers *vis-à-vis* all the Union's decisions and the strengthening of the powers of the national parliaments *vis-à-vis* their respective governments.

> (European Parliament 2002).

A similar resolution from 2009 notes the impending introduction of the Early Warning Mechanism but, regarding the legitimisation role of national parliaments, it only repeats the latter statement from the 2002 resolution. Moreover, the only substantial reference to the future of relations with national parliaments relates to strengthening national parliaments 'to hold national governments to account for their management of the spending of EU funds' and possible innovations by national parliaments, such as giving MEPs the right to be invited once a year to speak in plenary and to participate in meetings of EACs on a consultative basis (European Parliament 2009a).

Conclusions

National parliaments are one of the two channels of democratic representation of the EU. Although this chapter does not pay much attention to the EP, it has used the concept of the European multilevel parliamentary field to analyse the character of interparliamentary relations in the context of the interaction between national parliaments, other European institutions and the European-level incentives for this cooperation. It has also attempted to assess whether national parliaments' activities at the European level fulfil the criteria of collective actorness at the European level, as defined in the second section of this chapter.

Although the need for greater involvement of national parliaments in European decision-making has been acknowledged for at least twenty years, no informal, declarative or communicative impulses have been sufficient to substantially boost interparliamentary cooperation. The most relevant impetus came with the introduction of formal powers of national parliaments to enter into the legislative decision-making process of the EU. After the draft Constitutional Treaty that first suggested these powers, three things occurred: the European Commission started to monitor and report its relations with national parliaments, COSAC initiated tests of the new powers, and the IPEX database was launched. However, even if national parliaments gradually started to use these opportunities, the substantial increase in communication towards the European level (i.e. the European Commission) or towards one another via IPEX occurred only when the entry into force of these new formal powers became more certain. The number of parliaments that participate and the level of their participation have increased over time.

Despite these developments, the level of interparliamentary cooperation has yet to increase further if national parliaments are to make full use of these new powers. There are substantial differences among individual national parliaments and their involvement in interparliamentary cooperation. Nonetheless, whilst launching the above aforementioned initiatives, national parliaments have acted as a collective and not just as a group of peers. Also, the thresholds required to raise the yellow or orange cards in the EWM will probably require that national parliaments look for ways to further improve their cooperation.

This limited success raises questions about the abilities of national parliaments to work together to legitimise the EU at the European level, not just individually in their respective member states. The national parliaments meet two out of the three criteria of the collective actorness required for such legitimisation. National parliaments perceive one another as sharing the same function, and they have the means to be (and, to a certain degree, are) aware of the various scrutiny processes and positions held by other members of the national parliamentary collective.

Having said this, the question of their ability to execute coordinated efforts to influence the European decision-making process is still pending. However, the recent first-time-ever successful use of the yellow card by national parliaments[8] demonstrates that even this does not have to be out of their reach (although at this point it is difficult to say what coordination, if any, occurred prior to achieving the necessary threshold). Any conclusive proof of coordinated effort is still missing and the added value of national parliaments for the European-level legitimisation of European integration remains an open question.

---

8. Regarding the Proposal for a Council Regulation on the exercise of the right to take collective action within the context of the freedom of establishment and the freedom to provide services, COM/2012/0130. Available Online: http://www.ipex.eu/IPEXL-WEB/dossier/document/COM20120130.do (accessed July 4 2012).

chapter four | deliberation in the multilevel parliamentary field: the seasonal workers directive as a test case

Ian Cooper

Introduction: Of mechanisms, chambers and fields

The Treaty of Lisbon was hailed as the 'treaty of parliaments' because it significantly bolstered not only the EP's powers but also those of national parliaments (NPs) within the EU. In this, the treaty contributed to a broader trend of changes – already underway before Lisbon, still in progress today – in the relationships *between* parliaments. These changes are taking place in two dimensions, horizontal (among NPs) and vertical (between NPs and the EP), that are well captured in two novel theoretical concepts. In the horizontal dimension, relations among NPs have intensified; as they now have a collective role in the scrutiny of EU legislation, they have been characterised as a 'virtual third chamber' (Cooper 2012), performing many of the functions of a parliamentary chamber at the EU level without meeting together in the same physical space. In the vertical dimension, relations between NPs (individually and as a group) and the EP have also intensified, to the point that they may be characterised as constituting a 'multilevel parliamentary field' (Crum and Fossum 2009) in which representative bodies at multiple levels may reinforce one another.[1] These two concepts suggest two vital and overlapping research questions which will be explored below. First, have NPs used their new powers under the Treaty of Lisbon to exert influence over policy deliberation at the EU level? And second, have the interventions of NPs influenced policy deliberations in the EP more than in other EU institutions? The latter question, in particular, frames the analysis in this chapter as it provides a kind of empirical test for the concept of the multilevel parliamentary field that is the focus of this volume.

One important instrument which NPs could use to influence EU policy is the EWM which has in effect turned them into 'subsidiarity watchdogs' (Cooper 2006) empowered to raise objections to EU legislative proposals which they believe violate the principle of subsidiarity. This mechanism has drawn the interest of many EU scholars, some of whom welcome it as enhancing the role of NPs and alleviating the democratic deficit (Barrett 2008; Dougan 2008; Louis 2008; Maurer 2008; Piris 2010), whereas others remain sceptical of its merits (de Wilde 2012; Fraga 2005; Kiiver 2006b, 2008; Raunio 2007, 2011). For the first time, the EWM

---

1.   The notion of a 'deliberative system' (Parkinson and Mansbridge 2012) may also capture the relationship of these parliamentary bodies at national and EU levels.

does give NPs a modicum of leverage, though not a veto, in the EU's legislative process: if one third of NPs raise objections to an EU legislative proposal (a 'yellow card'), it must be reviewed (after which it may be amended, withdrawn or maintained unchanged); and if a majority of NPs raise such objections (an 'orange card') then the proposal is put to an early vote in the Council and the EP, either of which may reject it.[2] In terms of legislative impact, however, the early results of the EWM have been modest: the first two and a half years after the Lisbon Treaty entered into force (in December 2009) yielded no orange cards. It did, however, yield one yellow card in late May 2012, on the 'Monti II' proposal concerning collective action in the context of the single market;[3] in response to the opposition of numerous NPs, the Commission withdrew the proposal.[4] Yet, apart from this one episode, there is – in line with the expectations of sceptical academic observers – little evidence that NPs have gained significant legislative influence as a result of the EWM.

There is, however, another way of assessing the influence of NPs in the EU's legislative process: by focusing on the EWM as a deliberative exchange between NPs and EU institutions. The deliberative character of the exchange is particularly in evidence in NPs' interaction with the Commission, the institution which receives and is required to respond to the concerns of NPs. This exchange is structured much like an argument: the Commission is required to provide reasoned justifications for its legislative proposal, NPs must respond to the proposal with reasoned opinions stating their objections, and the Commission must respond to NPs' objections with further reasons to justify its position regarding the proposal.[5] Within the context of the EWM, the argument is confined to the question of the subsidiarity compliance of new legislative proposals. However, the Commission

---

2.   In the EWM, each national parliamentary system is allotted two 'votes' – two votes for unicameral parliaments, one vote for each chamber in bicameral parliaments – for a total of fifty-four votes in the EU 27. There is an eight-week deadline. The threshold for a yellow card is (with some exceptions) eighteen votes, and the threshold for an orange card is twenty-eight votes. After an orange card, the proposal may be rejected either by a vote of 55 per cent of Council members or a majority of votes cast in the EP.

3.   'National parliaments show "yellow card" to EU law on strikes,' *EuObserver*, 29 May 2012. Online. Available: http://euobserver.com/social/116405 (accessed 30 June 2013).

4.   'EU anti-strike rules sink as parliaments wield Lisbon powers,' *EuObserver*, 12 September 2012. Online. Available: http://euobserver.com/news/117523 (accessed 30 June 2013).

5.   In Cooper (2006), it is posited that the exchange between NPs and the Commission could conform more to the 'logic of arguing' (Risse 2000) in which two sides put forward reasoned arguments, than to the 'logic of consequences' which normally characterises legislative bargaining. After all, the interlocutors are in effect arguing about the applied meaning of a political principle – subsidiarity – which is at the same time an argument about whether the EU should take action in a given circumstance. This chapter builds on this idea by examining not only the exchange between NPs and the Commission, but also between other EU institutions. While the parties to this exchange might be unlikely to reach a purely rational consensus, they might arrive at what Eriksen calls a *working agreement*, 'an outcome that might fall short of a rational consensus,' but is nevertheless '[…] the result of a deliberative process based on inter-subjectively justifiable reasons' (Eriksen 2009: 51).

also engages in a 'political dialogue' with NPs which is less formal (no yellow or orange cards) but broader in scope, encompassing discussion of the proportionality compliance and policy wisdom of a proposal. Moreover, whereas the NPs' principal interlocutor in the EWM is the Commission, other EU institutions – notably the EP and the Council – are also expected to take heed of their opinions. Insofar as the EWM spurs NPs to scrutinise EU legislation, it more generally lends legitimacy to their engagement in an ongoing policy dialogue with EU institutions. What must be investigated is whether and to what extent the opinions of NPs are reflected in policy deliberations at the EU level.

This investigation into the EWM is aided by the two notions mentioned above, the virtual third chamber and the multilevel parliamentary field, each of which captures a dimension of the evolving role of NPs in the EU. Structurally, the two concepts are not antithetical but complementary, in that the virtual third chamber may be thought of as an instance of particularly robust interparliamentary cooperation embedded *within* the multilevel parliamentary field. Each concept relies on a holistic methodological approach, depicting a form of interparliamentary interaction creating a collective entity that is more than the sum of its individual parts. In the virtual third chamber, NPs come together (in the horizontal dimension) as a collective entity that functions as a parliamentary chamber. Similarly, in the multilevel parliamentary field, NPs and the EP come together (in the vertical dimension) to form an 'integrated structure' with 'systemic properties' (Crum and Fossum 2009). Both concepts involve the structural integration of parliaments – rather than merely their members – into a common entity. In these ways, both concepts contrast strongly with, for example, the much looser notion of an international 'network' of parliamentarians (cf. Slaughter 2004).

Moreover, both concepts are multifunctional. The virtual third chamber performs at least three parliamentary functions at the EU level: it has a hand in the EU legislative process (legislation), it provides a new link between the citizen and the EU (representation), and it provides a forum for the debate of salient public policy issues (deliberation).[6] Similarly, all three of these functions are apparent, though perhaps not in equal measure, in the workings of the multilevel parliamentary field. The notion of a multilevel parliamentary field is focused mainly on the *representative* functions of parliaments at both levels – and how these interact with and perhaps reinforce one another – but it also involves *deliberation*, in that it engages with deliberative aspects of democratic theory. As for legislation, the virtual third chamber has a legislative function insofar as NPs can intervene directly in the EU's legislative process; it can even exhibit an element of collective agency, in particular on those rare occasions when a majority of NPs act in concert to wield an orange card. It is uncertain whether the multilevel parliamentary field could perform a legislative function or display a similar element of collective agency, although in the case of an orange card it would be possible for a majority of NPs and a majority of MEPs to act in concert

6. For a full explication of this argument, see Cooper 2012.

to defeat a legislative proposal. Even so, the multilevel parliamentary field is more a system of relations between parliaments and an arena in which they interact than it is itself an 'actor'. Relations between the EP and the NPs may be characterised either by cooperation or rivalry: despite the fact that MEPs and MPs 'all share the same role conception as *parliamentarians*', whether they 'reinforce each other or [...] operate as competitors for authority' is still an open question (Crum and Fossum 2009). This leads to the question that animates the empirical analysis that follows: does their coexistence within the field cause the EP and NPs to cooperate – for example, to work together towards commonly agreed legislative outcomes – or to compete?

Of the three parliamentary functions mentioned above – legislation, representation and deliberation – the focus of the empirical analysis in this chapter is on deliberation. It is too soon to say what the impact of the EWM – or more generally, the increased involvement of NPs – will have on the other two functions. In *legislative* terms, its impact has been minimal: while a number of legislative proposals have provoked reasoned opinions, none have reached the orange card threshold that would trigger a vote in the Council and EP, and only one has reached the yellow card threshold that triggers a formal review. As for the long term, aside from the withdrawn 'Monti II' proposal, none of the most contested proposals has yet reached the final stages of the legislative process, at which point it would be possible to assess whether NPs' interventions contributed to the final outcome (e.g. if the measure were rejected or significantly amended as a result of concerns raised by NPs). The *representative* function of the virtual third chamber is also difficult to assess at this point as it concerns the effect of NPs' involvement on the long-term democratic legitimacy of the EU. However, it is possible to make at least a preliminary assessment of the effect of the EWM on *deliberation* – i.e. whether the involvement of NPs leads to an improvement of public discussion of salient public policy issues in the EU. The question then is, has there been an increase either in the quantity (i.e. frequency of interaction) or quality (i.e. substantive depth) of the deliberative exchange between NPs and the EP? By way of comparison, we could look at the way in which the three main political institutions of the EU – the Commission, EP and Council – have responded to and interacted with NPs since they gained new powers under the Treaty of Lisbon. In other words, the empirical task is to compare the extent to which EU institutions were *procedurally* responsive to NPs' concerns (explicitly addressing them) and *substantively* responsive (reflecting such concerns in subsequent internal deliberation). That is the aim of this chapter.

The main body of this chapter is a case study of the early legislative progress of one legislative proposal, the Seasonal Workers Directive. Using a process-tracing analysis, I detail (1) the Commission proposal, and how it was explicitly justified on subsidiarity grounds; (2) how NPs reacted to the proposal, raising subsidiarity-based objections and other concerns; and (3) how each of the three main political institutions – Commission, EP and Council (and, briefly, two minor ones: the Committee of the Regions (CoR) and the European Economic and Social Committee (EESC)) – responded to the concerns raised by NPs. This last point allows me to compare the responses of the Commission, EP and Council. I will compare their procedural and substantive responses – first, whether they actually addressed the concerns of NPs, and second, whether they adopted them. In this way we can assess the deliberative exchange between NPs and EU institutions and compare the EU institutions' responses. This can at least give us a rough and ready early assessment of how deliberation occurs within the multilevel parliamentary field. This concept might be thought to imply an expectation that there would be more or better deliberative interaction between NPs and the EP than between NPs and other EU institutions. However, this turned out not to be the case. The institution with which NPs had the most extensive deliberative interaction was in fact the Commission, which is surely a consequence of its self-imposed obligation to respond individually to every communication it receives from an NP. However, while the Commission did respond individually to NPs' concerns – often by augmenting its subsidiarity-based justifications for the legislative proposal in the process – those concerns were not reflected in the proposal itself, which was not substantively altered. By contrast, the substantive concerns of NPs *were* reflected in the subsequent internal deliberations of the Council. In comparison, the deliberative exchange between NPs and the EP was less extensive than that with the Commission, and the substantive concerns of NPs were not reflected in the subsequent internal deliberations of the EP as they were in the Council. This conclusion does not belie the existence of the multilevel parliamentary field, but it does indicate that the field might be characterised as much by rivalry as by cooperation between the parliaments at different levels.

The Seasonal Workers Directive: EU institutions' responses to national parliaments

The legislative proposal that provoked by far the largest reaction from NPs in the first year[7] after Lisbon was the 'Seasonal Workers Directive' (SWD).[8] Nine chambers issued reasoned opinions under the Early Warning Mechanism[9] and a

---

7. The SWD is the only proposal that meets two criteria: it provoked a significant reaction from NPs, and it occurred in 2010, early enough in the history of the EWM for us to trace subsequent deliberations in EU institutions. (The 'Monti II' proposal of 2012 was quickly withdrawn after the first yellow card, so in that case there is no subsequent legislative history to trace). Only one other proposal, in 2011, attracted a large reaction from national parliaments, namely, the Proposal for a Council Directive on a Common Consolidated Corporate Tax Base (CCCTB) (COM(2011) 121, 16.3.2011). Compared to the SWD, this measure provoked the same number of reasoned opinions (nine) and a greater number of votes (thirteen) under the EWM. However, as it is a more recent proposal, it is less far along in the legislative process. Moreover, as its legal basis entails the 'consultation' procedure, the EP only has limited input in the legislative process (and agreement in the Council must be unanimous), which makes it a poor test case for the notion of a multilevel parliamentary field.

8. 'Proposal of a Directive of the European Parliament and of the Council on the conditions of entry and residence of third-country nationals for the purposes of seasonal employment' (COM(2010) 379).'

9. Austrian *Nationalrat* and *Bundesrat*, Czech *Poslanecká sněmovna* and *Senát*, Lithuanian *Seimas*, Netherlands *Tweede Kamer* and *Eerste Kamer*, Polish *Senat*, UK *House of Lords*. In its reasoned

further nine sent contributions to the Commission in the context of the political dialogue.[10] This proposal is controversial because it not only involves migration – already a sensitive topic for member states – but the migration of low-skilled workers. Also, it is a policy area that, since the Treaty of Lisbon, is covered by the Ordinary Legislative Procedure (co-decision) in which the EP enjoys new powers and seems eager to use them. At the time of writing, the fate of the legislation remained uncertain. By mid-2012, the EP had reached a common negotiating position on the legislation, but the Council had not. It is unknown what the results of negotiations between the Commission, Council and EP would be, should they occur; it is entirely possible that the legislation could fail altogether. But the legislative process is far enough along that we can assess the early interaction between NPs and the EU institutions.

It should be emphasised that this is chosen because it is an extreme, rather than representative, case. It is the instance in which '[...] the European Commission encountered for the first time significant direct opposition to one of its initiatives from NPs' under the EWM (Monar 2011). NPs were largely quiescent in the first year after Lisbon, making little use of their new powers: in response to the eighty-two draft legislative acts subject to subsidiarity scrutiny under the EWM, they issued only thirty-four reasoned opinions (Commission 2011a). While it is far from typical, it is the one case where the interventions of NPs are likely to be noticed and taken seriously by EU institutions: for example, in this case the responsible EP committee took the highly unusual step of inviting national parliamentarians to speak in person and air their subsidiarity concerns. For this reason, it can give us a sense of what the impact of NPs can be, not in a typical case but in the rare case where they have been roused into action. If it is true that NPs' interventions open up new 'deliberative spaces', both among themselves and with EU institutions, then examining this case can give us a sense of what the size and dimensions of those spaces are. To this end, here I will sketch out the interaction between NPs and the various EU institutions pertaining to this measure. My aim is not to pass judgment on the wisdom of the policy proposal at issue, but to compare how the various EU institutions attended to NPs' views on the matter. Above all, this will show how the deliberation between NPs and the EP – within the multilevel parliamentary field – compares to their deliberations with the Commission and the Council.

---

opinion, the Lithuanian Parliament only raised concerns regarding proportionality, not subsidiarity. *See* European Commission (2011: 11).

10. Finnish *Eduskunta*, German *Bundesrat*, Italian *Senato* and *Camera dei Deputati*, Latvian *Saeima*, Portuguese *Assembleia* and Spanish *Congreso de los Diputados and Senado*, UK *House of Commons*. The UK House of Commons raised subsidiarity concerns, which I include in the discussion below, but its contribution was not technically a 'reasoned opinion'. *See* European Commission (2011a: 7).

The Seasonal Workers Directive Proposal, with Subsidiarity Justifications

The Commission proposed the Seasonal Workers Directive in July 2010.[11] Part of a broader effort to develop a comprehensive immigration policy for the EU, the proposal is intended to create a common legal framework to govern low-skilled workers from third countries entering the EU to do seasonal work in industries such as tourism and agriculture. However, the legal basis of the EU's power in this area is limited and ambiguous because much power remains in the hands of the member states. The treaty clearly empowers the EU to develop a common immigration policy to ensure 'the efficient management of migration flows' and 'fair treatment of third-country nationals residing legally in Member States' (Art. 79(1) TFEU). Yet, in the case of third-country nationals, it has the power to set policy regarding their rights and conditions of entry and residence (Art. 79(2) (a) and (b) TFEU) but the member states retain the power to determine volumes of admission (Art. 79(5) TFEU). There are three main elements to the proposal: simplified admission procedures for seasonal workers; common rules regarding their rights and residency conditions during the working period; and measures to encourage their departure afterwards (such as the promise of future re-entry).

As usual, the proposal was accompanied by an explanatory memorandum explaining its purpose, as well as a detailed impact assessment.[12] Of particular interest for our purposes is the section of the explanatory memorandum that explicitly justifies the action on subsidiarity grounds – i.e. as necessary and therefore not violating subsidiarity. The Commission presents four points, paraphrased below, to support the argument that the status quo (member state action alone) is insufficient to address the problem, making action at the EU level necessary:

S1. Most member states experience a need for seasonal workers; moreover, the decisions of any one member state on the rights of third-country nationals could affect other member states and possibly cause distortions of migratory flows;

S2. in the Schengen area, common minimum rules are needed, because lax or diverse rules could lead to overstaying and illegal entries;

S3. seasonal workers must be granted socioeconomic rights in a binding, enforceable EU-level instrument to prevent exploitation and sub-standard working conditions;

S4. an EU instrument will facilitate cooperation with third countries because removing obstacles to legal migration of their nationals will strengthen their commitment to tackling irregular immigration.

---

11. COM(2010)0379 FIN.
12. SEC/2010/08879 FIN. *See also* summary: SEC/2010/0888 FIN.

In addition, the Commission makes an explicit two-point justification on proportionality grounds: the legal instrument chosen is a Directive which allows member states flexibility in its implementation; and the proposal is a relatively small change from the status quo in terms of the legislative action required and the burden on prospective employers. In this way the Commission has discharged its initial obligation to justify the legislative proposal on subsidiarity and proportionality grounds.

National Parliaments' responses

The nine parliaments claiming that the proposal breaches subsidiarity vary in the extent of their response. Some are short, such as the Czech Chamber of Deputies, which asserts with little elaboration its finding that the proposal 'is not in compliance with the principle of subsidiarity' (2010). Most, however, are long and detailed, and some – the Austrian and UK Parliaments' opinions in particular – refute the Commission's justifications point by point, and so bear closer examination here.

In response to S1, the House of Lords (2010) responds that while most member states need seasonal workers their needs differ greatly with respect to numbers, time and length of service, type of work, etc. The Austrian Chambers (whose opinions are separate but identical) argue that because member states remain responsible for the volumes of admission, 'the admission procedure is not therefore a transborder problem' requiring EU-level legislation (Austrian National Council 2010). As for the argument that the patchwork of national laws could cause 'distortions of migratory flows' – by making working conditions more attractive in some member states than in others – the UK House of Commons (2010) questions whether this is the principal cause of the difference in demand for seasonal workers, remarking that this competition is 'a sign of a healthy labour market'. Against S2, the Austrian Chambers point out that the existence of the Schengen area does not overburden the member states and the House of Lords does not see why having common rules for seasonal workers should necessarily reduce the risk of overstaying or illegal entry. Regarding S3, the Austrian Chambers acknowledge that aiming to combat exploitation and social dumping is important, but argue that there is 'no transborder problem,' and that 'every Member State may at its own discretion grant seasonal workers the same rights as their own nationals' (Austrian National Council 2010). The House of Commons notes drily that this justification is 'somewhat at odds with the first justification advanced by the Commission that Member States are competing with each other to offer more attractive conditions', then goes on to argue that the problem lies with 'deficiencies in national legislation and lax enforcement' (House of Commons 2010). Similarly, the House of Lords (2010) does not see the need for a binding EU-level instrument because 'measures of national law are of course binding and enforceable, and at least as effective as EU measures in overcoming exploitation'. As for S4, the House of Commons (2010) understands the argument that 'opening up opportunities for legal migration [...] may make it easier to secure co-operation on illegal immigration from source countries', but does not see how EU-level legislation is necessary, given that the treaty 'does not empower the EU to determine how many labour migrants to admit'. Others merely reject this as 'unpersuasive' (House of Lords 2010) and 'not an adequate argument' (Austrian National Council 2010).

Those national chambers which found a subsidiarity breach also raised objections on other grounds. The Austrian Chambers voiced their concerns that the legal basis of the proposal was faulty. They also claimed – and the UK House of Commons and the Nerherland Chambers voiced similar concerns – that the proposal was formally in breach of subsidiarity because the reasoning of the Commission was inadequate. Noting that the Commission cited 'anecdotal evidence' in its Impact Assessment, the UK House of Commons (2010) remarked, '[w]e doubt whether anecdotal evidence constitutes the qualitative indicator required under the Subsidiarity Protocol'. The Lithuanian Parliament and the Polish Senate raised objections to the proposal on proportionality grounds. Moreover, many of these objections also overlapped with concerns about policy. These policy-based concerns were sometimes normative: for example, the Czech Senate questioned whether the proposal fully upheld the principle of EU preference, wherein EU nationals should have priority over third-country nationals when these jobs are awarded. More often, the objections challenged the policy effectiveness of the proposal, questioning whether it would even achieve its stated goals: for example, the House of Lords notes that the legislation would not actually solve the problem of distorted migratory flows because it does not make member states equally attractive to seasonal workers but only imposes minimum standards.

In addition to those parliaments who submitted reasoned opinions, nine chambers sent 'contributions' to the Commission within the framework of the political dialogue. These opinions are even more varied, ranging from those that in effect claim a substantive breach of subsidiarity without formally alleging it (UK House of Commons, Finnish Parliament), to statements of support for the proposal and even a desire to see it strengthened (Italian Chambers).[13] In between these extremes many parliaments raised (explicit or implicit) proportionality concerns, arguing that elements of the proposal would impose undue administrative burdens or financial costs. One such element was Article 14, which stipulates that member states must require employers '[…] to provide evidence that the seasonal worker will benefit from accommodation that ensures an adequate standard of living'. The Latvian Parliament in particular singled out this provision as 'redundant' and excessive, potentially imposing 'new administrative costs with [a] higher risk of corruption' and leading to '[…] a higher level of protection of seasonal workers from third countries than of the citizens from the Member States' (Latvian

---

13. Indeed, two views of this kind can coexist within a single opinion without necessarily contradicting one another. The French Senate's European Affairs Committee made an 'observation' (not an official reasoned opinion) that the Commission's justifications with regard to subsidiarity were insufficient, but then went on to claim that the proposal did not provide sufficient protection to seasonal workers against exploitation and should therefore be strengthened. Online. Available at: http://www.senat.fr/compte-rendu-commissions/20101013/2010–10–13.html #toc6 (accessed 30 June 2013).

Parliament 2010).[14] Others raised policy objections. Both Italian Chambers thought that member states should be able to offer permits up to nine, rather than six, months, given the varying length of seasons (and associated work) in different countries; while this was presented as a point about policy, it could also be read as a proportionality-based call for a more flexible Directive. The German *Bundesrat*, while generally expressing approval of the proposal, nevertheless called for 'clarifications' to the text that would restrict the scope of the EU legislation in a way that increased national authorities' discretion and limited the rights granted to seasonal workers: national authorities should not be required to make a decision within a thirty day deadline, to issue a multi-year permit, or to keep more than minimal statistical data. Meanwhile, it should be 'clarified' that seasonal workers do not have the 'right' to a work permit, to compensation if the deadline is not met, to work in a member state other than the one which issued the permit, or to family reunification.

The Commission's response

In response to the large number of reasoned opinions, the Commission produced a six-page 'Commission reply to opinions concerning subsidiarity' (2011b) which addressed most of the concerns raised by NPs. This generic 'reply' was attached to an individualised two-page letter sent to each parliamentary chamber, addressing its specific concerns that were not related to subsidiarity.

With respect to subsidiarity, the Commission defends the proposal, stressing as a first point that it is one piece of a broader policy plan on legal migration which has been endorsed by all member governments, most recently by the European Council in 2009. In other words, when NPs argue that no legislation is necessary in this case, the Commission reminds them that their respective governments have already agreed in principle that some legislation is needed. Responding to the formal objection made by the Austrian and Netherlands Chambers that the justifications for the proposal were inadequately argued, the Commission points to its detailed Impact Assessment accompanying the proposal to demonstrate that its analysis was thoroughgoing.

As for the specific, substantive complaints regarding its subsidiarity reasoning (see S1-S4, above), the Commission does, for the most part, develop and elaborate its original justifications. The exception is S2, in which case it merely 'reiterates its assessment' (2011) – i.e. restates its one-sentence justification with respect to the Schengen area. The other complaints are given a more substantive response. Regarding S1, the Commission points out that even though member states determine the volume of admissions, 'distortions of migratory flows' can still occur due to variations in the attractiveness of the national schemes. With respect to S3, it makes the additional argument that seasonal workers must be granted socioeconomic rights not only to prevent exploitation but to ensure that they 'do not unfairly compete with Union citizens' (2011). Furthermore,

---

14. This point was also made by the Czech Senate and the Polish Senate.

in response to the observation that demand for third-country seasonal workers varies among member states, the Commission responds that the proposal takes account of this by including provisions that allow them to 'accommodate their national specificities' (2011). Finally, regarding S4, the Commission explains the logic of its argument concerning international cooperation: some third countries have 'long awaited' a common EU legal regime on seasonal workers, which they see as linked to EU development policy. Moreover, the Commission defends the concept of 'circular migration' – the promotion of legal migration by promising re-entry to exiting seasonal workers – which it says can contribute to 'triple-win' outcomes, benefiting the sending and receiving countries, and the migrants themselves (2011).

The Commission also responded to non-subsidiarity-related concerns, both in its generic 'reply' and in its individual letters to various NPs. It defends the legal basis of the measure as the appropriate one. Against proportionality-related concerns, it shows that there is some flexibility in the proposal – allowing national authorities to uphold the principle of EU preference, issue visas for stays shorter than three months, or choose whether to issue a multi-year permit or to provide a facilitated procedure for readmission of returning workers. On policy grounds it defends other less flexible provisions – the requirement of proof of a contract or job offer specifying hours and pay, the requirement of proof of accommodation, and the provision allowing seasonal workers to change employer – as necessary to prevent exploitation. It makes a similar point regarding its proposed maximum duration of stay: work that exceeds six months is not really 'seasonal' and, by implication, the worker in that situation should be able to obtain a more long-term immigration status.

The European Parliament

Members of NPs were invited to take part in the EP's first public deliberations on the Seasonal Workers Directive. The main committee responsible for the legislation, the Committee on Civil Liberties, Justice and Home Affairs (LIBE), first took it up on 29 November 2010.[15] After a Commission representative presented the legislation, and a representative from the Belgian Presidency presented the main points of discussion in the Council, representatives from three national chambers which had issued reasoned opinions – Tomáš Grulich (Czech Senate), Hannes Weninger (Austrian Nationalrat), and Lord Roper (UK House

---

15. The national parliaments' opinions on the measure were not published in the 'Meeting Documents' section of the LIBE committee's website, despite their obvious relevance for that day's agenda. According to the EP's amended Rules of Procedure, reasoned opinions received from national parliaments 'shall be referred to the committee responsible for the subject-matter and forwarded for information to the committee responsible for respect of the principle of subsidiarity' (Art. 38a(3)). The latter is the Committee on Legal Affairs (JURI) which publishes them on its 'Meeting Documents' website but apparently does not review them substantively. According to its *2010 Yearbook* on relations with national parliaments, the EP 'makes a clear reference to all reasoned opinions' when it adopts a resolution on the same subject matter (EP 2011).

of Lords) – were given the floor to present their arguments that the measure was in breach of subsidiarity insofar as no EU legislation was warranted in this area. After a response from the Commission representative, who noted pointedly that several other national chambers had in fact communicated a *positive* response to the proposal, MEPs discussed the measure.

In the subsequent debate, MEPs showed a marked willingness to address, if not be convinced by, NPs' objections to the proposal. Even at this early stage, opinion in the EP was already manifestly in favour of legislation: among the eleven MEPs who spoke, nine – including the *rapporteur*, Claude Moraes (S and D, UK) – were positively disposed towards the measure and only two were negatively disposed.[16] But despite this imbalance, the exchange was nevertheless largely framed by the subsidiarity question – not in terms of what form the legislation should take, but whether any legislation was necessary at all. The pro-legislation MEPs felt compelled to state why they believed EU action was indeed necessary before going on to address the substantive provisions of the measure still up for negotiation. With the visiting national parliamentarians looking on, MEPs promised to take their concerns into account – also making positive remarks about interparliamentary cooperation – even as they argued that legislation was necessary. For example, Salvatore Iacolino (EPP, Italy) said, '[...] of course we should take account of interparliamentary cooperation which can only enrich us mutually [...]', but he also said, 'Okay we've got the subsidiarity principle but we've also got the need to guarantee a uniform approach [...]'; Renate Weber (ALDE-Romania) was less conciliatory, saying, 'Are we going to have common rules, even minimum rules, or are we going to invoke the principle of subsidiarity all the time?' Meanwhile, the two dissenters were not decidedly opposed to the measure but said they were yet to be convinced by the arguments of the Commission that EU action was necessary and that the arguments of the national parliaments (NPs) should be taken seriously. For example, Simon Busuttil (EPP, Malta) said, 'I think that our colleagues from national parliaments have raised some compelling arguments on the principle of subsidiarity which cannot just be wished away [...] The European Commission has not fully convinced us that the principle of subsidiarity is being respected.'

Yet, some months after this extraordinary exchange, when the EP again took up the issue of seasonal workers, the concerns of NPs were largely ignored. At a public hearing held on the subject in April 2011, in addition to MEPs there were numerous invited speakers including representatives of social partners

---

16. Speakers broadly in favour of legislation were varied in their party affiliation and national origin. They were: Claude Moraes (S and D, UK), Georgios Papanikolaou (EPP, Greece), Judith Sargentini (Greens-EFA, Netherlands), Renate Weber (ALDE, Romania), Salvatore Iacolino (EPP, Italy), Carmen Romero López (S and D, Spain), Axel Voss (EPP, Germany), Jean Lambert (Greens-EFA, UK), Cornelia Ernst (GUE/NGL, Germany). Speakers sceptical of legislation were: Simon Busuttil (EPP, Malta), Jan Mulder (ALDE, Netherlands). The entire debate (including quotes cited below, in unofficial translation) can be viewed on the Europarl TV website. Online. Available: http://www.europarl.europa.eu/ep-live/en/committees/video?event=20101129–1500-COMMITTEE-LIBE&category=COMMITTEE&format=wmv (accessed 26 June 2012). For minutes of the meeting, see LIBE_PV(2010)1129_1.

(business and labour), international organisations and civil society – but not national parliaments.[17] Moreover, NPs' substantive concerns were also essentially absent from subsequent deliberations as the proposal made its way through the EP committees. In fact, in all three committees that have considered it, opinion has overwhelmingly favoured *strengthening* the Directive. First, in November 2010 the EP Committee on Women's Rights and Gender Equality (FEMM) produced an opinion[18] proposing amendments that would prevent the exploitation of (particularly female) seasonal workers, such as making them aware of their rights and providing for inspections of their accommodation to be sure their living conditions were adequate. Next, in November 2011 the Committee on Employment and Social Affairs (EMPL) also produced an opinion[19] which recommended that the proposal be strengthened to ensure that seasonal workers be accorded equal treatment to EU nationals with respect to social security coverage and collective agreements; it also favoured a system of monitoring and inspections of the working and living conditions of seasonal workers, with sanctions against employers that engaged in exploitation.

Finally, in April 2012 the legislation was approved by LIBE, the main committee responsible for it, after considerable behind-the-scenes negotiations between the *rapporteur* and the 'shadow *rapporteurs*' (MEPs from other political groups responsible for this legislation). It was approved overwhelmingly (fifty-two in favour, none against, one abstention) in an 'orientation vote' giving the *rapporteur* a mandate to begin negotiations with the Council with a view to a first-reading agreement.[20] The final vote incorporated numerous amendments that would, in essence, strengthen the legislation – with respect to information and a new regime of monitoring, inspections and sanctions against employers. Most controversially, it also proposed expanding the scope of the legislation by adding a transitional measure to allow third-country nationals already residing illegally in the EU to apply for employment as seasonal workers.[21] These amendments point in the opposite direction to the concerns of NPs. Indeed, it is difficult to find a single instance where the substantive concerns of NPs on the proposal were reflected in the opinions of the EP committees.[22] Even in the case of the section of the proposal concerning accommodation, which was flagged by the Latvian Parliament and other chambers as infringing the principle of proportionality, all three EP committees favoured language that would make the requirements more, not less, stringent.

17. See draft programme: Hearing: Legal Migration After Lisbon: Seasonal Workers and Intra-Corporate Transferees, LIBE_(2011) 0420_1.
18. FEMM Committee, 2010/0210(COD), 18.11.2010.
19. EMPL Committee, 2010/0210(COD) 1.12.2011.
20. 'Better working conditions and social rights for seasonal workers', LIBE Committee press release, 23 April 2012.
21. LIBE Committee, Orientation Vote result, 2010/0210(COD), 4.5.2012.
22. This is even true of most of the hundreds of amendments suggested by individual MEPs to the LIBE committee's draft report.

The Council

It is difficult to give a detailed account of the closed deliberations of the Council, but information that is publicly available indicates that the concerns of NPs were noted there. Indeed, in the first exchange of views on the proposal in the Council in October 2010,[23] a number of delegations questioned whether it was compatible with subsidiarity. In addition, many of the other points aired touched on concerns related to proportionality, insofar as they reflected a demand for greater flexibility – relating to duration of stay, the time limit for the decision on an application, ability to take national labour markets into account, and to call the travel document a 'visa' rather than a 'permit'. After this, it seems to have received little attention at the ministerial level with the exception of a subsequent meeting in June 2011, where the issues still unresolved included '[…] the definition of seasonal work, the admission criteria, permits or visas for seasonal workers and seasonal workers' rights'.[24] Beyond this, discussions were carried out at a lower level.

In July 2011[25] and February 2012[26], the Council Presidency circulated new texts with compromise language that incorporated a number of amendments echoing the initial concerns of NPs. These included the following amendments (noted with the national chambers that raised the issues):

- the right of a member state to determine the volumes of admission is by itself sufficient grounds to reject an application (Art. 5a) (German *Bundesrat*);

- the duration of stay has been changed from 'a maximum of six months' to 'a maximum of five to nine months' (Art. 11(1)) (Italian Chamber of Deputies, Italian Senate);

- the time in which the competent authorities must make a decision has been changed from thirty days to sixty or ninety days (Art. 13(1)) (Italian Senate, German *Bundesrat*);

- regarding accommodation, it is 'the applicant' – not, as previously, 'employers of seasonal workers' – who must provide '[…] evidence that the seasonal worker will benefit from accommodation that ensures an adequate standard of living'; the member state determines whether the application is made by the worker and/or the employer (Art. 14) (Latvian Parliament);

- there is an explicit statement that the Directive does not allow for family reunification (Recital 22) (German *Bundesrat*).

---

23. A summary of the exchange available online at: http://europa.eu/rapid/pressReleasesAction.do?reference=PRES/10/262&format=HTML&aged=0&lg=en&guiLanguage=en (accessed 30 June 2013).

24. Online. Available at: http://europa.eu/rapid/pressReleasesAction.do?reference=PRES/11/161&format=HTML&aged=0&lg=en&guiLanguage=en (accessed 30 June 2013).

25. Council of the European Union, 'Interinstitutional File: 2010/0210 (COD)' Brussels, 26 July 2011.

26. Council of the European Union, 'Interinstitutional File: 2010/0210 (COD)' Brussels, 1 February 2012.

All of the above changes would have the effect of giving national authorities greater flexibility in applying the Directive. It should be emphasised that the Council has yet to come to a final position on this legislation, and so none of these amendments has yet been approved; but given that they are suggestions for compromise from the Presidency, they are likely to be part of an emerging consensus on the proposal. In any case, they provide evidence that many of the substantive concerns raised by NPs were the subject of deliberations in the Council.

CoR and EESC

Two minor bodies also bear mentioning in this context; they are both quasi-parliamentary assemblies within the EU, and thus could perhaps be thought to occupy the periphery of the multilevel parliamentary field. Both the CoR and the EESC produced advisory opinions on the draft Directive that duly took note of NPs' reasoned opinions. Interestingly, the CoR, an assembly of representatives of regional and local governments, considers itself to be – like NPs – a subsidiarity watchdog; its modest powers in this regard were increased by the Treaty of Lisbon. Yet, in this case, the CoR disagreed with the dissenting NPs and found the legislative proposal to be compatible with the principle of subsidiarity, arguing that, '[…] the added value of EU legislation must lie mainly in its ability to prevent national systems from engaging in a race to the bottom with regard to the protection of seasonal workers'.[27] However, they recommended on policy grounds that the maximum duration of stay should be extended to nine months. By contrast, the EESC, an assembly of representatives of various socioeconomic interests, found that the Directive may be in violation of the principle of subsidiarity precisely because the six-month duration of stay is too rigid: 'In order to take account of the NPs' concerns about compliance with the subsidiarity principle, the Committee recommends that the duration of the residency permit be dealt with at national level so as to reflect national conditions'.[28] Thus, the two bodies interpreted subsidiarity in very different ways but reached the same substantive conclusion regarding the duration of stay of seasonal workers.

Conclusion

It is now possible to compare the response of the three main political institutions to NPs' concerns about the Seasonal Workers Directive. Of the three, the Commission has been the most responsive to NPs, at least in procedural terms. In the absence of a yellow or orange card, the Commission is only required by the treaty to 'take account' of NPs' reasoned opinions. Even so, it voluntarily responds individually

---

27. Online. Available at: http://coropinions.cor.europa.eu/coropiniondocument.aspx?language=en&d ocnr=354&year=2010 (accessed 30 June 2013).

28. Online. Available at: http://eescopinions.eesc.europa.eu/eescopiniondocument.aspx?language=e n&docnr=801&year=2011 (accessed 30 June 2013).

to every communication from NPs, whether or not they qualify as 'reasoned opinions' under the treaty; this political dialogue has grown into a large and continuously increasing correspondence. In substantive terms, the Commission has only been responsive in a limited way. On the one hand, it takes pains to explain its substantive position to NPs, at times bolstering its arguments with better – or at least more extensive – justifications of the proposal. Yet, regarding the key substantive question of whether a proposal should be amended or withdrawn in response to NPs' concerns, the Commission has proven largely inflexible.

The exchange on the Seasonal Workers Directive has broadly conformed to this pattern. As we have seen, the Commission responded individually to the eighteen communications from NPs but it did not change its position either on the need for, or the substance of, the legislation. This is not surprising, given that the Commission received an equal number (nine each) of 'negative' opinions (objecting, on subsidiarity grounds, to any legislation) and 'positive' ones (agreeing that some legislation was necessary, but not necessarily in the form proposed). There is no 'consensus' opinion among NPs – indeed, a majority of chambers, twenty-two out of forty, did not formally transmit an opinion on the measure. As the reasoned opinions only represent a small minority of the votes of NPs under the EWM (10/54 in EU 27), it would have been premature for the Commission to voluntarily withdraw the measure before the EP or the Council had considered it. Furthermore, the 'positive opinions' (which also represent a minority of NPs) are in disagreement as to how the measure should be amended, even if the Commission were inclined to do so. At this early stage in the process, before the EP and the Council have intervened, the Commission would be essentially caving in if it were to concede that the measure should be withdrawn or amended. A principal role of the Commission is to propose legislation; arguably, the Commission would be remiss if it failed to push forward those legislative proposals it deemed necessary to achieve the goals of the Treaty. Thus, it should not be criticised for refusing to change its position in this case.

The EP does not undertake to respond individually to the concerns of NPs, and so it is procedurally much less responsive than the Commission. Even so, the LIBE committee of the EP, in an unusual gesture of interparliamentary cooperation, invited members of some NPs which had issued reasoned opinions to present their objections in person. The extraordinary debate that followed was framed by the subsidiarity question of whether any EU action was necessary in this case. However, despite the fact that a new deliberative space had opened up between the EP and NPs, this had no lasting effect on subsequent debates on the Directive. In future cases where the legislation was discussed, it was more or less taken for granted that EU action in some form was necessary, and that the subsidiarity question was therefore moot. Moreover, even the proportionality concerns raised by NPs – agreeing that legislation was necessary, but that it should allow greater flexibility to national authorities – were ignored by MEPs, whose proposed amendments would almost without exception involve strengthening the Directive.

The Council is the least responsive to NPs in procedural terms, but the most responsive in substantive terms. Given the closed nature of the Council proceedings, there is very little scope for open deliberation with NPs on the question of subsidiarity or anything else. Of course, many NPs are regularly in contact with their respective governments on matters of EU policy – EACs will often question ministers as part of their scrutiny of a legislative proposal – but there is little scope for interaction with the Council as a body. And yet, substantively, it is clear that the concerns raised by NPs in their communications with the Commission were also raised by representatives of national governments in the Council. This was true regarding subsidiarity, as some national representatives questioned whether any legislation was necessary at all. But it was also true concerning more specific substantive concerns – which could be described as policy-based or proportionality-based – that found their way into conciliatory language on proposed amendments to the Directive.

How does this story fit with the notion of the multilevel parliamentary field? Recall that we are inquiring in particular into the MLPF as a deliberative space in which NPs and the EP can engage in a meaningful exchange on salient public policy questions. When the question is defined broadly in this way, there are some indications that such a space has opened up, at least in this case. The extraordinary exchange which occurred in the LIBE committee of the EP would probably not have happened if the EWM had not facilitated and legitimised the active participation of national parliamentarians in the legislative process at the European level. This was in part enabled by the fact that it involved interparliamentary cooperation across different levels. Yet, if the concept of the multilevel parliamentary field implies that there should be greater deliberative interaction between these bodies simply by dint of their being institutionally alike, this may be tested by broadening the comparison. When the interaction between the NPs and the EP is compared to that between the NPs and other non-parliamentary EU institutions, then a much more nuanced picture emerges. Much more than the EP, the Commission was responsive to NPs both procedurally (responding individually to their concerns) and in a minimally substantive way (addressing their substantive objections, while not yielding to them). The Council, on the other hand, while being unresponsive in procedural terms (hardly responding to NPs' opinions), was quite receptive to them in substantive terms, to the point that many of their substantive concerns about the legislation were incorporated into later conciliatory texts (and is likely to be incorporated into the final Council position on the legislation). The EP, by comparison, had little meaningful interaction with NPs. Thus, while the multilevel parliamentary field shows some promise as a deliberative forum, at this point it remains underdeveloped.

part ii. interparliamentary interaction in different policy domains

chapter | interparliamentary coordination
five | in single market policy-making:
| the EU services directive[*]

Ben Crum and Eric Miklin

Introduction

The structure of the EU can be considered particularly conducive to interparliamentary coordination given its distinctive character as a system of 'multilevel government': rather than that the EU operates as a supranational political system in its own right, its decision-making processes are premised upon those of its member states. Such a system of multilevel government challenges standard conceptions of parliamentary representation as it does not concentrate parliamentary authority in a single institution but, rather, leaves it dispersed over multiple parliamentary sites. Even if the EU has a directly elected supranational parliament, the EP, this parliament shares its legislative powers with the EU governments in the Council of Ministers, and each of these governments is again accountable to its respective national parliament. Moreover, while the EP holds a distinctive position because it is the only parliament that can credibly claim to represent all EU citizens, each national parliament retains an autonomous claim to represent its national people and, generally, can command more popular legitimacy and engagement. Importantly, there are various means through which these parliaments interact at the national and European levels, ranging from formal get-togethers in, for instance, COSAC, to informal contacts in European party group gatherings. It is this condition of dispersed parliamentary authority combined with interparliamentary interaction in a system of multilevel government that is captured by the notion of a 'multilevel parliamentary field' (Crum and Fossum 2009).

In principle, the dynamics between parliaments in this multilevel parliamentary field can operate in either a vicious or a virtuous way. The very dispersion of

[*] Earlier versions of this chapter were presented at the RECON WP3 Workshop on Representative Theory at the Austrian Academy of Sciences, Vienna, 22 May 2009, the 5th ECPR General Conference in Potsdam, 10–12 September 2009, and the ECPR Joint Sessions in Münster, 22–27 March 2010. We thank the participants of these events, and particularly Berthold Rittberger, John Erik Fossum, Pieter de Wilde and Aron Buzogány, for their helpful comments. We thank Stijn van Kessel for allowing us to draw on his previous research. Research for this chapter has been undertaken as part of the RECON Integrated Project sponsored by the European Commission under its sixth Framework Programme, contract nr. FP 6–028698.

parliamentary authority can have vicious effects as parliaments may operate at cross-purposes or even compete with one another over power so as to weaken overall parliamentary impact on decision making. For instance, one can imagine the EP seeking to transfer power to the European level while this was opposed by the national parliaments, and this setting off a destructive struggle. Alternatively, if some EU parliaments pursue right-wing EU policies while others push for more left-wing alternatives, these differences may cancel each other out and, in fact, allow governments to ignore both.

By contrast, one can also imagine more virtuous dynamics in the multilevel parliamentary field in which parliaments benefit from one another. For instance, parliaments may profit from the exchange of ideas with other parliaments via institutional learning and emulation (see Buzogány in this volume) and use this as a means to strengthen their position *vis-à-vis* their executives. Also, considering the extremely heterogeneous societal basis on which EU decisions have to rely, bringing in different ideological and national points of view extends the scope of arguments on which they are based and, ultimately, may serve to increase their legitimacy. Clearly, however, such benefits are more likely to be reaped if EU parliaments actually coordinate their input with one another.

This chapter explores the ability of EU parliaments to exploit the potential benefits of the multilevel parliamentary field of the EU. More specifically, it examines the extent to which EU parliaments can operate along the same lines, reinforce one another's positions and, eventually, amount to a coherent force in EU decision-making. It does so by looking at a likely case in which we would expect parliaments to be aware of one another's positions and to actively engage with one another. The issue selected is taken from the sphere of decision making in the EU single market as this is the domain in which the powers of the EP have been developed most. In this sphere, ever since the Maastricht Treaty, the EP has operated as an equal co-legislator with the Council of Ministers. It can propose amendments, and all directives eventually require its consent (together with that of the Council).

Sticking to the aim of examining a very likely case of virtuous parliamentary interaction within the EU's multilevel parliamentary field, we have selected a single market Directive that has been one of the most visible EU decisions of the last decade: the EU Services Directive (2004–2006). As the Directive has been one of the most politicised pieces of EU legislation in recent years, it provides a particularly promising case for revealing the possible effects of interparliamentary coordination, and for indications of the level of cohesion that can be reached in the EU multilevel parliamentary field. Obviously, this choice for a most likely case implies that the findings from this particular case cannot automatically be generalised to all EU law-making. Rather, it gives an indication of what *can* be achieved in other instances of EU decision-making and what mechanisms may help to maximise the collective leverage of parliaments in that decision making.

The structure of the chapter is as follows. The next section draws on the notion of the 'multilevel parliamentary field' to identify standards of virtuous interparliamentary dynamics and appropriate indicators. Then, the first empirical section reviews the way the Services Directive has been processed by the EP. This analysis serves to introduce the dossier and provides a benchmark for the handling of the Directive as the eventual outcome was very much determined in the EP. The subsequent section then turns to a selection of four national parliaments (Austria, Germany, Sweden and the Netherlands) and reviews their engagement with the Services Directive in terms of the indicators adopted. The conclusion summarises the main findings as regards interparliamentary coordination in this most likely case and reflects upon their implications.

Estimating interparliamentary dynamics in the multilevel parliamentary field

The concept of a 'multilevel parliamentary field' underlines how, together with the emergence of multilevel government in Europe, democratic representation has become dispersed across multiple sites (Crum and Fossum 2009). Concretely, the notion of a 'multilevel parliamentary field' is inspired by the way that the EU's political system has come to rely on a double system of democratic representation. On the one hand, European citizens are represented directly in the EP which increasingly serves as a co-legislator on a par with the Council. Yet, however much the EP's powers have expanded over time, it cannot shoulder the democratic legitimacy of the EU on its own. This does not merely reflect the incompleteness of its powers since not all competences that have been lifted to the EU level are, as yet, under (full) EP control. It follows, more fundamentally, from the fact that the EU political system remains premised on the capabilities and democratic authority of its member states and that, hence, democratic representation also requires national interests to be properly represented in the process (Crum 2012).

The limitations of the EP's authority bring back into focus the indirect representation of European citizens in EU decision-making which runs through their national parliaments that control the governments that, in turn, decide over EU issues in the Council of the EU and the European Council. These national parliaments continue to play a key role in the democratic legitimation of EU decision-making because collective political will-formation for most European citizens still very much takes place within national confines; any indications of public spheres transcending national boundaries point to cross-national (horizontal) exchanges between them rather than to the emergence of a supranational, pan-European public sphere (Koopmans and Erbe 2004; Risse and van de Steeg 2003). The double system of political representation in EU decision-making that thus emerges, combining direct and indirect representation, is anything but a transitional phenomenon; it has developed over time and has by now become well-entrenched in the EU's institutional structure (cf. Lord and Pollak 2010).[1]

Crucially, the concept of the multilevel parliamentary field not only thematises the multi-sited character of EU decision-making but also seeks to retain the value

---

1.   *See* Article 8A.2 of the EU Treaty of Lisbon.

of parliamentary representation. The main reason for this is that parliamentary representation has so far proven to be the most effective institutional way of guaranteeing political equality and inclusion. The focus on parliaments as sites for democratic representation and deliberation is further justified by the view that parliaments are, and remain, quintessential as *strong publics,* that is, spheres of institutionalised deliberation *and* decision making (Fraser 1992; Eriksen and Fossum 2002). As embodiments of popular sovereignty, parliaments are generally regarded as the source of all political power in modern-day democracies. Formally at least, parliaments fulfil an indispensable role in authorising public norm-making, be it directly or indirectly, by setting and monitoring the overarching legislative framework. For this reason they also continue to be a major focal point for public deliberation. Ultimately, the key role of parliaments is backed up by the fact that they effectively institutionalise the fundamental democratic norm of the political equality of all citizens by being composed on the basis of the 'one person, one vote' principle.

The multilevel parliamentary field thus serves to gauge the overall interplay between multiple sites of democratic representation. Following up on the normative observations just made, the fundamental question with regard to the quality of parliamentary representation under conditions of multilevel government is whether different parliamentary channels and activities within the EU add up in vicious or virtuous ways. This involves the consideration of more specific questions such as: Do the interventions of parliaments in EU decision-making processes reinforce or weaken other parliamentary positions? Are there actors that have a higher standing in the field and that are therefore in a position to impose their views on others? Does the sheer variety of parliamentary interests in fact allow for effective interparliamentary coordination?

To answer these questions and to estimate the cohesion of the EU's multilevel parliamentary field, it does not suffice to merely review the formal arrangements that are in place. Instead, the analysis has to go beyond the formal arrangements to look at the actual inputs of parliaments in the decision-making process and the way they combine and, ultimately, impact upon the eventual EU decision. Specifically, we propose to look at four empirical indicators, which, depending on the 'value' they take, hint at either virtuous or vicious dynamics in the field.

A first focus of the comparison of the different parliamentary sites concerns *timing*: the later parliaments become engaged in the EU decision-making process, the less likely it would seem for them to make a difference.

While the timing of parliamentary engagement provides a first indication of the saliency of a decision *per se*, the second indicator looks more closely at the specific issues concerning the decision that become salient in parliaments' debates. The question is whether these issues are the same across the different sites, or whether they differ. If parliaments raise similar concerns, their interventions reinforce one another. This serves to underline the importance of these issues and increases the chances that the parliaments involved will have an impact on the process. By contrast, if an issue is only raised by a single or a few parliamentary chambers, it is less likely to be taken up.

However, the importance of an issue is not merely a function of the number of occasions on which it is raised. Ultimately, it requires a substantive assessment. In that light, if different issues become salient in different parliaments, this may contribute to a broader understanding of the proposal and therefore allow for a better – more balanced – outcome. Thus, the questions are rather whether all the issues salient in the different parliaments find their way into the process; whether they are equally and adequately balanced in the process; and, if they do not make it into the eventual decision, whether adequate grounds are provided for excluding them.

Complementary to registering which issues come to the fore in the different parliaments, it is also useful to determine the main lines of debate. Hence, we consider the inter-party divides that are central to parliamentary debates. The analysis of these divides is all the more important since, even if the aggregate interests of twenty-eight parliaments find their way into the process (in a field marked by 'perfect' parliamentary control), the question remains what happens to views that are not held by a parliamentary majority but that nevertheless reflect the interests of important national minorities. Due to the EU's institutional structure, such views are at risk of not being represented by a country's government in the Council and, hence, of remaining invisible at EU level. Do these views play any role in the EU parliamentary field and to what extent can they be accommodated in the eventual decision?

Finally, vicious dynamics are, of course, much less likely when parliaments not only pursue their aims in isolation but, rather, try to pool their resources and coordinate their activities amongst one another. Hence, we have to review any evidence of parliamentarians seeking to strengthen their role in the EU decision-making process through *actual interparliamentary engagement*, like interparliamentary contacts with one another and with the EP.

To sum up, we distinguish four indicators to establish the quality of the interparliamentary dynamics of the EU's multilevel parliamentary field:

- timing of parliamentary engagement
- nature of salient issues
- inter-party divides
- interparliamentary contacts

The analysis of the parliamentary input is eased in the case of the EU Services Directive since we can take the substance and the structure of the debate in the EP as a proxy for the eventual decision. In general, the EP claims a unique place in the EU multilevel parliamentary field because it enjoys a formal veto position under the EU's co-decision procedure. Still, it often finds its position compromised as it has to be reconciled with that of the Council of Ministers. However, in the case of the Services Directive, the role of the EP was decisive as its first reading very much determined the eventual substance of the Directive.

To analyse all national parliaments in the EU would be a step too far. Instead, a sample of the national parliaments of Austria, Germany, Sweden and the Netherlands is analysed.[2] This sample includes bigger and smaller EU member states, with some variation in the *intensity* (Maurer and Wessels 2001; Raunio 2005) and *format* with which their parliaments engage in EU affairs (with mandating systems in Austria and Sweden, document based systems in Germany and in the Second Chamber of the Dutch Parliament, and a mixed system in the Netherlands' first chamber). Also, the sample contains some important variation in terms of socio-economic outlook, as it involves more Social-Democratic (Sweden) and more Christian-Conservative welfare state systems, as well as governing coalitions that were, at the time, both left of centre (Sweden and Germany, although this changed towards the end of the process) and right of centre (Austria and the Netherlands). Admittedly though, the range of variation between the parliaments selected is limited as the sample does not contain any parliaments from Southern Europe or from countries with a determinately liberal political outlook. Also excluded are the new EU member states from Central and Eastern Europe because the decision-making process on the Services Directive had already been set in motion when these acceded in May 2004.

The Services Directive in the European Parliament

On 6 February 2004, the European Commission published its draft on a 'Directive of Services in the Internal Market' (COM2004/02 final), which had as its central objective the removal of obstacles hampering intra-EU trade in services. The handling of the Services Directive by the EP proved to be crucial for the decision that was eventually adopted. A key role in this process was played by the EP *rapporteur* on the Directive: Evelyne Gebhardt, German Social-Democrat and prominent member of the EP's Committee for Internal Market and Consumer Protection (IMCO). After extensive consultations inside and outside the Parliament, she delivered her draft report in May 2005.

Two issues stood out among the concerns that Gebhardt highlighted in her draft report: the 'Country of Origin Principle' (CoOP) and the scope of the Directive. The CoOP provided that a service company would, with certain exceptions, only have to follow its homeland's regulations when providing services in other member states on a temporary basis. The report raised the fear that this principle could lead to social dumping and to a 'race to the bottom' in regulatory areas like environmental law, consumer protection, taxation and, most notably, labour law. The Directive was considered too weak in providing for control and sanction mechanisms with regard to foreign service providers. Hence, it was expected to

---

2.   The case studies of the debates in national parliaments draw on the PhD dissertation of Eric Miklin (2008) for the cases of Germany, Austria and Sweden and on the work on the Dutch case by Stijn van Kessel (van Kessel 2006; van Kessel and Pelkmans 2007). Data used for the analysis are drawn from official documents and protocols from the Council, national parliaments and governments, as well as position papers and press releases from various national actors and the national news coverage. In addition, semi-structured expert interviews were conducted with actors directly involved in the discussions both at European and national levels.

facilitate social dumping by allowing companies to legally circumvent (higher) standards as well as by inviting them to work around these standards illegally.

The second major issue concerned the scope of the Directive and, in particular, whether it would include services of general economic interest. Gebhardt argued that the draft Directive remained ambiguous on the point of whether or not it would affect social services. More specifically, she criticised that the actual inclusion of a number of services of general economic interest (healthcare, audio-visual services, postal services, electricity services, gas and water services) within its scope would force member states to liberalise these sensitive sectors.

Initially, the EP's IMCO divided along a clear ideological left-right divide. On the left, the Party of European Socialists (PES), the Greens–European Free Alliance (Greens) and the GUE/NGL were very critical of the Commission's draft and endorsed the amendments proposed by Gebhardt. These three party-groups opposed the inclusion of the CoOP and favoured a narrow scope for the Directive (e.g. the complete exclusion of all services of general economic interest). By contrast, on the right, the European People's Party-European Democrats (EPP-ED), the Alliance of Liberals and Democrats for Europe (ALDE) and the Union for Europe of the Nations (UEN) were rather pleased with the Commission's draft and were critical of Gebhardt's report. Not only were these groups in favour of the CoOP, they also advocated a broad scope of the Directive (i.e. the inclusion of services of general economic interest).

This ideological divide became manifest when the Committee voted on the Gebhardt report in November 2005. A majority of the EPP-ED and ALDE groups voted down most of the amendments and safeguards proposed by Gebhardt and others, and approved a draft that came much closer to the original Commission's proposal than Gebhardt's report had foreseen. The final report of the Committee was adopted by twenty-five votes in favour, ten against and five abstentions (including Gebhardt).

However, this centre-right majority was not sustained due to two developments. For one, the EPP-ED group recognised that it would be undesirable for the EP to adopt the Services Directive with a slim and distinctively right-wing coalition. This might undermine the EP's credibility both in its interactions with other EU institutions (Council and Commission) and also in the eyes of the wider European public. Secondly, reconsiderations were triggered by Commissioner McCreevy's comments to IMCO that if the EP could reach a *broad* agreement on the Directive, he would make sure that the Commission approved its position and, further,would try to ensure an agreement in the Council. However, if no such agreement was achieved, it was unlikely there would be any Directive at all.

After the Committee vote of November 2005, these considerations led to negotiations between the two large party-groups, EPP-ED and PES, with the aim of seeking a compromise between them. The day before the first reading in the Plenum on 16 February 2006, they reached an inter-party agreement (Mardell 2006). The deal involved the EPP-ED accepting the rejection of the CoOP (and its replacement with a principle about the 'freedom to provide services'), and the PES accepting the inclusion of services of general economic interests under the scope of the Directive. Among the smaller EP party-groups, this compromise was severely criticised. While ALDE and UEN would have preferred a more liberal compromise, the Greens and GUE/NGL considered the compromise too liberal still.

This new divide between the big party-groups in the political centre and the smaller ones on the periphery was clearly visible in the vote on the EP's first reading. As agreed between the big party-groups, the CoOP was replaced by a principle on the 'freedom to provide services', while services of general economic interest (but for healthcare, social and audiovisual services) were not generally excluded from the scope of the Directive. Thus revised, the EP position was adopted with 392 'yes'-votes, 216 'no' -votes, and thirty-four abstentions. While the vote was carried by strong majorities in the EPP-ED and PES, they also faced some internal dissent (Lindberg 2008). Thus, a quarter of the PES-delegation, composed mainly of its French and Belgian members, opposed the final report. They considered the scope of the Directive (especially with regard to services of general economic interest) to be too broad still. Within the EPP-ED, 80 per cent of the members supported the amended draft, with defection concentrated among delegations from Central and Eastern Europe. Also, within the ALDE group, a majority voted in favour of the compromise, even if the group would have preferred a more liberal Directive. Here the German Free Democratic Party (FDP) — being the most prominent pro-liberalisation force in the group — defected as, did, again, some representatives of East European countries (Lindberg 2008). On the other hand, the 'no'-vote included the complete groups of the GUE/NGL and the Greens, as well as the greater majorities of the UEN and the ID party-groups.

The EP's first reading turned out to be decisive for the eventual fate of the Services Directive as the compromise reached there, by and large, laid down the basis for the Commission's revised draft, which again was, for the most part, confirmed by the Competitiveness Council of 24 July 2006. As a result, there was only modest discussion within the EP on the Commission's revised draft Directive. No new issues or cleavages emerged. This was also the case because none of the major party-groups wanted to risk the overall compromise by opening the package deal again. Hence, with a couple of very minor additions, on 15 November the EP came to endorse the Council's position on its second reading.

National parliaments and the Services Directive

This section discusses the way the Services Directive was handled in the four national parliaments along the four indicators that were identified above: timing, issue-salience, inter-party divides and interparliamentary contacts. Notably, this analysis reveals many parallels, both between the four parliaments as well as with the handling in the EP. Nonetheless, some notable differences between the parliaments also emerge. Such differences may become vicious if the eventual decision comes to address some of them at the cost of excluding or ignoring others. However, they may also be virtuous to the extent that addressing one does not necessarily preclude addressing the others. Indeed, if they become the object of substantive deliberation, differences between parliaments may even be productive.

Timing of Parliamentary Engagement

For most national parliaments it took some time before they came to scrutinise the Services Directive. The first country by far in which the Directive attracted attention was Sweden. Already by mid-March 2004, little over a month after the publication of the draft, the Swedish Parliament's EU Committee had its first discussion of the Directive. This very early start of the debate was mostly due to the Swedish trade unions having been on early alert for the draft Directive. These signals were then fed to the left-wing factions in parliament, the governing Social-Democratic Party, the Green Party and the Left Party.

In Germany, it took some months longer before the first party took action on the Services Directive. Here the Social Democrats (SPD) set up an internal working group to discuss the Directive (SPD-Bundestagsfraktion 2004), an example that was soon followed by its junior coalition partner, the Greens. Events in Austria followed a similar pattern, but with a further time lag of about three months. By contrast, in the Netherlands, parties postponed their engagement with the Directive until the Government had officially communicated its position.[3] In the parliamentary debate that followed in November 2004, parties raised various concerns about the Directive but, rather than committing themselves to a clear position, they asked the Government to request an advisory opinion from the Dutch Social and Economic Council (SER) so as to furnish them with more reliable information on the Directive's potential implications.

The finding that most parliaments were relatively slow in picking up on the Directive, suggests that parliamentary debates trailed behind the agenda-setting debate in the EP as well as behind the position-taking processes of their national governments (cf. Miklin 2009). Seen from that perspective, the debate on the European level basically set the terms in which the subsequent national debates came to be framed. Still, it was not merely 'Brussels' that put the Services Directive on national political agendas. Notably, trade unions played an important role in bringing the Directive to the attention of national parliamentarians. Thus, debate about the Services Directive in Europe was not merely imposed vertically, from above, but rather spread as a ripple, horizontally, through the different national spheres. In this process, left-wing parties and social movements were driving forces. They were also the actors most likely to instigate debates and to raise criticisms against the Commission's draft text.

The differences between the four parliaments increase when it comes to the way that they eventually dealt with the Services Directive. A decisive factor in this was whether or not the (centre-) left parties that were critical of the Directive were part of the governing coalition. In Sweden, the Social-Democratic minority Government very much maintained the lead in the debate, even though it was followed critically by the parliament's EU committee and, in particular, by the Left Party faction. Similarly, in Germany, it was a motion prepared by the left-wing

---

3.   TK 21501–30 (2004), Nr. 59.

government coalition in the *Bundestag* that essentially determined the national position on the Directive.

By contrast, being in opposition in Austria and the Netherlands, the left-wing parties had to struggle their way through parliament to put their concerns about the Services Directive on the political agenda. In Austria, the SPÖ addressed a series of parliamentary inquiries to various ministers[4] and also brought a motion that addressed the Services Directive (amongst others). Eventually, in September 2005, it managed to have a plenary debate on the Directive in the first chamber in which various parliamentary motions from the governing and the opposition parties were discussed (plenary protocol XXII/124). Also, in that same month, the Dutch Parliament determined its official position, following up on the advisory report from the Social-Economic Council that it had received in July.

To sum up, even if some of them had been slow to get started, all four national parliaments had their positions more or less determined well before the first reading in the EP and certainly well before the common position of the Council of Ministers. Most parliaments saw little need to revisit the Directive once the EP had adopted its first reading in February 2005 and the Council had to determine its common position on it. Indeed, many parties across all four countries welcomed the compromise developed in the EP and saw it meeting many of the concerns that had been raised earlier. Especially in Germany, the EP compromise was warmly welcomed as it came much to the relief of the new government coalition (the Christian Democratic Union/Christian Social Union of Bavaria (CDU/CSU) and the SPD) for which the Services Directive had been a source of tension. Only in the Netherlands did the EP's amendments of the Directive find little support. The centre-right coalition in government as well as the Dutch Labour Party (PvdA) in opposition regarded them as watering down the main purpose of the Directive. For this reason, the Parliament remained involved with the Government throughout the spring of 2006 as it sought to re-insert some aspects of the original draft into the final text.

The nature of salient issues

We also find many similarities in the substance of the concerns that were raised against the draft directive. In fact, they tend to reflect the two issues that were also central in the debate in the EP: the CoOP and the scope of the Directive. However, one notable exception was the prevailing consensus in the Dutch parliamentary debate that, notwithstanding some substantial concerns, European services liberalisation would eventually be conducive to economic growth.

Throughout, the main concern was the CoOP. In all four 'Western' European countries analysed there were major concerns about unequal competition putting national standards under pressure and inviting social dumping from countries where lower standards obtained. In Sweden, the debate was driven mainly by

---

4.   Documents 2686/J XXII.GP; 2752/J XXII. GP; 2687/J XXII. GP; 2688/J XXII. GP; 2685/J XXII. GP.

the trade unions who considered the CoOP to be incompatible with the Swedish system of labour law regulation (TCO/LO 2004). They feared that the principle would exempt foreign companies from complying with the labour standards agreed in Swedish collective agreements. In particular, they were concerned that it would be impossible to protect the relatively high wage level of Swedish workers from being undercut by foreign providers.

The German debate ran very much parallel to that in Sweden as it focussed on the perceived incompatibility between, on the one hand, the CoOP and the German system of labour law (DGB 2005) and, on the other, the possible downward pressures on wage levels in service sectors. Fears that the CoOP would lead to social dumping and to the lowering of German standards of regulation were amplified by the country's proximity to a number of new member states (most notably Poland) with relatively low standards and wages. Similarly, in the Dutch debate, there was fear that the CoOP would contribute to the detriment of national labour conditions due to the appearance of cheap workers from Eastern Europe, a situation that raised the spectre of social dumping.

Trade unions' concerns also very much framed the debate in Austria (Austrian Chamber of Labour 2005). Besides fears that the CoOP would permit service companies to *legally* circumvent the comparatively high Austrian labour standards, there were also concerns that it would allow these providers to evade Austrian standards *illegally* because of the limited possibilities that the Directive provided for controlling and monitoring foreign services. Other reasons for which the CoOP was criticised in Austria included its potential effects on the country's environmental and consumer-protection standards, the sphere of professional qualifications, and the unclear distinction between temporary deliveries of services and the actual settlement of service companies, etc.

Besides the concerns about the CoOP, in all four countries we also encounter debates about the scope of the Directive, even if the sectors that were highlighted reflect some notable variation in the national preoccupations. In Sweden, the scope issue focussed in particular on some services where the Swedish state still had a monopoly at the time. In Germany and Austria, the principal concerns in the debate on scope came to be framed in terms of protecting the existing systems of *Daseinsvorsorge* ('services of general interest'). In turn, in the Netherlands, sectors like healthcare and pension funds figured prominently in debates about the scope of the Directive.

Inter-party divides

The Services Directive tended to divide national parliaments along left-right lines, just as it did in the EP. In all four countries, criticism of the Commission's draft came first and foremost from the Social-Democratic, Green, and Socialist parties on the left. On the other hand, liberal and (Christian-) conservative parties were generally sympathetic towards the Commission's draft.

However, these ideological divisions were refracted by the government-opposition dynamic. Among left-wing (Social-Democratic) parties in government, the criticisms were especially likely to be balanced with some endorsement of the

Commission's proposal. For instance, the Swedish Social Democrats were rather critical of the Directive's deregulatory character and its likely negative effects on the Swedish public services sector. Still, as the party was convinced of the overall desirability of a Directive, it was reluctant to challenge the Directive as a whole (Interview Four) and thus adopted a more moderate position than the Left Party and the Green Party on its left-wing flank.

In Germany, the Social Democrats initially banded together with the Greens as, together, they formed the governing coalition. Their factions in the *Bundestag* adopted a motion (*Bundestag Drucksache* 15/5832) that strongly criticised the Directive and urged the Government to advocate its comprehensive revision while rejecting a much more supportive one that had been put forward by the FDP (with the endorsement of the CDU/CSU) (*Bundestag Drucksache* 15/5131). However, once the SPD joined the new government coalition with the CDU/CSU in 2005, it happily rallied around the EP compromise position, leaving the opposition against the Directive to the Greens and the Left Party.

Also, it is notable that whenever the Social Democrats were in opposition, their position was crucial: first, in prompting the debate and articulating the criticisms, later, in adopting a 'responsible' stance and coming round to an acceptable compromise position. Thus, in Austria, criticisms of the Services Directive came from the Social Democrats (SPÖ) and the Greens. Yet, from the start, the position of the SPÖ was more nuanced than that of the Greens, since it recognised that any Directive would need to be based on a compromise between the Social Democrats and the Conservative parties, both in the EP and in the Council (Interview Seven; Interview Eight). As a consequence, once the EP compromise had been forged, the SPÖ was happy to endorse it, leaving the Greens as the only parliamentary party to persist in opposing it. Similarly, in the Netherlands, the PvdA, being in opposition, adopted a critical stance but never opposed the very concept of an EU services directive. It was happy to support the EP compromise but, notably, even considered some of the concessions as going further than needed. Operating from the opposition, the Green parties in Sweden and the Netherlands followed the same path as the Social-Democrats: critical at first, but eventually welcoming the EP compromise. However, in Germany and Austria the Green parties continued to resist the Directive.

Thus, ultimately, in all four countries analysed, the eventual Directive was supported by a very wide majority, a 'grand coalition', that included the more right-wing parties as well as the Social Democrats. Still, however broad the consensus, the eventual decision left some positions less accommodated. For one, there were those who supported a full-blown liberalisation along the lines of the Commission's initial draft. In Sweden this concerned, for instance, the Moderate Party and the Liberal Party who expected the country to profit from the liberalisation of the monopolies in the public services sector. Similarly, the German FDP considered the watering down of the Commission's draft Directive as a missed opportunity for comprehensive liberalisation. In Austria the ruling People's Party (ÖVP) would, ideally, have preferred a more liberal Directive (Interview Six). Notably, in the Netherlands, this sentiment was not only shared by the governing coalition parties VVD, D66 and CDA, but even the PvdA considered that the EP's amendments went further than desired. Thus, parties committed to liberalisation were forced to make concessions by the course of the process. Even if they eventually endorsed the compromise as better than nothing, this outcome fell below what they might have hoped for initially.

The other position that failed to be accommodated in the process was the extreme left that opposed any EU-wide framework for the services market in principle. This applied to the Left parties in Sweden and Germany, the Socialist Party in the Netherlands and the Green parties in Germany and Austria. Indeed, this position was probably beyond accommodation from the very moment that a draft Directive was tabled. The only way that they might have been placated would have been if the process had become completely stalled due to irreconcilable interests.

Interparliamentary contacts

German national parties benefited from the prominent positions their European colleagues enjoyed in the EP debate. Most notably, the SPD benefited from having party member Evelyne Gebhardt as the EP *rapporteur* for the Directive. National representatives of the SPD closely cooperated with Gebhardt, who joined several party meetings at national level to discuss it (Interview Two). Additionally, the SPD cooperated with national MPs and MEPs from the Social Democratic parties of other member states, e.g. at a meeting organised especially for this purpose in Berlin in December 2004. The main contact of the CDU/CSU in the EP was Joachim Würmeling (CDU), who was the *rapporteur* for the Directive in the EP's constitutional committee. Also, the Greens coordinated their position with their representatives in the EP (Interview One).

In Austria, contacts with other parliaments were reported, especially by representatives of the SPÖ and the Greens. MPs from the SPÖ joined a meeting of the PES party-group in the EP as well as the SPD meeting in Berlin. Additionally, the SPÖ mobilized its members to support a petition initiated by Belgian Social Democrats (Interview Five). Members of the Green Party discussed the Directive not only with their own MEPs but also with MPs and MEPs from other member states at meetings of the European Green Party (EGP) (Interview Seven).

In the Dutch debate on the Services Directive, MEPs played a prominent role. Left-wing MEPs were especially crucial in publicly articulating the criticisms of the Directive. Labour MEP Ieke van den Burg formed a partnership with her socialist colleague Roeline Knottnerus (Socialist Party) to publish a critical manifesto against the Directive entitled *The Bolkesteinbubble* (van den Burg and Knottnerus 2005). In this booklet, the two left-wing MEPs questioned the positive effects that the draft Directive was estimated to have on the Dutch economy and argued that the Directive might invite unfair competition and 'social dumping' instead. In March 2005 van den Burg attended a meeting of the Dutch parliamentary committee to explain and defend the EP's position. In the Dutch press, the criticisms of van den Burg and Knottnerus were countered by D66 MEP Sophie in't Veld, who underlined the economic benefits implied by the Directive. Ultimately, the PvdA-SP tandem parted company, as van den Burg endorsed the EP position while her SP-colleagues remained fundamentally opposed to it.

Conclusion

So, can parliaments combine in a virtuous way into a coherent voice under conditions of multilevel government? In this chapter we explored the quality of the EU multilevel parliamentary field by way of a case study of position taking and decision making on the EU Services Directive across five parliamentary sites in the EU: the EP and the national parliaments of Austria, Germany, Sweden and the Netherlands. This case study gives evidence of the distinctively deliberative and inclusive character of the EU multilevel parliamentary field (cf. Benz 2003). Certainly, in all parliaments, votes were taken in which majorities formally imposed their views at the cost of those of the minorities. Yet, in very few cases did this imply the definitive exclusion of positions from the process. On the contrary, many minority concerns that were outvoted in one place found a way to be heard elsewhere in the process. Thus, the concerns of the Social Democrats and the Greens that were outvoted in Austria can in many respects be said to have been taken up by the centre-left Swedish majority. At the same time, while the liberal-right opposition in Sweden was unable to impose its views on its Government, many of its concerns were articulated by the Dutch majority.

These findings shed some light on the mechanisms of interest aggregation in the EU decision-making process. As any votes that are taken are premised on broad deliberation, and actors that are outvoted may well find their interests being taken up through alternative channels, the impact of formal differences in voting weights in EU decision-making (as they have so often been the object of political haggling in treaty negotiations) is restricted. For the same reason, we find that no parliamentary actors are structurally excluded from the EU multilevel parliamentary field. In fact, any parliamentary actor who takes a distinct interest in the issue at stake can turn to multiple entry points in the field to bring it to bear upon the decision-making process. Indeed, the crucial condition would seem to be that actors do actually take an interest in EU policy-making in the first place. While this may be self-evident in the EP, it does not necessarily seem to be the case for national parliaments. Even in the rather politicised case of the Services Directive, most of them were relatively slow in taking it up.

At the same time, the opportunities in the field are not fully equal for each and every actor. On the one hand, some parliamentarians appear better connected than others. For instance, the German parties seem particularly well-connected to the EP, especially since the size of their delegations makes it likely that they can claim prominent positions in the decision-making process. On the other hand, while we did not find any issues that were salient in any one of the national parliaments that were to be excluded from the EU decision-making process, in the end some actors have had to make more concessions than others or even found the eventual decision imposed against their will. The interests that eventually failed to be accommodated in the decision found themselves in that position because of their extreme character. This applies in particular to extreme-left opponents who were unwilling to accept a services Directive of any sort and, to a lesser extent, to those who advocated services liberalisation across the board. Accommodation is less likely if one's own position allows for little reconciliation. In that sense, many liberal-right parties were eventually willing to endorse the compromise outcome, while the extreme left remained stubbornly and consistently opposed to the Directive, however it was revised.

In the case of the Services Directive, the EP, as the EU's supranational parliament, played a particularly notable role. To a considerable extent, the way it picked up on the Commission's draft Directive set the terms in which the subsequent national debates came to be framed. Even more importantly, it was in the EP that most of the eventual compromise was determined through intense public debates about the various arguments for and against the Directive. In a way, the EP can thus be seen to fulfil the role of a clearinghouse for the political arguments as they have emerged throughout the parliaments of the Union.

The empirical analysis thus demonstrates how the EU's multilevel parliamentary field can operate as a coherent whole that serves to carry and accommodate a broad range of concerns into the decision-making process. At the same time, while there were very different views – not only between parliaments and other actors but also between parliaments themselves and even within parliaments – the overall process allowed these divides to be overcome and encouraged all concerned to agree on a proposal that was supported by a broad majority. This is an important finding because strong and active national parliaments are sometimes just seen negatively, as additional veto players that make legislative progress within the EU even more difficult than it already is. However, despite the considerable involvement of national parliaments, the decision-making process on the Services Directive was eventually a virtuous one that led to a substantively better-justified Directive that commanded broad support among the European nations and the different parties.

While this article highlights the capacity of EU parliaments to act as a coherent and constructive voice in the EU's political system, it is obviously by no means guaranteed that this capacity is always (fully) realised. The exceptionally politicised character of the Services Directive makes it a particularly suitable case to demonstrate the potential of the EU's multilevel parliamentary field. However, this potential would seem much less likely to come out on less politicised issues. Such issues may simply be ignored by national parliaments or only picked up by some, who then either exert disproportional influence or, just the opposite, are easily ignored. Also, the positions of the national parliaments and that of the EP may be much less compatible in cases where subsidiarity concerns become particularly prominent, as, for instance, in the case of the Seasonal Workers Directive (see Cooper in this volume). Indeed, as the powers granted to national parliaments under the Treaty of Lisbon are particularly geared towards the principle of subsidiarity, they risk pitting the national parliaments and the EP against each other and, hence, decreasing the cohesion of the multilevel parliamentary field. Finally, the present analysis only looked at a limited number of national parliaments. Further research may want to probe whether, indeed, all EU national parliaments are effectively connected to and accommodated within the EU's multilevel parliamentary field, in particular the ones of member states that are smaller and that joined the EU only recently, or that have more deviant interest structures which may make them particularly vulnerable to exclusion.

chapter six | coordination practices in the parliamentary control of justice and home affairs agencies: the case of Europol

Daniel Ruiz de Garibay

Introduction

The increasing role of national parliaments at EU level opens greater possibilities for interparliamentary coordination. However, there has been little research on how this coordination is evolving in practice. This chapter focuses on interparliamentary practices developed in the context of the parliamentary control of Europol, the European Police Agency.

Europol has evolved from its original institutional design as an intergovernmental body established by an international convention among the member states into a supranational agency fully integrated into the EU. Against this background, this chapter looks at the evolution of the parliamentary control of Europol as a case of institutional development within EU representative-democratic institutions. Thus, the chapter discusses the relationship between integration (as institutional incorporation) and democratisation.

Established in 1999 by the Europol Convention – an international convention – Europol was an intergovernmental institution. Parliamentary control was provided indirectly by national parliaments via the scrutiny of ministers sitting at the JHA Council. The EP did not have any scrutiny role over the agency. However, since then, Europol has undergone significant legal changes. The most significant was in 2010 when it was transformed from a supranational body into an EU agency, allowing the EP, among other things, some degree of control over the Europol budget. Currently, the Lisbon Treaty provides for the political monitoring of Europol by national parliaments and the EP together (TFEU Art. 88). A new regulation would need to be drafted in order to implement the provisions of the Lisbon Treaty regarding Europol. The form the parliamentary control of Europol will take has not yet been decided. However, changes in parliamentary practices have already taken place in preparation for the new modality in which both national parliaments and the EP will be involved.

Given this background, the key question is, how is the involvement of national parliaments and the EU in the parliamentary control of Europol best balanced? This chapter provides insights into the relative salience of interparliamentary coordination as compared to a strengthened role for the EP in the process of the institutional incorporation of Europol. A focus on the evolution of the parliamentary control of Europol allows us to study why and how interparliamentary coordination is developed and why interparliamentary coordination takes one form and not another.

The first section of this chapter provides an overview of Europol's evolution, paying attention to the balance between its increased parliamentary control by the EP and the different forms of interparliamentary coordination suggested at different points in time. The next three sections analyse the different forms of interparliamentary coordination that have flourished. Section Two looks at interparliamentary networking initiatives. Section Three examines the coordination achieved through COSAC; and Section Four studies the different kinds of interparliamentary meetings between national parliaments and the EP. To conclude, this chapter discusses the way forward for the parliamentary control of Europol, considering that the three different modes of coordination need not exclude one another and that the real challenge for the regulation that will implement the Lisbon Treaty's requirement – that 'the political monitoring of Europol [...] be done by national parliaments and the European Parliament together' (TFEU Art. 88) – is how the different coordination modes can best be connected and calibrated.

The history of Europol: From Convention to EU body

Europol was created in 1999 by the Europol Convention.[1] However, Europol has evolved from its original institutional design, as an international body established by an international convention among the member states, into a supranational agency, fully integrated into the EU. The Council Decision of 6 April 2009 replaced the Europol Convention and transformed Europol into an EU body from 1 January 2010 onwards.[2] At that moment, a new regulation was to replace the Council Decision in order to implement the new provisions of the Lisbon Treaty, notably, those referring to the participation of national parliaments and the EP in the political monitoring of the agency (TFEU Art. 88). For this reason, Europol's legal framework is subject to an ongoing debate regarding the different forms in which the provisions of the Lisbon Treaty could be put in place.

The following section analyses the evolution of Europol in order to understand how its transition from an intergovernmental agency on the fringes of the EU to a fully fledged EU agency with more powers led, on the one hand, to improving the parliamentary control over Europol by the EP and, on the other, to finding a balance between the role of national parliaments and the EP in providing parliamentary control. Three different stages can be identified in Europol's development. The first stage runs from 1999 until 2006. Based on the then new provisions of the Treaty of Maastricht for cooperation in the field of JHA, the member states

---

1. Convention based on Article K.3 of the Treaty on the European Union, on the Establishment of a European Police Office (Europol Convention), adopted on 26 July 1995.
2. Council Decision 2009/371/JHA of 6 April 2009 establishing the European Police Office (OJ L 121/37, 15.05.2009).

signed the Europol Convention providing Europol with a legal framework. At that time, police cooperation was still largely dominated by intergovernmental decision-making. For this reason, and because of the intergovernmental origins of the police cooperation structures that preceded Europol, the role of the EP in the parliamentary supervision of Europol was limited. During this phase a series of incremental increases in Europol's powers and competences came about via the creation of successive Protocols modifying the Europol Convention.[3]

In a second stage, from 2006 until 2009, Europol's legal framework was recast altogether and a Council Decision transformed Europol into an agency of the EU, financed from the Community budget and not from the contributions of the member states, as had been the case under the Europol Convention.[4] A third phase is currently being developed. In this phase the future of Europol will be defined. The Council Decision on Europol will be replaced by a Council Regulation that will implement the legal provisions of the Lisbon Treaty regarding Europol's structure, operation, field of action, tasks and parliamentary control. Particularly interesting for the subject matter of this research is that one of these provisions mentions specifically that the 'political monitoring of Europol' will be carried out by the EP 'together' with national parliaments (TFEU Art. 88).

The Europol Convention established Europol in order to support EU member states in combating serious, organised crime. Europol was originally created with limited tasks and with the competence to apply those powers only to limited forms of crime. Its initial tasks concerned the gathering, exchange and analysis of information and intelligence on criminal cases. To that end, Europol established specified systems and databases containing personal data on criminal suspects, persons convicted of crimes and persons who might commit crimes. However, both its powers and the types of crimes in its remit were extended soon after its creation by the 1999 Europol Convention. Already, in 1999, this remit was extended to terrorism and counterfeiting. In 2006, Europol's powers were extended further with the request that member states start investigations and participate in joint investigation teams. Developments such as these point to a shift from an initial focus on specific crimes towards organised crime in general, and from an initial role of handling information towards operative powers, showing a tendency towards a more executive Europol.[5] In view of these developments, and due

---

3. The Protocols entered into force in 2007. Protocol One: the Protocol drawn up on the basis of Article 43(1) of the Europol Convention amending Article Two and the Appendix to that Convention — (the 'Money Laundering Protocol'), OJ C 358, 13.12.2000, p.2. Protocol Two: the Protocol amending the Europol Convention and the Protocol on the privileges and immunities of Europol, the members of its organs, the deputy directors and the employees of Europol — (the 'JIT Protocol'), OJ C 312, 16.12.2002, p.2. Protocol Three: the Protocol drawn up on the basis of Article 43(1) of the Europol Convention amending that Convention — (the 'Danish Protocol'), OJ C 002, 06.01.2004 p.3.

4. Council Decision 2009/371/JHA of 6 April 2009, establishing the European Police Office (OJ L 121/37, 15.05.2009).

5. From the intervention of Prof. Dr. W. Bruggeman at the European Parliament public seminar: 'An Efficient and Accountable Police cooperation in the EU: The way forward'. 18 December 2006.

to the important and sensitive nature of Europol's activities, the question of its accountability seemed unavoidable.

Debates on the parliamentary control of Europol followed a parallel trajectory. Process tracing shows that the incorporation of Europol into the EU established the basis for both national parliaments and the EP to be involved *together* in the parliamentary control of Europol. This confirms the findings of previous research showing that the primary interests of parliaments when taking part in the interparliamentary coordination of parliamentary control practices is that their interests are served (Westlake 1995) and that increasing parliamentary control is not the main objective when taking part in cooperation (Larhant 2005). In fact, by developing parliamentary coordination practices, both national parliaments and the EP promoted their interests. Successive reforms of Europol's legal framework never included interparliamentary bodies for the parliamentary control of Europol. Only the Lisbon Treaty dealt with that issue. However, it should be noted that the Treaty only refers to the development of future regulations to 'lay down the procedures for scrutiny of Europol's activities by the European Parliament, together with national parliaments' (TFEU Art. 88(2b)). This should be done in accordance with the so-called ordinary legislative procedure (previously, co-decision) in which the Council and the EP are 'co-legislators'. This implies that the development of future cooperation will need to have the support of the EP.

As regards national parliaments, an increase in the tasks performed at EU level that the creation of supervisory structures for Europol would have involved was not something that national parliaments had an interest in. The findings presented in this chapter regarding this point are contradictory. The MEPs, MPs and parliamentary officials interviewed in this research agree on the limited interest the scrutiny of EU affairs raises in national parliaments. However, the same parliamentary officials and MPs mention that national parliaments are very interested in shaping the future development of parliamentary cooperation and that the issue of the control of Europol is being followed with interest. A loose form of cooperation is a solution that avoids investing resources as it provides national parliaments with the advantage of benefiting from the EP's higher expertise and its full-time focus on the EU arena. At the same time, nothing in the EU Treaty prevents national parliaments from arranging their own scrutiny at national level if they would like a greater degree of involvement.

Under the Europol Convention the Council officially appoints Europol's Director for a period of four years, renewable once, and can dismiss him/her after consulting the Management Board, composed of one representative from each member state and chaired by the state holding the EU presidency.[6] Member states set Europol's funding, appoint its senior staff and define its priorities through the Management Board. National parliaments provided indirect democratic control via the control of their ministers in charge of Justice or the Interior who are in the Council. It should be noted that the Council's control over Europol was only indirect. Europol's

---

6.   A representative of the Commission is also allowed to attend the meeting.

Management Board provided annual reports to the JHA Council on Europol's activities but the Council did not supervise Europol's activities. Despite Europol's structure and its markedly intergovernmental character, the Europol Convention also mentions a role for the EP. Article 34 of the Europol Convention provided for Europol to report to the EP. However, the effect of this measure was rather limited.

With this legal framework it is not surprising that when, in June 2001, the Dutch Parliament invited parliamentarians from national parliaments and the EP to discuss the parliamentary supervision of Europol, the conclusion of the discussion was that the scrutiny of Europol by national parliaments was rather non-existent and that the EP lacked the competencies to balance the control deficit of national parliaments (Dutch Parliament 2001; Fijnaut 2002). The perceived lack of parliamentary control was addressed several times. The EP called, on several occasions, for the establishment of democratic and parliamentary control of Europol. Already, in 1999, the EP formulated proposals for enhancing parliamentary control over Europol in a recommendation regarding the extension of Europol's powers (European Parliament 1999). The EP also expressed its concern over the democratic control of Europol in two resolutions dealing with the extension of Europol's remit (European Parliament 2001b) and the future establishment of Europol as a Community Agency (European Parliament 2000). The following suggestions have been put forward in these documents: (1) to provide for adequate parliamentary control in the event of Europol being given operational powers; (2) to provide for the creation of a European public prosecutor in the event of Europol being given cross-border operational powers; (3) to make the Europol Director accountable to the competent parliamentary committee.

Another suggestion for the improvement of the parliamentary control of Europol has been the establishment of interparliamentary bodies to oversee its activities. The first so-called 'interparliamentary' conference on Europol was organised at the Dutch Senate and House of Representatives in June 2001. At that meeting JHA Commissioner Antonio Vitorino called for greater democratic control of Europol. In particular, he suggested the creation of a joint committee comprising members of both the EP and national parliaments to supervise Europol. This committee would meet twice a year. In the same conference a Dutch initiative suggested the creation of PARLOPOL, a network of national and European parliamentarians concerned with police and justice affairs (Dutch Parliament 2001). The aim of this network was, on the one hand, to overcome information deficits and, on the other, to serve as a basis for the coordination of the parliaments' positions.

Following this interparliamentary conference, on 26 February 2002 the European Commission issued a communication to the EP and the Council on the democratic control of Europol in which it recommended the establishment of 'a formal mechanism for information exchange and coordination between national parliaments and the EP' in the form of 'a joint committee' consisting of both MPs and MEPs (European Commission 2002). Whereas, at The Hague conference, the proposal was to create a 'network' for the exchange of information, the Commission went further by suggesting the creation of a 'joint committee' of MPs and MEPs.

According to the Commission, 'this joint committee could meet twice a year to exchange information and experience and to discuss matters relating to Europol following the example of the Community and European Affairs Committees of the Parliaments of the European Union (COSAC)' (European Commission 2002). The creation of a joint supervisory committee was broadly supported and included in one of the draft protocols modifying the Europol Convention, what was known as the Danish Protocol.[7] However, in the end the proposal of a joint committee was not included in the version upon which general agreement was reached in December 2002.

The creation of a joint supervisory committee was again discussed in 2006 when the Council agreed that a council decision should replace the Europol Convention. In its Draft Council Conclusions of 6 April 2006 the Council encouraged the EP 'to set up a joint EP-national parliaments mechanism to follow Europol's activities' (Council of the European Union 2006a). An 'options paper' submitted to the JHA Council of 1–2 June 2006 by the Friends of the Presidency Group discussing the possibilities of future changes to the Europol Convention also mentioned that '[a] joint supervisory committee could be set up by the EP and national parliaments' (Council of the European Union 2006b).

Although discussed at an early stage of the negotiations, the proposal never made it into the Council Decision. However, the idea of establishing a body for the joint supervision of Europol by the EP and national parliaments was never forgotten and its eventual development is totally in line with current legal provisions. The Lisbon Treaty makes specific reference to the interparliamentary cooperation, both among national parliaments and between them and the EP (TEU Art. 12 and Protocol 1, Arts. 9 and 10) and it provides for the involvement of all these parliaments in the 'political monitoring of Europol' (TFEU Art. 88).

What can explain the limited importance attached to this proposal? Why were interparliamentary structures not developed sooner to achieve better parliamentary control? Process tracing of the evolution of Europol's legal framework shows that the interparliamentary structures were perceived to risk hampering the increase in the EP's parliamentary control powers. In this scenario, interparliamentary practices could only be developed later on, once the EP had acquired greater control powers, as a way to accommodate national parliaments' role at EU level without jeopardising that of the EP.

In the early stages of Europol's development the EP was concerned with increasing its own parliamentary control powers. For this reason the EP saw national parliaments as potential competitors. In 2002, in a recommendation to the Council on the future development of Europol, the EP clearly stated its position regarding the role of national parliaments: 'as a European organ, Europol must be monitored by another European organ – the European Parliament – and not by national parliaments' (European Parliament 2002b). In the same recommendation

---

7. Protocol drawn up on the basis of Article 43(1) of the Europol Convention amending that Convention (the 'Danish Protocol'), OJ C 002, 06.01.2004, p.3.

the EP asked for a number of improvements in the parliamentary control of Europol, including the right to receive the same activity report as the Council and the formal right to hold an exchange of views with the Council Presidency and the Europol Director on the annual activity report (European Parliament 2002b). However, there is no mention of any need to set up a joint supervisory meeting with national parliaments. Moreover, according to the EP, parliamentary control of Europol at the national level has proved overly cumbersome and ineffective as a result of intergovernmental mechanisms. In the EP's view, a solution to this problem would be 'to place Europol under the direction and supervision of a member of the European Commission, fully answerable to the EP' (European Parliament 1999).

Table 6.1 shows the preferences of different actors regarding Europol. National parliaments were closer to the *status quo*, while the EP and the Commission held a more pro-integration position. The integrationist end of the spectrum implies that Europol should become an EU agency financed by the Community budget under the scrutiny of the EP. The non-integrationist position would entail that Europol continues to be an intergovernmental body and that any amendment to its Convention needs the ratification of national parliaments. The Council of Ministers, meanwhile, adopted an intermediate position. It is difficult to know the positions of each and every member of the Council due to the secrecy of Council negotiations. However, Council documents (Council of the European Union 2006c) suggest that the Council's main priority was to obtain a legal framework for Europol that would be easier to amend in the future than an international convention such as the Europol Convention. The Council agreed that this could be achieved by transforming Europol into an EU agency. Being an international convention, any amendment to the Europol Convention requires the ratification of national parliaments. If a Council Decision regulates the agency, this will not be the case for any further amendments to Europol.

As seen in Table 6.1 the main initial disagreements between actors were over whether or not Europol should be financed by the EU's general budget and whether or not there should be national parliamentary scrutiny. Due to their loss of budgetary control, national parliaments showed initial resistance to EU financing but, ultimately, the need to find a new legal basis for Europol was prioritised. In

Table 6.1: Preferences of actors at the start of the Europol negotiations

	- Integration		+Integration →
Preferences	**National Parliaments**	**Council**	**EP/COM**
Europol's Status	intergovernmental body	EU agency	EU agency
Parliamentary Control	national parliaments	national parliaments	EP
Budget	national finance	national finance	EU finance

fact, the idea of establishing a legal framework for Europol, one that could easily be updated, was not a trivial matter if one considers that it took an average of more than five years to ratify the Protocols to the Europol Convention that were adopted in 2000, 2002 and 2003.

Despite their potential power loss, there is no empirical evidence that allows us to suggest that national parliaments used the scrutiny of the Council Decision on Europol to resist the transformation of Europol into an EU agency. A possible explanation for national parliaments' acceptance of a reduction in their control powers is that the *status quo* was not so satisfactory in the end. The Europol Convention allowed national parliaments some control in their role as those responsible for the ratification of Europol's amendment protocols. However, despite having a formal ratification role, national parliaments faced a situation in which approval was basically the only possible outcome because ratification happened after agreements at the level of the Council were already reached. On the other hand, the negotiation process of the Protocols was a long process and was considered inadequate for an agency like Europol which dealt with criminality; hence the need to find a new legal basis for Europol. The only solution in this case was the transformation of the Europol Convention into a Council Decision. This implied accepting EU financing and therefore a role for the EP in the parliamentary scrutiny of Europol. Accepting a stronger position for the EP was inevitable as it was not possible to replace the Europol Convention by a Council Decision without providing for EU financing of Europol. At that point the negotiation changed its focus from the need to find a solution to the democratic control of Europol within the Europol Convention to a broader issue regarding the establishment of an EU agency. In a parallel process the issue of national parliaments' control was pushed away and dealt with separately in the context of the negotiations of the Lisbon Treaty. Article 88 of the Lisbon Treaty provides for the involvement of national parliaments, together with the EP, in the political monitoring of Europol.

The Provisions of the Lisbon Treaty still need to be implemented. Europol's legal framework will soon be modified again in order to include the changes required by the Treaty's legal provisions, in particular those referring to the participation of national parliaments and the EP in the political monitoring of the agency. The Commission intends to make a proposal for a new regulation on Europol, including all changes on its parliamentary control, by 2013 (European Commission 2010). In light of these future changes, a number of initiatives have discussed the future parliamentary control of Europol and several interparliamentary practices have already taken place. Particularly relevant are the networking initiatives, the meetings of COSAC and the interparliamentary meetings between national parliaments and the EP. The following sections analyse these interparliamentary modes in turn.

Networking initiatives

Most of the parliaments of the twenty-seven member states have by now some type of representation in Brussels.[8] With the creation of a representative office, national parliaments seek to increase their influence in decision making in the EU. One of the main activities of these representatives is to follow the EU legislative process from the initial phase and inform their respective parliaments of the development process. This information is important because it is in the initial stages when the possibility of influencing the final decision is higher. The presence of representatives *in situ* provides accurate and updated information in an expeditious manner. On the other hand, a representative is able to establish contacts, which are part of an incipient culture of interparliamentary practices. Representatives of national parliaments have a formal meeting every week, the so called MMM (Monday Morning Meeting) '[b]ut there are lots of informal meetings' (Interview Seventeen) National representatives have their offices at the EP building and 'it is common to simply go to the office of another representative in order to ask something needed' (Interview Seventeen).

Issues regarding the parliamentary control of Europol have been discussed in those meetings. However, the meetings have not served the purpose of coordinating any scrutiny activity. Moreover, although information exchanges occurred, little of this information regarded precise legal measures affecting Europol. This research has, however, discovered that groups of parliaments tend to work together towards some objectives and this work is coordinated by their representatives in Brussels. For instance, the Danish Parliament has managed to obtain the support of other parliaments to suggest to the Commission a proposal for an interinstitutional agreement which would arrange the relations between the EP and national parliaments regarding the parliamentary control of Europol (Interview Eighteen). Although this suggestion is unlikely to be successful, the fact that parliaments have coordinated their views is a sign of the importance of interparliamentary practices and it is an indication of the important role played by national parliaments' representatives in Brussels.

Representatives of national parliaments in Brussels have started to circulate information via email regarding the scrutiny undertaken in other parliaments. These emails are mainly intended to inform other national parliaments about the parliament's intention to raise concerns over the issue of subsidiarity on proposals from the Commission. This is an interesting development that could be used in the future in the case of the scrutiny of Europol. Some parliaments are indeed demanding something along these lines in order to exchange information 'in real time' (European Parliament 2009b). And COSAC, a forum that brings together members of EACs from all national parliaments as well as representatives of the EP, has, in one of its biannual reports, investigated

---

8. The parliaments of Slovakia and Malta and the upper houses of Germany and Slovenia have no representatives in Brussels. Source. Online. Available: http://www.europarl.europa.eu/webnp/cms/lang/en/pid/18 (last accessed 3 September 2012).

the improvements required 'to support real-time information exchange between [p]arliaments' (COSAC 2010b).

Representatives in Brussels also use the electronic platform, IPEX, for the exchange of information. IPEX has a database where parliaments can upload documents in order to share them with other parliaments. However, IPEX is mainly intended for the exchange of reports regarding the scrutiny of legal acts. This minimises its potential as an instrument for the exchange of non-legal act related information. Looking in particular at the scrutiny of Europol's legal framework, this research has found that 45 per cent of the EU's national chambers shared via IPEX the report of the scrutiny they carried out on the Council Decision on Europol. Considering that not every chamber may have written a report, this percentage is quite high. However, there is no evidence to suggest that these reports influenced the scrutiny of other parliaments. Interviews with MEPs, MPs and parliamentary officials suggest that the use of IPEX is rather limited, which rules out that information shared in IPEX will have much influence in the scrutiny work of parliaments. This finding is similar to the results of the analysis of debates and reports, which showed little evidence of information being retrieved from IPEX in order to inform the scrutiny of parliaments.

Over the years there have been more structured networking initiatives such as PARLOPOL, essentially a network for the exchange of information, together with a meeting of MPs and MEPs in charge of Justice and Home Affairs. However, they came to nothing (Interview Nineteen). In the case of PARLOPOL in particular, there were only two meetings between 2001–2002, one in The Hague and one in Brussels. The next meeting should have been organised by the Danish Parliament, but was not.

Some of the MEPs and MPs working on the issue admit they welcome interparliamentary initiatives but they doubt their efficiency (Interview Twenty). They believe that real interparliamentary work is done informally, in many cases through informal networking and contacts, most of the time along party lines (Interview Twenty-One). Ms Sophia in 't Veld MEP gives an example of how this works:

What we do is [...] try to tackle the same subject at the same time both at the EP and in the national parliament. For example if I table a parliamentary question on a particular topic then I ask my colleagues in the national parliament to put in the same question or a similar question at the same moment [...] or when the national parliament has to debate about a European topic, I will provide input. And the same when we are having a debate. I ask them for input on the national situation. We also do that with parliaments from other member states, not only my own national parliament (Interview Twenty-One).

Coordination along party lines is increasingly important and most people see the added value of working with party colleagues. However, there are good reasons to have formal coordination structures as well because, as Lord Bowness put it, 'you cannot guarantee that members of your own party are the chairmen or *rapporteurs* of a relevant committee' (Interview Twenty) but formal structures will at least guarantee some form of access to all the actors.

Interparliamentary fora have also dealt with the parliamentary control of Europol. Perhaps the most structured ones have been COSAC, and the several interparliamentary meetings organised at the premises of the EP in Brussels. The next sections analyse these two interparliamentary fora and their relevance to the scrutiny of Europol.

The Conference of European Affairs Committees (COSAC)

COSAC, the Conference of European Affairs Committees, was created in May 1989. It currently brings together representatives from national parliaments and the EP and its biannual meetings have provided the most structured interparliamentary forum in the EU. It currently has a permanent Secretariat that produces biannual reports on issues of interest to national parliaments. Discussions regarding the future parliamentary control of Europol and an increasing exchange of information regarding its current scrutiny has taken place within COSAC.

In its early years the effectiveness of COSAC was questioned (Maurer and Wessels 2001), but its potential importance as a forum that could serve as a tool for parliamentary scrutiny has grown since it originated. In 2003, COSAC changed its rules of procedure. This change enabled the adoption of contributions voted under majority rule, allowing it the possibility of articulating views and formulating opinions.

COSAC's potential regarding the scrutiny of Europol has also increased. The Lisbon Treaty provides for COSAC to address to the Union institutional contributions on the legislative activities of the Union, notably in relation to the application of the principle of subsidiarity; the Area of Freedom, Security and Justice (AFSJ); and questions regarding fundamental rights (TEU Art. 69). Regarding Europol, it should be said that Protocol No.1 of the Lisbon Treaty, which amends the provisions on COSAC, gives COSAC an official role with regard to the exchange of information and good practice between parliaments and extends that role to 'specialised committees'. The Protocol also provides for COSAC to 'organise interparliamentary conferences on specific topics' (TEU Art. 10 Protocol No.1). This modification in the COSAC Protocol opens the door for specific interparliamentary coordination between JHA sectoral committees that can cooperate through COSAC. These are significant improvements. On the one hand, the exchange of information at the level of specialised committees helps to reduce the lack of expertise, which has been one of the major problems of an interparliamentary forum like COSAC. On the other hand, the possibility of direct contributions to the European institutions is also a significant improvement because this way the discussions that take place in COSAC can have concrete results, such as an opinion that can be sent to the Commission or the Council.

However, even though, formally, the Treaty seems to provide COSAC with the necessary tools to become an important forum for scrutiny, including that related to the parliamentary control of Europol, not every parliament sympathises with this option. Moreover, some national parliaments, as well as the EP, do not seem convinced that COSAC should evolve from a forum merely for the exchange of best practice to an active forum for the scrutiny of EU policies. For instance, the Estonian *Riigikogu*, the French *Assemblée Nationale* and the Polish *Sejm* and *Senat* support the idea of adding the topic of the political monitoring of Europol as a recurrent issue on the COSAC agenda. However, several national parliamentary chambers, such as the German *Bundestag*, the Dutch *Tweede Kamer*, the Spanish *Cortes Generales*, the Swedish *Riksdag* and the EP, do not favour the idea of holding regular debates on Europol within COSAC's framework (COSAC 2010c). While there have been no mini-COSAC or specialised COSAC meetings, the parliamentary control of Europol has been part of the agenda of four COSAC meetings between 2008 and 2010. Also, COSAC biannual reports which are compiled by the COSAC Secretariat have served as a way for national parliaments to share their scrutiny best practice and their opinions on the interparliamentary dimension of the future parliamentary control of Europol.

COSAC's fortieth meeting (November 2008) dealt with the issue of Europol control and the involvement of national parliaments in it. In the conclusions to the meeting, COSAC recalled 'the role of national parliaments in scrutinising police activities' and affirmed 'the necessity to submit cooperation in these fields for scrutiny by the EP, in association with national parliaments' (Fortieth COSAC Meeting, Paris, 2–4 November 2008). Contributions to COSAC's forty-first meeting (May 2009) also stressed that oversight of Europol can only be carried out by national parliaments in conjunction with the EP and mentioned that COSAC had agreed to use the existing interparliamentary forms of coordination for this purpose (COSAC 2009). Of course, this includes COSAC but also shows a reluctance to mention it as the principal forum for that purpose. Apart from COSAC, meetings between national parliaments and the EP in the context of regular parliamentary cooperation have also discussed the parliamentary control of Europol.

Interparliamentary meetings between national parliaments and the European Parliament

Originally, meetings between the EP and national parliaments took two different formats: Joint Committee meetings and Joint Parliamentary meetings. However, a new form of meeting is emerging, the so-called Interparliamentary Committee meetings with national parliaments. Both the Joint Committee meeting and Interparliamentary Committee meetings with national parliaments are gatherings between sectoral committees of the EP and committees of the national parliaments. The difference between these two types of meetings is that Joint Committee meetings are organised by the EP and the parliament of the country holding the EU presidency, whereas Interparliamentary Committee meetings are proposed on the initiative of the individual parliamentary committees of the EP which invite national colleagues from their corresponding committees. These meetings are a continuation of existing practice and mainly cover the policy areas where the EU has legislative powers in accordance with the co-decision procedure. This difference is mainly procedural but it makes the process of organising meetings easier compared to the one required for joint meetings. In the last few years the number of Interparliamentary Committee meetings dealing with the issue of the parliamentary control of Europol has increased (Interviews Twenty and Twenty-One). Between 2005 and 2011 there were at least six meetings between national parliaments and the EP in which the parliamentary control of Europol and the role played by national parliaments was on the agenda.[9]

These meetings display a tendency to at least discuss issues related to the parliamentary control of JHA agencies between national parliaments and the EP. But another, more interesting, practice is that, in most cases, a questionnaire is sent to every parliament prior to the meeting. These questionnaires are a genuine tool for the exchange of information and the sharing of good practice. As an example, the questionnaire sent in 2005 included the following questions:

1. How is national parliamentary scrutiny of JHA matters organised in your country?
2. Have there been recent reports/resolutions/debates in your national parliament on one or more of the four issues mentioned above?
3. Could you give us names of any parliamentary committees and/or Members of Parliament who, in your opinion, have a direct involvement or interest in the four issues described above (please specify which issue)?
4. Could you identify the relevant officials in your parliament who deal with these issues and provide us with their contact details for further information?

Questions One and Two are clear examples of the sharing of best practice. Questions Three and, especially, Four are interesting because they show that in 2005 there was already a tendency to focus parliamentary coordination on personal exchanges, mainly between parliamentary officials. In the same vein, in the programme of this meeting the EP expressed its 'desire to improve coordination between national parliaments and the EP in their scrutiny of measures to implement the area of freedom, security and justice' and to find 'ways in which informal exchanges of information and networks of interested parliamentarians and parliamentary officials could be established in the field of the AFSJ'. For this particular questionnaire, fourteen parliaments provided answers. Even if this was not a huge percentage, it shows a clear attempt, already in 2005, to share information and to start building working networks.

---

9.   -- 17–18 October 2005 Joint Parliamentary Meeting 'Liberty and Security: Improving Parliamentary Scrutiny of Judicial and Police Cooperation in Europe'.
      -- October 2006 Joint Parliamentary Meeting 'The future development of the AFSJ'.
      November 2007 Joint Committee Meeting (LIBE Committee – national parliaments) 'The future of the EU as an AFSJ'.
      -- 16–17 November 2009 'Joint Parliamentary Meeting: Building a Citizen's Europe',
      -- 4–5 October 2010 Evaluation of Europol, Eurojust, FRONTEX and Schengen,
      -- 5–6 October 2011 'Democratic accountability of the internal security strategy and the role of Europol, Eurojust and Frontex'.

Due to their sectoral nature there is a lot of potential in these meetings and they may become a forum for interparliamentary scrutiny. However, two main problems have been identified. On the one hand, the legal basis for parliamentary control to take place in such fora is not yet ready, thus, these arrangements have been informal so far. Second, the MPs attending these meetings vary frequently, a situation that is not conducive to a cohesive working dynamic. Some national parliaments are trying to solve this problem by making sure that it is always the same MPs who attend such meetings (Interview Twenty-Three). Despite these two problems, the meetings have provided opportunities to 'share information and to debate' (Interview Twenty-Two).

The future parliamentary control of Europol

The precise form in which national parliaments and the EP will take part in the scrutiny of Europol will be defined by a regulation subject to the ordinary legislative procedure (former co-decision) in which the EP and the Council are co-legislators. Most parliaments agree that 'no new forum should be created' (COSAC 2009b). Among the already existing fora, the most discussed interparliamentary formats are the Joint Committee meetings and COSAC. Each forum has its supporters and opponents. The EP, for instance, is quite keen to have Europol scrutiny carried out at a Joint Committee meeting of its LIBE Committee together with the corresponding committees in national parliaments: 'The EP is offering the premises; they are also offering the Secretariat support' (Interview Twenty-Four). For instance, Mr Agustín Diaz de Mera MEP, a member of the LIBE Committee and *rapporteur* for the Council Decision on Europol, has proposed a meeting in Brussels of only the chairpersons of the JHA committees (Interview Twenty-Two). In his view, a forum like this has the advantage of reducing costs significantly and would also provide Europol with a forum in which information can be revealed without the risk of jeopardising Europol's work, as might sometimes be the case if the agency reported to more open fora. The committee could work in the following manner:

> The committee would meet three times a year. One time in order to evaluate Europol's budget. Another time in order to evaluate the use of the budget. And the third time in order to evaluate the activity plan. There should also be the possibility of establishing control mechanisms for extraordinary events and for when the Europol Director would ask at his own initiative to speak before the committee (Interview Twenty-Two).

The EP has already made a move by organising a number of Joint Committee meetings in an attempt to 'establish the practice' and be able to present it as an option for the future (Interview Nineteen).

Some national parliaments, such as those of Italy and Denmark, support this option (Interviews Eighteen and Twenty-Three). 'Normally we do not like that, we prefer COSAC', explains the representative of the Danish Parliament in Brussels. However, he recognises that, due to the greater expertise of the LIBE Committee, a Joint Committee meeting with the LIBE Committee 'will be for the benefit of national parliaments'. Another reason the Danish Parliament follows the EP's idea and agrees with its leading role in this matter is that it trusts in the work of the LIBE Committee which, it says, is working 'quite well' (Interview Eighteen). The representative of the Italian Senate also mentioned such trust in the LIBE Committee, particularly in its Secretariat (Interview Twenty-Three); 'The question is whether the House of Lords, the *Bundestag* and the French *Assemblée Nationale* will agree with this clear dominance and leadership of the EP in matters like this' (Interview Twenty-Four). When asked about such a possibility, Lord Bowness said: '[M]aybe the EP has a role to pull all that together at the end, maybe they do. Or alternatively because we are talking about national parliaments maybe that is another reason for COSAC to do it.' (Interview Twenty).

According to Lord Bowness, Interparliamentary Committee meetings, whichever form they may take, are only going to be 'the end of the process'. What he proposes is for national parliaments to individually scrutinise Europol's report before a meeting with other parliaments takes place. During this process each national parliament would be able, individually, to pose questions and to analyse detailed information. The particular feature of the proposal made by Lord Bowness is that it introduces a preliminary phase in which national parliaments individually assess the work of Europol. Indeed, there is nothing in the Treaty preventing national parliaments from organising their involvement on the 'political monitoring of Europol' (TEU Art. 12) as they wish.

Conclusion

Although solutions for the interparliamentary control of Europol have been discussed since 2001, there was not enough political will to formalise them. It was only with the entry into force of the Lisbon Treaty that coordination started to be taken seriously. Process tracing shows that successive reforms of Europol's legal framework never included interparliamentary bodies for its parliamentary control. Only the Lisbon Treaty dealt with that issue. We might have expected interparliamentary coordination to flourish because neither the EP nor the national parliaments could, on their own, provide adequate parliamentary control over Europol. However, evidence presented in this chapter shows that it was precisely the improvement of the parliamentary control of Europol *vis-à-vis* the EP that established the basis for the possibility of interparliamentary practices of control to be developed.

With the replacement of the Europol Convention by a Council Decision, the EP's role in the parliamentary control of Europol increased. In particular, the EP acquired a significant function in adopting the budget of the agency and the right to request and receive information from the Europol Director. It was only once this new legal framework was in place that the EP's discourse regarding interparliamentary coordination started to change, including with regard to the control of Europol. Before these developments the EP had expressed itself in the following terms: 'as a European organ, Europol must be monitored by another European organ – the EP – and not by national parliaments' (European Parliament 2002b). By contrast, once the Council Decision had been adopted, the EP asked the Commission to come forward with a legislative proposal outlining the involvement of the EP and national parliaments in the evaluation of the AFSJ agencies, including Europol (European Parliament 2009b). In the early stages of Europol's development the EP was concerned with increasing its own parliamentary control powers. Interparliamentary solutions for the parliamentary control of Europol were perceived more as a threat to the position of the EP than anything else. This research has found that to a certain extent this perception is still held by some MEPs and it may be one of the issues that could prevent the development of certain types of interparliamentary coordination.

Due to the failure of specific instruments to channel interparliamentary coordination regarding this issue of control, this coordination has been limited and it has been conducted via instruments for general parliamentary coordination. The work done by the national parliaments' offices at the EP's premises in Brussels is perhaps one of the most successful initiatives regarding interparliamentary coordination. According to those interviewed for this research, representatives in Brussels establish regular formal and informal contact among themselves and with EP officials, including an incipient practice of circulating information via email regarding the scrutiny carried out in other parliaments. This is an interesting development that could be used in the future scrutiny of Europol. Indeed, some parliaments are demanding something along these lines in order to exchange information 'in real time' (European Parliament 2009b).

National parliaments have used COSAC as a forum to express and discuss their views regarding the future parliamentary control of Europol. In particular, COSAC bi-annual reports and the questionnaires circulated to compile these reports have served as tools for the exchange of best practice in different policies including the scrutiny of EU agencies like Europol. Moreover, this research has found evidence of national parliaments using these reports to express their views on the future of parliamentary coordination regarding the parliamentary control of both Europol and other JHA agencies. Technically, COSAC has the (good) potential to establish itself as the forum around which interparliamentary coordination for the parliamentary control of Europol would be arranged. However, some parliaments, including the EP, are not convinced that COSAC is the right forum for the organisation's scrutiny and consider that COSAC should simply remain a forum for the exchange of good practice. These parliaments would prefer a forum like the Joint Committee meetings organised between the EP's sectoral committee dealing with JHA, the EP's Committee on Civil Liberties (LIBE), and its corresponding committees in national parliaments. In fact, the LIBE Committee and its Secretariat have managed to push for this type of fora by offering secretarial support and the premises for this purpose. They initiated these Joint Committee meetings in order to present the practice as already established in the future. The trust in the work of the LIBE Committee has led some parliaments to believe that this could be the way forward but evidence suggests that other options may still be considered. For instance in a move similar to the LIBE Committee's, COSAC has discussed the monitoring of Europol repeatedly since 2008 and the COSAC Secretariat has explored the potential of that option in four of its biannual reports (cf. COSAC 2009a; 2009c; 2010a; 2010c).

Interparliamentary activities have increased since the entry into force of the Lisbon Treaty. However, the extent to which these activities serve the purpose of parliamentary control seems to be rather limited. It is possible that most of the coordination regarding scrutiny happens in informal meetings between representatives of national parliaments. Further, interparliamentary coordination seems to be limited to the exchange of best practice among national parliaments. For this purpose COSAC, and in particular its biannual reports, seems to be the preferred option. In the view of those interviewed for this research, 'real scrutiny' takes place at 'home'. Therefore, it can be said that the parliamentary control of Europol has provided opportunities for interparliamentary coordination, although this coordination has not been oriented to scrutiny itself but, rather, to the sharing of best practice regarding scrutiny. Yet, this research has found several examples of interparliamentary coordination oriented towards scrutiny, which takes place along political lines in the form of MEPs attending meetings at national parliaments, or by coordination of scrutiny mechanisms such as asking parliamentary questions on the same issues at the EP and in national parliaments.

Why did interparliamentary coordination for the parliamentary control of Europol only start to develop once the Council Decision on Europol had already decreased the oversight gap (by measures like the recognition of the EP as a budgetary authority)?

The inclusion of national parliaments via coordination might have been the only way to advance on further integration. As some MEPs put it, the inclusion of national parliaments via parliamentary coordination provides an argument against those worries related to the EU 'becoming a super state' (Interview Twenty-One). In this sense, parliamentary coordination can be understood as a side effect of the enhanced role that the Council Decision provided for Europol. In other words, despite the numerous discussions on the need to improve parliamentary control, the real need to improve it was not realised until Europol became a fully-fledged European agency. Another explanation is that parliamentary control has evolved in line with the role of Europol. This idea was already expressed in 2001 at The Hague during the first parliamentary meeting to discuss the democratic control of Europol. There, Mr Hugo Coveliers, at the time a member of the Belgian House of Representatives, warned that 'parliamentary control on the national or European level will be different depending on the tasks of Europol' (Dutch Senate 2002). Nevertheless, some see a third explanation. As a permanent member of COSAC's Secretariat, Ms Loreta Raulinaitytè, explains 'parliamentary democracy has been developed (compared to) twenty years ago [when] there was not a single reference to national parliaments in the body of the Treaty. Now we have references to national parliaments all over in the Lisbon Treaty (Interview Twenty-Four). Thus, the current development of interparliamentary practices emerges as a consequence of the new role that the Lisbon Treaty ascribes to national parliaments and the need to actualise models of control according to the Treaty's requirements.

chapter seven | parliaments at the water's edge: the EU's naval mission Atalanta[*]

Dirk Peters, Wolfgang Wagner and Cosima Glahn

Introduction

Security and defence policy is not an obvious issue area for the study of parliaments and interparliamentary cooperation. According to some, the involvement of parliament is simply incompatible with the secrecy that military operations require. Moreover, concerns about national sovereignty have set limits to the internationalisation and Europeanisation of this issue area. Therefore, even in the EU, security and defence policy has retained intergovernmental characteristics: unanimity prevails for decisions on military deployments, and the Commission's competencies pale in comparison with the powerful position it has in Common Market governance. This may appear to imply that parliamentary control is primarily a task for national parliaments.

Indeed, parliamentary control of EU security policy has always been much more centred on national parliaments than in other policy fields (see, for example, on the EU Services Directive, Crum and Miklin in this volume). Yet, the establishment of the European Security and Defence Policy and the newly acquired ability of the EU to conduct military operations for crisis management has increased the pressure to rethink the focus on national control procedures and led to some institutional adjustments. Above all, the increasing significance of role specialisation and of tightly integrated multinational forces (brought about by the ambition to spend shrinking defence budgets as efficiently as possible) has made national parliamentary control procedures problematic. The more integrated security policy becomes, the more difficult it is to control it through national parliaments that act independently from one another (Wagner 2006a). Consequently, the pressures on parliamentarians to cooperate across borders and across levels of governance have increased in the security realm as well. Thus, security and defence policy in the multilevel polity of the EU may not be the most obvious choice, but it is certainly a very interesting case study of parliamentary activity and interparliamentary cooperation.

[*] This chapter emanates from RECON (Reconstituting Democracy in Europe), an integrated project supported by the European Commission's Sixth Framework Programme (contract no. CIT4-CT-2006–028698). The empirical sections of this chapter are based on Peters *et al.* (2011), which also includes a detailed chronology, a list of interviewees and additional sources. The authors wish to thank Anna Herranz, Espen Olsen, Marianne Riddervold, Anne Elizabeth Stie, and Sophie Vanhoonacker for helpful comments and suggestions, Sjirk Prins for research assistance and Berenike Schott for careful proofreading.

In this chapter, we employ the notion of the parliamentary field to provide an analysis of parliamentary involvement for one particular segment of the EU's Common Security and Defence Policy (CSDP): military missions. Our goal is to provide insights into both general parliamentary competences and actual parliamentary practice in the control of EU military operations. In the following section we will first describe our analytical lens, the notion of the parliamentary field, and three configurations of the field. In the next section, we provide some background information on the planning and implementation process for EU operations and on one particular operation: the EU's anti-piracy mission, Atalanta, off the Somali coast, which we will use to examine the practice of parliamentary control. We then go on to analyse the parliamentary field in the last section before our conclusions. These will show that the field is characterised by a patchwork of control levels and procedures at the member state level. The EP primarily serves a scrutinising role, and transnational assemblies and interparliamentary networks provide for information exchange between parliamentarians across borders and levels.

Multilevel parliamentary fields

According to John Erik Fossum and Ben Crum (2012), a 'multi-level parliamentary organisational field' denotes a field in which parliaments are in some way interconnected in a specific area on and across different levels of political organisation. The advantage of this notion is that it does not focus exclusively on separate channels of parliamentary control but directs research towards the totality of relevant parliamentary actors and also includes their interaction across different levels. Examining a parliamentary field requires the researcher to take into account both its formal institutional set-up, i.e. the competences that parliaments have at the various levels; and the practices that fill this model with life, i.e. the actions and interactions taking place on and across the levels. This distinction is very similar to Born and Hänggi's (2005) distinction between the 'authority' and the 'attitude' that parliamentarians possess in the control of military operations. The 'authority' to hold the government accountable in deployment questions refers to formal parliamentary competences. These are the legislative, budgetary, elective, representative, scrutiny and oversight rights of the parliament. Parliamentarians may be equipped with a variety of formal competences to control the executive but equally they need the willingness to use these means. Their 'attitude' (in Born and Hänggi's terms) towards controlling the government may vary as it might be affected, for example, by party pressure, public or media opinion. We therefore need to examine actual control practices to assess whether and how MPs make use of the competences they possess.[1]

---

1.   Born and Hänggi add 'ability' as a third dimension. It refers to parliaments' resources for scruti-nising government. As the level of authority and/or attitude, on the one hand, and that of ability, on the other, are usually closely related, we disregard the 'ability' dimension here.

A multilevel parliamentary field can be institutionalised in a variety of ways. For the EU, Fossum and Crum (2012) distinguish three types of institutional layout, each of which is connected to a particular conception of the EU as a polity. Conceiving of the EU as a functional regime, the parliamentary field would have its prime locus at the level of national parliaments whereas the European level would serve to complement national arrangements and fulfil what they term an 'audit function'. From this perspective, the EU is simply a collaborative arrangement that has been created by member states to help them solve collective action problems. Member states delegate competences to the European level but decision making remains in the hands of member states (intergovernmentalism) and, consequently, democratic legitimacy continues to be derived from legitimising mechanisms at the national level. The EP, in this view, would not play a representative role in its own right since the sovereign remains located at the member state level. Rather, the EP would, 'through standing committees and special enquiries, through debates and hearings, and so forth, shed light on the nooks and crannies of the EU system, and thereby aid the national parliaments in their efforts to hold their executives accountable when they operate at the EU level' (Fossum and Crum 2012). The EP would thus serve a deliberative audit function, further enabling the national parliaments to hold executives accountable.

If, instead, the EU is conceived of as a federal state in the making, the parliamentary field would be organised in functionally specific domains. Both member state parliaments and the EP would serve the same functions (deliberation and decision making), but in different policy areas. As a state in the making, policies may be made according to different procedures. Where policies are made primarily through intergovernmental decision-making, as is by and large the case in the EU's security policy, the structure would resemble that of the functional regime type just described, with national parliaments playing the dominant role. However, in areas where there is supranational European policy-making, parliamentary control would have to involve a strong EP.

Whereas the two types discussed so far are intimately related to the idea of the nation-state, a third type draws more on cosmopolitan democracy, steeped in a deliberative conception of democracy. Deliberative democracy is seen as a particularly promising concept for democratising the EU as it does not presuppose substantial social prerequisites like rich collective identities but, rather, holds the promise of producing those elements of community it relies on (Eriksen 2006). Deliberative democracy is an attempt to integrate input and output legitimacy into one model by aligning participation in decision making with the rationalisation of decisions to ensure individual autonomy (Cohen and Sabel 1997; Habermas 1996; Niesen 2008). Parliaments play a crucial role in conceptions of deliberative democracy. A parliamentary field reflecting the idea of deliberative democracy beyond the nation state would require interaction among parliaments across different levels. In contrast to the preceding models, any parliament would no longer be 'the main institutional manifestation of a given, sovereign, democratic *demos*, but [...] rather one among a chain of strong publics who *together* seek to accommodate the interests and concerns of a multitude of interdependent *demoi*'

(Fossum and Crum 2012). Relations on and across the different levels would thus be institutionalised, in contrast to the preceding models where the different levels possess more or less clearly delineated spheres of competence. The EU would then be neither a functional regime nor a federal state in the making. Rather, it could be perceived as part of a larger deliberative cosmopolitan order.

EU Operation Atalanta: Mission and decision making

To study parliamentary control in action, we will examine parliamentary involvement in one particular operation: Operation Atalanta. This was launched in 2008 and, at the time of writing, is one of the EU's most recent military operations. It therefore enables us to analyse the parliamentary field in its most current form. This is all the more important as (especially) national provisions for the control of military operations have been in flux since the end of the Cold War (Peters and Wagner 2011) and appear to have somewhat consolidated in the second half of the 2000s. Atalanta constitutes the EU's contribution to the international community's attempt to combat piracy off the Somali coast. International efforts to protect ships in this area gained momentum in 2008 after the number of attacks on World Food Programme (WFP) ships and international cargo vessels increased significantly, from forty-one in 2006 and 2007 combined, to 217 in 2009 (Zimmer 2009). As the humanitarian situation in Somalia is precarious and as most of the population is dependent on WFP deliveries, the protection of relief supplies is highly important and constitutes a major goal of the military mission. Moreover, most Euro-Asian trade is conveyed through the Gulf of Aden, one of the most important sea lanes worldwide. Bypassing the Somali coast via the Cape of Good Hope is costly for ship owners and prolongs the journey by up to several days (Zimmer 2009).

The mandate of the Atalanta mission stipulates that the participating forces are allowed to 'take the necessary measures, including the use of force, to deter, prevent and intervene in order to bring to an end acts of piracy and armed robbery' (Council Joint Action 2008/851/CFSP). Atalanta's main objective is the protection of WFP ships. Vessels from the African Union's Mission to Somalia (AMISOM) are also protected, whereas the protection of commercial cargo ships has only lower priority. The force is made up of national contributions and does not comprise integrated multinational units. Its size fluctuates somewhat. It usually consists of four to seven vessels, two to three reconnaissance aircraft and, overall, around 1,500 military personnel.[2]

Atalanta was launched only after several other attempts had been made to tackle the problem. After a request by the International Maritime Organization (IMO) and the WFP, France, Denmark, the Netherlands and Canada began a one-off operation for the protection of WFP ships in 2007 and 2008 (Helly 2009). After this mission ended, French ships stayed in the Gulf to protect vulnerable vessels.

---

2.   EU NAVFOR Website http://eunavfor.eu/ (accessed 11 July 2012).

Starting in May 2008, the United Nations Security Council adopted a series of resolutions under Chapter VII of the UN Charter (Resolutions 1814, 1816, 1838, 1846 and 1897) that condemned piracy and, among other things, authorised the use of military means to combat this problem in Somali territorial waters. The EU set up a coordination cell (NAVCO) in September 2008 to coordinate the naval activities of its member states in the region and, in October 2008, NATO started a maritime mission there. Finally, the EU launched its own operation Atalanta in December of the same year (Council Joint Action 2008/851/CFSP). The EU mission did not aim to replace but to complement various operations by NATO, by 'Operation Enduring Freedom' contingents (Combined Task Force 150 and 151) and by several other states including Russia, China, Japan and India. Atalanta's rapid operational readiness can be traced back to the fact that some national contingents of EU member states had already been stationed off the Somali coast as well as to its cooperation with the other missions on site (Weber 2009). Although the mission has successfully escorted WFP vessels to Somalia, critical voices highlight, among other things, the inability of the mission to stop piracy in the area and, generally, the lack of a political element, which would focus on creating stable political conditions in Somalia (see, for example, Ehrhart and Petretto 2012).

In order to explore in detail the involvement of parliaments in decision making on, and implementation of Operation Atalanta, it is of course important to understand the decision-making process that underlies EU military operations. In general, the formal decision to launch any EU military mission is taken by the foreign ministers in the 'Foreign Affairs Council' (previously the 'General Affairs and External Relations Council'). With a view to parliamentary control, however, it is essential to understand the preceding processes of advance planning and crisis response planning, because it is during this planning phase that crucial strategic decisions are made. We limit our overview of the EU planning process to the political-strategic level which is also of prime interest to parliaments. We thus exclude the operational level that is concerned with the implementation of the political mandate, including the mission's organisation and 'enabling requirements such as logistics and communication and information systems' (Grevi 2009).

Advance planning is carried out by the EU Military Staff (EUMS) under the direction of the EU Military Committee (EUMC)[3] and often starts many months before a military mission is launched. In the case of Atalanta, advance planning started around March/April 2008 when both the High Representative and NATO's Secretary General expected the EU to assume a lead role in the combat of piracy. Whereas no political decision is required to begin advance planning, a decision that EU action is appropriate needs to be taken by the Political and Security

---

3. The EUMC is composed of the Chiefs of Staff of the member states but usually works on the level of the Military Representatives. It advises the PSC and instructs the EUMS which consists of some 200 military experts. If necessary, the EUMS can draw on resources of the much larger military staff of NATO.

Committee (PSC)[4] to switch from advance to more concrete crisis response planning; in the case of Atalanta, this was done in the summer of 2008.

Crisis response planning then takes the form of 'an iterative dialogue between political authorities and supporting staffs' (Mattelaer 2010), overseen by a 'Crisis Response Coordination Team' (CRCT) which is composed of the relevant units in the Council Secretariat and the Commission (merged into the 'European External Action Service' (EEAS) with the Treaty of Lisbon) and meets on an *ad hoc* basis. The first milestone in this crisis response planning process is the 'Crisis Management Concept' (CMC) which gives an assessment of the situation and reviews various options for the EU to react to the crisis (Mattelaer 2010). The CMC is drafted by the Military Staff and passed on to the Military Committee, the PSC and, finally, the Council which has to formally endorse it. In the case of Atalanta, the draft CMC was sent to the Council on 31 July 2008, which adopted it on 5 August 2008.

On the basis of the CMC, 'Military Strategic Options' (MSOs) are worked out by the Military Staff which outline a number of military alternatives, including an estimate of the common costs of the operation (Dijkstra 2011). The MSOs are discussed in the Military Committee and the PSC and forwarded to the Council, which chooses one among them. In the case of Atalanta, the options were: (1) maritime surveillance without close protection ('deterrence by presence'); (2) convoy escorts; and (3) surveillance with close protection. These were discussed in the MSOs and sent to the PSC on 11 August 2008. The document already indicated a preference for the third option and, on 15 September 2008, the Council decided that Atalanta would indeed carry out surveillance and close protection. A few days later, on 19 September 2008, the Council adopted a Joint Action launching the EU coordination mission NAVCO[5]. The decision to launch a full-blown military operation was taken by the Council on 10 November 2008,[6] and was followed by the adoption of the Concept of Operations (CONOPS) and the Operational Plan (OPLAN). The Council Decision actually launching Atalanta followed on 8 December 2008.[7]

---

4. The PSC is composed of representatives of the member states at ambassador level and is tasked with 'the political control and strategic direction of the crisis management operations' (Art. 28 TEU-L). The PSC has therefore been considered to be 'the political mind' of the CSDP (Thym 2006: 110).

5. Council Joint Action 2008/749/CFSP.

6. Council Joint Action 2008/851/CFSP.

7. Council Decision 2008/918/CFSP.

The parliamentary field in action

The national level: Member state parliaments and European security policy

We start our examination of parliamentary control competences and practice at the national level. Probably the most characteristic feature of parliamentary involvement at the member state level is the absence of any standard way in which member state parliaments are engaged in European security affairs and, indeed, of any guarantee that national parliaments are involved at all. Instead, there exist a wide variety of arrangements for the national control of European security policy, ranging from an *ex ante* veto power over troop deployments in Germany and Spain to a complete lack of parliamentary involvement in Belgium or Greece.[8]

It is interesting to note that the involvement of parliaments in EU security policy bears hardly any resemblance to parliamentary involvement in the scrutiny of other EU policies (see Buzogány in this volume). This is due to the intergovernmental character of the policy field and to the fact that oversight mechanisms in the military realm have historically developed independently from those concerned with EC/EU issues. Moreover, they were tailored to controlling or scrutinising national policies rather than Europeanised ones. Strong parliamentary influence is usually institutionalised in the form of a veto over national troop deployments. In contrast to other policy fields, therefore, some national parliaments formally have the ability to stop the implementation of a decision at the EU level. However, few parliaments have such strong powers, whereas others can only scrutinise deployment decisions but do not possess co-decision rights.

To illustrate the heterogeneity of parliamentary involvement in decision making over EU military missions we take a closer look at the parliaments in Germany, Spain, the Netherlands and Belgium. These countries are all major contributors to Atalanta but, at the same time, vary significantly in terms of national deployment legislation and practice. Whereas, in Germany and Spain, parliament enjoys *ex ante* veto power over military missions, the Dutch and Belgian Parliaments lack such power. However, the Dutch *Staten Generaal* is still more powerful than its Belgian counterpart as the Dutch Government has comprehensive obligations to inform and consult its Parliament. Our analysis is based on thirty background interviews which we conducted mostly with MPs and some parliamentary staff (for a full list of interviews, see Peters *et al.* 2011).[9]

---

8. For overviews on national deployment procedures, *see* Anghel *et al.* 2008; Dieterich *et al.* 2010; Wagner *et al.* 2010.

9. We do not attribute quotes to individual MPs in the sections that follow as most interviewees asked that direct quotations not be attributed to them.

Germany

The German troop deployment law stipulates that troops can only be deployed *after* the *Bundestag* has given its explicit consent. Thus, in Germany, the Government could commit troops to Atalanta only after the *Bundestag's* approval on 19 December 2008, i.e. eleven days after the EU Council decision to launch the mission.[10] The approval of the *Bundestag* is also required for any prolongation of Atalanta as well as any significant change in its mandate. Thus, the *Bundestag* endorsed the enlargement of the area of operations as far as the Seychelles on 18 June 2009[11] and extended the mandate for another year on 17 December 2009 (BT Drucksache 17/179) and for two more years on 2 December 2010 (BT Drucksache 17/3691).

Information about the operation and the planning process to guide the decisions was obtained by MPs through various channels. First, the government, usually at the level of a state secretary, regularly briefed the defence committee and answered questions. In addition, MPs posed questions to the government, mostly seeking detailed information about the numbers of participating soldiers and escorted WFP ships and about the procedure for detaining suspected pirates. Finally, German MPs made use of their right to visit troops at the military mission on site. Two parliamentary delegations have visited the Atalanta mission in the headquarters in Djibouti: one parliamentary delegation went to Djibouti with Franz Josef Jung, the German Minister of Defence, immediately after the start of the mission in December 2008[12] and another one in February 2010, when state secretary Thomas Kossendey was accompanied by several MPs from the Defence Committee (Deutscher Bundestag 2010).

German MPs generally agree in their assessment that they can wield influence on government positions before the text of the mandate is written. Usually, the government communicates with its parliamentary majority and thus gets an idea of whether a majority supports a deployment of troops for a military mission or not. This way, 'the government usually gets a feeling for how a mandate has to be written'.[13] The 'flow of information' is less intense with the parliamentary opposition. One opposition parliamentarian revealed in an interview that it was 'very uncommon that the government informs us about planned projects [on the European Union level] of its own accord'. Therefore, inter-party communication is clearly an important factor concerning the information about international

---

10. The Cabinet had decided that it would ask the *Bundestag* for approval the day after the Council meeting and forwarded a proposal on 10 December 2008 (BT Drucksache 16/11337). The *Bundestag's* Foreign Affairs Committee recommended participation on 17 December 2008 (BT Drucksache 16/11416) and the plenary debated the issue on 17 and 19 December.

11. The PSC decided on 19 May 2009 to spatially enlarge the mission, and the government forwarded a respective request to parliament on 27 May 2009 (BT Drucksache 16/13187).

12. *See* http://www.nouripour.de/fileadmin/pdfs/international/0901_Reisebericht_Djibouti.pdf (accessed 1 June 2011).

13. All quotations in this subsection are from interviews with German MPs, conducted between April and June 2010.

negotiations in general, and the planning of military missions in particular. As in other policy areas, then, government usually informs its own parliamentary majority much earlier than it notifies the opposition.

According to the assessments of the MPs we interviewed, their primary resource for influencing government lies in the *Bundestag's* constitutional right to actually veto troop deployments. All of the interviewees stated that this provision constrains the government's position during negotiations at the international level. As 'the members of the *Bundestag* are usually very sensitive concerning the deployment of troops' the government cannot single-handedly confirm a German military contribution at the international level. Rather, it is 'very well-advised to consider the various parliamentary positions in advance'. German MPs also referred to the Parliament's veto position as something special and unique which 'should be defended'. Overall, although the information flow may sometimes discriminate against the opposition and although the *Bundestag* may sometimes be informed only *after* international negotiations have taken place, the parliamentary veto position is considered to have a 'constraining effect' on the executive's decision.

Spain

The Spanish deployment law was modified significantly in 2005 after the deployment of troops to the Iraq war. The Spanish Parliament now plays a key role in deploying the military, as its prior approval before troops participate in military missions is required. Remarkably, the 'Organic Law of Defence 5/2005' does not specify whether or not the additional deployment of troops or the modification and prolongation of a mandate needs further parliamentary approval. Until today, political practice has shown that the deployment of additional troops has been mandated by the Defence Committee, while the prolongation and the modification of missions have been decided by the executive alone. As the deployment law remains silent about the detailed rules of procedure for the deployment of troops, parliament still debates about its exact competences.[14]

In the case of the Atalanta mission, parliament approved the deployment of a Spanish frigate to the mission on 21 January 2009. The mandate was given on a Tuesday and military personnel had already begun to contribute to the mission on the following Friday. There was no formal parliamentary approval of the extension of the Atalanta mission (in terms of both area and duration). The total number of Spanish military personnel, however, may not exceed 395, as has been specified in the Spanish mandate.

In comparison to other CSDP deployments, the Atalanta mission has attracted a remarkable amount of attention from parliament. The mission itself has not been discussed critically in Spain, which can mainly be traced back to the fact that there has barely been any political disagreement surrounding this mission and

---

14. For this and the following details on the Spanish deployment, see Herranz-Surrallés (2010).

only a few MPs from leftist parties actually criticised the mission as a whole. Additionally, Spain possesses a tuna fishing fleet in the Indian Ocean and the hijacking of Spanish vessels in 2008 and 2009 had raised public awareness. Political discussions about Atalanta were not focused on the mission's general desirability but rather on its efficacy, on the employed means to stop and prevent piracy, the parliamentary rules of procedure, the field of action, the supplied protection to the vessels and the handling of suspected pirates. MPs have raised a high number of oral and written questions, and requests for appearance have been important tools for the parliament to force the government to comment on certain aspects of the mission. Furthermore, it is worthwhile to note that parliamentarians referred to interparliamentary meetings to back up their arguments, as in the case, for example, of the NATO-PA meeting in Edinburgh on 17 November 2009 where the issue of piracy was discussed. Last but not least, MPs visited the command centre of the air and naval forces of the Atalanta mission. A delegation of seven members of the Spanish Defence Committee of both Houses of Parliament accompanied the Defence Minister to visit the operational headquarters during the Spanish leadership of the mission between April and August 2009. The President of the Somali Parliament also visited the Spanish Parliament in February 2010 by invitation of the Association of European Parliamentarians with Africa.

Of course, *informal* interactions have also been important channels through which parliamentarians gain information about the Atalanta mission. During plenary discussions, MPs sometimes referred to communications with the Defence Minister, other officials from that ministry, or parties' spokespersons, even though they did not elaborate on the information they had received through these informal contacts.

The Netherlands

The Dutch Parliament cannot veto any military mission but since a new Article 100 was introduced to the Dutch constitution in 2000, government is obliged to inform parliament in advance of any planned military mission. Moreover, once government has decided to send troops, it is obliged to notify parliament and add an explanatory note that outlines the legal basis, military aspects, risks, and underlying political rationale. Between government's first information and the actual decision, parliament's standing committees on Foreign Affairs and Defence usually have a discussion with the respective ministers. When deciding about participating in a military mission, government is therefore well aware of any particular concerns as well as the general degree of support among the political parties. Once a military mission is completed, government sends an evaluation report to parliament.

Among Dutch Members of Parliament, the absence of a formal veto power is not necessarily regarded as a shortcoming. According to Henk Jan Ormel, MP, Christen Democratisch Appél (CDA), co-decision making with the government over military missions may even compromise parliament's ability to effectively criticise the mission later on.[15]

---

15. Interview on 30 May 2010.

Dutch contributions to the combat of piracy had already started in March 2008 in response to a request by the director of the World Food Programme. At this time, neither NATO nor the EU was involved. As a consequence, the debate in the Standing Committee on Foreign Affairs and Defence was not concerned with the institutional framework. In accordance with Dutch tradition, the debate ended with statements by the representatives of all political parties, indicating whether their faction supported the military mission. This indication of support, of course, was not binding but the Dutch Government normally refrains from any military deployment if there is no majority in support of such a mission. At the end of the debate of 1 April 2008, representatives of all political groups present declared their support. On 22 October 2008, twelve days after the Government had informed its Parliament about its decision to send another frigate to guard WFP ships, a similar debate took place. As in April, the representatives of the parties present (i.e. of all parties except the Dutch Party for Freedom (PVV); the Democrats 66; and the PvdA) all declared their support for the decision. Ten days before the Council decision to launch Atalanta, the Dutch Government informed Parliament that it was looking into the possibility and desirability of contributing to such a mission. On 19 December 2008, it informed Parliament about its decision to send a frigate to Atalanta in the second half of 2009. Given the thorough discussion in Parliament earlier that year, these letters were not followed by any further debate. As a consequence, representatives of the political groups did not explicitly indicate their support for Atalanta as such, but it can be concluded from the earlier debates that support was widespread in Parliament.

Since the initial decision to participate in Atalanta, the Dutch Government has sent additional letters to Parliament whenever it has considered or decided to deploy another ship. Furthermore, once a particular frigate was deployed, the Government forwarded to Parliament an evaluation which was then debated. These debates focused on issues of military equipment (most importantly the absence of a board helicopter) and on the release of pirates (because Kenya failed to put them on trial). In addition, the Government shared the report on piracy by the Advisory Council on International Affairs (2010) with Parliament.

In sum, even though the Dutch Parliament lacks a formal *ex ante* veto power, it has succeeded in being well informed about governmental intentions and plans. Moreover, the Dutch Government almost acts as if its Parliament had formal veto powers in that it normally refrains from sending troops without majority support. In the case of Atalanta, however, there was a broad consensus on the desirability of such a military mission.

Belgium

In Belgium, the Government is not obliged to consult parliament before it decides to deploy troops. However, MPs may make use of question time to engage in a dialogue with government about planned deployments. In the case of Atalanta, MP Ludo van Campenhout used the question time on 20 November 2008 to demand military action against piracy off the Somali coast. In his response, Belgian minister Jo Vandeurzen referred to the planned EU maritime mission and to the Belgian Government's intention to contribute a frigate in the second half of 2009 (Belgische Kamer van Volksvertegenwoordigers 2008). On 19 May 2009, during a joint meeting with the Foreign Affairs and Defence Committee, the Defence Minister, Pieter de Crem, and the Minister of Foreign Affairs, Karel de Gucht, together informed the House of Representatives that Belgium would send the frigate 'Louise-Marie' from September to December 2009 (Belgische Kamer van Volksvertegenwoordigers, CRABV 52 COM 561). On a further meeting with the Defence Committee on 28 October 2009, the Defence Minister mentioned that he had already proposed to the Government that Belgium take over the command of the mission during its EU Council presidency in the second half of 2010 (Belgische Kamer van Volksvertegenwoordigers, CRIV 52 COM 683). Belgium participated with a frigate until the end of December 2009.

Subsequent parliamentary discussions about Atalanta were mainly focused around the handling of captured pirates and the existing legal regulations relating to that issue. Furthermore, MPs asked questions concerning the financing of the mission, the protection of merchant ships and the lack of a political component to stop piracy on the Somali mainland. MPs asked the Defence Minister in various meetings with the Defence Committee about the status of the Belgian contribution to Atalanta. At the beginning of 2010, parliamentarians were particularly interested to learn more about the forthcoming Belgian EU Council Presidency and the operational command of Atalanta by Belgium. Parliamentarians used these means to control the Belgian Government frequently, as the Parliament had no formal control competences and parliamentary questions seemed to be the sole channel of influence available to MPs.

Nevertheless, the Parliament approved a governmental motion for an anti-piracy law, which mainly regulated the treatment of captured pirates. The government proposal was introduced on 21 October 2009, debated, and approved by the Chamber on 17 December and afterwards by the Senate. Although the Atalanta mission was discussed within the context of this law, the operation was not its primary focus and parliamentary control competences concerning the mission were not addressed. Piracy had also already been an issue at the end of 2004, when the Government had proposed a law concerning 'the suppression of unlawful acts against the safety of maritime navigation' (Belgische Kamer van Volksvertegenwoordigers, DOC 51 1524/001). All in all, it can be seen that MPs had only limited influence on the Belgian Government's decision to deploy troops to the Atalanta mission. Apparently, the only possibility for Belgian parliamentarians to scrutinise their executive is through raising parliamentary questions *ex post,* whereas formal decision-making competences do not exist, or at least did not exist in the case of Atalanta.

Taken together, then, member state parliaments differ vastly in both their formal authority and in the attitudes that MPs bring to the scrutiny of EU military operations. It appears that possessing a certain degree of formal competences is helpful for MPs to assert their influence, even though – as the Dutch case indicates – formal veto power is not required when MPs' inquisitive attitude meets with formal obligations for the government to forward information to parliament in a timely manner. Moreover, even though formal veto power may be an important tool for parliamentarians, it may especially benefit a subset of MPs, namely, those that belong to the parliamentary majority – as the German case demonstrates. All in all, then, parliaments' authority matters but so does the attitude of MPs – their effects cannot be assessed in isolation from each other.

The supranational level: The European Parliament

The EP has only very limited formal powers when it comes to military deployments. It does not have veto power over military missions. The High Representative is only obliged to

> regularly consult the EP on the main aspects and the basic choices of the common foreign and security policy and the common security and defence policy and inform it of how those policies evolve. The views of the EP are duly taken into consideration. (Article 36, TEU)

However, the EP has not been satisfied with the implementation of this provision in general. Atalanta is a case in point. In a resolution on the mission, the EP

> regret[s] the lack of consultation by the Council of the European Parliament on the decision to launch this operation and to provide information to the EP about the scope of this action and the exact tasks that the 'EU coordination cell' in the Council will undertake in support of EU NAVCO. (European Parliament 2008b).[16]

The formal position of the EP is further weakened by the fact that its budgetary powers are also rather limited. Most importantly, parliament has no influence whatsoever over expenditure arising from military operations. These are not charged to the Community budget but are covered by member states following a 'costs lie where they fall' principle ('Athena mechanism'). From Parliament's perspective, military expenditure appears as a shadow budget which increases the Council's discretion in financial matters (Brok and Gresch 2004).

Despite these formal obstacles, the EP has, in practice, developed a quite active approach to scrutinising EU military deployments. It is interesting to note, though, that the problem of piracy off the Somali coast was first put on the EP's agenda not by a security expert but by a member of the committee on fisheries in May 2008. After the Spanish fishing trawler 'Playa de Bakio' had been hijacked, Spanish MP Daniel Varela Suanzes-Carpegna (PPE) (People's Party of Spain) sent a written question[17] to the Commission inquiring about future action of the EU to improve

---

16. *See also* the press release. Online. Available at: http://www.europarl.europa.eu/sides/getDoc.do?language=EN&type=IM-PRESS&reference=20081022IPR40410 (accessed 8 August 2010).

17. E-2585/08.

the situation off the Somali coast. Members of the Committees for Fisheries and for Transport and Tourism also dominated the plenary debate on piracy that was held on 23 September 2008. Geoffrey van Orden was one of the few members of the EP's subcommittee on Security and Defence (SEDE) to speak in this debate. Remarkably, he questioned why the EU should get militarily involved at all, saying, 'this is a job for NATO' (European Parliament 2008a). Although the committees on fisheries and transport took the initial lead on the combat of piracy, SEDE took up the issue shortly afterwards and organised an exchange of views with the Head of the Council Secretariat's Crisis Management Unit, Claude-France Arnould, and the Head of NAVCO, Capt. (N) Andrés Breijo Claúr, on 15 October 2008. At the same meeting, the committee also discussed a draft motion for a resolution, sponsored by the Committee for Transport and Tourism that the plenary then adopted on 23 October 2008. In this resolution, the EP

> [c]alls on the Commission to seek ways to provide protection against piracy for EU-flagged and other fishing vessels that operate in international waters in the north-western Indian Ocean.
>
> (European Parliament 2008b)

Although the Council is not formally obliged to ask the EP for its position towards a CSDP military action, the EP has developed a political practice of commenting on a military mission, preferably before its commencement. The EP has even held votes on CSDP missions through resolutions during the planning process. This 'highly symbolic practice' (Herranz-Surrallés 2011) was encouraged by Karl von Wogau, former Chairman of SEDE. In the case of the Atalanta mission, however, the EP adopted the abovementioned resolution only after crisis response planning was already well under way and the coordination mission, EU NAVCO, had already been launched. In its resolution, it welcomed the planning of a military mission in the Gulf of Aden (European Parliament 2008).

Once Atalanta had been launched, the EP took an increased interest in its course as reflected in hearings, field trips, questions, debates and reports. In November 2009, for example, the European People's Party (EPP) held a hearing with various high-ranking experts, discussing Atalanta in the broader context of the situation in Somalia, and piracy in particular. Furthermore, MEPs have made various on-site visits: to the operational headquarters in Northwood in January 2009 and May 2010; and the Djibouti headquarters in October 2009 and November 2010. MEPs appreciate the direct contact with the military staff and the possibility to talk to the soldiers on site as important instruments for learning more about the situation and the mission's current problems.[18] After a delegation has visited the mission's headquarters, a detailed report is discussed in the subcommittee. In a similar vein, the EP has invited a number of high-ranking officers of the Atalanta mission to report about the ongoing mission and to answer questions on critical issues. The

---

18. Interviews with MEPs and parliamentary assistants to MEPs in May 2011.

Committee on Fisheries also invited members of a number of French and Spanish shipowners' organisations and an Atalanta Navy Commander representing the mission to talk about piracy and the situation of European fishing fleets in the Indian Ocean.

Moreover, the EP kept posing questions to both the Council and the Commission. Most of the questions asked for information about the command and control procedure of the mission, the role of piracy in Somalia in general and the procedure after suspected pirates have been detained by military personnel. Finally, the EP has adopted a variety of reports and texts concerning the role of piracy off the Somali coast and the tasks of a military mission in this respect (for example, see European Parliament 2009c; 2009d). Resolutions and texts adopted have generally welcomed common action by the EU to tackle the problem of piracy, although some MEPs from various parliamentary groups also raised criticisms. The EP frequently criticised the fact that military action did not address the roots of piracy, a problem which would also require a political response to the conflict in Somalia and the humanitarian situation on the mainland.

From the beginning, MEPs have asked that European fishing vessels be protected by Atalanta ships, a task which was not covered by the initial mandate. In addition to the resolution of October 2008, various interpellations have highlighted this point. When the Council extended the mission's mandate in December 2009, Atalanta was also tasked with monitoring fishing activities off the Somali coast (*see* Council Decision 2009/907/CFSP).

Taken together, MEPs did not pay much attention to the initial decision to launch a maritime mission combating piracy off the Somali coast. Instead, the EP, and SEDE in particular, only became involved after key decisions of crisis response planning had already been made. Once the mission was under way, however, the EP assumed an active role in monitoring the EU's military activities off the Somali coast. In particular, it made ample use of its opportunities to exchange views with the responsible militaries and key political decision-makers. Furthermore, various field trips to the Atalanta headquarters were used to get first-hand information about the mission.

The EP also added a transnational dimension to the various cleavages in EU decision-making. Parliamentary debates demonstrated EU-wide transnational cleavages with most political groups supporting EU action but the GUE/NGL parliamentary group being sceptical. The activities of the EP also indicate the importance of the 'attitude' dimension of parliamentary control as opposed to the dimension of 'authority'. Even though it lacks (co-)decision-making powers, and even though the Council has not been proactive in involving the EP in CSDP, the EP's ambition to assume a prominent role in CSDP made it assume an active role in monitoring the mission once it was under way.

Crossing the levels: Interparliamentary cooperation

Between the national and the supranational levels, interparliamentary cooperation has emerged as an additional parliamentary layer in European security affairs. Interparliamentary cooperation in security affairs within the EU framework is obviously a rather young phenomenon and has not yet reached the same degree of complexity as the networks between parliaments' EACs (see Buzogány in this volume). As a matter of fact, the revised version of the protocol on the role of national parliaments that is appended to the Lisbon Treaty explicitly mentions, for the first time, foreign, security and defence policy as a subject of cooperation between parliaments in the European Union interparliamentary system.

Nonetheless, there are linkages between parliaments in the realm of EU security policy.[19] Some of these have emerged with the EU's foreign and security policy, others were created in different contexts, primarily NATO and WEU. They take on similar forms as those between EU scrutiny committees, that is to say, we find formal and informal, bilateral and multilateral linkages between national parliaments and between national parliaments and the EP (see Buzogány in this volume). There are, on the one hand, some fora which have no firm organisational framework and bring together members of national parliaments and the EP. Member state parliaments' committees on foreign and defence affairs, for example, are invited twice a year by the EP's Foreign Affairs Committee to discuss foreign and security affairs. Moreover, there is a Conference of Defence Committee Chairs, in which the EP is also represented. On the other hand, interparliamentary cooperation also takes place in more firmly organised and publicly visible transnational parliamentary assemblies. These can be defined as 'transnational, multilateral actors which are constituted by groups of members of national parliaments' (Marschall 2005 (our translation)). Two such parliamentary assemblies exist(ed) in the realm of European security policy, the WEU Assembly (which was dissolved in May 2011 as a consequence of WEU's dissolution) and NATO's Parliamentary Assembly (NATO-PA) (Hilger 2008; Marschall 2008).

Operation Atalanta was discussed in both assemblies, mainly in the context of general debates about piracy in the Gulf of Aden and in its relation to other military missions off the Somali coast. The WEU Assembly, for example, adopted a report which dealt with 'the role of the European Union in combating piracy' in June 2009. In the debate preceding its adoption, MPs frequently argued that piracy could only be eradicated if EU member states established a broader approach towards Somalia to eliminate the causes of piracy (e.g. illegal fishing by European fishing fleets, the negative economic and humanitarian situation in Somalia, the absence of the rule of law, and so on). The mission was also a topic of discussion at the December 2009 meeting of the Assembly in the context of talks about 'European Maritime Surveillance'. In addition to plenary debates and official reports which were adopted, the WEU Assembly organised a seminar

---

19. For a detailed discussion of these forms of interparliamentary cooperation, see Barbé and Herranz-Surrallés 2008; Hilger 2008.

on 'European Maritime Surveillance' in May 2010 in Athens. Two high ranking military commanders of the mission visited the meeting and reported about the Atalanta mission. Additionally, one representative of the NATO headquarters (SHAPE) represented Operation 'Ocean Shield' during the seminar.

During the annual session of the NATO-PA in 2009, one report, which deals with the question of piracy and discusses the Atalanta mission in this respect, was adopted. The report outlines the coordination between the various NATO contingents on site and the development of the Atalanta mission (NATO-PA 2009). Another report was presented in the NATO-PA Spring Session of 2010, dealing especially with the coordination between the different anti-piracy and anti-terrorism missions off the Somali coast (NATO-PA 2010). Furthermore, in November 2009, the mission was discussed in the meeting of two NATO-PA committees, the Committee on the Civil Dimension of Security, and the Defence and Security Committee. One representative of the mission had been invited, namely, Rear Admiral Peter Hudson, who briefed the two committees about the military efforts of Atalanta and presented the mission's progress in combating piracy.

By and large, the MPs we interviewed considered interparliamentary meetings as quite important forums for connecting with other parliamentarians. When asked about the significance of interparliamentary meetings for their work, they first of all emphasised the opportunities the meetings offer to interact with MPs from other countries. In the second place, the interviewees highlighted the possibility of exchanging information during these meetings. Thirdly, MPs judged interparliamentary meetings as useful for familiarising themselves with the national positions towards certain issues in much more detail, both through discussions in the plenary and through informal contacts. The informal side of the meetings was reported to be of particular value. Thus, joint dinners or receptions in the evenings are opportunities for discussing political topics and communicating ideas. This happens within the established party-groups (e.g. during official dinners), but also across party borders (e.g. during evening events, receptions and breaks).

Most interviewees stated that interparliamentary contacts continue after the Assembly meetings. Thus, it appears quite common for parliamentarians to call or e-mail their colleagues from other European countries in order to gather information on specific topics or to ask for support in preparing the next interparliamentary meeting. For example, Dutch MP Haverkamp used the contacts he had established with parliamentarians in other EU states to inquire into the possibility of stationing armed forces on ships that pass the Somali coast. The Dutch Minister of Defence had argued that this was not a feasible way of enhancing the security of vessels. Haverkamp used his interparliamentary contacts to develop the well-informed counter-argument that stationing armed forces on ships was considered feasible or even practiced in some other countries. This episode illustrates how interparliamentary cooperation can improve MPs' position *vis-à-vis* their government. Without the information obtained via other countries' parliaments, the government would have had a near monopoly of interpretation over the menu of choices available.

To some extent, however, the arrangement of this 'Europe-wide network' depends on the existing transnational party-networks. One interviewee, for example, noted that there is less networking between the parties of the left, compared to those of the centre and the centre-left.

One MP of the German *Bundestag* also reported that MEPs sometimes pass on information about the planning and status of military missions at an early stage. For the EU military training mission of Somali security forces in Uganda (EUTM Somalia), 'colleagues from the EP called and told us that a new military mission was being planned'.[20] This enabled the German MPs to ask questions concerning the envisioned mission via the Defence Committee earlier than would have been the case normally. Another interviewee highlighted the importance of the information exchange between the corresponding parliamentary groups in the EP and the *Bundestag;* this not only helps MPs at both levels to attain additional knowledge about the issues at stake but also contributes to the coordination of positions and activities. German interviewees indicated that they generally consider the NATO-PA more useful than its WEU counterpart. Among the greatest benefits of being a member of the NATO-PA, interviewees report, is being able to go on field visits to conflict zones (an opportunity that has not (yet) been used in the case of anti-piracy missions).

Conclusion

The previous sections have mapped the general competences and, in the case of Atalanta, the specific activities of national parliaments, the EP and various transnational networks and assemblies. In conclusion, four points are worth highlighting: first, none of the parliaments we studied was actively involved in the decision-making process before the main decisions had been made on whether, and in what form, to launch an EU-led maritime mission. Second, the competences and activities of national parliaments vary widely, resulting in a patchwork of parliamentary control at the national level. Whereas some parliaments are very well informed and closely monitor government policy, others are, by and large, left in the dark. Third, the EP has had no influence on the initial decision to launch an EU military mission. However, once Atalanta had begun, the EP scrutinised the mission through questions, debates, hearings and field trips. In doing so, it benefited from its access to top militaries and key decision makers who frequently visited the EP and its committees. Fourth, transnational Parliamentary Assemblies as well as more informal networks provide opportunities to gain information about military missions and about other countries' preferences, concerns, and so on. Party groups are an important medium for establishing such informal contacts across national boundaries. A closer look reveals, however, that these opportunities are used to greatly varying degrees within different party groups, by different national delegations and by individual MPs.

---

20. Interview with a German MP in 2010.

Concerning the relative importance of the authority of parliaments and the attitude of MPs in employing these competences, our study suggests that there is no clear hierarchy. Obviously, formal veto power can be a very strong tool in the hands of parliamentarians and the self-assessments of German MPs show that this tool can be considered a key instrument in constraining the executive's freedom of action. However, absence of veto power cannot be equated with absence of parliamentary influence. The Dutch case demonstrates that strong political traditions and tacit (or formalised) agreements between government and parliament can make up for the lack of legal competences to a certain degree. Certainly, parliamentary influence based solely on established practice remains precarious. Yet it still can provide a powerful constraint on governmental policies. The absence of such agreements between government and parliament, however, makes yielding influence even more difficult, even if parliamentarians are very active in scrutinising policies. MEPs attempt to assert their influence through their political will and activities based on the little competences they have in the security and defence field. Their success is mixed at best, especially when compared with the influence national MPs can gain over their governments.

With a view to the three institutional lay-outs of the parliamentary field and to the particular conceptions of the EU as a polity that come with them, the role of parliaments in CSDP clearly indicates the importance of the member state level in the security and defence domain. Because decision making remains in the hands of member states (intergovernmentalism), the prime locus of parliamentary activity is at the national level; the European level is limited to a 'deliberate audit function'.[21] Overall, this is most compatible with the first and second models outlined above. Depending on the role of parliaments in other policy fields, the EU would thus have to be conceptualised either as a functional regime, in which legitimacy is created generally at the national level; or as a federal state in the making, in which security and defence, in contrast to most economic policy fields, for instance, are in the competence sphere of the member states making up the federation and thus still require democratic legitimisation to be provided primarily through national control procedures.

---

21. In our previous work, we emphasised that the empirical reality of parliaments in CSDP appeared to be out of sync with the developments in the executive realm, especially the high level of military integration in Battlegroups etc. (*see* Peters *et al.* 2008). However, such a misfit is hardly discernible in the case of Atalanta because the degree of military integration of this maritime mission is low when compared to tightly integrated multinational units like the EU Battlegroups. Further, individual member states' decisions about national contributions have little if any effect on the feasibility of the mission as such.

chapter eight | an asymmetric two-level game: parliaments in the Euro crisis

Arthur Benz

Introduction: executive governance in fiscal crisis?

The Lisbon Treaty ended a decade of constitutional policy in the EU. This process, determined to improve democratic legitimacy, resulted in an extended role for the EP in legislation and amendment of treaties. In addition, national parliaments are now explicitly mentioned as part of the EU polity. They gained new powers in subsidiarity control and extended their rights to obtain information. Despite the failure of the constitutional project of the Convention, at the end of the decade the institutional foundation of democratic legitimacy had been advanced significantly.

The Euro crisis has changed the conditions for democracy dramatically. As in every crisis, quick decisions about difficult problems have to be made; governments are confronted with a turbulent environment and uncertainties about further development; the public expects leadership and bold decisions instead of protracted deliberation. Usually, crises are times of the executive and cause a centralisation and concentration of powers in a political system. Where there is no central government, as in the EU, small groups of heads of governments and their experts take the lead. This is indeed what we observe in the Euro crisis. The conclusion could be that parliaments both at the European and at the national level have lost what they achieved during the previous decade.

However, such a conclusion draws from an over-simplified perception of reality. In order to assess the consequences of the crisis for democracy in general and for the power of parliaments in particular, we have to refer to an appropriate normative and empirical conception of the structures and the processes which make parliamentary democracy work in the EU. Moreover, it has to be taken into account that reactions to the crisis affect the EU's legislative powers and the budgets of the member states. In both areas, parliaments have a say according to constitutional rules. In a nation state a government can usually rely on the majority of its parliament to accept decisions of crisis management. In the multilevel system of the EU, many parliaments at different levels must agree, and this makes executive leadership more complicated. Leaders who must coordinate their actions still act in a two-level game of national and European politics (which in federal member states may turn into a three-level game). This setting has changed with the Lisbon Treaty into what Crum and Fossum have termed a 'multilevel parliamentary field' (Crum and Fossum 2009). But as I will explain in the following sections, this field and the strategic interaction of governments and parliaments have been significantly affected by the fiscal crisis. Yet, parliaments have not generally lost power. As my analysis reveals, the handling of the crisis has caused a different and probably more serious problem in European democracy.

In the following sections, I outline the pattern of democracy in the EU as it has evolved during the last decade, with particular emphasis on the multilevel character of parliamentary democracy. After outlining the emerging 'multilevel parliamentary field' in Europe, I suggest an analytical framework to cover different trends and changes in this field. This framework combines the model of a 'two-level game' based on rational choice theory and a normative concept of a parliamentary democracy in a multilevel context. The ensuing third section describes the impacts of the crisis on the role and power of parliaments, with particular emphasis on national parliaments, and the resulting effects on multilevel parliamentary democracy. I conclude with a brief assessment of the consequences of the changes observed.

Multilevel democracy in the European Union

While scholars still disagree on how to conceptualise the political system of the EU, there is hardly any doubt that parliaments have gained ground during the last two decades.[1] During this period, the powers of the EP increased incrementally, but significantly. At the same time, national parliaments became more assertive and improved their capacities to control the national executives in European affairs. Finally, national parliaments were acknowledged as constitutive institutions in EU democracy and achieved the right to control the integration process by the new mechanism of subsidiarity control. In order to appropriately understand the changes in the democratic system of the EU, we have to consider the interplay of parliamentary politics at the national and the European level in what Crum and Fossum have called a dynamic and open 'field' of interaction (Crum and Fossum 2009).

The emerging 'multilevel parliamentary field'

Introduced as a 'heuristic for capturing the distinctive traits of the EU's structure of democratic representation' (Crum and Fossum 2009), the concept of a 'multilevel parliamentary field' can be used to derive analytical tools for comprehending the evolution of democratic governance in the EU. For this purpose, three structural dimensions should be distinguished: the supranational dimension relating to the representation of European citizens includes internal structures of the EP and its relations to the Council, to the Commission and to national parliaments; relations between national parliaments are captured by the horizontal, *inter*governmental dimension; and the *intra*governmental dimension consists of the relations between each national parliament and the national executive. It goes without saying that all three dimensions are closely connected in reality.

---

1. For a summary of research, see Maurer 2002; Raunio 2009.

At the supranational level, the EP has profited from a series of treaty changes since 1988. The European legislature now exists as a 'two-chamber' system not unlike those we find in federal states. It combines a supranational institution, the EP, and an intergovernmental body, the Council. In ordinary legislation where the EP has a co-decision right, both institutions have to cooperate in policy making. With the Commission setting the agenda, it is up to the EP and the Council to come to a joint decision. Provided that the ordinary procedure applies, members of the EP are now included in discussions on treaty changes, although treaty ratification remains the responsibility of the member states.[2]

Resulting from this particular system of government constituting a kind of 'consensus democracy', structures and processes inside the EP clearly differ from what we can observe in national parliaments, regardless of which type of political system we consider. Majorities on policy issues have to be negotiated in structures which are characterised by fluctuating, cross-cutting cleavages. The Lisbon Treaty advanced external linkages to institutions outside the EP. Co-decision with the Council requires coordination between both institutions. The EP is also engaged in cooperation with the Commission. Finally, the new subsidiarity control can boost relations with national parliaments. Given the increasing tasks and the interlinked patterns of internal and external negotiations, parliamentary work has become more and more like committee work and a matter for policy specialists (Costello and Thomson 2011; Jensen and Winzen 2012). In this way, the EP has enhanced its capacities to decide and control the executive. It has turned from an arena of public deliberation into a working parliament where policies are made via a division of labour. Yet, for policy specialists and committees, support from European party-groups and national parties is highly important.

Although representatives in the EP still lack close linkages to citizens, party politics increasingly shapes the action orientations of MEPs and decision making within the Parliament. However, in contrast to what we observe in national parliaments, structures seem to be in flux. Some scholars have revealed an increasing impact of the traditional left-right cleavage (Hix *et al.* 2007), while others have pointed to how the party system has become fragmented and multidimensional (Coman 2009; Maurer *et al.* 2009). Even if MEPs are organised in factions formed by European parties, voting behaviour is not determined solely by affiliation to these groups but is also influenced by national parties or governments. Party discipline is still limited. With the extended use of the co-decision procedure, party membership has an increasing impact on the negotiation process, on the allocation of powerful committee positions (*rapporteurs*), and on voting behaviour. But national orientations continue to play a role even if MEPs increasingly support European against national interests.

---

2. Beyond its legislative powers, the EP achieved supervision rights in Comitology procedures and in the Open Method of Coordination, as well as the right to participate in the selection of members of the Commission and to pass a vote of no confidence against the incumbent Commission. For the following analysis, these powers can be disregarded.

These internal structures reflect the EP's intense external relations to other institutions in the multilevel parliamentary field. They go beyond those established by legislative procedures. Linkages between the EP and national parliaments have emerged since the 1990s (Neunreither 2005). Some parliaments of member states invite MEPs representing their respective country to participate in EACs. Moreover, a kind of parliamentary diplomacy has developed. Through more or less regular visits to Brussels, national delegations of parliaments meet with the Commission or groups of the EP. These patterns of communication add to the existing linkages inside parties. Moreover, the EP has tried to install a regular 'interparliamentary dialogue'. This concept comes close to the model of the 'Assises' which was recently revived by the British Hansard Society (Fox 2012). However, so far it has been practiced on an *ad-hoc* basis only (Maurer 2009a).

The intragovernmental dimension of the multilevel parliamentary field, i.e. the power of national parliaments *vis-à-vis* the executive, was also supported by the Lisbon Treaty. Responding to the actual revival of national parliaments in European politics, the Treaty endorsed their right to control and hold accountable the respective national representatives in the Council. Governments of member states have to comprehensively inform their parliaments on European policies as early as possible. Meanwhile, all national parliaments established special committees for European Affairs, determined as they were to cope with the rising tide of issues and documents. Quite a number of them explicitly confirmed their veto power over their governments in European legislation and put in place specific procedures to control the executive. Others systematically scrutinise European documents and the behaviour of their national representative in the Council (Kiiver 2006; O'Brennan and Raunio 2007). The effective impact of these procedures may vary between member states, but no government can ignore the voice of its national parliament when negotiating at the European level.

Members of national parliaments have realised that they cannot tie the hands of their respective governments in European negotiations but need to intervene in a strategic way based on information regarding the different negotiating positions of other member state governments (Benz 2004). To gain the relevant information, national parliaments extended their engagement in interparliamentary relations (Bengtson 2007; Fasone 2011). They established contacts with other parliaments, mostly with those from neighbouring member states. They set up bureaus in Brussels in order to have access to European actors. Moreover, they met, on a more or less regular basis, with members of the EP. At the same time, COSAC has become an important institution. Established as a forum for information sharing, COSAC evolved into a kind of service institution for national parliaments, but increasingly organises exchanges of opinions. Following a recommendation of regular meetings of speakers of EU parliaments in 2000, the EU established IPEX. All these interparliamentary relations contribute to integrating the different national parliamentary systems into a multilevel parliamentary field.

The Treaty on the European Union explicitly mentioned this horizontal parliamentary dimension of multilevel governance (Art. 12, Section F TEU). It supported its evolution by introducing the subsidiarity control mechanism. The

Commission has to forward all initiatives for legislation directly to national parliaments. They can check whether an initiative conforms to the principle of subsidiarity and issue their opinion to the Commission. In order to make its opinion effective, a national parliament has to obtain support from other parliaments. The Treaty also states that national parliaments, together with the EP, control and evaluate measures of the EU taken in the areas of security and law, i.e. in policies affecting the core powers of nation states and the identity of national societies. In addition, national parliaments have a say when it comes to the application of flexibility clauses concerning majority rules or legislative procedures. Finally, representatives of national parliaments will participate in those Conventions that are called for preparing treaty amendments according to the ordinary procedure. Still, the rule holds that treaty amendments have to be ratified by all member states according to their constitutional provisions, which gives each national parliament a veto right.

So far, national parliaments have only started to apply their new rights against the European institutions. Since the Convention on the Future of Europe, they have had no opportunity to participate in Treaty amendments. However, they have used the subsidiarity control mechanism, although not yet in a coordinated way. In a number of cases, national parliaments or chambers of national legislatures have issued a 'reasoned opinion' on subsidiarity. As of August 2012, only one of the addressed drafts has been rejected by a sufficient number of parliaments/chambers to challenge the legislative act.[3] The informal dialogue initiated by the Commission in 2006 allows national parliaments to submit statements on policies but the intensity of communication is limited. Although national parliaments cooperate in a variety of ways, their relations are still fragmented and unstable.

Nonetheless, from a normative point of view, the supranational and intergovernmental dimensions of the multilevel parliamentary field are essential to generating democratic legitimacy. 'Hard powers' to control the executive and to veto a negotiation position of the national representative in the Council of Ministers or the ratification of Treaty amendments have to be supported by those 'soft powers' of national parliaments constituted by the Lisbon Treaty. By vetoing European legislative acts, national parliaments risk blocking European legislation or preventing the national executive from influencing Council decisions (Benz 2004). To avoid this risk, they usually support their government in European affairs but if they simply leave it to the government to define the

---

3.   This 'yellow card' was shown in case of a proposal to regulate strikes (EUobserver, 29 May 2012. Online. Available http://euobserver.com/social/116405 (30 September 2012) According to COSAC's sixteenth bi-annual report, twenty-nine out of forty national parliaments/chambers have adopted at least one reasoned opinion since the entry into force of the Treaty of Lisbon. 'The largest number of reasoned opinions, i.e. eight, has been adopted by the Polish *Senat*. The Polish *Sejm* has adopted seven reasoned opinions, the Swedish *Riksdag* and the Luxembourg *Chambre des Députés* - five, the Italian *Senato della Repubblica* - four, the Danish *Folketing*, the French *Sénat*, the Lithuanian *Seimas*, the Dutch *Tweede Kamer*, the Dutch *Eerste Kamer* and the Romanian *Senatul* - three each. The remaining eighteen national parliaments/chambers have adopted one or two reasoned opinions' (COSAC 2011b).

national position, European policy-making and legislation would continue to be dominated by executives. Therefore, the new soft powers founded in multilevel and interparliamentary relations are important in order to effectively apply intragovernmental powers. Moreover, the new rights to influence the deliberations of European institutions are applied 'in the shadow' of powers which national parliaments can directly exert against their governments or use by taking legal action in the ECJ. From this point of view, 'horizontal' interparliamentary relations induced by the participation of members of parliaments in treaty negotiations, and by the subsidiarity control procedure, are of particular significance. Not only can they lead to a more balanced allocation of powers between levels of the European polity, they also make representative democracy in a multilevel setting possible (Crum and Fossum 2009).

In the multilevel democracy of the EU, national parliaments act as representatives of national communities of citizens, but by themselves they are also represented in the Council by their government. Certainly, each government that is participating in European decision-making is accountable to its parliament, and this should be anticipated by its partners in negotiations. On the other hand, when scrutinising their government, national parliaments conform to the normative requirements of democratic representation only if they consider national interests in the light of interests of other member states and with a concern for a common European public interest. That these 'double-barrelled conditions' (Savage and Weale 2009) are fulfilled can only be supposed if not only governments, but also parliaments, develop horizontal structures that constitute an essential element in every form of democratic representation. And for this very reason, interparliamentary relations are an important element of European representative democracy coming to fruition in 'Multilevel Parliamentarism'.

Multilevel parliamentarism and the two-level game of European politics

The normative concept of Multilevel Parliamentarism (Benz 2011) draws upon suggestions that the democratic legitimacy of European governance can be advanced if parliaments fulfil shared functions (Eppler 2012; Maurer 2002; Maurer 2009a). It provides a standard that the reality of governance in the EU more or less deviates from. This reality is driven by the strategic 'two-level game' of actors trying to coordinate national and European policy-making (Evans *et al.* 1993; Putnam 1988). Strategic interactions of executives and parliaments in particular policies have repercussions for how the multilevel parliamentary field, as a 'field of power' (Crum and Fossum 2009), evolves. In order to capture this power dynamic, it seems appropriate to distinguish between parliaments with strong versus those with weak power regarding their positions in the different relations, the stability of these relations, and parliaments' impact on governance. We can theoretically categorise them into a set of constellations to guide the research and evaluation of changes and developments associated with the Euro crisis. Given my interest in those constellations that are likely to occur in practice, I focus on the following combinations of strong and weak powers of parliaments, steeped within different relations in the European two-level game. These configurations yield different degrees of field-ness coupled with parliamentary control/influence.

1. As a standard of representative democracy in the EU, '*Multilevel Parliamentarism*' assumes intense interaction among parliaments across levels of government, but also a rather balanced structure in horizontal relations. In addition, parliaments are assumed to influence legislation on the different levels, to hold executives accountable and to define their policy positions in meaningful parliamentary discourses open to the public (Benz 2011). Communication between parliaments may be organised in regular meetings or by special organisations (like COSAC). They may also be supported due to an integration of national and European party organisations. Finally, the interpenetration of national and European discourses (Schmidt 2006) supports the evolution of multilevel parliamentary relations.

2. In cases where interparliamentary relations are weak both between levels and in the horizontal dimension, but where the EP and national parliaments have strong powers against the executive in the governmental systems at each level, the structure of multilevel democracy comes close to what we find in democratic federations. Accordingly, Sergio Fabbrini (Fabbrini 2008) has compared the EU to the US model of a '*Compound Democracy*'. It divides powers both between levels and between executive and legislative institutions, at least at the centre, but with an EP endowed with powers to participate in legislation. Division of power does not rule out interparliamentary relations, but they are considered as weak and not supported by an integrated party system.

3. A similar constellation, but with a weak EP, can be labelled as *joint decision making*, according to the model elaborated by Fritz W. Scharpf (Scharpf 1988). He used this term to characterise the European Community as it existed in the 1970s and 1980s. In this case, governments represented in the Council are bound to the will of national parliaments determining policy positions on European affairs. The EP had only limited co-decision rights in those days. Interparliamentary relations did not exist, and party associations at the European level had not linked parliamentary work in an effective way. This model is still relevant for particular policy areas of the EU and cannot be ruled out as a relevant tool to comprehend real two-level politics.

4. Strong interparliamentary relations may contribute to increasing the divide between national parliaments and their executive, a situation which has been described as '*Presidentialisation*' in parliamentary democracies (Poguntke and Webb 2005). Compared to the Compound Democracy Model, this constellation arises due to a divergence between formal rules and effective power. In the US, government powers are separated between legislatives and executives but they are also balanced, with the legislature being in a strong position. In the case of Presidentialisation, parliaments cooperate across levels and borders of states, but they lack the power to

Table 8.1: Possible constellations of the Multilevel Parliamentary Field

	Power of the EP to influence decisions	Power of national parliament to control the executive	Intensity of interparliamentary relations
Multilevel Parliamentarism	strong	strong	strong; multilateral
Compound Democracy	strong	strong	weak (bi- or multilateral)
Joint Decision-Making	weak	strong	weak (bi- or multilateral)
Presidentialisation	strong or weak	weak	strong (bi- or multilateral)
Executive Politics	weak	weak	weak (bi- or multilateral)

hold the executive effectively accountable due to a parallel evolution of parliamentary and executive intergovernmental relations.

5. Finally, where parliaments are weak in all dimensions, we have the constellation of '*Executive Politics*', often assumed as typical for cooperative federalism. In the EU, common foreign policy comes closest to this pattern of the two-level game, where the EP has no right to participate in decisions; national parliaments play mainly a symbolic role; and interparliamentary relations are hardly relevant.

It goes without saying that these constellations are theoretical constructions. As indicated, in the differentiated polity of the EU all patterns can be expected to co-exist. Variations can be observed between policy areas, either due to different rules or to a different salience of issues for elections. They can also occur due to the dynamics of European integration and multilevel governance over time. Of particular relevance for the quality of democracy is a third aspect: with the exception of multilevel parliamentarism, interparliamentary relations can be more or less exclusive, i.e. include all member states, a group of member states, or only two of them in bilateral contacts, with the degree of inclusion varying from time to time and from policy to policy.

The multilevel parliamentary field in the Euro Crisis

The label 'Euro crisis' refers to an extreme fiscal imbalance in the Euro-area that finds expression in excessive debts in some member states and soaring interest rates burdening the governments of these states. Whether this crisis is caused by market failure or state failure need not be discussed here. There is no doubt that the imbalance not only threatens the single currency in the Euro-area but also economic and social stability in the EU. Moreover, regardless of which solutions are considered appropriate, the crisis and crisis management have significant redistributive consequences and the potential to change the power structure in the

EU multilevel system. Therefore, decisions in multilevel governance are difficult to make and any policy selected is highly significant for democratic legitimacy. Therefore, the Euro crisis implies a serious challenge for democracy in the EU and its member states.

Decisions taken to fight the Euro crisis are certainly decisive for parliamentary processes, party competition, and elections in member states. They first and foremost relate to monetary and fiscal policies. In this case we have to take into account that important instruments are controlled by the European Central Bank (ECB), an independent institution not accountable to parliaments. However, significant decisions relate to fiscal policies of the EU and the member states. In this area, parliaments are strongly involved due to their right to decide on the budget and on taxes. Proposals to supervise fiscal and economic policies of member states or to establish a European economic government concern the powers of the EP. Institutional rules require participation of parliaments at the European and the national level in one way or another. Moreover, in order to strategically decide on measures negotiated by governments and on proposals to extend the powers of the EU, we need to take interparliamenary relations into account as well, because they will also be affected. Therefore, there are good reasons to assume that the normative concept of multilevel parliamentarism figures in some of the economic and fiscal policies that are debated to address the Euro crisis. Nonetheless, and not surprisingly, the two-level game played in practical policy-making deviates from the normative standard implied by this model. However, as a closer look reveals, real patterns do not turn out as purely executive politics.

Governing the Euro crisis

The management of the crisis triggered activities at all levels of government and in all institutions. Until about June 2012, the predominant perception focused on high public debts and the rising interest rates burdening southern European countries. Apart from the activities of the ECB, core measures included guarantees of national credits by EU member states and the IMF, amended rules of the Stability Pact and new procedures for monitoring national budgeting and fiscal planning. Only extensive research could uncover the real complexity of policy-making. Yet, a preliminary account is possible. The following analysis is based on documents and media reports and only considers selected member states. Nonetheless, with some plausibility the changes in the patterns of parliamentary involvement in multilevel governance can be outlined. They point out serious risks for the European model of representative democracy caused by changes in multilevel governance during the crisis.

The short term responses to the Euro crisis aimed at avoiding the bankruptcy of individual member states after Greece, Ireland and Portugal had come under severe pressure from the financial markets. They included the market operations of the ECB, credit guarantees by the European Financial Stability Facility (EFSF), which is to be replaced by the European Stability Mechanism (ESM), and an 'Economic Adjustment Programme for Greece' of the European Commission, which certainly affected policy changes in other countries. These measures were negotiated between heads of governments and ministers of member states under the leadership of France and Germany, the Commission and the ECB. Thus, immediate crisis management was mainly a matter of executive governance. Besides conflicts about measures that should be taken, the process also revealed a power game between the ECB, the European Commission, and member state governments. The Bank, after serious internal disputes, adopted a policy which has been criticised as driven by politics rather than by independent economic expertise. The Commission fought for extended powers in a European economic government, but to no avail. In the end, an intergovernmentalist governance approach prevailed. This had consequences for the involvement of parliaments.

Beyond this continuing crisis management, governance in economic and fiscal policy was revised. In June 2010, the Commission initiated a 'European Semester', a new procedure to coordinate economic and budgetary policies between the EU and member states of the Euro-area. Based on an annual growth survey, the Commission proposes and the Council decides on recommendations for the budgetry policy of member states. To reinforce coordination, a reform of the Stability and Growth Pact was launched by the Commission and the European Council in order to avoid future crises. The policy package included a Directive and five regulations (the so-called 'six-pack'). Approved by the heads of all twenty-seven member state governments and the EP in October 2011, these legal acts entered into force in December of that year. The new rules allowed for easier sanctions against member states with excessive deficits. They formulated more precise criteria defining debt limits. A new monitoring mechanism was introduced and enforceability of the Pact was improved in order to avoid the lenient implementation of the past. The Directive and regulations resulted from legislative processes at the European level, with the EP applying the 'fast track' procedure (the informal 'trialogue') after interventions from France had delayed the process. This way of policy-making resembled a centralist version of the Compound Democracy model. It provided an opportunity for the EP to demonstrate its significance and to gain influence in close cooperation with the Commission, while the relations between the Parliament and the Council revealed a competitive mode.

As a next step of reform, the European Council initiated a 'Treaty on Stability, Coordination and Governance' (Fiscal Stability Treaty). Since the Governments of the UK and the Czech Republic abstained from signing an amendment to the existing Treaties, the Council decided to proceed with an intergovernmental treaty. If ratified, the treaty will commit the participating member states to balance their budgets. These rules

> shall take effect in the national law of the Contracting Parties at the latest one year after the entry into force of this Treaty through provisions of binding force and permanent character, preferably constitutional, or otherwise guaranteed to be fully respected and adhered to throughout the national budgetary processes.
>
> (FST 2012)[4]

---

4.   Article 3, Section 2.

As a consequence, national parliaments not only have to ratify this Treaty, they will also be committed to amend national (constitutional) law. Moreover, they are responsible for implementing the new rules when deciding on fiscal planning and budgets. The Treaty will empower the Commission and the ECJ to monitor national fiscal policies and to impose sanctions on member states exceeding the debt limits. Governments of the member states will meet in summits at least twice a year to discuss issues regarding the Euro-area. The president of the EP 'may be invited to be heard' (FST 2012),[5] but the Parliament as an institution is excluded from decision-making.

With the negotiation, ratification and implementation of this Treaty, governance in the Euro-area changed to joint decision-making mode. In negotiations on the Treaty, heads of governments agreed on the lowest common denominator, well aware of the veto power of their parliaments. They excluded any decision on a fiscal trade tax and they also avoided a formal transfer of power in economic policy to the EU. If parliaments ratify the Treaty, they also tie their own hands in future fiscal policy and reinforce the intergovernmental policy-making of their executive. However, they are not excluded from decisions in general. Some national parliaments, the German *Bundestag* in particular, emerged as decisive players in joint decision-making. In contrast, the voice of the EP has weakened, although it is still engaged in the policy area, e.g. in reforming the regulation of financial markets (Dorn 2012).

Divided democracy

Regarding the role of national parliaments, the selection of the intergovernmental mode of governance to regulate national debt is remarkable in both substantive and procedural terms. First, the policies to be implemented in member states emulate rules that had been written into constitutional law in Germany two years before. The German Government strongly pushed for extending these requirements to other member states. Second, combining short term crisis management with a reform of the treaties opened opportunities for national parliaments to discuss and decide on issues. However, the effective power of parliaments in individual member states varies. Notably, those in states under pressure from the financial markets (such as Greece, Italy and Spain) followed suit, with Spain taking the lead in amending its constitution and the Greek Parliament being the first to ratify the Fiscal Stability Treaty. On the other hand, ratification was intensely debated in Germany and is still pending due to proceedings in the Federal Constitutional Court instituted by MPs and citizens. This indicates that the gap between strong and weak parliaments demonstrated in earlier research (Raunio 2005) has widened during the Euro crisis. The German Parliament in particular exploited its power with considerable consequences for the policy-making process at the European level.

---

5.   Article 12, section 5.

During the 1990s, scholars regarded the German Parliament, the *Bundestag*, as a laggard in European affairs (Maurer and Wessels 2001). In fact it was not before a constitutional reform in 1994 that the rights of the *Bundestag* were anchored in the Basic Law. Even after this amendment came into force, the upper house of the legislature representing German *Länder*, the *Bundesrat*, more actively controlled European policies than the Federal Parliament. Since the Lisbon Treaty was passed, this has definitely changed. The Parliament now not only profits from information rights established by the Treaty (like all national parliaments), it has also become more assertive than before in European affairs at the national level. Yet it was not the Parliament itself but the Federal Constitutional Court which was the driving force behind these changes. The Court had to decide on the Lisbon Treaty and later on the participation of the *Bundestag* in emergency measures during the Euro crisis. In all its decisions the Court expressed its sceptical stance on the question of multilevel democracy and supported representative democracy at the national level. Accordingly, it required an extensive participation of the *Bundestag*, in particular when the core powers of the state to decide on its own finances are at stake. This process of strengthening the Parliament by the Court will probably continue. As mentioned, prominent citizens, including a former minister of justice, and MPs from majority and opposition parties filed a constitutional complaint against the ESM. They argued in particular that the limited powers of the Parliament in European economic governance infringe on the principle of democracy entrenched in the German constitution. In view of public debates triggered by these initiatives and earlier court proceedings, the Parliament is now compelled to demonstrate its powers in European policies.

As a consequence, the German representative in the Council has to see to it that it finds the support of a majority in the *Bundestag* before it agrees on fiscal policies and reforms in the Euro-area. While Chancellor Angela Merkel was ascribed a leading role in negotiations, she was constrained by the majority coalition in parliament. The coalition included the Liberal Party and the Bavarian CSU, the sister party of the federal Christian Democrats. Both parties strongly opposed bailout measures and pressed for austerity programmes in states with high public debts. Certainly, Angela Merkel agreed to these policy proposals anyway. Yet regardless of her intentions, her coalition in parliament left her little room for manoeuvre. Moreover, the conservative CSU opposed any extension of EU powers affecting the budgetary autonomy of the nation state. In view of their own budgetary constraints by the new debt rule, a majority of *Länder* governments supported this position and defined budget consolidation as a 'central political priority' (COSAC 2011a). For this reason, the German Government negotiated at the European level with tied hands. The Social Democrats and the Green Party supported the Chancellor, but they always requested participation of the Parliament. German debate about the opaque style of European crisis management and the presumed executive dominance (Wendler 2012) should be interpreted as strategic communication in the two-level game determined to strengthen the *Bundestag*. Under the pressure of the crisis which required decisions, the presumed weakness at the national level against a powerful parliament and an equally powerful second chamber turned into strength at the European level. Consequently, the reform of the Fiscal Stability Pact conformed to the model of fiscal federalism laid down in the 2009 amendment of the German constitution. This was not only due to the leadership of the German Chancellor and her close cooperation with the French President, but due to the particular role played by the national parliament in Germany, a parliament which owes its power not least to an active Federal Constitutional Court.

The French president, Nicolas Sarkozy, the second major player in negotiations on measures against the crisis, was no less compelled to include the French Parliament. As Amandine Crespy and Vivien Schmidt demonstrate, he was more successful in gaining support from the majority in parliament by intensely communicating his position to the public, whereas Merkel prevailed in European negotiations (Crespy and Schmidt 2012). Evidently, the different strategies in the two-level game translated into the package deal between both leaders. In a similar vein, the Finnish and Austrian national parliaments tried to tie the hands of their respective governments and carefully scrutinise the evolution of crisis management and the consequences for their countries. Therefore, the power of national parliaments needs to be included in the explanation of the outcome of policy-making in the Euro crisis.

However, the power of national parliaments has divided member states. In Greece, Italy, Spain and Portugal, there are indications that joint decision-making has turned into executive politics, although parliaments like the German *Bundestag* and the French *Assemblée Nationale* hold veto powers in ratifying the new treaty and in implementing the crisis related policies. Under the pressure of financial markets and in view of the rigid negotiation positions of the German and French Governments, these countries had to accept strict measures to consolidate their budgets. The reactions of voters had problematic consequences for parliamentary democracy. In Italy, the Parliament elected a new coalition government lead by Mario Monti, an experienced expert in economic policy and European politics. In Spain, elections led to a change in government, reducing the legitimacy of the new majority rather than punishing the former socialist government. In Greece, the fragmentation of the party system further undermined parliamentary influence. Given the constraints in fiscal policy-making, parliaments in these countries had to comply with austerity programmes and with new rules set up at the European level or induced by European policies. Therefore, the crisis further weakened national parliaments in some of those member states which, according to research findings, had been assessed as comparatively weak in any case (Raunio 2005). As a consequence, the imbalance in the multilevel parliamentary system of the EU resulting, among other things, from the varieties of national democracies, has increased significantly due to governments' strategies in crisis management.

Certainly, the two-level game in the Euro crisis dominated by German and French politics constituted only part of a multifaceted process. Worth mentioning are attempts to reinforce the interparliamentary dialogue, i.e. to further develop the horizontal dimension of the multilevel parliamentary field. For example, COSAC made efforts to distribute information on the procedures of national parliaments.

In addition, the IPEX calendar lists regular conferences of national parliament committee chairpersons, including the finance committees in September 2010 and the economic affairs committees in July 2011, as well as an interparliamentary conference organised by the EP on monitoring of national fiscal policy (the so-called 'European Semester') in February 2012.

However, interparliamentary relations in the Euro crisis seem to reflect the economic divide among member states and the political divide among their governments. As indicated by the responses of national parliaments to the COSAC questionnaire, parliaments issue different opinions on the future of economic and fiscal policies and on European economic governance. Even more striking are changes in patterns of interparliamentary relations. Beyond the multilateral meetings, bilateral communication seems to have gained ground. In October 2011, the German *Bundestag* and the French *Assemblée Nationale* established a working group to discuss the treaty changes proposed by the heads of government. In February 2012, the group met for the fourth time and further meetings were not ruled out.[6] Thus, the close cooperation between the governments of these two countries gave rise to a corresponding intensification of bilateral interparliamentary relations. This practice clearly deviated from the ideal of multilevel parliamentarism since it reflected exclusive communication and an imbalance of power. Notably, it was due to the intervention of this working group that a proposal for continuous multilateral meetings of budget committees of national parliaments was not written down in the Fiscal Stability Treaty.

The EP does not seem able to countervail this trend of an imbalanced reinforcement or weakening of national parliaments. In view of the volatile nature of its internal structures described above, external shocks like the Euro crisis are likely to have more significant impacts on the functioning of the EP than can be observed in well-established national parliamentary systems. However, the consequences are not yet clear and need to be investigated. The leader of the EP tried to exploit the crisis to make the voice of the EP heard. Since the Euro crisis relates not only to economics but also affects the legitimacy of the European project, it may be up to the EP to restore confidence among citizens. On the other hand, MEPs and party groups are challenged by the rising Euro-scepticism in member states. And in view of the redistributive conflicts, negotiating majorities in the EP becomes difficult. At any rate, the Parliament has lost influence due to the intergovernmentalist approach of crisis management.

---

6. *Das Parlament*, No. 4, 23 January 2012, p. 11; *Deutscher Bundestag*, 'Abgeordnete wollen Fiskalpakt zügig ratifizieren'. Online. Available at: http://www.bundestag.de/dokumente/textarchiv/2012/37783646_kw07_deutsch_franz_gruppe/index.jsp (accessed 10 April 2012).

Consequences: A new democratic deficit

As expressed in the concept of a multilevel parliamentary field, representative democracy in the EU materialises in multidimensional and dynamic relations between citizens, parliaments and executives. Beyond the dual representation of European citizens in the EP and national citizenries in the Council institutionalised by the Treaty of the European Union, interparliamentary relations have evolved linking the two levels of representation. From a normative perspective, communication among parliaments helps to integrate *multiple demoi* (Sørensen 2011). It is essential to prevent a polity being divided between national and European public interests, a politics riven by a confrontation of national interests, and policy-making that is dominated by colluding executives which cannot be held accountable in a meaningful way. Discursive processes in an interparliamentary arena constitute a forum of the European public in a multinational federation from which the EP can draw opinions; they also enable national parliaments to hold accountable their executive and their delegates in the Council on the basis of reflected positions. To conform to principles of democratic legitimacy, interparliamentary communication must be 'shaped by a sense of fairness' (Savage and Weale 2009); it must provide equal opportunities for all national parliaments to make their voices heard. It goes without saying that even before the crisis there was a significant gap between what would be required by democratic theory and by real politics. Nonetheless, the emerging multilevel parliamentary field in Europe, and the provisions of the Lisbon Treaty, evolved in the direction of the normative concept of multilevel parliamentarism.

During the course of the Euro crisis, the multilevel parliamentary field not only fell back into a pattern of joint decision-making, this pattern also showed signs of a divide in relations between national parliaments and, thus, an imbalance of power. The intergovernmentalist mode of crisis management weakened the EP, while national parliaments turned into independent external veto-players (Benz 2004). However, while parliaments in member states like France and, in particular, Germany profited from the strategies of their executive in the two-level game, with the German *Bundestag* getting additional support from the Constitutional Court, those in Southern European member states surrendered to strong executives and external pressure.

Accordingly, redistributive conflicts were not discussed in a fair public discourse, but were dealt with in power politics. In public debates, solidarity among European nations was an issue – in reality, governments, supported by their national parliaments, framed policies as a question of winning and losing. In Germany, for instance, talks about solidarity often implied that some member states should pay for others that were blamed for inefficient governance, if not fraud, when getting access to the Euro-area; economic imbalances, the redistributive effects of monetary union and market failure (i.e. problems that had to be tackled by cooperative action) hardly mattered. In addition, redistributive conflicts in fiscal policy were reinforced due to conflicts about power when reforms of the Stability and Growth Pact put constitutional policy on the agenda. This strengthened the role of national parliaments, in particular where, as in Germany, the constitutional court was involved, and weakened the EP because governments circumvented the ordinary procedure of treaty amendment.

As a consequence, the crisis is no longer confined to the realm of economics and fiscal policy-making; it has turned into a political crisis of the EU. However, in contrast to scenarios drawn in public debates, this crisis does not find expression in disintegrative tendencies. Still, member states are mutually dependent in economic terms and compelled to negotiate joint solutions. There are no indications so far that the Union will fall apart, although anti-European parties have succeeded in elections. Even a failure of the Euro need not cause the end of the European project. What is at stake, however, is the quality of the European type of representative democracy that has evolved over the last two decades. While the fundament of a multilevel pattern of democracy erodes due to the divide and imbalance of power in the relations among national parliaments, populist forces appealing to the will of the people, supporting direct democracy and igniting protests against European politics are on the rise. Indeed, leading German politicians especially have been forthright in joining those populist voices demanding a referendum on the new fiscal stability regime. Against these opinions it needs to be emphasised that national parliaments in general have not lost out as a result of the crisis. Rather, it is the asymmetry of parliamentary involvement in the member states and the degradation of multilateral relations among parliaments that has caused a new democratic deficit. However, this does not prove that representative democracy has failed in the EU. As careful analysis shows, the new democratic deficit has been caused by the power games and political tactics of the actors in multilevel governance.

part iii. actor perspectives

chapter nine | EU parliaments after the Treaty of Lisbon: towards a parliamentary field?

Johannes Pollak and Peter Slominski

Introduction

The Lisbon Treaty marks a watershed in the parliamentary development of the EU. Although we have become quite used to the extension of parliamentary rights with every new treaty, Lisbon brings a new quality to the EU by further enhancing the role of national parliaments, substantially extending the rights of the EP and potentially opening the door for collaboration between the two legislative bodies. A total of forty chambers with around 9,500 Members of Parliament is a force to reckon with. So, it seems that the chance for supranational democratic politics has never been better. As with every reform of the EU's primary law, however, black letter law needs to be filled with political life. While the EP has in the past been very skilled in using the smallest nook or cranny in the treaties to apply its leverage and thereby wrest rights from the European executives, national parliaments have had considerable difficulties in keeping pace with EU politics. The hearings of European Commission candidates, the trilogue meetings, and various interinstitutional agreements have served to establish an EP whose powers go beyond mere treaty law. National parliaments, on the other hand, be it individually, in the form of European assizes, or in COSAC, have so far seemed incapable of either controlling their executives or substantially influencing the European policy-making process.

This chapter will address the following questions: What is the exact scope and breadth of the EP's new rights? Does the new treaty give national parliaments the opportunity to influence European policy-making? Can national parliaments deal with their new tasks? How have they done so far? And finally, can there be a meaningful cooperation between the EP and national parliaments?

The next section will briefly review the main themes of parliamentary involvement in the EU which serve as a background for depicting, in the subsequent section, the changes the Treaty of Lisbon brings for the EP, and in the section thereafter, for the national parliaments. We will also report on the case of the Austrian Parliament, usually described as a member state parliament with extraordinarily strong formal rights concerning European politics. How did it use those rights in the past and how have those rights been adapted since the Treaty's inception? The Austrian Parliament serves as an example for testing how national parliaments, based on their past performance, may actually use their new rights. It stands to reason that if a strong parliament quickly adapts to the new rules and uses them efficiently, we will see a substantial transformation of the European parliamentary landscape amounting to a definite democratisation of the Union. If, however, even a strong parliament cannot use its participation and control rights sufficiently to leave its imprint on European policy-making, we may see a further advance of executive decision-making. The final section sums up our argument and provides suggestions for further, urgently needed, research.

Parliamentary involvement in EU affairs

A glance into the literature shows that the assessment of parliamentary involvement in EU affairs oscillates between despair and glimmers of hope. While for some the European integration process is a kind of crop duster, slowly but efficiently eroding national democracy and leading to a democratic deficit or even a double democratic deficit, others have drawn attention to the fact that most parliaments have managed to acquire new rights with regard to European policy-making. Systematising the literature, we can differentiate between three phases in the assessment of parliamentary politics in the EU.

(1) At least since the Single European Act (1987), the implementation of which brought renewed vigour into the project of finalising the internal market, the question of the EU's democratic credentials has been tabled. This vigour was translated into intensified regulatory activity and triggered a discussion about a potential democratic deficit of the Union, a deficit expressed in the lamentable loss of control and legislative authority of national parliaments (e.g. Birkinshaw and Ashiagbor 1996; Newman 1996; Norton 1995; Weiler *at al.* 1995; Wincott 1998). The main conclusion of those early discussions was that, compared to the Council of the European Union, the EP's legislative position was embarrassingly weak. The ever rising transfer of competences from the national to the European level led to a 'double democratic deficit' (Lodge 1996) and to a creeping deparliamentarisation: national parliaments lose legislative authority which is not taken over by the EP. Rather, these competences are absorbed by the European Commission and the Council, thus being removed from any parliamentary control. As long as there is no substantial strengthening of the EP's rights or an effective control over the Council of Ministers by national parliaments, the democratic quality of the EU will be suboptimal at best and the 'systematic erosion' (Andersen and Burns 1996) of parliamentary rights will continue.

(2) It is somewhat ironic that, parallel to this criticism, the EP has enjoyed an ever-increasing strengthening of its power through all treaty amendments since the Single European Act. The same partially holds true for national parliaments. Since the late 1990s scholars critical of the deparliamentarisation thesis heralded the second phase which focused on the process of 'reparliamentarisation' in the sense of the extensive new rights of national parliaments in the determination of national European

politics (e.g. Raunio and Hix 2000; Auel and Benz 2005; Benz 2004; Maurer and Wessels 2001; Maurer 2002; Saalfeld 2005; Raunio 2005; O'Brennan and Raunio 2007).

(3) More recently, a discussion about a new form of parliamentarism in the EU envisions a novel form of horizontal or multilevel parliamentarism (Maurer 2001a) or the development of a multilevel parliamentary field (Crum and Fossum 2009). While horizontal parliamentarism describes the (as yet infrequent) working together of member states' parliaments on issues of common interest, whether in COSAC or in a less institutionalised environment, the notion of a parliamentary field might represent a democratic innovation. Like a giant ant colony, a plethora of links between supranational, national and subnational assemblies have not only brought about a more efficient system of checks on the Council and tacit but consistent pressure for more parliamentary rights in primary law and national regulations but this system also heralds an entirely new form of democracy stretching beyond the confines of territorial representation. Scholars are still struggling to pin down the exact dimensions, characteristics and effects of this development but the rising cooperation between national parliaments (for figures, *see* Maurer 2001) is undisputed.

What changes for the European Parliament?

With a few exceptions the Lisbon Treaty follows the Constitutional Treaty when it comes to the stipulations concerning the EP: co-decision is extended to around forty new issue areas and becomes (more or less) the rule as – in the words of the Treaty – the 'ordinary legislative procedure' (Arts. 289 and 294 TFEU; Best 2008). According to estimates, this procedure applies to around 95 per cent of all legislative acts in the EU (Leinen 2010). In addition to the former third pillar, the ordinary legislative procedure has been extended to structural funds, transport, external trade, agriculture and fisheries. Despite this formal strengthening of EP powers it must not be overlooked that the Treaty also introduced so-called 'emergency brakes' providing member states with the possibility to suspend co-decision in areas they regard as too politically sensitive and to refer the issue in question to the European Council (Joint Study 2007; Maurer 2008b).[1] In EU budgetary politics the Treaty of Lisbon has abandoned the differentiation between compulsory and non-compulsory expenditures, which means that the entire range of the annual EU budget is now under the control of the EP (Art. 14 TEU).[2] However, despite its significance we should bear in mind that the annual EU budget has to comply with

---

1. Issue areas where the ordinary legislative procedure can be suspended are for example decisions on criminal procedure, the establishment of a European Public Prosecutor's Office or operational cooperation between national police.

2. This is especially relevant for expenditures related to agriculture which now fall under the competences of the EP.

the broader multiannual financial framework adopted by the Council (Art. 312 TFEU) – a practice which has informally been established since the late 1980s by interinstitutional agreements (Eiselt *et al.*2007). Without doubt the abolishment of the differentiation between compulsory and non-compulsory expenditures is one of the most important changes in the institutional structure of the Union. The EP, since it is now truly on a par with the Council, will use – and has already done so in the process of establishing a Common Foreign Action Service – its new budgetary rights to influence all areas of European policy-making.

Apart from this indirect way to influence the Common Foreign and Security Policy via budgetary matters, the EP's formal powers in this field remain modest. It is the investiture of the Vice President of the Commission (who at the same time wears the hat of High Representative of the Union for Foreign Affairs and Security Policy) and the extended budgetary rights (Maurer *et al.* 2005) that give the EP some considerable leeway. By using its budgetary powers as leverage, the EP has traditionally tried to gain influence in policy fields where it has had little or no formal say (Kietz and Maurer 2007). While an interinstitutional agreement adopted in 1999 has established some budgetary rights within, and influence over, the EP in foreign affairs, funding external actions has proven a controversial issue between the Parliament and the Council. However, there are several legal loopholes for the Council to minimise the EP's influence in foreign affairs. In particular, it should be noted that the EP has no right to influence expenditures which arise from military operations and that are not covered by the Community budget (Peters *et al.* 2008).

In sum, the legislative rights of the EP have increased since the Single European Act and this trend continued with the enactment of the Lisbon Treaty. However, we should also bear in mind that the EU – as the crosshatched bar in Figure 9.1 shows – still covers a number of policy fields in which the EP is not entitled to play a significant role or participate in at all. These include issues ranging from economic policy (Art. 121 and Art. 121.4 TFEU), member states' budgetary situations (Art. 126 TFEU), the 'Luxembourg Process' (Art. 148 TFEU) and the passerelle (Art. 31 TEU) where there is no need to inform or consult national parliaments.

The Lisbon Treaty also strengthens the EP's power of investiture. The EP has the right to elect the Commission President (Art. 14 TEU) proposed by the European Council, taking into account his/her election to the EP (Art. 17 para 7 TEU). It remains to be seen whether the political parties have the willingness to select suitable candidates prior to the next EP election and whether these personalities will play a relevant role in the political debate during the campaign (Joint Study 2007). If the political parties succeed in Europeanising the election campaign it will be an important step away from the established argument that EP elections should be conceived of as 'second order national elections' (Reif and Schmitt 1980) and mark significant progress towards a 'more politicised' Union (Hix 2006).

Since the High Representative for Foreign Affairs and Security Policy is also Vice President of the Commission, the EP significantly extends its reach into that realm. Besides the power to appoint or dismiss the whole Commission, the High Representative 'shall regularly consult the EP on the main aspects and the basic choices of the common foreign and security policy and the common security and defence policy and inform it of how those policies evolve' (Art. 36 TEU).

Figure 9.1: Distribution of decision-making procedures on EU competences

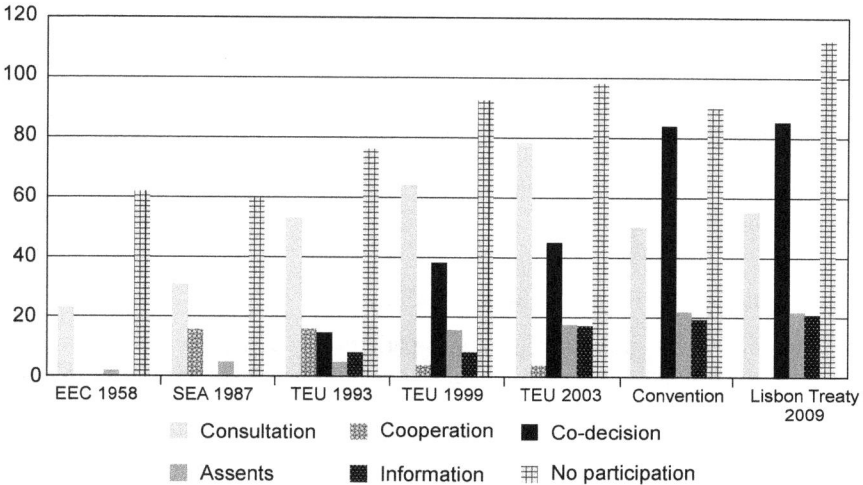

Based on Maurer (2009b) and own data.

However, since the EP has had budgetary oversight over the newly created EEAS there has been severe pressure by the EP to get more rights with regard to the operations part of the diplomatic service (European Parliament 2010).

The entire Commission can be dismissed by a two-thirds majority in the Parliament (Art. 234 TFEU). This rule, which was already established in prior treaty law, has been widely criticised as being rather toothless since it can only be used against the entire Commission and not against individual commissioners.[3] Since it is difficult to argue that the dismissal of the Commission requires a larger majority in the Parliament than was needed for its election, this also raises serious doubts about the EU's commitment to representative majoritarian democracy.

In addition to the legislative and executive powers, the EP – along with the Commission and the government of any member state – can initiate treaty amendments via a convention, subject to approval by the European Council (Art. 48 TEU). In this so-called ordinary revision procedure EP representatives will play an important role, since a convention adopts its final recommendation only by consensus. Furthermore, the EP also enjoys a formal veto if the member states' governments want a treaty revision without the Convention procedure.

And finally, if at least a third of EU member states want to cooperate (enhanced cooperation), the EP has to give its prior approval to this cooperation (Art. 329 TFEU).[4] Since this procedure has never been used it remains to be seen to what

---

3.   The resignation of the Santer Commission in 1999 is a case in point.

4.   If enhanced cooperation deals with foreign and security policy the EP will only be consulted.

extent the EP will be involved once enhanced cooperation is envisaged. Some scholars (see Maurer 2009b) argue that, according to Article 20 TEU, member states that want to establish enhanced cooperation between themselves 'may make use of its institutions and exercise those competences by applying the relevant provisions of the Treaties'. This implies that the EP, along with the Council consisting of the participating member states' governments, will act as the ordinary EU legislator. This, however, creates delicate problems since the full participation of the EP also means that MEPs from non-participating states are involved in affairs concerning enhanced cooperation.

What changes for the national parliaments?

Prior to the Treaty of Lisbon, national parliaments could perform only three functions within the EU's multilevel system of governance: the ratification of treaty amendments, transposition of EC directives into national law, and influencing the performance of 'their' national minister in the Council. The extent to which national parliaments were allowed to exert power with regard to the latter two functions depends on the national constitution and the political culture of the member state. Despite the fact that previous treaties recognised the importance that national parliaments play in maintaining the legitimacy of the EU [5], national parliaments have not played a major role in EU treaties. Nonetheless, the mere incorporation of their role into EU primary law by the Maastricht Treaty as well as their legal upgrading into a legally binding protocol has been considered as a 'political breakthrough' (O'Brennan and Raunio 2007). Additional developments aimed at strengthening the impact of national parliaments on the European policy-making process have also occurred outside the EU's legal framework. Among these were the establishment of COSAC in 1989 and the Laeken Declaration in 2001, both of which paved the way for the European Convention where the majority of participants were representatives from national parliaments and in which particular emphasis was placed upon the role of national legislative assemblies within the EU.

However, evolving from the failed Constitutional Treaty, the Lisbon Treaty now provides ample space dedicated to national parliaments (Articles 5, 10, 12, 48 and 49 TEU). While the German Constitutional Court (BVerG 2009) is convinced that the increase of participation rights for national parliaments 'cannot compensate for the deficit in the strand of legitimation of the European public authority', it also acknowledges that this development has to be welcomed and may 'increase the level of legitimation'.[6] In particular, the new Article 12 TEU strengthens the role of national parliaments. Some rights have already been stipulated in protocols but only with the Treaty of Lisbon have these rights been established on the level of primary law and with the Early Warning Mechanism extended into previously

---

5. Declarations 13 and 14 attached to the Maastricht Treaty; Protocol D 3 attached to the Amsterdam Treaty; Declaration 23 of the Treaty of Nice.

6. BVerG 2009; paragraphs 293–4.

unknown territory. According to Article 12, national parliaments contribute to the functioning of the Union by being informed about draft legislative acts.[7] An additional Protocol (No. 1) requires other EU institutions, in particular the Commission, to forward all consultation documents (i.e. Green and White Papers; communications), as well as the annual legislative programme, to the national parliaments. National parliaments have the right to issue a reasoned opinion on whether a draft legislative act complies with the principle of subsidiarity within a period of eight weeks instead of six weeks as foreseen in the Constitutional Treaty. A further protocol on subsidiarity (No. 2) stipulates that when a reasoned opinion represents at least one third of all national parliaments[8] the draft must be reviewed by the Commission which has the right to maintain, amend or withdraw the draft concerned. If, however, the reasoned opinion represents the majority of the national parliaments, the proposal must again be reviewed by the Commission. If it chooses to maintain the draft it has to issue a reasoned opinion and argue its case for why the draft is in accordance with the principle of subsidiarity. If the EP, along with the Council, considers the proposal compatible with the principle of subsidiarity it can adopt the legislative act. While this Early Warning Mechanism may be regarded as a negative rather than a positive instrument (Sonnicksen 2010) it also reflects the opinion that EU institutions are probably more inclined to adhere to the principle of subsidiarity by an *ex ante* political review carried out by national parliaments than a judicial *ex post* review once the legal act has been adopted. However, it remains to be seen whether this timetable will be sufficient for a serious scrutiny of legislative drafts and, if necessary, for the required amount of coordination among various national assemblies. In any case, in order to cope with those new rights, national parliaments will find themselves under considerable pressure to make their internal working procedures more efficient as well as to establish new and viable institutional arrangements as soon as possible (Dougan 2008).

Apart from the Early Warning Mechanism, member states are also entitled 'on behalf of their national [p]arliament' (Art. 8, Protocol No. 2) to bring alleged infringements of the principle of subsidiarity before the European Court of Justice. So far, subsidiarity can be regarded as an extremely vague concept which makes it virtually impossible to limit or define the correct EU competences. This explains why the European Court of Justice may be reluctant to review EU legislation from the subsidiarity angle (Konstadinides 2009; Barents 2010). This new endorsement of subsidiarity by the Treaty of Lisbon, as well as the likelihood of increased submissions of reasoned opinions by national parliaments to the Court of Justice, may provide new opportunities for the Court to intensify the legal discourse on subsidiarity and transform it into a forceful political weapon beyond mere rhetorical affirmation (Dougan 2008).

---

7.   The term 'draft legislative acts' has to be broadly understood and covers all Commission proposals, initiatives from group of member states and the European Parliament as well as requests from the European Court of Justice, the European Central Bank and the European Investment Bank for the adoption of a legislative act.

8.   Each national parliament has two votes (Art. 7, Protocol No. 2).

Another aspect deals with the relationship between national parliaments and their respective governments. Will parliaments be able to emancipate themselves from 'their' governments and establish themselves as independent political actors or will national governments merely instrumentalise 'their' national parliament and reinforce their political argument *vis-à-vis* other member states by using this new layer of political action (Maurer 2008a)? Given the dominance of party politics in most of the EU's member states it remains highly unlikely that a parliament will be able to transform itself into an independent and self-confident political actor tabling opinions divergent from its own government line (Raunio 2009; also, see below with regard to the Austrian case). While the Early Warning Mechanism makes it legally impossible to force the EU legislator to discard a legislative draft, we should bear in mind that even a smaller number of national parliaments than the third or half envisaged in the Treaty may play a politically relevant role. It seems highly unlikely that the EU legislator whose standard operation procedure is based on consensus would risk adopting a legal act if, say, a quarter of all national parliaments raised the concern that that piece of legislation breached the principle of subsidiarity (Hix quoted in House of Commons 2008).

Apart from the *ex ante* and *ex post* control of subsidiarity, national parliaments are also expected to play a significant part in the evaluation mechanism for its implementation in the field of Freedom, Security and Justice, and they are involved in the political monitoring of Europol and the evaluation of the activities of Eurojust (see the chapter by Garibay in this volume). Finally, national parliaments will also increase their role in the course of future treaty amendments. Apart from ratifying already adopted treaties, national parliaments will now be engaged in an earlier stage of the revision process and play an active part both in the ordinary revision procedure, especially through their engagement in the European Convention, and its simplified version under Article 48 TEU. Additionally, national parliaments have the right to be notified of future membership applications (Art. 49 TEU).

In addition to the question of whether a national parliament will succeed in emerging as an independent political actor, there is also the procedural challenge of whether they are prepared to cooperate with one another. Experiences with interparliamentary or horizontal cooperation are rare. However, COSAC organised eight subsidiarity tests between 2005 and 2010 in which national parliaments had the opportunity to scrutinise legislative drafts under the rules of the Early Warning Mechanism (Cooper 2010; Knutelská in this volume). These test cases revealed a number of problems indicating that it does not seem likely that national parliaments will be able to operate under the Early Warning Mechanism. Among these problems were that national parliaments found it extremely difficult to comply with the eight week deadline, a lack of knowledge, language problems and low parliamentary response rates. In particular, the eight weeks' time limit put severe constraints on their ability to scrutinise the legislative proposal concerned. For instance, during the summer of 2009 the COSAC Secretariat organised a subsidiarity check on the Proposal for a Council Framework Decision on the right to interpretation and translation in criminal proceedings (COM (2009)). Twenty-one parliaments from seventeen member states succeeded in completing the subsidiarity check while ten additional parliaments started the process but proved unable to finish it within the given time frame. Other parliaments were not interested in participating in the subsidiarity check due to domestic reasons (such as general elections in the case of Greece). While eleven participating parliaments did not have any difficulty in meeting the eight-week time limit, a significant number of parliaments had problems operating within the set time limit. The concrete problems may take many different forms ranging from being unable to 'involve specialised committees or to hear [the] opinions of interested [p]arties' (Cypriot *Vouli ton Antiprosopon*); the impossibility 'to mediate between both Chambers of the Parliament' (the Dutch *Tweede Kamer*); to the problem of coping with the eight-week deadline when it falls during summer recess (COSAC 2009d).

In order to facilitate interparliamentary cooperation the IPEX website was established in 2006. According to its website, IPEX is a 'platform for the electronic exchange of EU related information between parliaments in the Union'[9] and contains two types of documents: first, all documents which are adopted at the EU level, notably Commission proposals which usually start the EU legislative process and, secondly, documents uploaded from individual national parliaments which scrutinise EU documents, especially if they are in accordance with the principle of subsidiarity. While COSAC acknowledges that an increasing number of parliaments use IPEX, it is also clear that parliamentary use of IPEX is currently uneven, sporadic, and offers, in many cases, outdated or no data, a situation which obviously hampers horizontal cooperation between national parliaments.

The main problem is that it is up to national parliaments whether they upload a specific document or not and even if they do so these documents may differ in format, scope or content (IPEX 2006). So far (as at June 2012), a total of 4,879 documents have been uploaded. In addition, most parliaments upload their documents only in the original language which makes it extremely hard for MPs from other member states to consult and use them. As a consequence of these problems, the COSAC report of 2009 found that only eight out of the twenty-one participating parliaments are actively using IPEX, i.e. following the activities of other parliaments or informing other parliaments about their own scrutiny (COSAC 2009d). A tentative solution to this problem may be that national parliaments at least provide English or French summaries of their main arguments or decisions which may alert MPs from other parliaments to take a closer look at these documents, which in turn may trigger a lasting relationship between parliaments on a given issue area. In order to handle the logistical challenges of interparliamentary cooperation, national parliaments have also to increase their human as well as financial resources in order to make IPEX a useful, workable and up-to-date database (*see also* Knutelská in this volume). Besides IPEX, the network of national parliaments' representatives in Brussels may also serve as an important platform for informal dialogue and cooperation (Šefčovič 2010). Furthermore, most national parliaments also suffer from the fact that most

---

9.   Online. Available at: www.ipex.eu (25 June 2013)

Figure 9.2: Number of documents filed on IPEX by parliamentary chamber
Data based on IPEX, June 2012

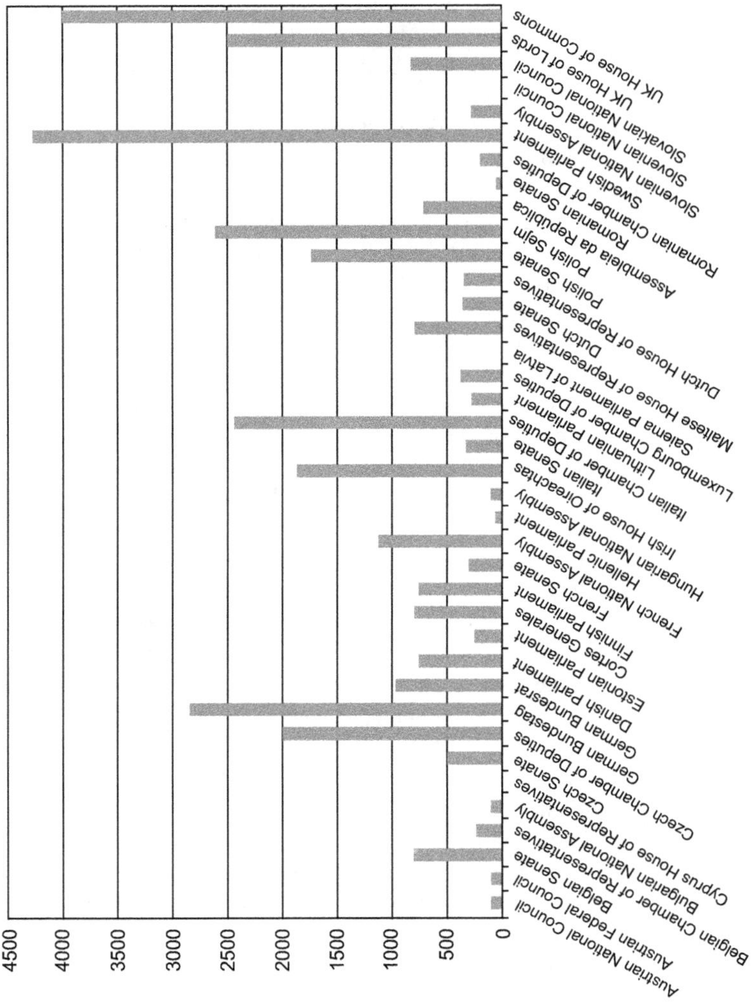

agreements at the European level are reached at first and second reading stages through the use of informal trilogues:[10] small, private meetings between the Commission, Council and EP – this is where the real negotiation takes place and why national parliaments are left on the outside. This results in parliaments seeing the first proposal but being unable to follow up the amendments negotiated in the trilogues. Given that 94 per cent of codecision bills (201 out of 219 agreements between 2004–2009) were discussed via the informal trilogue procedure before open deliberations and votes could take place in committee meetings, we can imagine how important those meetings are (Lieb and Maurer 2009).

Last but not least, national parliaments lack a common definition of subsidiarity which also makes it difficult to assume that the required number of national parliaments will be able to formulate a common and coherent argument substantiating their claim of an alleged breach of the principle of subsidiarity. Despite all these problems, it seems easy to dismiss these new parliamentary powers as merely symbolic or toothless. One author even argues that national parliaments sending complaints to the Commission is not a 'real' new right (Kiiver 2008). No one can prevent MPs from confronting EU institutions with concerns of all kinds. However, it cannot be ruled out that the new provisions will unfold a fresh dynamic among national parliaments, further integrating MPs into EU decision-making and enhancing not only their degree of Europeanisation but also their opportunity and motivation structure (Töller 2010) – a development which will be more likely to occur if it is accompanied by a significant reorganisation of the inner procedures of national parliaments (to make scrutinising and communication with fellow MPs more efficient). Parliamentary cooperation, however, does more than merely control the adherence to the subsidiarity principle. Over the last two decades, a wide range of interparliamentary activities and cooperations have emerged, both inside and outside the EU context, comprising not only well-known fora such as COSAC, the Interparliamentarian Union, the parliamentary assemblies of the OSCE and the Council of Europe but also the Conference of Speakers of the EU Parliaments, the Conference of the Presidents of EU Parliaments and the Parliamentary Assembly of the Union for the Mediterranean.

Any assessment of the future role of national parliaments has to take into account the lessons of previous involvement by national parliaments. In the next section we will provide empirical evidence of the performance of the Austrian parliament which is considered to have exceptionally strong, constitutionally granted participation rights.

---

10. Contrary to popular belief, these meetings are not small. Although numbers vary, usually they are attended by the Parliament's *rapporteur*, shadow *rapporteurs* and support staff, staff from the Council Presidency and staff from the Commission. In total there may be some twenty to forty people in attendance. They are a vital part of the co-decision procedure because they allow frank, face-to-face discussions between those leading on the proposal under discussion from each of the institutions.

The buck stops with national parliaments – the Austrian case[11]

The Austrian Parliament has two standing committees dealing with EU affairs: the Main Committee (*Hauptausschuss*) and the Subcommittee (*Unterausschuss*). Work between them is divided along the high-politics – low-politics partition, the latter being processed by the Subcommittee.[12] Both committees are entitled to pass binding opinions. In such a case the respective member of the government is obliged to follow this mandate in all negotiations and acts of voting at the supranational level. It was clear from the very beginning that respective parliaments had to take care to achieve a balance between the necessary control of their governments and the total paralysis of the Council. A mandate that was too narrow or detailed would considerably hamper the executive's room for manoeuvre and could be detrimental to the decision-making capability of the entire Council. How did the Austrian Parliament use its rights? Did those rights leave any imprint on the (1) legislative and (2) control and information function exerted by the Austrian Parliament?

Figure 9.3 shows that a striking decline in the use of this instrument has taken place. The reasons are that the parliament is an instrument of the government and not a controlling institution. These data reflect an important insight that national parliaments are – as Maurer (2008a), above, argues – less independent political actors but, rather, political agents of 'their' government. This insight has already been elaborated by Anthony King (1976) who, in his seminal article, criticised the so-called 'two-body image' as being part of the mythical and theoretical past of democracy rather than a description of reality. A simple differentiation between executive and legislative bodies does not do justice to the complex relations between those two state powers and, moreover, would neglect the development of party government and cartel parties (Blondel and Cotta 2000; Katz and Mair 1995). Especially in Western Europe, parties are the dominant actors in political systems since the 'behaviour of both MPs and ministers may be more conditioned by their membership of a party than by their belonging to either party or government' (Andeweg and Nijzink 1995). Thus, it is not a case of parliament and government facing each other in political battle; we have to conceive of the relationship between the executive and the legislative, firstly, as a *Handlungsverbund* (Beyme 1997) between the government and its supporting parliamentary groups and, secondly, as a more or less conflict-oriented relationship between this powerful *Handlungsverbund* and the opposition.

As a corollary, the legislative function of the Austrian Parliament (expressed in the sheer number of adopted binding opinions) dropped significantly after the

11. The following section is largely based on Pollak and Slominski (2003; 2009). In addition to quantitative data provided by the website of the Austrian Parliament, we conducted semi-standardised interviews with relevant MPs and party officials in two periods (2001–2002 and 2008). For reasons of anonymity, interviewees are not mentioned by name or party affiliation but only by 'I' and a specific number (e.g. I-1 for the first interview period or I-2 for the second one).

12. A third committee is the so-called Fire Brigade Committee which has the task of providing 'on-the-spot' parliamentary monitoring of European Councils.

Figure 9.3: Total number of binding opinions in both Austrian EU affairs committees

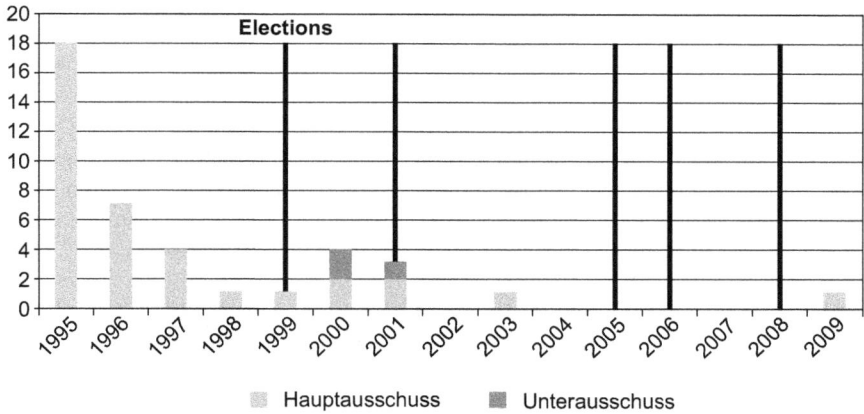

Figure 9.4: Total number of meetings, incoming and discussed documents in the main committee

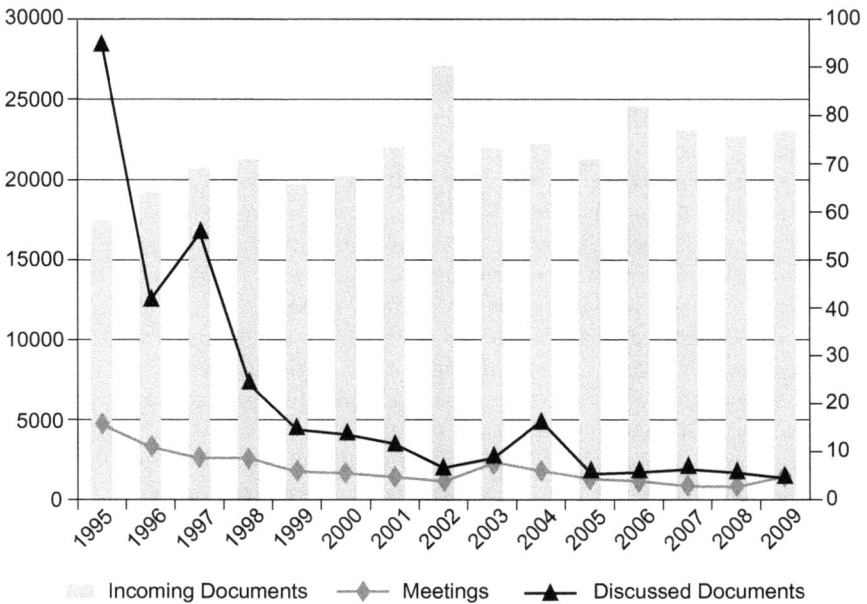

first two years and now hardly plays any relevant political role at all. Now, even when such an opinion is adopted (usually by government majority or unanimity) it is either politically vague and/or is used mainly for symbolic reasons to impress the Austrian constituency rather than influence EU decision-making.

The legislative function is only one of the activities bestowed upon committees by legal provisions (Mattson and Strøm 1995). In addition we have to pay attention to the information and the control function which has gained importance over the last years.

One precondition of adequate control is access to and quality of information. The number of EU-related documents reaching the Austrian Parliament is impressive: according to information from the Parliamentary Administration (*Parlamentsdirektion*), the annual number lies between 17,000 and nearly 22,000 single documents.

To cope with this enormous number of documents a database was established in 1996. All incoming documents are provided with a date of receipt and a file number. While IPEX suffers from uneven inputs and/or updates by national parliaments, the Austrian database enables not only the Austrian Parliament to monitor the EU policy-making process but it is also frequently used by the Federal Ministries and other member states' parliaments. However, the transmission of uncommented EU-relevant documents proves to be a mixed blessing: on the one hand, the complete and thorough information is a central precondition for the opinion formation of the individual MP. On the other hand, practice shows that the procedure applied today leads to an information overkill and thus to a serious complication of the EU Main Committee's work (Rack *et al.* 1997; Schefbeck 1998).

While it goes without saying that comprehensive legislative and information rights are a prerequisite for effective parliamentary involvement in EU affairs, the most important changes have occurred beyond formal legal provisions. For example, a series of reforms – which also might be of interest both to other national parliaments and the operation of the IPEX database – significantly improved the working conditions for the Austrian Parliament. Firstly, a decision adopted by the Austrian Government stipulates that for the documents on the agenda of the subcommittee an introductory page (*Vorblatt*) has to be delivered. It usually comprises four to five pages, its form varies and it is compiled by the responsible ministry describing the Austrian position on the discussed legislative project. Secondly, every federal ministry, at the beginning of each year, has to submit a catalogue (around twenty pages) of legislative projects for the relevant parliamentary committee in which the supranational plans for the coming years, and the Austrian position, are charted. The timely announcement of legislative projects and the summary of their impacts on the Austrian situation facilitate the Parliament's control function. But probably the most important development has occurred on the level of socialisation, creating a new quality of knowledge and better awareness of EU politics among Austrian MPs (Pollak and Slominski 2009) which may also be indicative of the 'catalyst potential' of the parliament-friendly provisions of the Lisbon Treaty (Kiiver 2008).

While, at the beginning of Austria's EU membership, all parties lamented the lack of MP's 'European consciousness', the gradual Europeanisation of MPs is a remarkable development. Fifteen years after accession the interviewees confirmed a steep 'learning process' of MPs which may not only be the result of their daily work as MPs of an EU Parliament but also the outcome of a considerably denser web of institutionalised activities among MPs from other member states involving regular meetings and deliberations about various policy issues. In particular, the regular exchange with the EP has increased in the last few years. Data for the years 2009 to 2011 show that a modest but nonetheless increasing number of Austrian MPs (2009: 6; 2010: 20; 2011: 36)[13] participated in EP committee meetings discussing not only general issues of interparliamentary cooperation but also specific policy issues, especially in the context of the EU's current economic and financial crisis. More than fifteen years of membership have thus left their imprint on the MPs and most of them nowadays seem to understand the relevance of the supranational level. A central difference since the first years of membership is to be found in the assessment of the working climate in the committees. The interviewees talked about a 'very constructive atmosphere' in the committees which show a 'considerable quality' and enable the MPs to learn about policy processes and decision making in the EU, thus 'socialising the MPs'. One reason for this positive assessment might be that they can deliberate and discuss matters more freely beyond binding opinions. In other words, if the binding opinion is not always seen as a Damocles' Sword, MPs are willing to forget about party strategies. Ironically, the style of deliberation, described by the interviewees as based on argument, is encouraged by the lack of media attention. Because the MPs do not argue in the light of the mass public, they do not need to advance their own arguments at all costs but can transcend their own position (Eriksen 2000) thereby facilitating political compromise. It is a kind of 'communicative-cooperative problem-solving style' (Joerges 2002) that builds on convincing the other (Risse 2000) and in which rational arguments and adequate solutions are more important than the enforcement of party interests (Bessette 1994).

What does this mean for the new rights bestowed upon national parliaments as stipulated in the Lisbon Treaty? How would they impact on the role of the Austrian Parliament in EU affairs? Firstly, parliaments may have learned to send the documents not only to the special EU committees but to other specialised standing committees. This would be the optimistic interpretation which, in interviews, has failed to materialise itself strongly so far. Secondly, parliaments refrain from using strong binding instruments but, rather, rely on such committees as meeting and information points. This could be seen as control under the shadow of binding opinions which would of course only be effective if a parliament could muster the courage to stand up to a government. Lisbon does not make this more likely; if parliaments could not hitherto control their governments, why should they be able to do so now?

---

13. Data were provided by the Austrian parliamentary administration.

However, in light of the experiences of the Austrian assembly, an effective and efficient participation of national parliaments – national differences and traditions notwithstanding – requires certain principal changes: firstly, a coherent strategy for the efficient use of existing MP expertise in EU committees is needed. In the Austrian case, members of the committees can be changed according to topic, however, up until now, this has worked on an *ad hoc* basis and has not followed a coherent strategy. This would also lead to an exchange of expertise between the two European committees and other standing committees of the parliament, thus increasing efficiency and effectiveness. Secondly, MEPs should be given a more prominent role in the national context to report on developments, plans and the state of the art in the EP. Also, from a very early stage, one could also consider including in the parliamentary activities those civil servants who are part of the European policy process, i.e. civil servants from the permanent representation in Brussels. So far, MPs have complained about their late involvement in the policy process. Thirdly, EU committees should have the right to draw up their own reports (and thereby follow the example of the British Parliament) and make them accessible to a wider public. Such reports could involve the hearing of experts and parliamentary *enquetes* which would increase public awareness and interest in European topics. The last suggestion concerns parliamentary resources: without a considerable investment into the development of cross-national, interparliamentary databases (e.g. horizontally connecting national databases) an efficient use of newly gained information and the right to subsidiarity checking will be unlikely to occur.

Conclusions

Although the Lisbon Treaty introduces a lot of features which were, for a long time, requested by parliaments it remains to be seen how they will be implemented. Empirical evidence suggests that the EP has used its increased legislative powers wisely and has developed a reputation as a competent and consensus-seeking co-legislator. But the discreet and professional use of ever increasing legislative powers has not corresponded with the impact it has on public opinion, leading to a somewhat paradoxical situation in which the EP is increasingly affecting the lives of citizens who still regard it as a powerless institution. Apart from some notable exceptions, such as the controversial debate about the so-called Bolkestein-Directive or the Working Time Directive, the EP is more oriented to finding political consensus between the major political parties and with the Council and the Commission than to acting as a strong and coherent political voice conceived of as relevant by EU citizens. It has been argued elsewhere that the future challenge for the EP will not lie in the continuing increase of further legislative rights but in an increased level of political and controversial debates on concrete policy issues. To make this happen we do not need new treaties but reforms of the internal proceedings, especially a reorganisation of the plenary debates (*Common Market Law Review* 2009)

Moreover, in a parliamentary field we would also expect to see strong horizontal as well as vertical cooperation between the different legislative bodies, i.e.

between the EP and national parliaments. Meetings of national parliamentarians would facilitate the sharing of best practices and the identification of mutual problems and, through regular dialogue with the EP, national MPs would receive information that contributes to effective government scrutiny. Indeed, we see a certain convergence when it comes to national scrutiny systems: COSAC is becoming an important hub (but currently maintains an advisory capacity only) and cross country party ties are becoming a little stronger. However, there are also limits to this kind of cooperation. This is firstly because of the limited interest that national MPs have in European politics. In their minds, power and office are traded at the national level; secondly, while contacts between the EP and national parliaments have become more institutionalised and regular over the years, there is little reason to expect that such contacts would intensify in the near future merely because of the new Treaty. It is probable that we will need to wait for the emergence of true European parties before this happens; thirdly, the calendars of both sets of parliamentarians are quite full, and timetable problems are one of the reasons why most national parliaments and their committees seldom invite MEPs to their meetings. Nonetheless, as long as national MPs have no political incentive to increase their involvement in EU affairs, and if any engagement is hampered by inadequate institutional conditions (see e.g. IPEX), it is unlikely that the Lisbon Treaty will lead to a further parliamentary turn in EU policy-making.

chapter ten | the 'back door' to national politics: the French Greens and the 2009 European Parliament elections[*]

Yoav Shemer-Kunz

Introduction

The defining characteristic of the model of multilevel governance in the EU is the shift of authority – from public to private actors and from the central state to subnational authorities and supranational institutions (Hooghe and Marks 2001). States no longer monopolise EU-level policy-making as authority is dispersed and shared by a large variety of actors at different levels. Democratic representation in the EU has also come to be dispersed across different sites, interconnected in various, formal and informal, ways in one 'multilevel parliamentary field' (Crum and Fossum 2009). Operating through this multilevel parliamentary field, national parliaments continue to play important roles in shaping and legitimising EU decision-making. This chapter demonstrates how the dynamics of multilevel democratic representation in Europe also re-enter decision making at the national level by providing new political parties with access and influence.

As the different political arenas in Europe are interconnected, an actor's access to power at the EU level of democratic representation may help them to access legislative and executive power at the national level. This does not happen directly through formal institutional arrangements but, rather, indirectly through the mobilisation of political resources and the building of social relations with other actors in the field. It is the combined interactions and structures obtaining between the actors in the field that offer opportunities for new political parties. These interactions and structures are influenced by external changes in the institutional environment.

Specifically, European integration has changed the environment of national political actors. The EU, as an emerging political field, offers numerous resources, both material and immaterial, to political actors who connect to it (Kauppi 2005). Looking more closely at political parties, this environmental evolution does not impact all political parties in the same way. For the established, cartel parties (Katz and Mair 1995), it is not that crucial, since they already have numerous resources at the national level. However, for new and emerging parties, this environmental

---
[*] I would like to thank Niilo Kauppi (CNRS/University of Strasbourg, SAGE laboratory, UMR 7363) and the editors for their very useful comments on previous drafts of this chapter.

change can be very significant. Unlike cartel-parties, emerging parties suffer from resource scarcity at the national level. These actors seek to break into the political system, hoping to put new issues on the social and political agenda. For these marginal actors on the national stage, the multilevel context of the EU provides new opportunities. The emergence of the EP and the introduction of direct elections to the EP in 1979 represent important changes in the political parties' respective environments. The peripheral position of the EP in national politics generally makes it less attractive to dominant political elites at the national level (see Beauvallet and Michon in this volume). However, EP elections provide a significant political opportunity for some actors, whether nationally represented or not. Emerging political parties can use EP elections as a new entry point into politics, in a similar way to which the subnational level is used in federal settings (see Deschouwer 2000, 2003). EP elections, in turn, can have significant implications for these parties' roles and power in the national political field. The ensuing change in the national power structure then affects not only the new parties but the political system as a whole.

EP elections trigger a more pluralist representation at the national level and a more open structure of competition among closed national political systems (Mair 2006). Indirectly, EP elections open up closed political systems, such as bipartisan systems. This change towards a more pluralist structure of competition allows emerging parties access to national parliaments and governments, thus providing them with effective influence on decision making at the national level. This is not happening through a formal, institutional change but, rather, through the way in which the addition of a new layer of governance encourages 'bottom-up' dynamics through reconfiguring actors' incentives, strategies and practices.

Political scientists have overlooked this usage of EP elections, both as a significant entry point into politics for emerging parties, and in terms of the implications of this on the nature of the national political system. Scholars studying the influence of the European integration process on political parties have generally found that it has only limited effects (*see* Pogunkte *et al.* 2007; Ladrech 2010). EP elections have mostly been analysed as 'second-order national elections' (*see* Reif and Schmitt 1980; Marsh 1998; Hix and Marsh 2007). In this model, EP elections are considered 'second-order' in contrast to 'first-order' national elections.

Some scholars have, however, pointed out that EP elections have particular importance to new and small parties. For instance, Simon Hix and Christopher Lord observe that 'European elections have also influenced the entry of new parties to the field of serious political contestation. The 1984 election was crucial to the rise of the Front National (FN) in France' (Hix and Lord 1997). However, how the emerging parties' role in EP elections feeds back on power relations within the national political system, and the nature of the national party system itself, remains under-researched.

This chapter offers an in-depth analysis of how EP elections open up closed political systems for emerging parties, taking the case of the Green Party in France in the context of the 2009 EP elections. It is based upon a political sociology approach to European studies (*see* Kauppi 2005; Georgakakis 2008; Saurugger

2008; Mérand and Saurugger 2010; Favell and Guiraudon 2011; Zimmermann and Favell 2011). The sociological approach is useful in that it permits the analyst to take fully into account the actors' strategies and practices. The empirical data consist of ten semi-structured interviews with French Green Party's candidates for the 2009 EP elections, the party's MEPs, local party officials and electoral campaign staff; participant observations within the party's campaign team; and numerous informal discussions with party staff and members.

The chapter proceeds as follows. First, I provide an overview of the French Greens' limited political resources at the national level and its relative success in EP elections. In the second section I analyse how the party seized the 2009 EP elections as a political opportunity to recruit external candidates from civil society. The third section analyses how its success in the 2009 EP elections enabled the party to modify its power relations in national politics. I finish with some concluding remarks.

The French Greens: Weak at national level, good in EP elections

France's political system is relatively closed and immobile, characterised by centripetal tendencies. French politics is dominated by two established, bureaucratised parties, a 'circumscribed cartel of political actors' (Kitschelt 1986). The conservative party, *Union pour la Majorité Présidentielle* (UMP), was in power from 1995 until 2012, when the *Parti Socialiste* (PS) returned to power. The French bipartisan system leaves little place for emerging political forces, protest movements and 'outsiders'. The inaccessibility of the existing political structure drove the French anti-nuclear movement of the 1970s to support independent candidates for presidential elections as early as 1974, and to officially found the French Green Party, *Les Verts*, in 1984.

The French Greens are a small political party, relatively marginalised in French politics. They are often considered too utopian and not credible (*see* Sainteny, 1987, 1997, 2000). The French Greens often used elections more as a platform to spread their ideas than as a means to get to power and influence decision making.

The French Greens suffered from weak results in national elections. In fact, the party had no MPs in France's two national parliaments, the National Assembly and the Senate, until as late as 1997.[1] In 2009 the party still had only three MPs out of 577 in the National Assembly, and only five Senators out of 343. In both chambers the Green representatives were affiliated with the PS, as they were not numerous enough to establish a political group of their own. In presidential elections the French Greens' fortunes have been quite poor, taking between 1 to 5 per cent of the vote (*see* Table 10.1).

---

1. At the 1997 parliamentary elections the Greens joined the left bloc (*la gauche plurielle*) led by the PS. This cooperation enabled the Greens to obtain six MPs as well as the Ministry of Environment (1997–2002).

Table 10.1: Green candidates in presidential elections in France (1974–2012)

Election year	Candidate	% of the vote	Number of votes
1974	René Dumont	1.32	337,800
1981	Brice Lalonde	3.88	1,126,254
1988	Antoine Waechter	3.78	1,149,897
1995	Dominique Voynet	3.32	1,010,738
2002	Noël Mamère	5.25	1,495,724
2007	Dominique Voynet	1.57	576,666
2012	Eva Joly	2.31	828,345

Source: http://www.france-politique.fr; http://www.interieur.gouv.fr (accessed 23 May 2012)

The French Greens gained a certain stability of around 3 per cent in each of the three consecutive presidential elections of 1981, 1988 and 1995, and an historic 5 per cent in the 2002 elections. But their results in the 2007 presidential elections came at an unprecedented low, with only 1.57 per cent of the vote.

While the French Green Party thus scores quite poorly in national elections, it obtains relatively good scores in EP elections (*see* Table 10.2). In fact, the party attained its first MEPs as early as 1989, seven years before it secured its first MPs.

Table 10.2: Green lists in EP elections (1979–2009)

Election year	List	% of the vote	Number of votes	MEPs
1979	Europe Ecologie	4.39	888,134	0
1984	Les Verts	3.37	680,080	0
1989	Les Verts	10.59	1,922,945	9
1994	Les Verts	2.95	574,806	0
1999	Les Verts	9.72	1,715,450	9
2004	Les Verts	7.41	1,271,394	6
2009	Europe Ecologie	16.28	2,803,759	14

Source: http://www.france-politique.fr; http://www.interieur.gouv.fr (accessed 17 November 2009)

Still, even in EP elections, the French Greens' results have been quite unstable over the years. This can be explained by the dispersion of votes among different ecological lists. In the very first EP elections in 1979, an independent green list, *Europe Ecologie*, led by Mrs Solange Fernex, obtained almost 5 per cent of the vote. Five years later, in the 1984 EP elections, the ecological electorate was split between two lists: the official list of the newly founded Green Party and an independent list led by Mr Brice Lalonde, who was a candidate in the 1981 presidential elections where he attained 4 per cent of the vote. Each list secured only 3 per cent of the vote and no MEPs. But in the 1989 EP elections the French Greens, united under the leadership of Mr Antoine Waechter, attained an historic success in a national vote: 10 per cent of the vote and nine MEPs. However, this success did not endure as the French Greens failed to win seats in the EP in the following 1994 elections. Waechter had left the Green Party a short time before that and ran for the EP elections separately, leading the list *Génération Ecologie*. Neither of the ecological lists obtained any MEPs. In the 1999 EP elections the Greens were led by Mr Daniel Cohn-Bendit and again attained 10 per cent of the vote and nine MEPs, the same result as ten years earlier. In 2004 the Greens were once more facing harsh competition on the ecology issue. For instance, an independent ecological list, CAP21, led by Mrs Corinne Lepage, a former Minister of the Environment, obtained 3 per cent of the vote. In the 2004 EP elections the Greens attained 7 per cent of the vote and six MEPs. The internal division within the political ecology movement was often a disadvantage for the French Greens. However, when united, they achieved good results in EP elections: around 10 per cent of the vote. This was not the case in national elections.

Why such a gap between different levels of elections?

How can we explain these great differences, throughout the years, in the results of the same political party at these two election levels?

The particular success of green parties in EP elections is often explained by their secondary importance in relation to national elections. According to the 'second-order' model (Reif and Schmitt 1980), voters feel that there is less at stake and thus allow themselves to vote according to conviction. After all, the EP election outcomes do not determine the executive body at the European level and the EP itself, as well as its legislative activities, are largely unknown to the public. Therefore, in EP elections, voters can follow their convictions and take risks that they would not take at national elections that determine the choice of leaders. This is a possible explanation for the success of the French Greens in EP elections.

But there are alternative explanations for the success of green parties in EP elections that have nothing to do with the notion of 'second-order elections'. The first is the role of the environmental issue. Voters might actually vote for green parties in EP elections because they are in favour of a common environmental policy at the European level (see Curtice 1989; Carruba and Timpone 2005; Hix and Marsh 2007; Hobolt *et al.* 2008). The environmental issue might be an emerging 'European issue', perceived by the public as an issue which is better dealt with at the EU level than at the national one.

A second explanation for the success of the French Greens in EP elections is the electoral rule. The rule of EP elections in France is proportional representation (PR) in one round only, whereas the electoral rule generally used in France's presidential or parliamentary elections is a majority vote in two rounds. The latter majority vote system tends to favour the big parties and gives little possibility for small parties to acquire MPs. In line with the second-order model, French citizens often vote tactically in national elections, relying on rational utility calculations (*le vote utile*) to eliminate a specific opponent from the second round of elections. For instance, many French citizens tend to vote for the socialist candidates in majority elections but for Green ones in PR elections (Mayer and Perrineau 1992).

Notably, in the first round of the presidential elections on 21 April 2002, Jean-Marie Le Pen, the leader of FN, the extreme right-wing party, moved up to the second round together with Jacques Chirac due to the large dispersion of votes among various left and centre candidates. Henceforth, French Green voters tend to vote for the socialist candidate in the first round of elections in order to prevent a second '21 April', which became a reference to the political power of the extreme right in France. In fact, the French Socialists explicitly use this possibility in their call to vote for their candidate in the first round of presidential elections. This tendency does not exist in EP elections, as a local Green official explains:

> When people vote according to their convictions, we have good scores [...] [I]n presidential elections part of the green electorate did not vote according to their beliefs but in relation to the second round [...] I think there is a vote of conviction in European elections. That is why the greens always had good scores in these elections.

(Interview Nine)[2]

A third explanation for the French Greens' success in EP elections is the generally low turnout combined with relatively high green voter participation. Green voters seem to participate more in EP elections than the rest of the population. Citizens who take part in these elections are relatively supportive of the European integration process (*see* Blondel *et al.* 1997). Green voters in France are mainly young, educated and middle-class with a high proportion of higher education diplomas (*see* Boy 1994; Faucher-King 2005). A Green MEP described the traditional green electorate as 'Bobos' (Interview Ten). This population tends to be in favour of the EU. Another Green MEP said that the low turnout in EP elections is an advantage to the Greens 'because our electorate is relatively mobilised, pro-European, and will vote. However, the others [...] the people who are undecided, if they vote, will vote more easily for the big parties' (Interview Eleven). The high participation in EP elections among green voters, together with the low turnout from the general population, gives an important advantage to the Greens.

Finally, the French Greens' success in EP elections can be explained by the low salience of the left/right cleavage. This traditional cleavage is less dominant in EP elections than in other, national, elections in France where it tends to disadvantage the Green Party. The Greens build their political legitimacy around the emerging, post-materialist cleavage of economy *vs* nature: 'only the Greens correspond to a real European cleavage – opposing the 'all market' to the ecology – in which they

---

2. All citations are translated from French by the author.

clearly occupy one of the two poles' (Seiler 2005). In EP elections there is enough room for new, emergent political issues to be raised. The Greens may therefore compete in these elections as credible political rivals. For all these reasons, the French Greens do relatively well in EP elections.

I have shown that, for the French Greens, EP elections are an important political opportunity to get good electoral results and obtain seats in the EP. I will now demonstrate how the party seized the 2009 EP elections, both as a political opportunity to rescue itself from a state of crisis and as an entry point into national politics.

Background of the 2009 EP elections

In 2008, around a year before the EP elections, the French Greens were in a deep crisis. The party suffered from financial problems after the 2007 presidential campaign, which ended with catastrophic results; they achieved 1.57 per cent of the vote. They also suffered from lack of attractive national leadership and internal divisions. The divisions between different party currents were often visible to the public and contributed to the negative image of the party. At this point in time, after the 2007 presidential elections, two of the Greens' national leaders, Mr Yann Wehrling, the party's national secretary, and Mr Jean-Luc Bennahmias, one of the Greens' MEPs since 2004, left the party in order to join the ranks of *Mouvement Démocratique* (MoDem), a centre party on the rise and led by François Bayrou, who attained 18 per cent of the vote in the 2007 presidential elections. In addition, the French Greens faced competition from renewed parties on the radical left which also adopted environmental issues in their political agenda: the *Nouveau Parti Anti-capitaliste* (NPA) led by Olivier Besançenot, who secured 4 per cent of the vote in the 2007 presidential elections; and *Front de Gauche*, a new union between the French Communist party (PCF) and other small left parties and trade unions. Thus, one year before the EP elections, the French Green's general situation looked quite gloomy.

However, in French civil society, green issues were on the rise, receiving positive media coverage and legitimacy. This became particularly apparent in the *Grenelle de l'environnement* dialogue. In 2007, the French President, Nicolas Sarkozy, launched this large-scale public dialogue between the Government and ecological NGOs which was extensively covered by French national media and was a moment of both glory and disappointment for the participating NGOs. The dialogue provided civil society actors with national media coverage, public recognition and legitimacy as they were negotiating directly with the French Government about its future legislation and policy stance on issues of environmental protection. At the beginning of their negotiations with the Government, civil society actors were rather satisfied and enthusiastic with their political influence, as a Green MP explains:

During the 'Grenelle' the NGOs' were very satisfied. Some propositions were adopted by the 'Grenelle', there was a kind of derision among civil society, saying 'we don't need a political partner anymore, we can discuss directly with the Government'.

(Interview Thirteen)

However, these actors were soon disappointed as they noticed that the French Government did not implement the negotiated recommendations, which were pushed aside by the economic crisis of 2008. As a Green MEP elected in 2009 puts it:

All of those who participated were very enthusiastic, very motivated, they were very engaged in the *Grenelle de l'environnement* [...] and then, well, it was a disappointment to see that finally all the nice speeches, the nice promises of the Government, did not end up with either real concrete measures or strong decisions which are necessary. So these people were disappointed to see that the negotiations with the Government did not bear fruit. I think that also explains why they came into politics.

(Interview Eleven)

During the negotiations and working groups in the *Grenelle* the idea of a new ecological political offer came about. It was a kind of bilateral 'deal' between some representatives and spokespersons of large environmental NGOs and the Green Party in crisis. These individuals launched a professional political career using the organisational resources of the Green Party: the Greens offered these personalities top positions on their list to the coming EP elections, thus guaranteeing them good chances of becoming MEPs. In return, the party highlighted these external candidates as the leaders of a brand new political organisation, *Europe Ecologie*.

The Greens' strategy for the 2009 EP elections

In the 2008 Summer University of the Greens in Toulouse, Daniel Cohn-Bendit proposed to 'open up' the party and build a larger network of support. A Green local official comments:

Cohn-Bendit said we have to get out of the narrow framework of a party which failed in the presidential elections with the worst scores in ages [...]. Because Bové was a candidate, well, we were completely divided [...] so he said we have to bring together supporters beyond the Greens.

(Interview Twelve)

Indeed, to open up the party to new candidates and to attract new voters were the primary objectives of the 2009 EP election campaign. The French Greens ran for these elections with a new strategy and under a new name: *Europe Ecologie*. The French Greens' national leadership used the 2009 EP elections as an opportunity to launch a new political strategy. A key element of this strategy was the renovation of its political offer through the recruitment of external candidates from civil society.

The list of *Europe Ecologie* for the 2009 EP elections was led by three national leaders: Daniel Cohn-Bendit, Eva Joly and José Bové. They were the best known candidates nationally, and became the symbols of political engagement and unity for the French ecologists. As a candidate to the EP explains: 'Having strong personalities such as Cohn-Bendit, José Bové, Eva Joly, those are the most symbolic three, the best known in France, that goes a long way for many of our voters' (Interview Eleven). As a Green local official, who was coordinating the elections campaign in his city, explained (Interview Nine), the Green election result would largely depend on how the voters perceived the three personalities leading the list (and who had a national audience): Daniel Cohn-Bendit, Eva Joly and José Bové.

Daniel Cohn-Bendit is very familiar to the French public. He became famous for his role in the student revolt in Paris in May 1968 and was then expelled from France (during which time he was also known as *Dany le rouge*). He has a unique position, since he holds dual (French and German) citizenship and constantly moves between these two national political arenas. As a prominent leader of the German Greens, he became Vice-Mayor of Frankfurt in 1989. He has been a Green MEP since 1994, and has, by turns, been elected to the EP in France and in Germany. He also led the French Greens' list in the 1999 EP elections, in which they obtained 10 per cent of the vote. The personal charm and charisma of 'Dany', as he is also known, was a main factor of the French Greens' success in the 1999 EP elections (see Boy 1999). Even though measuring the role of a leadership scientifically is a difficult task, Boy observes that 'the oratory qualities of Cohn-Bendit, his capacity to speak in [...] 'ordinary' language or even his informal clothing [and] presentation probably attracted young voters, perhaps beyond the borders of political ecology' (Boy 1999). As a local Green politician put it when discussing the different candidates on the list for the EP elections: 'in any case the voters do not know these people, so they will see Cohn-Bendit and they will vote' (Interview Twelve). French voters seem to approve of 'Dany', a charismatic leader who brings innovative, fresh spirit into the traditional French political scene and enjoys positive coverage in national television. He played a decisive role in the creation of the new list, helped convince the party politicians to share eligible positions with external candidates, and contributed to the reconciliation of the Greens' internal conflicts. He was also instrumental in convincing civil society personalities to join this political adventure under his leadership.

Eva Joly was positioned after Cohn-Bendit in the constituency of the Paris region. As a magistrate, she is known in France for her judgements in the famous trial of the ELF scandal (*l'affaire ELF*) and her strong engagement against corruption in the highest political circles and tax havens. Born in Oslo, Norway, she moved to Paris when she was twenty years old. Like Cohn-Bendit, Joly moves between different national political fields: she has been a special advisor to the Norwegian Government (2002–2005) and to the Icelandic Government (since 2009), following the latter country's financial collapse. Joly launched her professional political career in France by joining the *Europe Ecologie* list for the 2009 EP elections, and later became the Green candidate for the 2012 presidential elections, which illustrates her strong position in the party.

José Bové became France's most famous farmer after his direct action against a McDonald's restaurant in 1999 - a symbolic act of resistance against Genetically Modified Organisms (GMO) and the food industry, for which he served some time in prison. Since this event he has often been present in the French national media and is considered a charismatic spokesperson of the developing alternative global movement (Bourad 2011). Bové is a spokesperson of a farmers' NGO, the *Confédération paysanne,* and was a prominent figure in the campaign against the proposed European constitution in the 2005 referendum. However, his attempt to enter professional politics has been unsuccessful so far: as an independent candidate in the 2007 presidential elections, Bové attained only 1 per cent of the vote. He was elected MEP in the 2009 EP elections.

Other civil society candidates were also positioned high on the list for the 2009 EP elections and were elected as MEPs. MEP Yannick Jadot was the campaign director of *Greenpeace*, an economist who was engaged in international solidarity and north-south relations, especially regarding the situation in Africa. MEP Sandrine Bélier was the director of *France Nature Environnement* (FNE), a national federation of French environmental NGOs. Before that, Bélier had been the regional director of *Alsace Nature*, a large regional NGO. Bélier is a specialist in environmental law and took part in the legislation of the European Directive 'Natura 2000'. MEP Jean-Paul Besset was the spokesperson of *Fondation Nicolas Hulot*, a famous NGO in France founded by Mr Nicolas Hulot, a former television star known in France for his public engagement in environmental protection. Hulot announced he would stand as an independent ecological candidate in the 2007 presidential elections but eventually did not run. Besset's presence on the list permitted the party to use Nicolas Hulot's name in their electoral campaign even though Hulot himself officially kept his distance from the new list. These civil society candidates enabled the Greens to present *Europe Ecologie* to the French public as a political organisation with much larger scope than the original Green Party, *Les Verts.*

In their communication strategy for the 2009 EP elections, the Greens highlighted the external candidates from civil society and their widely respected reputations in non-partisan activities. The Green Party used the labels of the NGOs that these candidates came from, NGOs that seemed to enjoy legitimacy among the French public, such as *Greenpeace, Confédération paysanne, FNE* and *Fondation Nicolas Hulot.*

In contrast to this, the party's own politicians were less visible in the electoral campaign strategy. The party politicians who were elected MEPs in the 2009 EP elections were relatively unknown at the national level and had only a little experience in politics. Hélène Flautre was the only incumbent MEP, elected in 1999. Michèle Rivasi was the only former MP (1997–2002). The other elected MEPs among the party politicians - Pascal Canfin, Nicole Kiil-Nielsen, Catherine Grèze, Malika Benarab-Attou, and Karima Delli - had mostly been engaged in politics at the local level and were relatively unknown to the French public.

The French Greens used the 2009 EP elections to 'open up' a party in decline;

it was an opportunity to recruit external candidates from civil society, and thus to improve the party's public image. Through these elections, the French Greens modified the power relations in national politics, both with their ecological rivals and with the PS.

Modifying the power relations in national politics

The Greens' strategy in the 2009 EP elections led to electoral success. *Europe Ecologie* took 16.28 per cent of the vote (nearly three million votes) in the 2009 EP elections. This equated to fourteen MEPs, the same number of seats as the PS. Subsequently, in the 2010 regional elections, the Greens continued using their new strategy. *Europe Ecologie* attained 12.18 per cent of the vote in the first round, or nearly two and a half million votes.[3] The Greens doubled their power in the regional councils, obtaining fifty-four regional councillors, against only twenty-four in 2008 elections. *Les Verts*, officially founded in 1984, and *Europe Ecologie*, an *ad-hoc* list conceived to compete in the 2009 EP elections, were officially united as a 'new' party named *Europe Ecologie - Les Verts* (EELV) in November 2010. In fact, EELV is not a new political party, but, rather, a transformation of an old one (*see* Barnea and Rahat 2011). In the 2011 partial elections to the French Senate, eleven EELV Senators were elected against only four incumbent Green ones. These eleven MPs established an independent, green parliamentary group for the first time in French history.

The Greens' success in the 2009 EP elections, and other elections that followed, modified their power relations with their rivals in national politics. The aim of the Greens' strategy in the 2009 EP elections was to create a unified force of political ecology in France. According to one Green MEP, the aim of the EP elections was not the EP itself, but 'to appear, to translate politically, in elections, the movement that manifested itself in society' (Interview Fifteen). As this MEP put it: 'The European elections were the first step. The second step is the regional elections' (Interview Fifteen).

The aim of the Greens' strategy and its strong investment in the 2009 EP elections did not concern the party's particular interest in the European level of politics. The idea behind the new list for the EP elections was to launch a new party of political ecology which would be more attractive to voters than the Greens.

A major difficulty for the French Greens throughout the years has been their competition with other ecologists. Through their success in the 2009 EP elections, the French Greens brought rival ecologists in to join them. They have integrated other green politicians, thus obtaining a monopoly on legitimate political ecology representation in French politics.

For instance, Mrs Corinne Lepage, a former Minister of the Environment, created her own independent ecologist party, CAP21, but did not succeed in being

---

3.   Source. Online. Available at: http://www.interieur.gouv.fr/sections/a_votre_service/resultats-elections/RG2010/FE.html (accessed 14 June 2010).

elected as an MEP in 2004. In the 2007 presidential elections she joined François Bayrou, the leader of MoDem, and was elected MEP in 2009 under the MoDem banner. However, Lepage left this party soon after the 2009 EP elections and joined *Europe Ecologie*. Another example is Antoine Waechter, a former leader of the Greens. Waechter had left the Greens in 1994 and created his own party, *Mouvement Ecologique Indépendant* (MEI). In the 1994 EP elections, MEI competed with a separate list, *Génération Ecologie*. Both this and the Green list failed to secure the necessary 5 per cent for getting seats in the EP. In 2009, Waechter negotiated joining Europe Ecologie, but eventually ran separately with MEI and failed to get elected to the EP. Waechter joined *Europe Ecologie* soon afterwards, becoming a regional counsellor in Alsace in the 2010 regional elections. Both Mrs Lepage of CAP21 and Mr Waechter of MEI were ancient rivals of the Greens. Both joined *Europe Ecologie* in the aftermath of the 2009 EP elections.

The main message to the French public was that the new political offer, *Europe Ecologie,* was larger than *Les Verts*, and went beyond the traditional left-right cleavage, as both Lepage and Waechter had criticised the French Greens for being too much of a leftist party. A member of the campaign staff for both the European and the regional elections in the Alsace region comments:

> In Alsace we have an old ecological movement but it is very divided: there was the MEI, *Les Verts*, *Génération Ecologie* [...]. Today through *Europe Ecologie* the big tendencies that had divided political ecology in Alsace are disappearing. *Les Verts,* MEI, maybe CAP21, are coming closer through *Europe Ecologie*.

(Interview Sixteen)

Nicolas Hulot, a prominent figure in political ecology in France, who had kept his distance from the Greens before the EP elections, officially joined EELV in April 2011. He was a candidate for the party's presidency investiture but lost the internal primaries to MEP Eva Joly.

Even more notably, the French Greens used the EP elections in order to modify the power relations with the PS. Daniel Cohn-Bendit had declared that the 2009 EP elections and the first round of the 2010 regional elections were a kind of electoral test of the power of political ecology *vis-à-vis* the PS.[4] He repeated this message in his closing speech at a large public meeting a few days before the regional elections of 2010: 'After the European vote, with the regional elections, we have the possibility to deeply transform the political landscape in France'.[5]

The electoral results since the 2009 EP elections served as a basis for the negotiations between the Greens and the Socialists. These negotiations were concluded in a signed agreement in November 2011 (*see* EELV-PS 2011). The two parties agreed on a common political programme for the years 2012–2017 in the case of a socialist government. But the first practical aspect of this agreement was

---

4.   Television programme 'à vous de juger', *France 2*, 17 September 2009.

5.   Participant observation, Strasbourg, 8 March 2010.

the division of constituencies between the two parties for the 2012 parliamentary elections. This was an attempt to regulate the parties' competition with each other: in sixty-three 'reserved' constituencies, the PS stands behind the Greens' candidate, thus giving them a chance to win a seat in the National Assembly. This arrangement modified, *de facto*, the official electoral rule of the majority vote in parliamentary elections in France. The division of the constituencies was a crucial factor in the Greens' chances of obtaining MPs in the 2012 parliamentary elections due to the electoral rule in these elections – that a majority vote must be achieved in two rounds. In the 2012 parliamentary elections, the party's candidates moved up to the second round in forty constituencies out of 557.[6] EELV won seats for eighteen MPs in the National Assembly, compared to only four incumbent MPs. For the first time in their history, the Greens had established an independent parliamentary group in the Bourbon Palace in Paris, as they passed the threshold of fifteen MPs needed.

In addition, EELV attained two ministries in the PS Government, after François Hollande's victory in the 2012 presidential elections. Pascal Canfin, elected an MEP in 2009, became minister in charge of development, while Cécile Duflot, who had been heavily engaged in the 2009 EP elections as the Greens' general secretary, was nominated Minister of Territorial Equality and Housing.

Conclusions

This chapter analysed EP elections as a 'back door' to politics for emerging parties, taking the case of the Green Party in France's bipartisan system. The French Greens suffer from weak political resources at the national level but this has not affected their standing in EP elections where they often attain good results. As a consequence of this, EP elections are a political opportunity of primary importance for the party. The French Greens used the 2009 EP elections as an opportunity to save the party from crisis by adopting a new strategy: recruiting external candidates from civil society. This use of the EP elections modified the party's power relations within France's national political arena, both with other green politicians and with the socialists.

Also, in the aftermath of the EP elections, the PS, one of the two main parties in the French bipartisan system, made an *ad-hoc* bilateral arrangement with the Greens. This arrangement concerned both policy making at the national level and the electoral competition in the coming parliamentary elections. The actors' newly created institutional setting enabled the Green Party to secure representation in the national parliament and to establish an independent parliamentary group in both the Senate and the National Assembly. In general, then, the presence of the EP facilitates the effective participation of a greater number of political parties in decision making at national level politics. It not only offers a political platform at

---

6. Ministère de l'Intérieur, 'Les résultats des élections'. Online. Available at: http://elections. interieur.gouv.fr/LG2012/FE.html (accessed 10 December 2012).

the supranational level but also provides emerging parties with a new platform to attain influence at the national level.

This case-study demonstrates that the process of European integration has significant effects for parties that are relatively excluded at the national level. The direct elections to the EP provide an additional entry point to politics for emerging actors who seek to break into the national political system. Emerging parties, facing difficult institutional environments at the national level, seize the opportunity to break into the political system through EP elections. This chapter demonstrates the degree to which EP elections and national elections are interconnected. Success in EP elections has significant effects on a party's power structure in domestic politics. Without these elections, these actors might have disappeared altogether as national, independent parties.

Even more notably, EP elections as an additional entry point into politics have effects beyond the emerging party in question. This chapter analysed how an emerging party's success in EP elections triggers a change in different actors' practices, including the most dominant ones nationally. Thus, indirectly, EP elections modify the nature of the political system as a whole. The success of emerging parties in EP elections gives momentum to increasingly pluralist representation and a more open structure of competition in relatively closed national political systems.

This is an indirect consequence of the multilevel character of the interparliamentary field in Europe. The EU level of democratic representation triggers a certain dynamic towards opening up bipartisan closed systems. In this more open multilevel political system, an emerging party can gain representation in the national parliament and the national government, and thus effectively influence decision making at the national level. Hence, the multilevel parliamentary field not only involves the inclusion of national parliaments in EU decision-making, it also affects the inclusiveness of national decision-making and the opportunities for emerging parties to gain access to it. In the EU, as a multilevel polity, states no longer monopolise EU-level policy making, but share their power with a variety of actors at different levels. In the same way, as part of a multilevel parliamentary field, even dominant political parties in closed national political systems tend to lose their absolute monopoly, sharing their power with emerging political parties.

chapter eleven | women in Europe: recruitment, practices and social institutionalisation of the European political field

Willy Beauvallet and Sébastien Michon

Introduction

The EU can be understood as a 'multilevel and multipolar field of power' (Kauppi 2005; Cohen 2012). Given its paradoxical position in the interparliamentary field in Europe, this applies in particular to the EP. On the one hand, the EP represents a central institution with important legislative powers over 'neo-federal' political activities. On the other hand, the EP has a peripheral position in the national political space. Indeed, there is a high level of electoral abstention, political distance to the center of national politics and lack of recognition by national politicians and commentators, such as journalists.

This peripheral position of the EP in the national political realm makes it less attractive to political elites. In turn, it favours a more open recruitment with greater engagement from actors who are less endowed with important political resources. For a growing number of politicians, the EP constitutes an opportunity for professionalisation and acquisition of political capital, especially since the increasing importance of the EP within the EU institutional triangle contributes to giving more value to parliamentary investment. This has led to the emergence of actors who are more directly specialised in European affairs, able to accumulate and concentrate enough internal resources to hold main leadership positions (Beauvallet and Michon 2010). The persistently high turnover of parliamentary personnel, the EP's strong heterogeneity linked to its multinational character and the diverse practical modalities of elections are partly compensated for by internal processes of closure of the space (Verzichelli and Edinger 2005). The clearest manifestation of closure of EP space is the strong specialisation of leadership positions within the EP.

The institutionalisation of the EP should be put into perspective with the emergence of a new category of political specialists. This process is the product of social and political processes, and not the result of ideological choices or a mechanical effect of legal rules (Beauvallet 2007). This applies notably to women who, as we show with the French case, represent a good example of the emergence of a new category of political professionals (Beauvallet and Michon 2008).

The feminisation of the EP has often been emphasised in the literature (Vallance and Davies 1986; Norris and Franklin 1997; Hix and Lord 1997; Bryder 1998; Norris 1999; Mather 2001; Freedman 2002). However, gender is seldom considered in relation to the EP's composition, for instance, in terms of political qualifications. Indeed, studies on gender differences in political personnel also need to focus on social and political properties (Kauppi 1999; Achin *et al.* 2007). Who are the women members of the EP (MEPs)? What are their social and political features, their former career paths, and their professional expertise? Does nationality influence these issues? Do women in the EP differ from men in their practices, involvements, and internal and external network positions? These questions have to be appreciated in the configuration formed by all MEPs, within the context of the institutionalisation of the EP, which changes according to different variables (political positioning, nationality, time, etc.) (Elias 1991; Georgakakis and Weisbein 2010). These questions are also related to the nature of political patterns and forms of interaction across levels, which is the specific theme of this book.

This chapter shows that MEP feminisation is an important aspect of the emergence of the EP as a space of political professionalisation and that this situation implies various consequences for practices inside and outside the institution. By political professionalisation, we mean the process by which an actor lives 'for' and 'of' political activity, as Max Weber said. It means that this actor gives most of his time for political activity and that political activity gives to him/her the most important part of his/her salary. In the sense of Pierre Bourdieu (1998), structures of social and political properties and resources can help us to understand the practices of political agents in European political arenas and institutions (Georgakakis 2009; Cohen 2012). The comparison between women and men underlines that women generally possess fewer properties that lead to political professionalisation - notably less political experience at the national level - than their male counterparts. For women, internal and external networks represent important opportunities for acquiring political resources (particularly informational) which compensate for their lack of experience and allow them to play the European political game. Women's participation in these networks favours permanent mediations between the EP and national political spaces.

This chapter consists of four main parts. First, we carry out a historical comparison of MEPs, focusing on the evolution of recruitment patterns. MEPs' profiles evolve: the analysis bears out the emergence of a new type of recruitment in which the ratio of women increases, in contrast to what occurs in most member states. Second, we compare the features of men and women elected to the EP. We try to explain the differences between national delegations, particularly between the 'old' countries and the 'new' countries that acceded to the EU in 2004 and 2007, respectively. Third, we focus on a more qualitative analysis and compare the women MEPs' involvements and practices with those of men. Finally, we explore how female MEPs' relatively low level of political resources leads them to a high degree of involvement inside the assembly and to the development of external political links.

The analysis is based on quantitative data, drawing on the biographies of the members of the sixth EP (2004–2009) using the EP website's 'Your MEPs' section and biographical dictionaries. There are indicators related to socio-demographical properties (gender, age, level and type of degree); dispositions for internationalisation (foreign degrees); political paths (types of mandates, career features); and professional careers (former profession). In addition to this, involvement in the European assembly includes: committees on which they sit; number of mandates and years in the EP; leadership positions (presidencies and vice-presidencies of committees, groups, membership in the Bureau, presidencies of delegations); number of reports; interventions in plenary sessions; questions asked; propositions of resolutions; and written statements, all over a three-year period (between June 2004 and June 2007).[1] Given the strategies of self-presentation used for part of this data, information was double-checked, notably via the Internet. Semi-directed interviews constitute another type of data. Those carried out with MEPs provide essential information and a first-hand approach. However, aside from the difficulties in securing appointments, it is hard to get MEPs to put aside their role of representative and to obtain a 'non-formatted' discourse. In this respect, the staff – parliamentary assistants – are useful for giving other information on the practices of MEPs and their staff. This work is also based on more than one hundred and fifty interviews with MEPs and personal parliamentary assistants of the fifth (1999–2004) and the sixth (2004–2009) term (realised during our research) of the EP.

Transformation and specialisation of MEP recruitment

In the 1980s, MEPs were mostly experienced political professionals (actual or ex-members of national parliaments). In the 1990s, the EP favoured the political professionalisation of actors with less political experience, such as local councillors or people with professional experience (business, art, sport, etc) but without political experience. There had therefore been an incumbency effect in MEPs' profiles and a convergence of their political and socio-demographic characteristics beyond national differences. There is also a Europeanisation of the selection processes, i.e. the emergence of explicit and codified norms, which apply to various national contexts. The gaps between MEPs from countries of the 2004 enlargement and the others confirm this early conclusion: the former, recently subjected to European regulations, resemble the characteristics of the majority of MEPs in the 1980s. The EP is increasingly considered as a political professionalisation area for a predominantly middle-aged intellectual elite, partly internationalised and feminised. Various elements illustrate this structural evolution, from a political and a sociological point of view.

First, mandates in the EP have become increasingly stable and durable: during the fifth term (1999–2004) less than 15 per cent of MEPs resigned during their mandate (and 24 per cent under the first term), and close to one out of two MEPs was re-elected (Bryder 1998; Corbett *et al.* 2000). From the fifteen pre-2004 EU member countries, 56 per cent of the MEPs in the sixth term (2004–2009) have already been MEPs (43 per cent in total). It is only since the third term (1989–1994)

---

1. Elements. Online. Available: http://www. europarl.europa.eu (accessed 1 August 2007).

that MEPs started joining the EP for longer periods (Marrel and Payre 2006). Halfway through the sixth term, the MEPs from the fifteen pre-2004 EU member countries had 7.5 years of experience each and, on average, 2 mandates (see Table 11.2).

In the 1980s, MEPs often had substantial political experience at the national level. By contrast, in the 1990s – and regardless of the country – the EP was more often a first substantial mandate (after a subnational mandate) or a first mandate (more than 40 per cent in the sixth term). A progressive differentiation in the paths to Europe can thus be observed: MEPs more rarely have national parliamentary and government experience. For instance, 45 per cent of MEPs from the first term had already been Members of Parliament in their home country, this dropped to 35 per cent for the second term, and was only 28 per cent by the fifth. If these proportions increased in 2004 (39 per cent were former MPs), it was largely because the MEPs from 2004 and 2007 enlargement countries tended to come from the centre of national political fields. As a matter of fact, as for the fifteen pre-2004 EU member countries, percentages are rather similar to those of the fifth EP term (31 per cent) (Table 11.1). MEPs with substantial political experience at national level tend to be older men, mostly from right-wing parties and from countries of the 2004 enlargement. Thus, 42.5 per cent of men have previously been elected in one of the national parliaments (against 32.5 per cent of women) and 18.5 per cent have occupied governmental positions (12 per cent of women).

Variations between national delegations tend otherwise to decrease: over time we see an overarching pattern emerging. This reality is more apparent within major delegations whose number of MEPs easily allows statistically significant historical comparisons. For example, between 1979 and 1994, 58 per cent of Britons and 43 per cent of Germans accumulated up to 7.5 years of presence at the EP against 25 per cent of French and 28 per cent of Italians (Scarrow 1997). In the sixth term, it is still the Germans and the British who have the longest seniority: during the 2004 elections, more than two German MEPs, and three or (close to) four out of five British are re-elected; they have on average 2.4 and 2.3 mandates per MEP against 2.0 for the French, 1.8 for the Italians, 1.4 for the Portuguese, 1.4 for the Swedes and 1.3 for the Greeks (Table 11.2). But this pattern also increasingly affects, for instance, the French (who went from 31 per cent of re-elected MEPs in 1999 to 45 per cent in 2004).

Second, the professional backgrounds tend to match those of the (national) politicians in general (Best and Cotta 2004). MEPs have a middle-class profile, with a predominance of lawyers and other academics (Norris and Franklin 1997; Hix and Lord 1997). The predominance of lawyers is significant in the European political space as it has historically been based on law and acquired more general expert competence (Vauchez 2008). The high level of degrees held by MEPs confirms their intellectual profile: in the sixth term, more than 80 per cent have a university degree, and 27 per cent have completed a PhD (Table 11.3). Better qualified MEPs from acceding countries have more often studied economics, science and technology and health, rather than law and humanities. They have held more positions in scientific professions and have been senior officials or diplomats.

Table 11.1: Proportions of sixth term MEPs having previously exercised a national mandate or having been a member of government, according to country of election

Country of election	National Parliament	Former members of Government
France	26 %	18 %
Germany	14 %	0 %
Italy	31 %	12 %
Belgium	42 %	33 %
Netherlands	7 %	0 %
Luxembourg	67 %	67 %
United Kingdom	16 %	5 %
Ireland	69 %	46 %
Denmark	42 %	8 %
Spain	43 %	9 %
Portugal	71 %	38 %
Greece	25 %	17 %
Sweden	50 %	5 %
Finland	77 %	31 %
Austria	44 %	6 %
Hungary	46 %	29 %
Slovakia	77 %	31 %
Poland	49 %	22 %
Czech Republic	50 %	13 %
Lithuania	54 %	31 %
Estonia	83 %	50 %
Latvia	100 %	78 %
Slovenia	57 %	43 %
Malta	20 %	20 %
Cyprus	67 %	17 %
Romania	100 %	24 %
Bulgaria	40 %	20 %
Total	**39 %**	**16 %**
(First EU 15 only)	(31%)	(12%)

Table 11.2: Indicators of seniority in the EP, according to country of election of the sixth term MEPs (in decreasing order)

Country of election	Total number of MEPs	Average number of mandates in the EP	Average number of years in the EP (in 2007)
Germany	99	2.4	10
United Kingdom	78	2.3	9.2
Austria	18	2.2	7.9
Belgium	24	2.0	7.3
France	78	2.0	7.4
Luxembourg	6	2.0	7.1
Denmark	14	1.9	7.3
Spain	54	1.9	7.3
Finland	14	1.9	6.7
Italy	78	1.8	6.7
Netherlands	27	1.8	6.7
Ireland	13	1.5	4.9
Portugal	24	1.4	4.8
Sweden	19	1.4	4.7
Greece	24	1.3	4.5
Cyprus	6	1.0	3
Estonia	6	1.0	3
Hungary	24	1.0	3
Latvia	9	1.0	3
Lithuania	13	1.0	3
Malta	5	1.0	3
Poland	54	1.0	3
Czech Republic	24	1.0	3
Slovakia	14	1.0	3
Slovenia	7	1.0	3
Bulgaria	18	1	0.5
Romania	35	1	0.5
Total	**785**	**1.7**	**6.1**
(First EU 15 only)		(2.0)	(7.5)

Table 11.3: Distribution of occupation and degree level of sixth term MEPs

	Total		First EU 15		Acceding countries	
	Number of MEPs	%	Number of MEPs	%	Number of MEPs	%
Farmer	12	2	10	2	2	1
Craftsman/retailer	7	1	7	1	0	0
Company manager	45	6	34	6	11	5
Liberal profession	71	9	51	9	20	9
High official/diplomat	49	6	29	5	20	9
Scientific profession	141	18	72	13	69	32
Primary/secondary teacher	61	8	51	9	10	5
Senior executive – public sector	40	5	30	5	10	5
Information/ communication/arts	84	11	59	10	25	12
Senior executive – private sector	92	12	67	12	25	12
Intermediary profession	36	5	35	6	1	0
Employee/worker	17	2	17	3	0	0
N/A	130	18	108	19	22	10
Total	**785**	**100**	**570**	**100**	**215**	**100**
Degree level:						
High school or lower	50	6	48	8	2	1
University (lower than PhD)	424	54	332	58	92	43
Doctorate	212	27	113	20	99	46
N/A	99	13	77	14	22	10
Total	**785**	**100**	**570**	**100**	**215**	**100**
Degree in:						
Law	158	20	128	22	30	14
Political science	55	7	42	7	13	6
Economics	106	14	63	11	43	20
Humanities	192	24	151	26	41	19
Science and technology	90	11	48	8	42	20
Health	39	5	18	3	21	10
N/A	145	18	120	21	25	12
Total	**785**	**100**	**570**	**100**	**215**	**100**

Because of the internationalisation of elites and academic job markets (Wagner 1998), MEPs have increasingly international profiles. Of the sixth EP term, 12 per cent of MEPs have attained a degree in a country other than their own (in Europe, the USA or even Russia for some Eastern European MEPs). Many of these MEPs come from countries with a more peripheral position in the EU: Hungary, the Czech Republic, Malta, Portugal and Greece. Going across borders and attending reputable schools in Europe or the United States allows elites from 'small' countries to receive the same training as future elites from 'big' countries, and therefore to be able to acquire resources that can be converted at the national or European level.

In terms of age, European representatives do not differ from other political professions, most of them being middle-aged (Best and Cotta 2004). In 2007, their mean age rose to 53.8 years (standard deviation of 10.1 years) – the oldest being eighty-three and the youngest, twenty-four; the modal age class was between fifty and sixty (40 per cent of MEPs). In fact, in 1979, European political personnel were older: the figure of the 'end-of-career' MEP was a prevalent one. During the late 1990s, it was the opposite: the majority of MEPs (73 per cent) was aged between forty and sixty, and only 14 per cent of the total were under the age of forty, while 13 per cent were over sixty (Hix and Lord 1997). Generally speaking, those who are slightly younger are MEPs from left wing political groups (51.7 years for the Greens/EFA, against 54.6 years for the EPP, 57.1 years for the ID (Independence/Democracy Group), and women (51.6 years against 54.8 years)).

The proportion of women is higher than in most national parliaments and has doubled between the first and the last two parliamentary terms: 16 per cent in 1979, 30 per cent in both 1999 and 2004, and 35 per cent in 2009. Whereas the EP is one of the most feminised parliaments in Europe, it has not yet achieved parity. Major variations remain between countries, indicating differences between national political spaces. There are fewer women amongst MEPs from Cyprus, Malta, Poland, Italy, the Czech Republic and Latvia (Table 11.4). Sweden is the only country where the number of women is the same as that of men. There are more than 40 per cent of women MEPs from the Netherlands, Denmark, Estonia, Romania, Slovenia and France. All in all, the proportion of women MEPs from countries of the 2004 and 2007 enlargements is somewhat lower than from the fifteen pre-2004 EU member countries (28 per cent against 32 per cent, respectively). However, the proportion of women in the EP turns out to be higher than in national parliaments. Data suggest that the EP provides an opportunity for political professionalisation for actors whose sociopolitical profiles are less favourable to political competition in national political spaces (Beauvallet and Michon 2008).

Table 11.4: Gender distribution depending on country of election of the sixth term MEPs (ranked in descending order of % of women)

Country of election	Men %	Women %
Sweden	47	53
Estonia	50	50
Netherlands	56	44
Bulgaria	56	44
Denmark	57	43
Slovenia	57	43
France	58	42
Ireland	62	38
Lithuania	62	38
Hungary	67	38
Finland	64	36
Slovakia	64	36
Romania	66	34
Austria	67	33
Spain	67	33
Luxembourg	67	33
Germany	68	32
Greece	71	29
United Kingdom	74	26
Belgium	75	25
Portugal	75	25
Latvia	78	22
Czech Republic	79	21
Italy	81	19
Poland	85	15
Cyprus	100	0
Malta	100	0
Total	**69**	**31**

Distinctive features of EP feminisation

In the EP, women MEPs distinguish themselves in two ways: first, their social and political backgrounds are less favorable to the exercise of a political mandate; and second, their involvement in parliamentary activity is quite differentiated. These differences are tied to their distinctive political and social resources.

The feminisation of European political personnel was, from its early stages, spurred by left wing parties (Norris and Franklin 1997). In the French delegation in 1979, women represented more than 22 per cent of socialist and communist MEPs. Since then, the feminisation rate of green, socialist and communist personnel has continually increased: 26.5 per cent in 1984, 32 per cent in 1989, 42 per cent in 1994, and 49 per cent in 1999. The feminisation of right-wing MEPs occurred much later and in a more random way. From 18 per cent in the first legislature, the rate dropped to 14.5 per cent during the second, and to below 12 per cent in the third. It progressed again after 1994 (16 per cent) and reached more than 31 per cent between 1999 and 2004, progressively attaining levels characteristic of left wing parties. There are more women in central left groups – 40 per cent for the PES, 47 per cent for the Greens/EFA (Greens/European Free Alliance) – than in the GUE/NGL (31 per cent), EPP (24 per cent) and, especially, ID (Independence/Democracy), UEN and non-attached (between 11 per cent and 16 per cent).

In contrast with the traditional weakness of female representation in political institutions – barring a few exceptions such as Sweden – the high proportion of women elected in the EP raises questions about the mechanisms of selection and recruitment of MEPs. Unlike in other assemblies, gender constitutes a positive and distinctive social property in the EP. Younger than men and endowed with less social resources, women MEPs also have less political responsibilities, notably among the most prestigious. These variations should be qualified for MEPs from countries of the 2004 enlargement.

On the whole, women MEPs do not distinguish themselves from the national political elites in this respect (Best and Cotta 2004); they mostly belong to the upper social tiers. Compared to men, women are less often company managers (3 to 9 per cent), high officials (4 to 9 per cent) or practising a profession as lawyers or doctors (7 to 12 per cent); they are more frequently teachers in primary or secondary schools (14 to 7 per cent), employees (4 to 1 per cent), with an intermediary profession (8 to 4 per cent) or a profession in information, communication or the arts (e.g. journalist, television presenter) (15 to 12 per cent) (Table 11.5). An examination of paths and educational properties leads to similar conclusions: female MEPs have less educational resources than their male counterparts. Despite the significant proportion of academic paths (more in political science and the human sciences than law, economy, health, science and technology), they have less educational capital than men. They have fewer PhDs (24 to 29 per cent) and are less likely to have completed five years of higher education (55.5 to 61 per cent), more often having studied at that level for three or four years. Once again, female MEPs from countries of the 2004 and 2007

Table 11.5: Distribution of occupation and degree level of the sixth term MEPs according to gender

	Total %	Men %	Women %
Farmer	2	1.5	0.5
Craftsman/retailer	1	1	0.5
Company manager	6	7	2
Liberal profession	9	10	7
High official/diplomat	6	7	4
Scientific profession	18	18	17
Primary or secondary school teacher	8	6	12
Senior executive – public sector	5	5	7
Information/communication/arts	11	10	12
Senior executive – private sector	12	11	13
Intermediary profession	5	4	7
Employee/worker	2	2	4
N/A	18	18	15
Total	**100**	**100**	**100**
Degree level:			
High school or lower	6	7	5
University (lower than PhD)	54	52	60
Doctorate	27	28	24
N/A	13	13	11
Total	**100**	**100**	**100**
Degree in:			
Law	20	21	17
Political science	7	7	8
Economics	14	14	12
Humanities	24	20	34
Science and technology	11	13	9
Health	5	6	3
N/A	18	19	17
Total	**100**	**100**	**100**

enlargements are an exception as they have higher degrees than their female and male counterparts in the fifteen pre-2004 EU member countries, as well as than their male counterparts from the new member states: 50 per cent of the women have PhDs – 16 per cent of women and 22 per cent of men from the pre-2004 members, 48 per cent of men from the new member states; 85.5 per cent of women have completed five or more years of higher education – respectively 45 per cent, 53 per cent and 79.5 per cent for the others.

Political paths are also divided along gender lines. Women MEPs are endowed with less symbolic properties, such as awards and distinctions at the international or national level, or those related to specific sectors (academic, professional, etc.) (18 to 26 per cent). They are also endowed with less political capital. Upon their entrance in the EP, women's political careers, both national and local, are shorter than men's. The case of French women illustrates this particularly well: 4 per cent of women MEPs have a national career of more than 15 years, with the figure standing at 19 per cent for their male counterparts; 15 per cent have a local career of more than 15 years, against 28 per cent for the men. Women MEPs have less frequently held a government function (12 per cent, against 18 per cent for their male counterparts), have less national parliamentary experience (32.5 per cent against 42.5 per cent of men) and local political experience (52 per cent, against 64 per cent). Women came to politics more often through positions as political collaborators (27.5 per cent, in contrast to 16.5 per cent of men) and associations (36 per cent, against 28 per cent of men). The right/left divide is not very relevant for social and educational properties but is more so in terms of political background. Right-wing women MEPs have more frequently been ministers (15 per cent, against 7.5 per cent left-wing) and members of national parliaments (33 per cent, compared to 29 per cent of men).

The distribution of former mandates, modes of accession to political careers and symbolic properties thus point to a differentiation along gender lines: women have less political capital. For women, the European mandate in itself more often represents an opportunity for political professionalisation. But once again, this observation should not be generalised too quickly. Women MEPs from the twelve countries of the 2004 and the 2007 enlargements distinguish themselves with more experience, including than the men from the pre-2004 members: 22.5 per cent of women MEPs from the twelve countries of the latest enlargements have been ministers – as compared to 9 per cent of the women from the pre-2004 members (respectively, 29 per cent and 14 per cent of the men); 48 per cent have been members of national parliaments – as compared to 27.5 per cent of women MEPs from the fifteen members before the 2004 enlargement (respectively, 67.5 per cent and 32 per cent of the men). While they are endowed with less of the most prestigious political resources than their male counterparts from new member states, they still have more resources than women MEPs from the pre-2004 members.

This comparison of the social and political properties of MEPs therefore suggests that Europe is a key space for the promotion, political involvement, and strengthening of the place of women in political life. Interviews and observations of women MEPs in the assembly enable us to continue the reflection on the modalities of their election, and to stress the social logics of involvement in the mandate and the construction of European parliamentary roles.

Practices of women MEPs in the EP: Eagerness to get involved in parliamentary activity

The study of the modes of female recruitment in the EP shows a relative weakness in their resources (social as well as cultural, notably educational or political), which distinguishes them from their male counterparts. To compensate for this less favourable social and political resource structure, many female MEPs tend to invest much in the EP and to conform as much as possible to the dominant role conception of their position. The dispositions of such MEPs, regardless of their political group (Aline Pailler, Françoise Grossetête and Marie-Claude Vayssade being French examples), are characterised by a form of 'goodwill' towards the institution and the roles that are prescribed within it. With fewer political resources, less familiarity (through their political and social paths) with the workings of political spaces and the know-how of professionals of representation, numerous women MEPs claim to be 'hard workers', even 'industrious', and almost like 'students' (for an analogical perspective on the social field, *see* Bourdieu 1984). They frequently emphasise the very 'time-consuming' aspect of their work, as in this example:

> When you arrive here, you have a lot of things to discover. You can't arrive thinking that you'll be familiar with everything right away. And you need to make your mark, the French don't always have [a] reputation [for being] hard workers, so on top of everything you need to make your mark by working hard. Here, if you work, there is no problem [...] I've worked an awful lot, for sure, I've worked very, very much. But I like what I do. I never pause to catch my breath all year, I never stop, I work all the time.[2]

Depending on their personal or political interests, such involvement can be embedded in highly diverse domains, and within different committees. Indeed, these forms of devotion to the institution and the over-involvement in their roles exhibited by newcomers in the political field offer the possibility to disassociate themselves from a sometimes fragile position in the political field, and comes with prospects of recognition and access to positions of leadership (i.e. vice-president of a group, a position held by Françoise Grossetête before 2004, and, as with Nicole Fontaine during the fifth legislature, the presidency of the EP). It also leads to the acquisition of political credit specific to the European institution, which can be reconverted in the national political field, at least insofar as it contributes to the renewal of the mandate. As long as the resources acquired within the institution can be reinvested in the party organisations, the European parliamentary space can provide an alternative path of political professionalisation.

The political approach of many women thus appears highly entrepreneurial in relation to social spaces outside the political field, as well as to the EP where involvements are intense. Given their political and social properties, women tend to join secondary committees, which are not the most important ones from the

---

2. Interview with a female MEP in 1998.

perspective of the traditional political hierarchy. These committees are, however, still liable to confer important gains in political capital, notably within the assembly itself. Along with the emergence of a European space of public policies, as well as the succession of treaties and the establishment of new legislative procedures, the Parliament's place in European policy-making has been strengthened together with the centrality of committees such as environment, public health and consumer policy, industry, foreign trade, research and energy, and internal market (Costa 2001). Co-decision procedures apply to these committees, providing strong margins of influence on policy making. These committees constitute areas of activities in which to invest intellectual resources and sociopolitical dispositions for political involvement with high chances of success. Indeed, they provide the possibility to follow issues and draft highly 'technical' reports; they occupy a valorised place in the institution's internal hierarchy.[3] Therefore, with the intensification of the European construction, from 1986 and especially 1992 onwards, opportunities to acquire a new type of political capital emerged for actors who were socially and politically inclined to 'play the game' and to be intensely involved, among which there were many women (Beauvallet 2007).

De facto, while men and women are not differentiated according to the average number of EP mandates (1.71 versus 1.705 year), this does not apply for the allocation of parliamentary committees, the positions of power within the assembly or legislative activity. In the sixth legislature, women MEPs are over-represented in committees that may be less prestigious, even if they are at the core of European legislative activity. These committees are: Internal Market (49 per cent of women – as compared to 31 per cent in the entire assembly), Environment, Public Health and Consumer Policy (48 per cent), Culture, Youth, Education, Media and Sport (46 per cent) and Civil Liberties (38 per cent). Conversely, they are under-represented in the most prestigious committees, where the MEPs endowed with the most political capital sit: Constitutional Affairs (16 per cent are women), Foreign Affairs (18 per cent), Economics and Monetary Affairs (27 per cent). Beyond sporting a prestigious name, it should be added that, in fact, some of these committees are, or were, less central in European political and legislative activity because, for example, their realm of action was not regulated by co-decision and they exerted very little influence on the key aspects of decisions.

The parliamentary practices of women MEPs thus cannot be understood outside of their social and political properties. More than a characteristic of femininity in politics, as some suggest, the forms of involvement in Europe should rather be related to the specificities of their political recruitment. The modes of involvement and modalities of appropriation of the mandate by women MEPs are not uniform. Indeed, women MEPs whose political paths are directly focused towards the centre of the political field (former ministers or national members of parliament, considered and considering themselves first and foremost as 'national'

---

3. On the role of the EP and the committee on Budgetary Control in the crisis of the Commission in 1998–1999, *see* Georgakakis 2004.

representatives) and who are generally waiting for a position in their national parliament or in the government, are not greatly involved in the EP. Entering the EP remains, for them, a secondary stage (the case of French MEP Roselyne Bachelot is interesting: she left the government in 2004, then entered the EP but left it before the term of her mandate expired in 2007 because she was elected to the French Parliament and nominated Health Minister). In the case of women with national political experience, the duration of the European mandate is generally short, from a few months to a few years, and resignations during the mandate are frequent following a national election or appointment to government (for example, Emma Bonino in 2006). Their effective presence in the EP is also more episodic, and their parliamentary activity often limited to votes in plenary sessions. The concrete practices of those women MEPs tend to be assimilated to dilettantism and are often denounced by the more involved women MEPs – a very similar process happens for men.

Otherwise, the fact remains – and this should be emphasised – that mechanisms of sexual discrimination specific to political life do not disappear within the EP regarding access to internal rewards in the institution, notably positions of power (presidency, vice-presidency of committees, groups, membership of the Bureau). According to our calculations for MEPs in the sixth term, women have less often held leadership positions than men (22 per cent of women in contrast to 28 per cent of men), be it as a member of the bureau (3.5 per cent *versus* 4.5 per cent), president of a group (1 per cent of the women MEPs, 2 per cent of the male MEPs), president of a committee (2.5 per cent, as compared to 5 per cent of the male MEPs), vice-president of a committee (12.5 per cent and 17 per cent, respectively). Whereas gender inequalities tend to decrease in the access to the EP, as the strong feminisation of certain delegations compared to the trends in national assemblies demonstrates, they tend to reappear within the institution itself (Kauppi 1999). These variations also illustrate the limits of legislative action in favour of the promotion of gender equality at all levels of political action. In this respect, we can suppose that the promotion of gender equality on the European political market partly reflects its instrumentalisation for electoral reasons by party organisations.

The effect of the differential distribution of political capital between men and women should not be overlooked either, as the distribution of the number of parliamentary reports tends to indicate. On the whole, men have drafted slightly more parliamentary reports (1.79) than women (1.74) despite similar lengths of mandate; women MEPs from new member countries who are endowed with more educational and political resources than their counterparts from the fifteen pre-2004 EU members countries have drafted an average of 1.28 reports – the figure is 0.90 for their male counterparts (1.85 for women from the Fifteen, 2.05 for men from the Fifteen). Thus, the analysis of the differences between men and women requires going beyond the gender variable and taking into account the related effects of political background.

Internal and external networks as opportunities for acquiring political resources

Political exchanges with non-institutional actors and even non-European actors increase over time. Although not specific to women, this fact is particularly apparent in their case, because the structures of these practices can be related to the structure of their social and political properties and resources. These exchanges are associated with a low level of political resources, albeit a high level of political entrepreneurship, and can take different forms.

The first form corresponds to information searches, political goods or political services offered in exchange for political support. Information is necessary to ensure parliamentary work, especially given the high level of expertise in the Commission or even in the Council and national administrations. This demand of expertise has increased over time, as the position of MEPs in the legislative process and in the European political game has become increasingly important. In this context, interests groups can provide very important resources to MEPs. They offer them counter-expertise or, perhaps more fundamentally, favour a better understanding of the political game, allowing MEPs to identify their rivals/partners' positions, to anticipate the immediate future, and so on. In other words, interest groups make political activities easier for MEPs, especially in a field of power that is less structured than in the national context, and one that is probably also more competitive (Bouwen 2004; Haroche 2009; Beauvallet 2010). As Jean-Louis Bourlanges, a French MEP elected between 1989 and 2009, once said, interest groups enable MEPs to avoid staying in 'weightlessness' on the European political planet. At the same time, MEPs can deliver important information regarding European legislative activities and provide interest groups with political access to the European decision-making field. Various examples show that, especially when they have less political capital or credibility, like women, MEPs make important use of this register of action because in this way they are able to reinforce social links and their level of political capital.

The second form of exchanges corresponds to the political links with national political parties and leaders. On the one hand, parliamentary professionalisation increases MEPs' autonomy. On the other hand, especially for women, transformations of social and political profiles generate more reliance on political parties and political leaders: many women are indeed younger and have acquired less political resources. Thus, they rely more on these national networks for the promotion of their career. Aware of this situation, they pay more attention to partisan structures, leaders and active members, in local as well as national contexts. This situation produces contradictory movements. In many cases, national political leaders control access to electoral lists. National political parties control MEPs who tend to vote less according to the European group than to the national delegation (Hix 2002). As the groups remain important spaces for political action and promotion in the EP, MEPs are, in fact, forced to play different games (national and European). Consequently, we observe a permanent work of political translation or reformulation from the European to the national game.

Contradictions between national and European political games are sometimes difficult to avoid, especially when tensions between both are strong, as in periods of high political conflict. The case of Pervenche Bérès, a member of the EP since 1994, is a good example of these difficulties. Bérès came to the EP with few national political resources: she had never been a member of a government, a Member of Parliament or a mayor. However, she became chairwoman of the EP's Employment and Social Affairs Committee (1999–2004) and head of the French socialist delegation (1997–2004). She was considered an important and recognised MEP and member of the new Progressive Alliance of Socialists and Democrats (PASD) Group. As a delegate for this group to the Convention on the future of Europe, she participated in writing the Treaty establishing a Constitution for Europe, signed on 29 October 2004. However, she declared herself against this document during the French ratification campaign. The reason was quite simple: she had to follow the position taken by Laurent Fabius, an important leader of the French Socialist Party (PS). The logic of this position was based on national concerns rather than on European stakes. For Fabius, the purpose was to challenge the general secretary of the party, François Hollande, who supported the treaty. Fabius followed this strategy in order to impose himself as the best socialist candidate for the next (2007) presidential election. Pervenche Bérès was close to Fabius, since she was his assistant when he was Chairman of the national parliament at the beginning of the nineties. Therefore, she relied on Fabius for her election and for her political career. Thus, she had to follow his position, even if this decision was completely unacceptable for other European socialists, and despite the fact that this decision had very negative consequences for her immediate position in the parliamentary group. Indeed, her position during the French campaign prevented (and still prevents) her from becoming president of the European Socialist Group or to be this group's candidate for EP president. These facts illustrate everyday links between European and national political fields. They are mainly informal and specific to relationships inside political parties.

Conclusion

The role of women MEPs provides a good illustration of the logic of the social institutionalisation of the European political field in general and of the interparliamentary field in particular. Our results indicate that women actively participate in developing social and political networks with actors from the European political space and from national political spaces. According to our analysis, such behavior is a consequence of their significant investment in the EP. This investment is linked to women-specific social and political trajectories and the structure and distribution of resources.

The study shows that, for women, Europe constitutes a privileged space of involvement and the acquisition of political resources. The weaker involvement in European levels by actors endowed with strong political capital, together with the widening of the EP's competences, create a structure of opportunities for representatives who access political professionalisation through the EP (including many women). Overall, women take advantage of the EP's lower centrality in the political field in order to circumvent the resistance they encounter to their being elected in national elections. At the level of EP elections, gender is a positive characteristic in political competition. Indeed, women access the European parliamentary arena more easily than men. The case of women in the EP also shows the effects that the emergence of a European level of electoral representation has on various political spheres. For many women, entering the EP represents a genuine opportunity for the advancement and acceleration of a political career otherwise subjected to strong constraints in their respective countries. The involvement of women members in the EP contributes to the development of the institution and to political exchanges with non-institutional actors and non-European political actors. Women's participation in these networks favours exchanges between the EP, the European political space and national political spaces, and thus furthers the EP's institutionalisation.

part iv. beyond the EU

chapter twelve | who is coming? attendance patterns in the NATO and WEU parliamentary assemblies*

Wolfgang Wagner

Introduction

For parliamentarians, meeting with colleagues from other countries has become a firmly established part of their work. Indeed, the number of parliamentary assemblies (PAs), i.e. 'transnational, multilateral actors which are constituted by groups of members of national parliaments' (Marschall 2005, my translation), has risen from one, in the late nineteenth century, to seven in the wake of WW II and forty-five in the 2000s (Marschall 2005). In addition, delegations from national parliaments regularly meet in various *ad-hoc* formats and bilateral settings. Network density of interparliamentary cooperation reaches its highest level among the parliaments of the EU's member countries.[1] Since 1989, the EACs met every six months in the form of COSAC. In addition, some parliamentary committees, e.g. on security and defence or JHA, have been meeting with their counterparts in national as well as in the EP at regular intervals.

At the same time, however, such transnational activities of parliamentarians have become the object of fierce criticism. Costs for translation, travel, accommodation, security and social programmes seem significant, especially in times of financial crisis and tight budgets. MPs report that they are under mounting pressure to justify travel to PA meetings which frequently take place in attractive locations, with critics claiming that the meetings are mainly for pleasure. Moreover, critics claim, the benefits of interparliamentary cooperation remain dubious. In particular, parliamentary assemblies are criticised for lacking real powers. For example, Uwe Jun and Ernst Kuper (1997) criticised the Western European Union's PA for having no independent decision-making competence and, in contrast to the EP's motion of censure,[2] for having no influence on the composition of the Council of

---

* This chapter emanates from RECON, an integrated project supported by the European Commission's Sixth Framework Programme (contract no. CIT4-CT-2006–028698). I would like to thank Salima Chebrek and Michael Hilger for providing data on attendance in Parliamentary Assemblies. Moreover, I am grateful to Stefan Marschall and Dirk Peters for valuable comments and suggestions and to Sjirk Prins and Michal Onderço for research assistance.

1. For an overview of these forms in Western Europe see Neunreiter 2005. *See also* Beisheim and Brunnengräber 2008.

2. According to Art 17 (8) TEU-L, 'European Parliament may vote on a motion of censure of the Commission. If such a motion is carried, the members of the Commission shall resign as a body

the WEU. In a similar vein, Nicolai von Onderza (2010) argued that the WEU-PA never managed to go beyond symbolic retrospective commentary of European security policies (*see also* Marschall 2008). To critics, therefore, PAs appear as useless talking shops. In 2010, such concerns were instrumental in deciding to dissolve the Western European Union's Parliamentary Assembly.[3]

However, the assumption that the value of parliamentary assemblies is best judged by assessing their decision–making powers is questionable, if not misleading. Historically, the main rationale for establishing parliamentary assemblies has been to foster close contacts between the political elites of countries in order to enhance mutual understanding and to avoid the escalation of conflicts into war. For this reason, no less than five Nobel Peace Prizes went to the pioneers of interparliamentary cooperation.[4] From the perspective of deliberative democratic theory, parliamentary assemblies contribute to a transnational public sphere (Blichner 2000). From this perspective, the lack of decision-making powers may even be an advantage: according to Lars Blichner,

> democratic legitimacy at the EU level is dependent on arenas where it is possible to talk relatively unrestrained by strategic considerations pertaining to national or party interests, interests which may be activated as soon as a concrete decision has to be taken.

> (Blichner 2000)

Parliamentary assemblies may serve as such a sorely needed public sphere (Blichner 2000).

In this chapter, I will focus on yet another function of parliamentary assemblies by treating them as instruments through which national parliaments can enhance their capacities to scrutinise government policies. This function gains in prominence as more and more competences are transferred to international institutions. The internationalisation of politics gives the executive privileged access to information,

---

and the High Representative of the Union for Foreign Affairs and Security Policy shall resign from the duties that he carries out in the Commission'.

3.   To be precise, the member states decided to dissolve the Western European Union, a move which inevitably put an end to its Parliamentary Assembly as well. However, all operational activities had already been transferred from the WEU to the EU in 2000, so the Parliamentary Assembly and the collective defence clause was all that were left from the WEU. The end of the WEU's operational activities had already led to calls to dissolve the WEU-PA as well. Yet, a majority in the PA wanted to prevent the transfer of activities to the EU leading to a decline of parliamentary scrutiny. Instead of dissolving the WEU-PA, they would therefore rather redefine its mandate to cover not only WEU activities but European security, broadly understood. This is reflected in the Assembly's renaming first as 'Interim European Security and Defence Assembly' (in 2000) and finally as 'Interparliamentary European Security and Defence Assembly' (2003). Hence, given the PA's persistence in the face of lacking operational WEU activities, it seems safe to assume that the main target of the WEU's dissolution was indeed its Parliamentary Assembly.

4.   Nobel Peace Prize laureates include one of the founders of the Inter-Parliamentary Union, Fré-déric Passy (1901), its first Secretary General, Charles Albert Gobat (1902), and IPU activists William Randall Cremer (1903), Fredrik Bajer (1908) and August Beernaert (1909).

and therefore tends to undermine the effectiveness of parliamentary control. Klaus Dieter Wolf (1999) has even argued that the redistribution of political resources to the benefit of the executive is one of the main driving forces of internationalisation (*see also* Moravcsik 1994; Wagner 2010). Empirical evidence for this 'collusive delegation thesis' has been presented by Matthias Koenig-Archibugi (2004) who demonstrated that government support for the Europeanisation of foreign and security policy is strongest in those countries in which government policy is tightly constrained by domestic actors (such as parliaments), whereas it is weakest in countries whose governments enjoy independent room for manoeuvre.

Faced with a transfer of competences from national to international institutions, parliaments may also engage in international networking to compensate for the loss of direct oversight. However, if the power of parliament impacts on the extent to which executives benefit from the internationalisation of policy making (as Koenig-Archibugi argues), then it can also be expected to influence parliaments' interest in international networking as a remedy.

This chapter examines data on the attendance of national MPs to the parliamentary assemblies of the WEU and NATO to test the plausibility of the thesis that interparliamentary cooperation is driven by parliamentarians' desire to compensate for the loss of effectiveness in scrutinising the government. The PAs of the WEU and of NATO were both established in the mid-1950s.[5] The establishment of the WEU-PA can only be understood in the context of the ambitious European Defence Community (EDC) that failed ratification in the French Parliament. In the hasty negotiations to find an alternative forum for German rearmament, the 'Brussels Pact' was transformed into the WEU. Because the prospective EDC member states had agreed on a parliamentary assembly and had even envisioned direct elections (Rittberger 2006), proponents of transnational parliamentary cooperation succeeded in endowing the WEU with its own parliamentary assembly. However, the new WEU-PA would be composed of the same MPs as the already established PA of the Council of Europe. The respective article IX of the Modified Brussels Treaty thus reads:

> The Council of Western European Union shall make an annual report on its activities and in particular concerning the control of armaments to an Assembly composed of representatives of the Brussels Treaty Powers to the Consultative Assembly of the Council of Europe.
>
> (Modified Brussels Treaty of 1954)

In contrast to the WEU-PA which is the parliamentary organ of an intergovernmental organisation, the NATO-PA has no foundation in an international treaty (Kissling 2011). Instead, its establishment was pushed by parliamentarians from various NATO states in order to promote NATO's cause in the member states. Thus, in contrast to the WEU-PA, the NATO-PA was not primarily designed to enhance parliamentary oversight of, and control over, security policies.

---

5.   For the following, *see also* Marschall 2008.

Both PAs meet twice a year for plenary sessions during which they adopt resolutions. Committees convene both at the occasion of plenary sessions and in between. The size of a country's delegation is the same in both PAs, ranging from three (Luxembourg) to eighteen (France, Germany, Italy and the UK) and, in the case of the NATO-PA, thirty-six (USA). Each delegate has a substitute who may participate independently of the attendance of the delegate, which *de facto* doubles the size of the delegations.

After the end of the Cold War, both PAs started to invite parliamentarians of the former Warsaw Pact countries and created new status groups to allow their systematic involvement in the PAs' work. In doing so, the PAs contributed to preparing some countries for future membership and in socialising them into liberal-democratic standards of civil-military relations (Flockhart 2004). Taken together, both PAs have not only been designed to provide parliamentary oversight but to serve multiple purposes such as building support for the tasks of NATO and WEU, socialising the political elites of potential new member states and mitigating security conflicts among member states. Notwithstanding this rich set of purposes, this chapter focuses on the PAs' contribution to the national parliamentary oversight of security policies.

The next section assumes a rationalist institutionalist perspective to examine the costs and benefits of interparliamentary cooperation. From this perspective, PA attendance is not only costly because expenses for travel and accommodation have to be covered, but mostly because valuable time is dedicated to activities that contribute little to re-election. On the other hand, PAs provide MPs with valuable first-hand information. From a rationalist institutionalist perspective, therefore, MPs should only be expected to attend PA meetings if the benefits exceed the costs. The subsequent section uses data on MPs' attendance of the PAs of WEU and NATO to examine the plausibility of this thesis. Taking the presence or absence of veto power over military missions as an indicator for a parliament's strength *vis-à-vis* its government, a comparison of mean attendance rates demonstrates that MPs from weak parliaments are indeed more likely to attend PA meetings. The final section concludes with some thoughts on the dissolution of the WEU-PA and the discussion about a follow-up institution.

The costs and benefits of transnational parliamentary cooperation

Establishing and maintaining international institutions is costly. Indeed, the costs for translation, travel, accommodation, security and social programmes figured prominently in the WEU member governments' decision to dissolve the WEU-PA. According to the Parliamentary Under-Secretary of State for Foreign and Commonwealth Affairs, Chris Bryan, the assembly's work does not justify 'the cost of over two million [Euros] a year to the UK alone'. Belgian diplomat Steven Vanackere seconded that from a 'budgetary point of view, keeping the WEU has become difficult to justify'.[6] The concept of 'costs', however, does not only apply

---

6. Both quotes from *European Diplomacy and Defence*, No 308 of 7 April 2010.

to such tangible expenses.[7] As Zlatko Šabič (2010) has documented with a view to members of the US Congress, the public can be highly suspicious of foreign travel to institutions with few if any decision-making powers. At minimum, members of parliament face opportunity costs since re-election prospects depend mostly on local and national activities rather than 'distant' problems (Šabič 2008).

With a view to these costs, rationalist institutionalist theory would thus lead us to expect that transnational parliamentary assemblies will only be established and maintained when the expected benefits exceed the costs. Let us therefore turn to the benefits that PAs provide to Members of Parliament.

The demand for such meetings has been interpreted as an adaptation of national parliaments to the internationalisation of politics: since more and more decisions are taken in intergovernmental fora, national parliaments find it more difficult to effectively scrutinise, let alone influence, government policies; instead, parliaments have been considered the main losers of internationalisation, especially with respect to European integration (see, among many others, Norton 1995; Rometsch and Wessels 1996).

The loss of national parliaments' capacity to oversee and control government policy has of course been most pronounced in policy areas in which competences have been delegated to supranational institutions such as the European Commission and in which decisions are no longer taken unanimously but by a (qualified) majority. Because decision making in security and defence has, by and large, remained intergovernmental,[8] one might not expect any changes in executive-legislative relations as a result of internationalisation. However, whereas the marginalisation of supranational institutions and the retaining of unanimity have left formal decision-making intergovernmental, the establishment of integrated, multinational armed forces have transformed the context in which national governments take decisions. The battle group concept, for example, implies that in the event of a decision to launch a military mission, the battle group currently on stand-by has to be sent abroad unless the EU refrains from intervening at all. If forces have been integrated, any state's decision against its participation in a mission *de facto* frustrates the entire deployment, because other states' forces cannot work effectively without the missing state's contribution. As a consequence, states whose forces have been integrated on an international level may come under heavy peer pressure from those states that advocate the use of joint forces (Wagner 2006a). The same effect results from any elaborate scheme of

---

7. In fact, in rational choice institutionalist analyses, the concept of costs mostly refers to transaction costs.

8. In the European Union, the High Representative, who is also a Vice-President of the European Commission, now chairs the meetings of the foreign ministers and appoints the permanent chairs of the PSC, the Military Committee and the Military Staff. However, in contrast to the governance of the common market, the member states retain a right to initiate policy. With a view to decision making, various attempts have been made to curb the national veto power, e.g. by providing for 'constructive abstention' or by agreeing unanimously what would be decided by qualified majority vote. However, none of these attempts abolished the national veto, let alone the deeply ingrained culture of deciding by consensus on security politics.

role specialisation: if capabilities are no longer held by all member states but only by a few or even a single one, the menu of choice for the member state concerned is severely transformed: instead of deciding about its country's participation in a particular military mission, it *de facto* bears the burden of deciding about whether the EU may become involved at all since no other member state could replace the capability under consideration.

Transnational cooperation with other national parliaments has been considered a promising strategy to mitigate the emerging democratic deficit (see, among others, Habegger 2010). Most importantly, transnational parliamentary cooperation helps to overcome information asymmetries that typically result from internationalisation. Because MPs do not participate directly in international negotiations, their knowledge about the preferences of other states, the feasibility of alternative solutions and the actual policy of their own government relies entirely on second-hand information from their government. Because the government in turn has strong incentives to present any negotiation outcome as the best possible one, parliamentarians' capacity for scrutiny is weakened. Transnational parliamentary cooperation provides MPs with valuable contacts through whom they can obtain additional information. For example, Dutch MP Haverkamp used the contacts he had established with parliamentarians in other EU states to inquire into the possibility of stationing armed forces on ships that pass the Somali coast. The Dutch Ministry of Defence had argued that this was not a feasible way of enhancing the security of vessels. Haverkamp used his interparliamentary contacts to develop the well-informed counter-argument that stationing armed forces on ships was considered feasible or even practiced in some other countries. This episode illustrates how interparliamentary cooperation can improve an MP's position *vis-à-vis* his government.[9] Without the information obtained via other countries' parliaments, governments would have had a near monopoly of interpretation over the menu of choices available.

Valuable first-hand information is not only provided via contacts with other MPs but also via high-ranking politicians and administrators who are invited to PA sessions and answer MPs' questions there. For example, at the NATO-PA's spring session in Riga in June 2010, Latvian Prime Minister Valdis Dombrovskis, Afghan Minister of Defence Abdul Rahim Wardak, NATO Secretary General Anders Fogh Rasmussen and the Commander of the Allied Joint Forces Command Brunssum, Egon Ramms, were among those addressing the assembly and answering questions from delegates.

Finally, some parliamentary assemblies also organise field trips to obtain first-hand impressions that would otherwise have been reserved for the executive. In 2010, for example, the missions of the various committees of the NATO-PA

---

9. Author's background talk with Maarten Haverkamp, on 21 June 2010 in Amsterdam. It is interesting to note that Haverkamp is a member of the CDA that, at the same time, was part of the governing coalition. While both the Prime Minister and the Foreign Minister were members of the CDA, the Minister of Defence belonged to the ChristenUnie (CU).

included Afghanistan, Azerbaijan, Georgia, Albania, Ethiopia, Japan, Serbia, Bosnia and Herzegovina and the Republic of Korea.

Anne-Marie Slaughter, in particular, has argued that transnational parliamentary networks 'provide their participants with professional and technical support, advice, and resources, thereby working to professionalise legislators and to help build parliamentarianism as an acquired skill or expertise rather than a mere political tool' (Slaughter 2004). Furthermore, working within parliamentary networks could 'enhance the ability of legislators working within national parliaments to monitor and regulate the activity of executive-branch officials engaged in international work. In other words, parliamentary committees responsible for trade, the environment, immigration – indeed, for any issue - could network with counterparts in other nations to better understand the issues before them and to counterbalance the claims that bureaucrats and regulators make on the same issue' (Slaughter 2004). This notion is shared by the former Secretary General of the WEU, Willem van Eekelen:

> The parliamentary assemblies of the Council of Europe, WEU, NATO and OSCE do not exercise parliamentary control as such, but rather contribute to consensus-building among parliamentarians of the participating countries. Working together on reports and resolutions enhances mutual understanding and provides a valuable basis for positions taken in national debates at home. Detailed knowledge of the arguments advanced by parliamentarians from allies and partners is a prerequisite for an informed and responsible debate. But these international assemblies control very little, at best their own budget.

(van Eekelen 2004)

Taken together, the rationalist institutionalist perspective adopted in this chapter puts the costs and benefits of establishing and maintaining PAs at the centre of the analysis. Costs include not only tangible expenses but, first and foremost, the time that MPs devote to PAs. Benefits are best understood as providing access to first-hand information from other MPs and high-ranking politicians and administrators. The following section assesses the plausibility of these assumptions by analysing which MPs tend to attend PA sessions and which do not.

Analysing attendance data[10]

To better understand the demand for PAs, this chapter examines data on attendance at sessions of the WEU and NATO-PAs. With the help of attendance data I examine the hypothesis that delegations from weak parliaments have higher rates of attendance than delegations from strong parliaments because the marginal benefits from attendance are higher. WEU and NATO-PAs are well suited for the study of attendance data because differences between weak and strong parliaments are

---

10. All data used for the analysis in this chapter can be found on my personal homepage.Online. Available: http://home.fsw.vu.nl/wm.wagner/data.html (accessed 20 June 2013).

particularly pronounced in the realm of security and defence politics (Peters and Wagner 2011); when the members of WEU or NATO decide on military missions, some governments can only commit troops once parliament has approved the deployment, whereas other governments can make such commitments without even informing parliament.

For NATO-PAs, data on national delegations' attendance rates have been obtained from the PA's Secretariat for all meetings between autumn 1998 and spring 2010. In the case of the PA of the WEU, a list of MPs who signed the register of attendance is published with the minutes of each sitting. An MP is considered to have attended a session of the WEU-PA if (s)he attended one or more sittings. However, until 2002, the register of attendance only records MPs from full member states. Thus, systematic data on attendance for all other delegations (e.g. associate members, observers and guests, see below) are only available from spring 2003 onwards.

The most important unit of analysis will be the attendance rate of a particular delegation, i.e. the share of a country's delegates that attends a particular session of a PA. Attendance rates can range from '0' (no MP attending) to '1' (all members of the delegation attending).[11]

In both PAs, attendance rates differ vastly. Whereas some member parliaments at times fail to send a single parliamentarian to a particular session (e.g. Denmark at the NATO-PA's spring session in 2002 or the USA at the NATO-PA's autumn session in 2004), other delegations attend in full (e.g. Luxemburg at the NATO-PA's spring session in 2008 or Bulgaria and Hungary at the WEU-PA's session in spring 2006).

Figure 12.1 depicts the attendance rates of NATO member states with the help of box plots. The thick lines represent the median, the boxes represent the middle 50 per cent of the data, with the second quartile above the mean and the third quartile below the mean. Whiskers, or long vertical lines, represent the spread of data up to one-and-a-half-fold of the interquartile range (the difference between the first and third quartile). The dots above (or below) represent outliers within the data, the asterisks represent extreme outliers. As Figure 12.1 illustrates, attendance rates for individual countries differ vastly across PA meetings. Luxemburg has had the highest fluctuation, ranging from complete absence (spring 1999 and spring 2000) to the presence of the full delegation plus all substitutes (in spring 2007 and spring 2008). At the same time – and more importantly in the context of this study – the graph also highlights country-specific patterns. Delegations from Norway and Portugal, for example, usually have higher attendance rates than those from Denmark. The USA also stands out for its very low attendance rate: on average, only a dozen members of Congress attended NATO-PA meetings. Even though a total of seventy-two congressmen and women could attend any NATO-PA session, sixteen MPs at the spring 1999 meeting in Warsaw was the largest US delegation in the period for which data is available.

---

11. In measuring the attendance rate I follow the practice in both PAs and count the substitutes as full members of the delegation because substitutes enjoy full rights independent of the presence or absence of the regular members of the delegation.

Figure 12.1: Member delegations' attendance rates at NATO-PA sessions

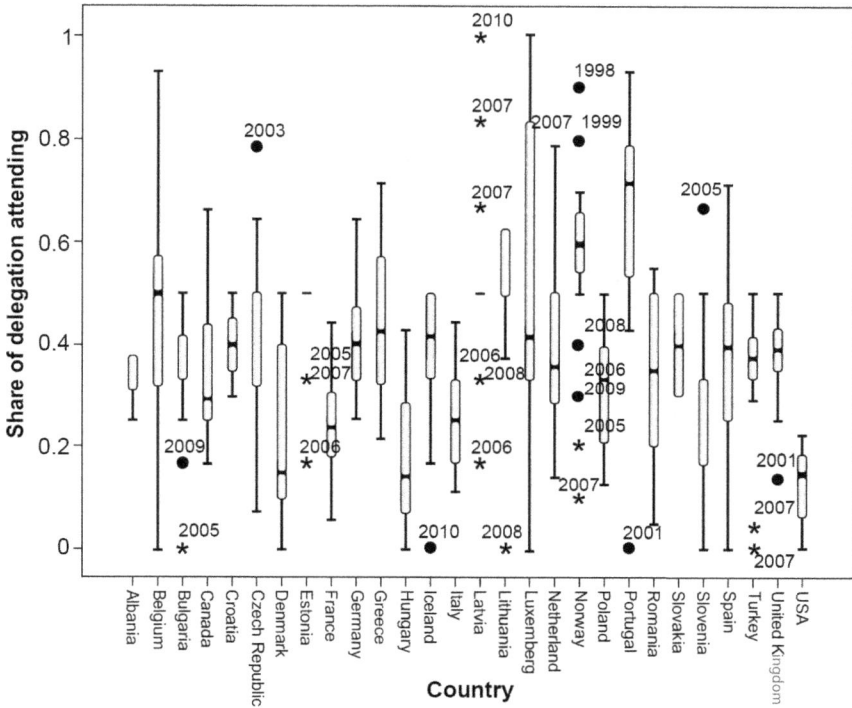

Measuring the strength of parliaments

In order to examine whether the country-specific attendance patterns result from the strength of the respective parliament, I use an issue-area-specific measure of parliamentary strength. Thus, instead of distinguishing between strong and weak parliaments *per se*, I distinguish between parliaments that are powerful or weak in the issue-area under consideration, i.e. security and defence policy. To measure the power of national parliaments in security and defence, I rely on the PARLCON dataset that assembles data on parliamentary war powers, i.e. the presence or absence of an *ex ante* veto power over military missions, for forty-nine democracies, 1989–2004 (cf. Wagner *et al.*2010). Although security and defence policy is not only concerned with military missions but also covers issues of (dis-)armament, troop levels, conscription and the like, the power to veto military deployments has been regarded as 'the strongest means of parliamentary oversight by far' (Hänggi 2004; *see also* Born 2004).

Table 12.1 ranks the mean attendance rates of NATO-PA members for which PARLCON data is available and adds information on the strength of the parliament. In the period under study, Bulgaria, the Czech Republic, Hungary and the Slovak Republic all abolished parliament's *ex ante* veto power over military missions. These countries are therefore listed twice, distinguishing periods with respectively weak and strong parliamentary war powers. N indicates the number of assembly meetings to which a delegation was invited (which depends on the status of a country).

At first glance, delegations from countries with weak parliaments seem indeed to have higher attendance rates than those from countries with powerful parliaments: among the ten countries with the highest attendance rates, only one has a parliamentary veto power over military missions. By contrast, six out of the countries with the ten lowest attendance rates have *ex ante* veto power. Quite remarkably, in three out of four cases, the abolishment of a parliamentary veto power comes with a rise in attendance at NATO-PA sessions: after the abolishment of the veto power, attendance rates more than doubled in the case of the Slovak Republic (from 14 per cent to 32.5 per cent) and rose from 37 per cent to 52 per cent in the case of the Czech Republic as well as from 25 per cent to 29 per cent in the case of Bulgaria. Only in the case of Hungary did the abolishment of the veto come with a slight drop in attendance rates (from 20.1 per cent to 17.8 per cent) but this finding is based on only two sessions in which Hungary participated in 2004.

The ranking's main methodological weakness, however, is that it does not take into account either differences in the number of NATO-PA sessions (which result from both invitations issued to the countries and from the availability of data in the PARLCON data-set), or differences in the status of delegations (i.e. full members, observers or special guests). Differences in status are important because they convey different sets of rights to delegations. Following the main assumption of this chapter (that an MP's likelihood to attend depends on the benefits s/he can expect from attending), status differences can be expected to have an impact as voting rights in particular are granted to different groups in differing degrees. Moreover, a delegation's status may also reflect how significant the international organisation in question is in a particular country - with full members having more at stake than observers.

In the following I therefore take delegations (instead of countries) as units of analysis. I run a series of *t*-tests to compare the mean attendance rates of delegations from weak with those from strong parliaments. For each PA, separate tests are then carried out for different status groups as well as on a year-by-year basis. Differentiating between status groups is necessary to ensure that differences in attendance do not result from differences in delegations' status. It could, for example, be the case, that delegations from associate members or observers expect to gain less from attending PA sessions as their countries lack the obligations of full members. However, attendance rates may also be influenced by the salience of the organisation at different time points. For example, exchanging information with other parliamentarians may be particularly beneficial on the eve of major decisions, such as the admission of new members, a change in the organisation's strategy, or a major new military deployment. Moreover, year-by-year comparisons are less susceptible to the different weights of countries in the sample than comparisons by status groups where, for example, long-term member

Table 12.1: Ranking of NATO-PA delegations by order of attendance rate (highest to lowest)

Country	N	mean	PARLCON
Norway	13	66.15	weak
Portugal	13	63.74	weak
Belgium	13	55.49	weak
Czech Republic, 2001–2003	8	52.68	weak
Greece	13	43.96	weak
Spain	13	42.95	weak
Germany	13	40.81	strong
Netherlands	13	39.56	weak
United Kingdom	13	37.39	weak
Canada	13	37.18	weak
Czech Republic, 1998–2000	5	37.14	strong
Lithuania	13	32.69	strong
Slovak Republic, 2001–2004	8	32.5	weak
Poland	13	30.77	weak
Bulgaria 2003–2004	4	29.17	weak
Former Yugoslav Republic of Macedonia (FYROM)	6	27.78	strong
Romania	2	27.5	weak
Switzerland	6	26.67	strong
Bulgaria 2001–2002	4	25	strong
Slovenia	13	24.36	weak
Denmark	13	23.08	strong
France	13	23.08	weak
Austria	13	22.31	strong
Finland	13	22.12	strong
Hungary, 1998–2003	11	20.13	strong
Hungary, 2004	2	17.86	weak
Slovak Republic, 1998–2000	5	14	strong
Sweden	13	13.08	strong
USA	13	12.82	weak
Japan	12	12.5	strong
Australia	9	0	weak

states' delegations have a bigger impact on the average attendance rate than delegations from states that were only recently admitted. Taken together, running a *series* of *t*-tests yields an empirically richer picture of the attendance patterns of PA delegations. Nevertheless, I would like to emphasise the explorative nature of the analysis as there are many additional factors that may influence MPs to attend, or be absent from, PA meetings.[12]

The NATO-PA distinguishes between full members, associate members and observers. Furthermore, there are parliamentary guests and Mediterranean Associate delegations but since PARLCON does not cover any country from these status groups, they are both left out of the analysis. By contrast, the WEU-PA has developed an extremely complex system that includes fourteen categories, namely: full members, members, affiliate members, associate members, affiliate associate members, partners, associate partners, observers, permanent observers, permanent observer members, affiliate observers, affiliate permanent observer member, permanent guests, and special guests. However, these fourteen categories can be grouped into three main status groups depending on the rights they enjoy (see Table 12.2). Thus, category one includes members, full members and affiliate members that are all entitled to vote in both committee and plenary. Category two comprises associate members, affiliate associate members, permanent observers, permanent observer members, affiliate permanent observer members that may only vote in committee but not in plenary. Finally, category three includes partners, associate partners, observers, affiliate observers, permanent guests and special guests that may speak in the plenary but may not vote either in committee or plenary.

Results

The hypothesis that delegations from weak parliaments tend to have a higher attendance rate than delegations from strong parliaments is first tested by comparing mean attendance rates across different status groups. Separate *t*-tests were run for the WEU-PA and the NATO-PA. In all cases, only delegations for which PARLCON data are available can be included. The results are reported in Tables 12.3 (for NATO-PA) and 12.4 (for the WEU-PA).

As the two tables demonstrate, MPs from weak parliaments are more likely to attend PA meetings than MPs from strong parliaments. This finding holds true across different status groups with the exception of the observers to the NATO-PA. However, a closer look at the attendance of observer countries at the NATO-PA reveals that the poor showing of MPs from weak parliaments is the exclusive result of Australian MPs who never attended a single meeting of the PA. An obvious explanation is the extraordinarily long distance that Australian MPs would have to

---

12. I owe this point to the editors who pointed to the material resources at a parliament's disposal that may also have an impact on attendance rates. Unfortunately, good time-series data for the countries under study here are in short supply.

Table 12.2: Status groups in the WEU-PA

Category	Status Group	Rights
I	Full members	right to vote in committees and plenary
	Members	
	Affiliate Members	
II	Associate members	right to vote in committees but not in plenary
	Affiliate associate members	
	Permanent observers	
	Permanent observer members	
	Affiliate permanent observer members	
III	Partners	No voting rights (but eligible to speak in plenary)
	Associate partners	
	Observers	
	Affiliate observers	
	Permanent guests	
	Special guests	

travel to attend NATO-PA meetings. However, the statistical significance of this finding varies widely between NATO-PA and WEU-PA. Because the WEU-PA is composed of delegations from weak parliaments to a much higher degree than the NATO-PA, the higher attendance rate of weak parliament delegations is not statistically significant in the case of the WEU-PA. By contrast, the differences in attendance between strong and weak parliaments' delegations to the NATO-PA are highly significant.

In addition to the two tests, I also compared the mean attendance rates on a yearly basis. Of course, the number of cases declines dramatically and even makes the test impossible for the WEU-PA in a number of years. For those years in which the test can be run, the results, by and large, again confirm the hypothesis that delegations from weak parliaments tend to have a higher attendance rate than delegations from strong parliaments. In the case of the NATO-PA, the mean attendance rate of parliamentarians from weak parliaments is always higher than the rate of those from strong parliaments. In three cases, this finding is even significant at the 0.01 level and in one case at the 0.005 level (see Table 12.5).

The test is more difficult to run for the WEU-PA because the number of delegations from strong parliaments is low in most of the years (resulting from the fact that before 2003, attendance data were only recorded for full members). Nevertheless, in all but one of the ten years for which it is possible, the comparison of mean attendance rates again confirms the hypothesis that delegations from weak parliaments tend to have a higher attendance rate than delegations from strong parliaments. The only exception is 1999. However, it must be noted that significance rates are generally low (with only one year significant at the 0.05 level).

Table 12.3: Comparative means NATO-PA

	All delegations		Full members		Associate members		Observers	
Strength of parliament	strong	weak	strong	weak	strong	weak	strong	weak
N	128	189	44	161	59	19	25	8
Attendance rate	**24.0%** (16.5)	**37.5%** (21.9)	**30.4%** (16.1)	**41.0%** (20.6)	**23.3%** (14.4)	**25.1%** (15.7)	**14.4%** (17.3)	**0** (0)
t-Test, significance	0.000		0.000		0.666		0.027	

Table 12.4: Comparative means WEU-PA

	All delegations		Category 1		Category 2		Category 3	
Strength of parliament	strong	weak	strong	weak	strong	weak	strong	weak
N	48	240	24	213	6	13	17	14
Attendance rate	**45.24%** (25.45)	**52.83%** (17.85)	**47.45%** (17.45)	**52.73%** (16.54)	**39.88%** (31.30)	**49.36%** (25.28)	**40.78%** (27.87)	**57.62%** (27.87)
t-Test, significance	0.53		0.169		0.533		0.105	

Table 12.5: Comparative means NATO-PA by year

Year	Weak parliaments		Strong parliaments		Significance
	Mean attendance rate	N	Mean attendance rate	N	
2004	33.88%	36	26.59%	18	0.194
2003	41.83%	32	24.65%	20	0.004
2002	38.47%	30	26.07%	22	0.024
2001	35.66%	29	18.21%	18	0.002
2000	33.66%	26	18.97%	20	0.031
1999	40.46%	24	26.14%	20	0.007
1998	41.88%	12	29.83%	10	0.138

Table 12.6: Comparative means WEU-PA by year

Year	Weak parliaments		Strong parliaments		Significance
	Mean attendance rate	N	Mean attendance rate	N	
2004	46.2%	30	42.85%	16	0.652
2003	51.88%	30	43.39%	16	0.361
2002	44.44%	14	34.72%	2	0.047
2001	47.08%	14	40.28%	2	0.168
2000	48.58%	14	44.44%	2	0.350
1999	50.61%	14	52.78%	2	0.726
1998	56.55%	14	50.00%	2	0.200
1997	59.48%	14	51.39%	2	0.433
1996	56.55%	14	54.17%	2	0.693
1995	48.53%	14	43.06%	2	0.390
1994	52.73%	12	n. a.	0	n. a.
1993	55.16%	12	n. a.	0	n. a.
1992	60.58%	12	n. a.	0	n. a.
1991	62.93%	12	n. a.	0	n. a.
1990	57.64%	12	n. a.	0	n. a.
1989	63%	8	n. a.	0	n. a.

Conclusion

The analysis of attendance data has provided some interesting insights into the functions of parliamentary assemblies. Most importantly, it has confirmed the hypothesis that members of weak parliaments who obtain little information from their respective governments attend PA sessions more frequently than members of strong parliaments. This pattern is best explained by the different marginal gains to be expected from attending PA meetings. Because MPs generally incur costs by attending PA meetings, those with lower marginal returns will be less likely to attend than those with higher marginal returns.

These findings resonate with an understanding of parliamentary assemblies as instruments of national parliaments that function to enhance their capacities in scrutinising government policy. It is not without irony that the initiative to dissolve the WEU-PA came from the United Kingdom because the British Parliament belongs to the group of parliaments with very few war powers. As expected from the perspective taken here, British delegations have always had high attendance rates (ranging from 50 to 86 per cent with an average of 67 per cent). However, the decision to dissolve the WEU-PA was of course not initiated by the Parliament but by the Government.

It may come to no surprise that the British Parliament has initiated the process of establishing a follow-up institution to the WEU-PA that would bring together delegations from EU national parliaments (with candidate countries as observers) convening twice a year (see House of Commons 2011). Interparliamentary cooperation on European security and defence policy is also stipulated by the Lisbon Treaty whose Article 12 states that 'national [p]arliaments contribute actively to the good functioning of the Union [...] by taking part in the interparliamentary cooperation between national [p]arliaments and with the European Parliament'. A protocol to the Treaty suggests security and defence policy as an area of interparliamentary cooperation. At the time of writing, however, the negotiations on the institutional setting have proved to be difficult[13] and the prospects of establishing a successor institution remain uncertain. The findings presented in this chapter demonstrate that judging the utility of a successor institution to the WEU-Assembly – and of transnational interparliamentary cooperation in general – on the basis of its competences *vis-à-vis* other institutions are misleading. Instead, the main purpose of transnational interparliamentary cooperation lies in the contribution to national parliaments' capacities to scrutinise and oversee national government policy.

---

13. For an excellent overview of the debate on a successor institution, *see* Herranz 2011.

Table 12.A1: Mean attendance of delegations to WEU-PA

Country	Number of sessions in sample[14]	Mean attendance rate (%)	PARLCON
Ireland	4	75	1
Norway	4	75	0
Lithuania	4	68.75	1
UK	32	67.62	0
Romania	4	67.5	0
Hungary, 2004	2	64.23	0
Greece	20	59.64	0
Spain	30	57.75	0
Turkey	4	56.25	1
Portugal	30	50.48	0
Netherlands	32	47.1	0
Germany	20	43.19	1
Slovenia	4	41.67	0
France	32	33.77	0
Slovakia	4	30	0
Poland	4	29.17	0
Sweden	4	8.33	1
Hungary, 2003	2	7.14	1

14. The number of sessions in sample results from the number of invitations for which PARLCON data were available.

chapter thirteen | the institutionalisation of a parliamentary dimension of the WTO*

Hilmar Rommetvedt

Introduction

Since its establishment in 1995 the World Trade Organization (WTO) has become one of the most important transnational organisations in the world. The increasing impact of the WTO is related to the importance of international trade and the powers that member states have entrusted to the organisation. First and foremost the WTO is an intergovernmental organisation. WTO negotiators represent the governments of the respective member states and, after ratification by national legislatures, the rules settled in the negotiated agreements are implemented by the national governments. So far, the WTO follows the 'standard' model of an international organisation. However, unlike most international organisations the WTO has an additional court-like institution: the dispute settlement system. Consequently, in the WTO there is a role to be played by national executives and by a supranational 'court', but what about *parliaments* and parliamentarians? Is there a role for them to play beyond the ratification of agreements?

For a number of reasons the WTO has encroached on the traditional domain of national legislatures and, as we will see, parliamentarians have emphasised the need for a 'parliamentary dimension' of the WTO. A 'Parliamentary Conference on the WTO' has been established with its own steering committee. In this chapter I will analyse the institutionalisation of the parliamentary dimension of the WTO. The following section presents theoretical perspectives that may enhance our understanding of national parliamentarians' engagement at the international level. The subsequent section takes a closer look at the history of the parliamentary dimension of the WTO. Finally, I will discuss questions for further research and – not least – for reflection among parliamentarians as well as in the WTO itself.

*   This chapter draws upon my article, Rommetvedt (2011) 'The institutionalization of a *parliamentary* dimension of an inter*governmental* organization: the WTO', *World Trade Review*, Volume 10(4), pp. 423–446, Cambridge University Press, reproduced with permission. I thank Ben Crum, Carsten Daugbjerg, Arild Farsund, John Erik Fossum, Christer Gulbrandsen, Oluf Langhelle, Amrita Narlikar, Johannes Pollak, Alan Swinbank, Serguei Tchelnokov, Ron Weber and the editor and referees of the *World Trade Review* for useful comments on earlier versions. The study has been funded by the Research Programme on Nature-Based Industry of the Research Council of Norway.

Theoretical perspectives

The development of a *parliamentary* dimension of an inter*governmental* organisation such as the WTO may seem paradoxical. In this section we have a look at theoretical perspectives that may contribute to the explanation of *why* parliamentarians engage in an intergovernmental organisation such as the WTO, and *how* they engage, that is, what kind of strategies they employ and what type of institution the parliamentary dimension of the WTO represents.

'Intermestic' affairs and the definition of the national interest(s)

According to constitutional theory, foreign affairs belong to the prerogatives of the executive, i.e. the monarch, president, or government in political systems based on the principle of parliamentarianism. To put it simply, the *formal* role of parliament is to ratify treaties negotiated by the government.[1] However, as we will see, the *actual practice* is somewhat different.

Traditionally, foreign affairs were matters of security and military defence. After the Cold War these concerns seemed to fade away. However, the 9/11 attack and the wars in Iraq and Afghanistan show that such concerns are still highly relevant, even though the character of the security problems has changed. Furthermore, a broad range of what used to be domestic policies are now involved in the ongoing process of internationalisation and globalisation. Internationalisation implies that political institutions, most notably the state, by law and international negotiations, open up the national economy for investments, co-production and international trade (Hveem 1998). The borderline between international and domestic affairs becomes more porous and, consequently, decision makers face a growing number of 'intermestic' affairs (Manning 1977; Langhelle forthcoming).

The 'intermestic' character of trade policy is acknowledged by, among others, the Canadian Parliament. A report on parliamentary oversight of international trade policies and negotiations states that 'trade policy increasingly intersects with areas of domestic and social policy' and consequently it has become 'increasingly vital that elected representatives' views influence the direction of international trade negotiations', and that parliamentarians 'demonstrate that they are keeping their government accountable on trade issues' (Berg and Schmitz 2006). The Canadian House of Commons Standing Committee on Foreign Affairs and International Trade and its trade subcommittee have undertaken a number of hearings on trade issues.

In international negotiations the national governments are supposed to attend to and safeguard the national interest. In relation to security and defence, the definition of the national interest would seem fairly straightforward. However, in highly internationalised societies the definition of the national interest is not at all

---

1. In some cases the parliament does not even ratify international agreements. In Canada for example, it is the prerogative of the federal government alone to enter into international treaties. There is no legal or constitutional requirement for parliamentary approval (Berg and Schmitz 2006).

straightforward. Milner (1997) argues that 'there is no single set of national policy preferences, no single national preference ranking on any issue, and no single national "interest"'. Trubowitz (1998) maintains that the definition of the national interest is 'a product of politics' and thus defined by the societal interests which have the power to work within the political system and to make winning coalitions and alliances, while in Frankel's (1970) words the definition of the national interest is an 'essentially political process'.

The involvement of various, more or less conflicting, domestic interests create a need for intermediation and trade-offs. In general, to prioritise and balance different domestic interests is among the most important roles to be played by parliaments. Consequently, the internationalisation of domestic policies makes the question of defining the role to be played by parliaments and parliamentarians in international relations topical.

Executive-legislative relations in two-level games

According to Putnam (1988) international negotiations can 'usefully be conceived as a two-level game' with a level I process taking place at the international level between the negotiating national delegations, and a level II process at the national level where each parliament discusses whether or not to ratify the outcome of the level I negotiations. At the national level, 'domestic groups pursue their interests by pressuring the government to adopt favourable policies, and politicians seek power by constructing coalitions among those groups'. At the international level, 'national governments seek to maximise their own ability to satisfy domestic pressures, while minimising the adverse consequences of foreign developments'.

Central decision-makers need to take the games at both levels into consideration. Most likely there will be 'prior consultations and bargaining at level II to hammer out an initial position for the level I negotiations', and 'the need for level II ratification is certain to affect the level I bargaining' (Putnam 1988). As Schelling (1973) points out, governments may 'create a bargaining position by public statements, statements calculated to arouse public opinion that permit no concessions to be made'. Milner (1997) argues that domestic and international politics are strongly interconnected and that political leaders are playing in the domestic and international arenas simultaneously. The behaviour of political leaders 'can only be understood when both internal and external factors are considered'.

It is reasonable to assume that such considerations will depend on, among other things, the strength of parliament *vis-à-vis* the executive. Over the years, numerous political scientists and observers have subscribed to the 'decline of legislature-thesis', dating back to Lord Bryce in 1921 (Norton 1990). However, more recently several researchers have questioned this thesis. Scandinavian studies indicate that parliaments have strengthened their position *vis-à-vis* the executives (Damgaard 1994, 2003; Rommetvedt 2003). De Puig (2008) maintains that 'parliaments, in the western world at least (and probably elsewhere too, always bearing in mind that we are talking about democratic systems), have never had such an important role in policy formulation and development as they have had in the last forty years'. According to the World Bank Institute, '[w]e are living in an "age of parliaments" with a revitalisation of legislatures that make them stronger and more relevant today than ever before' (WBI 2001). However, as suggested by Olsen (1983), an 'ebb-and-flow' perspective on the role of parliament may be more appropriate. Parliaments may also mobilise in order to avoid the risk of becoming losers in the internationalisation game where executives and experts are the main actors (cf. Crum and Fossum in the introduction to this volume).

The combined effect of the intertwinement of international and domestic politics and policies; the absence of a single national interest and the need for prioritisation among a variety of domestic interests; the two-level character of international negotiations; and the (re)vitalisation of parliaments in general should be expected to pave the way for a more active role to be played by national parliamentarians in international organisations and thus contribute to the explanation for the development of the WTO's parliamentary dimension.

The roles and strategies of parliaments

The discussion above has been related to the *influence* of parliaments and parliamentarians. Representing the voters and exerting influence on policy making on behalf of the citizens are core functions of democratically elected parliaments.[2] There are, however, more roles and functions for parliaments to fulfil.

In general, as Beer (1990) points out, '[o]ne of the oldest conceptions of the role of Parliament is that of controlling and restraining the executive'. It was not until later in history that the more positive role, 'to legislate, to make laws', became 'prominent'. Packenham (1990) draws attention to three main functions of legislatures: the 'legitimation function', the 'recruitment, socialisation and training function', and the 'decisional or influence function'. The latter includes law-making, interest articulation, conflict resolution, and administrative oversight.

The functions of parliaments in general are reflected in discussions on the role of parliaments in relation to the WTO as well. Legislation and scrutiny, together with the task of 'reconnecting the WTO with the people' were important roles pointed out by a study group arranged by the Commonwealth Parliamentary Assembly (CPA Study Group 2002). The Canadian report mentioned above listed five 'parliamentary oversight functions': delivering negotiating mandates to governments, monitoring negotiations, communicating with the public and responding to its concerns, ratifying multilateral agreements, and passing implementing legislation (Berg and Schmitz 2006).

To put it simply, two different strategies may be chosen by parliamentarians who seek to exert influence on international negotiations: a 'go-through-government'

---

2. We should bear in mind that not all the member states of the WTO have democratically elected parliaments or legislatures. There are many important questions that may – and should – be addressed in relation to non-democratic member states and assemblies, but it would be outside the remit of this chapter to deal with these questions here.

strategy and a 'bypass-government' strategy (Pedersen 2002). One could say that the go-through-government strategy is formally the 'correct' course of action. The WTO is an intergovernmental organisation and governments negotiate on behalf of their respective countries. If the negotiators reach an agreement, then the parliaments are supposed to ratify the treaty (if parliamentary approval is needed). If parliaments are to have real influence on the content of the treaty, then they will have to exert influence on the negotiating positions taken by the governments at earlier stages of the process.

The go-through-government option depends, however, on the strength of the parliament *vis-à-vis* the government. If the government is too strong, then the parliament will have little to say, and the threat of denying ratification will have little credibility. In this case the parliamentarians may try the bypass-government strategy. Other things being equal, we would expect relatively weak parliaments to be more inclined than strong parliaments to choose the bypass-government strategy, and to be active at the international level, including the WTO (cf. Wagner, this volume). However, a certain minimum of resources and capacity is necessary for parliaments to be able to engage at the international level.

The organisation of a transnational parliamentary dimension

The organisation of the roles to be played by parliamentarians in a transnational organisation such as the WTO is not straightforward. An inter- or transnational parliamentary dimension represents a challenge to the traditional assumption that democratic representation is based on one single *demos* and a single representative institution, namely the national parliament. National parliamentarians participate in parliamentary assemblies, committees and delegations in a number of international organisations (Rommetvedt *et al.* 2009), but there is no obvious or given model for the organisation of a parliamentary dimension in an intergovernmental organisation such as the WTO.

As pointed out by Crum and Fossum (2009), in the case of the EU, two channels of democratic representation have developed: direct representation through the EP, and indirect representation through national parliaments and governments. They review the EU on the basis of three 'conceptions of the structure of democratic representation'. The first two, the federal system and the parliamentary network, are fairly well established conceptions while the third, the multilevel parliamentary field, is a new conception introduced by Crum and Fossum themselves.

A federation is a highly institutionalised system with two channels of democratic representation. The two channels are 'incorporated in an integrated structure of representative bodies' at both the federal and the state level. The relations among these bodies are 'constitutionalized with a clear division of tasks'. The *network* notion is a more open concept which 'allows for more dispersed patterns of interaction' among the representative bodies. In some cases interactions may be 'quite intense and even become institutionalized' while in other cases 'the link can be quite weak' (Crum and Fossum 2009).

According to Crum and Fossum (2009), the multilevel parliamentary field shares 'the focus on the division of tasks and competences' with federalism. However, 'the field expands beyond federal organisational models, because it neither presupposes institutional symmetry among representative bodies, nor that that they need to fit into a clearly laid out (hierarchical) organisational structure'. The multilevel parliamentary field 'allows for greater variation among the component units and patterns of formal and informal parliamentary interaction (horizontally and vertically)' and it is 'compatible with less hierarchical and more loosely coupled patterns of interaction'. In a more recent publication, Crum and Fossum (2012) make a distinction between a parliamentary field and a *multilevel* parliamentary field. The former is 'likely only to encompass parliaments, and the structuring is mainly horizontal', while in the latter case 'it will also encompass parties and interest organisations and the structure will combine both horizontal and vertical traits'.

Putnam's conception of two-level games may indicate that a parliamentary dimension of an international organisation involves only two levels: the WTO and the national parliaments. However, as we will see, the parliamentary dimension of the WTO is a multilevel phenomenon. The parliamentary conferences on the WTO are organised by the Inter-Parliamentary Union (IPU) and the EP and the participants include not only national parliamentarians but representatives of other transnational parliamentary associations as well.[3]

I will return to the question of what type of transnational institution the parliamentary dimension of the WTO represents, but first it is necessary to take a closer look at the history of this dimension.

The parliamentary dimension of the WTO: A historical overview

In this section, I will consider how the 'Parliamentary Dimension of the WTO' has developed from the first informal meeting of parliamentarians in 1996 (via the institutionalisation of the 'Parliamentary Conference on the WTO') to the beginning of 2011. The first parliamentary meetings on the WTO concentrated on the role of parliaments and parliamentarians as such, but gradually the parliamentarians have become more concerned with the various substantive matters negotiated in the Doha round of WTO negotiations.

---

3. The Commonwealth Parliamentary Association (CPA) is one of these associations. In 2002 the CPA arranged a Study Group on Parliament and the International Trading System. The group listed a number of recommendations for parliamentarians and institutions (CPA Study Group 2002).

From Singapore 1996 to Geneva 2002[4]

Chutikul (2003) traces the origin of the parliamentary dimension of the WTO back to the first WTO Ministerial Conference in Singapore in December 1996. There was an informal and spontaneous meeting of MPs attending the conference, but no documents were adopted. Three years later, US Senator William V. Roth initiated a meeting of MPs attending the third Ministerial Conference in Seattle, USA, in November-December 1999. The MPs adopted an appeal for the establishment of a 'Standing Body of Parliamentarians' whereby members of parliaments could exchange views, be informed and monitor the WTO.

On the occasion of UNCTAD X (UN Conference on Trade and Development) in Bangkok, Thailand, in February 2000, the IPU organised a two-day meeting attended by members of fifty-three parliaments who adopted a declaration calling for a 'parliamentary dimension' enabling Members of Parliament 'to convey the concerns of peoples' in 'the field of trade, finance and development, in particular with WTO, UNCTAD and the Bretton Woods institutions'. In March of the same year, WTO Director-General Mike Moore addressed a letter to the speakers of parliament of the WTO members signalling a wish to 'involve more closely the parliaments and their representatives'.

In April 2001, the EP organised a seminar in Brussels, Belgium on 'Trade, Development and Democracy. The need for reform of the WTO'. In the closing statement the Chairman emphasised that the 'transparency and democratic legitimacy of the WTO should be strengthened by associating the parliaments of WTO members more closely with the activities of the WTO'. A Parliamentary Meeting on International Trade organised by the IPU in Geneva, Switzerland, in June reaffirmed the need to 'build a parliamentary dimension to international trade negotiations and arrangements'.

A Working Group to prepare a parliamentary meeting at the fourth WTO Ministerial Conference held its first session in Strasbourg in September 2001, hosted by the EP. In October, the IPU was granted observer status by the WTO, and two weeks later the EP passed a resolution on openness and democracy in international trade which proposed 'once again the creation of a parliamentary Assembly within the WTO'. At the Ministerial Conference in Doha, Qatar, in November 2001 the IPU and EP convened a one-day parliamentary meeting. Some of the participants wished to establish 'a Parliamentary Body formally linked to the WTO' whereas others argued that the parliamentary dimension of the WTO should be provided through the IPU. In the end, the attendees reached a consensus decision to establish a steering group to prepare options for the parliamentary dimension of the WTO.

At a public symposium on 'The Doha Development Agenda' organised by the WTO in Geneva in April-May 2002, there was a parliamentary workshop session moderated by Director-General Mike Moore. A month later the first session of

---

4. The presentation in this section and the quotations from various documents are based on Chutikul (2003).

the Post-Doha Steering Committee was convened jointly by the IPU and EP in Brussels in order to start preparations for the Second Parliamentary Conference on International Trade. In September Dr Supachai Panitchpakdi took over as WTO Director-General and in one of his first speeches he stated that civil society should be informed about the negotiations and that '[e]lected representatives, in particular, need to know about decisions which potentially affect the communities they represent and make their interest and concerns known'.

Interpreting the statements above, we see that they touch on several of the functions of parliaments mentioned in Section 12.2. The interest articulation function is visible in both Dr Panitchpakdi's speech and in the declaration from the IPU meeting on the occasion of UNCTAD X. The Chairman's closing statement in Brussels points to both the oversight function (need for transparency) and the legitimisation function. Furthermore, we see that the parliamentarians speak of a 'standing body' and 'parliamentary assembly' within the WTO, but at this early stage the ideas are not very well developed with regard to how to organise a parliamentary dimension of the WTO.

Geneva and Cancún 2003

Two parliamentary conferences on the WTO were organised by the IPU and the EP in 2003, the first in Geneva in February, and the second in September during the fifth WTO Ministerial Conference in Cancún, Mexico. In addition, a session on 'Parliaments and the WTO' was set up by the WTO and the IPU at the WTO Public Symposium, 'Challenges ahead on the road to Cancún' in Geneva in June.

The final declaration of the Geneva conference[5] in February 2003 emphasised that:

> International relations are shaping domestic policies, and external relations have become part of the domestic agenda. Without the introduction of substantive and procedural checks and balances similar to those that are usually applied to domestic policy-making, this tendency will inevitably cause a deficit in democracy at the international level. [...] We are thus acutely aware of the need for parliamentarians to participate in the running of public affairs that transcend national borders.

(Parliamentary Conference on the WTO 2003)

The participants were 'determined to push forward the interparliamentary process with the WTO which would evolve around regular parliamentary meetings held initially once a year and on the occasion of WTO Ministerial Conferences'. These events were to be called the *Parliamentary Conference on the WTO*.

---

5. Parliamentary Conference on the WTO: Final Declaration adopted by consensus on 18 February 2003. Online. Available at: http://www.ipu.org/splz-e/trade03/declaration.pdf (accessed 22 June 2013).

The declaration adopted in Cancún[6] stated that:

[...] the days when foreign policy, and more specifically trade policy was the exclusive domain of the executive branch are over. The WTO is rapidly becoming more than a mere trade organisation, having an ever growing impact on domestic policies. Consequently, we wish to contribute to making it more open, transparent, democratic and responsive to national policy objectives consistent with national sovereignty and international trade obligations.

(Parliamentary Conference on the WTO 2003)

The Cancún Declaration called on the respective governments 'to add the following paragraph to the final declaration: '*Transparency of the WTO should be enhanced by associating parliaments more closely with the activities of the WTO*'. WTO members were encouraged to 'include members of parliament in their official delegations to future Ministerial Conferences'.

With regard to substantive matters, the Geneva Declaration stated that the goal was 'to promote trade that benefits people everywhere, enhances development and reduces poverty'. The MPs applauded the 'intent to phase out agricultural export subsidies' and regretted that the deadlines had not been met with regard to 'special and differential treatment for developing countries' and 'making the TRIPS Agreement [on intellectual property rights] more flexible in order to improve access to medicines'. They were 'worried at the lack of advances on the fundamental issue of enhancing real access to markets' and underlined the need to reach an agreement on 'reducing barriers to trade in the field of agriculture, textiles and clothing'. With reference to 'agricultural support in wealthy countries' the Declaration stated that 'such trade distorting practices, and their social consequences are unacceptable'.

In Cancún, the MPs called on the Ministerial Conference 'to make a commitment to bring to an end all agricultural policies that have contributed to underdevelopment'. WTO members were asked to 'set forth a clear timetable for agreeing upon the phasing out of all forms of export subsidies and to agree upon substantial improvements in market access, taking into account special and differential treatment'. The parliamentarians recognised that 'agriculture has a multifunctional role which includes food safety, preservation of land, animal welfare, way of life, revitalisation of rural society and rural employment' and WTO members were invited to 'address those issues through non-trade-distorting means' and to 'respond positively to the sectoral initiative on cotton'.

In addition to agriculture, the Cancún Declaration paid attention to intellectual property rights TRIPS and trade in services GATS. The TRIPS agreement was to be interpreted in ways 'consistent with public health needs' in order to 'improve the present situation in which a third of the world population does not have access to essential medicines'. A 'cautious approach to liberalisation' was required in the

6. Cancún Session of the Parliamentary Conference on the WTO. Declaration adopted on 12 September 2003. Online. Available: http://www.ipu.org/splz-e/cancun/declaration.pdf (accessed 22 June 2013).

GATS negotiations, 'especially as far as services relating to basic human rights and needs are concerned'. Furthermore, the MPs declared that: 'all agreements require an appropriate assessment of their economic, social, cultural and gender impact as well as of their environmental sustainability'.

The declarations from Geneva and Cancún clearly reflect that international and domestic affairs are closely intertwined, and at this stage the parliamentarians are engaged in a variety of the substantive matters negotiated in the WTO. Foreign and trade policy have become 'intermestic' affairs and the MPs do not accept that such matters are the exclusive prerogatives of governments. Their participation is needed in order to safeguard democratic representation, transparency and oversight, and responsiveness to national interests. The parliamentary dimension of the WTO is on the way to being organised, not as a parliamentary assembly but primarily in the form of a parliamentary conference, supplemented by the recommended inclusion of MPs in the national delegations to Ministerial Conferences.

From Brussels 2004 to Hong Kong 2005

In November 2004, the IPU and EP organised a new session of the Parliamentary Conference in Brussels. The Conference – with the 'Adoption of Rules of Procedure of the Parliamentary Conference on the WTO' on the agenda – represented a major step in the process of institutionalising the parliamentary dimension of the WTO. The Rules[7] state that the Conference is 'a forum for the exchange of opinions, information and experience, as well as for the promotion of common action on topics related to the role of parliaments and the organisation of parliamentary functions in the area of international trade issues' (Article 1.1).

Furthermore, as with the Geneva Declaration, the Conference was tasked to 'promote free and fair trade that benefits people everywhere, enhances development and reduces poverty' (1.2), and 'provide a parliamentary dimension to the WTO' by (1.3):

(a) overseeing WTO activities and promoting their effectiveness and fairness – keeping in mind the original objectives of the WTO set in Marrakech;

(b) promoting the transparency of WTO procedures and improving the dialogue between governments, parliaments and civil society; *and*

(c) building capacity in parliaments in matters of international trade and exerting influence on the direction of discussions within the WTO.

Participants in the Conference are (Article 2.1):

- delegations designated by parliaments of sovereign States that are members of the WTO;

- delegations designated by IPU Member Parliaments from countries that are not represented in the WTO; and

---

7.   Rules of Procedure adopted during the Brussels session on 26 November 2004. Online. Available: http://www.ipu.org/splz-e/trade04/rules.pdf (accessed 22 June 2013).

- delegations designated by the European Parliament , the Parliamentary Assembly of the Council of Europe, the Commonwealth Parliamentary Association and the Assemblée parlementaire de la Francophonie.

The next Parliamentary Conference was held during the Ministerial Conference in Hong Kong in December 2005. The declaration that was adopted by the MPs comprises a considerable number of institutional and substantive matters related to the ongoing trade negotiations.[8] Institutional matters include technical assistance to developing countries, greater coherence between international economic actors like the WTO, the World Bank and the International Monetary Fund (IMF), and strengthening of the WTO with regard to openness, transparency, accountability and participation. Of particular interest here is paragraph 24 regarding, among other things, the *national* parliaments and their dealings with trade issues:

> We advocate assigning trade issues to an existing committee or, when needed, establishing a special committee on the WTO in national parliaments, regional and global parliamentary organizations. These committees could monitor developments in multilateral trade, including capacity-building of parliaments and parliamentarians in multilateral trade, and offer parliamentary oversight.

(Parliamentary Conference on the WTO. Declaration)

The declarations adopted by parliamentarians in Brussels 2004 and Hong Kong 2005 show a more wide-ranging engagement in the substantive matters negotiated in the WTO. The number of paragraphs in the Brussels and Hong Kong Declarations reached twenty-two and twenty-five paragraphs respectively, as compared to twelve and fifteen paragraphs in the Geneva and Cancún Declarations in 2003.

The Brussels Declaration stresses 'the importance of lower industrial tariffs' and 'better market access for non-agricultural products', reduction or elimination of 'tariff and non-tariff barriers to trade in environmental goods' and 'trade facilitation'. With regard to agriculture, the MPs called on WTO members to work on the 'elimination of all forms of export subsidies', a 'substantial reduction in trade-distorting domestic support' and market access. They pointed to the 'fundamental need to define and provide a framework for the notion of "sensitive products" and for the issues of special interest to developing countries'. The 'highest importance' was attached to the 'pressing needs of developing countries dependent on the export of tropical agricultural commodities, notably sugar, bananas and cotton'. The concerns of developing countries with regard to 'poverty reduction, food security and sustainable livelihoods' should be 'kept at the forefront' of the negotiations, and 'non-trade concerns of agriculture, which include food security, land conservation, revitalisation of rural society and rural

8. Hong Kong Session of the Parliamentary Conference on the WTO. Declaration. Adopted on 15 December 2005 by consensus (later the delegation of Australia expressed some reservations). Online. Available: http://www.ipu.org/splz-e/hk05/final.pdf (accessed 22 June 2013).

employment, as well as the issues of sustainable forestry and fisheries' should be 'addressed in a satisfactory manner'. The Declaration reiterated the need for caution with regard to the liberalisation of trade in services, especially services that relate to 'basic human rights and basic and essential needs such as those that provide for public health, education, culture, and social services'. The MPs in Brussels acknowledged each country's 'right to protect its cultural diversity and to conserve and develop public services', and underlined 'the importance of providing technical assistance to developing countries'.

The Hong Kong Declaration expresses a concern with 'the insufficient progress made in dealing with all key sectors, especially the major development issues'. With regard to agriculture, the Declaration emphasises that 'all forms of export subsidies' should be phased out, and that 'trade-distorting domestic support to agriculture by developed countries' should be reduced. Developed countries should open their markets for the world's poorest countries, and 'permanent provision of duty-free and quota-free market access for products originating from the least developed countries should be offered'. WTO rule-making and goals should be 'coherent with the obligations undertaken under multilateral environmental agreements' and the environmental legislation of WTO members 'should not be seen a non-tariff barrier to trade'.

The Hong Kong and Brussels Declarations illustrate the parliamentarians' preoccupation with the need to balance different concerns and interests such as trade liberalisation, non-trade concerns and the environment. The MPs argue that export subsidies should be eliminated and trade-distorting domestic support substantially reduced, and they are concerned with the needs of the developing countries. The Rules of Procedures that were adopted in Brussels include the oversight function, but also Packenham's socialisation and training function. The latter is expressed through the attention paid to the need for 'capacity-building'.

The establishment of a parliamentary dimension of the WTO indicates that the parliamentarians, to a certain degree at least, try to bypass their governments. However, in both Cancún and Brussels the bypass-government strategy was supplemented by an element of the go-through-government strategy when the parliamentarians argued that MPs should be included in the national delegations to the Ministerial Conferences. The national delegations are in fact the governments' delegations. It might also be said that a *go-through-the-WTO strategy* was added to the repertoire when the two WTO conferences recommended that MPs be included in the national delegations and when the Hong Kong conference advocated that national parliaments should assign trade issues either to an existing committee or to a new 'special committee on the WTO'.

The final point to be made at this stage is related to the organisation of and participation in the Parliamentary Conference on the WTO. As we have seen, the conference is organised by the IPU and the EP. The participants include not only national parliamentarians but also representatives of transnational parliamentary associations and assemblies, thus indicating that the concept of a multilevel parliamentary field is highly relevant.

Geneva 2006 – 2011

In July 2006, WTO Director-General Pascal Lamy concluded that the gap between key players was too wide, and that there was a need for a 'time out'. His recommendation that the negotiations should be suspended was adopted by the General Council. The Parliamentary Conference in Geneva in the beginning of December that year was marked by a standstill. The MPs expressed a particular concern with the 'lasting negative effects' of a 'prolonged suspension of the Doha talks' which could 'put poorer countries in a disadvantaged position', and repeated the 'commitment to provide a strong and effective parliamentary dimension to the WTO'.[9] However, nothing new was said with regard to the development of the dimension.

There was no Parliamentary Conference in 2007 but the Conference Steering Committee met twice and a parliamentary panel was organised at the WTO Public Forum in Geneva in October 2007. In June-July 2008 the negotiations seemed to progress, but once again the negotiators failed to reach an agreement. The Parliamentary Conference convened again in September 2008 and in the 'Outcome Document' the parliamentarians expressed their disappointment and concern about the failure.[10] The document stated that the WTO 'will need to engage in institutional reform aimed at improving its functioning and enhancing its accountability and democratic legitimacy'. Furthermore, the MPs declared that 'it is crucial for parliaments to exercise ever more vigorously and effectively their constitutional functions of oversight and scrutiny of government action', and that they were 'committed to play a far greater role than ever before in overseeing WTO activities'.

The amendments to the Rules of Procedure that were adopted by the conference in 2008 showed that a new step was taken in the process of institutionalising the parliamentary dimension of the WTO.[11] A specification of membership in the Steering Committee was included in paragraph 4.1. It stated that the committee should be composed of 'representatives of parliaments in Sovereign States, of the IPU and the European Parliament as the Conference co-organisers, of selected other regional and international parliamentary assemblies and structures, and of the WTO Secretariat'. Furthermore, five new paragraphs on continuity in representation (4.3), participation in the decision-making process (4.4), changes in the composition (4.5), term of office and rotation of seats (4.6), and a decision that the Steering Committee should define geographical regions for the purpose

9. Annual Session of the Parliamentary Conference on the WTO. Declaration adopted by consensus on 2 December 2006. Online. Available: http://www.ipu.org/splz-e/trade06/declaration.pdf (accessed 22 June 2013).

10. Annual 2008 Session of the Parliamentary Conference on the WTO. Outcome Document adopted by consensus on 12 September 2008. Online. Available: http://www.ipu.org/splz-e/trade08/ declaration.pdf (accessed 22 June 2013).

11. Rules of Procedure adopted on 26 November 2004, amended on 12 September 2008. Online. Available: http://www.ipu.org/splz-e/trade08/rules.pdf (accessed 22 June 2013).

of rotation (4.7), were added to the set of rules regarding the Steering Committee.

Of particular interest in our context are the new 'Guidelines for Relations between Governments and Parliaments on International Trade Issues' which were adopted at the 2008 conference.[12] The purpose was 'to provide all national parliaments with the opportunity to scrutinise and have an influence on governments' trade policy'. The guidelines should, it said, apply not only to the WTO but to 'international trade negotiations in the broader sense, i.e. both to multilateral and bilateral frameworks'. Three elements that were supposed to 'help to ensure that the national parliaments gain an influence on trade policy' were pointed out. It continued by stating that each parliament should receive 'relevant information on trade initiatives from the government in good time so that the parliament has an opportunity to take them into consideration before decisions are made'. Furthermore, parliaments should have 'real opportunity to use the information received to gain an influence on its own country's trade policy' and to 'follow up on its government's decisions'. The recommendations included easy access to information, original documents and draft agreements, and meetings with ministers 'well in advance' of both international trade meetings and decisions to be made on negotiating positions. Moreover, MPs 'specialising in international trade should be included, as a matter of rule, in their country's official national delegation to international trade events including WTO Ministerial Conferences'.

The guidelines state that it is up to each parliament 'to decide the extent to which the guidelines should be implemented', but we see that the *international* Parliamentary Conference on the WTO goes quite far in the specification of how *national* governments and parliaments should act, thus indicating that the national parliamentarians use a go-through-the-WTO strategy as an instrument in the struggle for influence *vis-à-vis* their respective national governments.

On substantive matters, the outcome document of the 2008 conference draws attention to the need to 'give priority to the vital interests of developing countries'. The MPs referred to 'the soaring prices of raw materials and agricultural products' and expressed worries about the financial and economic crises and the urgent need to address 'challenges relating to food security, energy and climate change'. However, the primary concern was the failure to reach an agreement, and the parliamentarians urged their government negotiators to close a deal so that the Doha Development Round could be concluded in 2009.

Shortly after the conference in September 2008 a new attempt to overcome the problems in the WTO negotiations was made by a group of countries and the EU, but the attempt failed. An enlarged session of the Steering Committee was organised on the occasion of the seventh Ministerial Conference in Geneva in November-December 2009 and a parliamentary panel was organised by the IPU and the EP at the WTO Public Forum in Geneva in September 2010. However, there were

---

12. Guidelines for Relations between Governments and Parliaments on International Trade Issues, adopted by consensus on 12 September 2008. Online. Available: http://www.ipu.org/splz-e/trade08/guidelines.pdf (accessed 22 June 2013).

no parliamentary conferences in 2009 and 2010 and the two meetings that were arranged cannot be characterised as anything but a pale reflection of what would normally qualify for the term 'parliamentary dimension'. The non-appearance of parliamentary conferences in 2007, 2009 and 2010 reflected the lack of progress in the WTO negotiations, and illustrates the relevance of an ebb-and-flow perspective on the development of the parliamentary dimension of the WTO.

The next Parliamentary Conference took place in Geneva in March 2011. For the first time ever the conference was held on the premises of the WTO. In the outcome document, the parliamentarians declared that 'multilateralism remains the best option to harness globalisation and manage interdependence'.[13] They reaffirmed their 'commitment to the universal, rule-based, open, non-discriminatory and fair multilateral trading system as embodied in the WTO' and declared that during the economic downturn 'the multilateral trading system has proven its value'. The WTO 'played a crucial role in weathering the threat of protectionism'.

The parliamentarians emphasised that '[t]he needs and interests of the developing countries, in particular the least developed countries, are at the heart of the Doha Development Agenda, which seeks to redress asymmetries and imbalances affecting them'. Consequently, 'special and differential treatment' of 'small and vulnerable economies' should, it said, be 'made more effective, meaningful and operational'. Developed countries should 'provide immediate, predictable, duty-free and quota-free market access [...] for all products originating from the least developed countries', and advanced developing countries 'should also contribute to this process'. The MPs emphasised that 'it is important to ensure that market opening and fair trade liberalisation go hand in hand with sustainable development, which contains three pillars: economic development, environmental protection and social development'.

Furthermore, the parliamentarians underscored the need to 'improve the functioning of the WTO as a negotiating forum' and 'rethink its processes and decision-making structure' in order to 'strengthen the democratic character and legitimacy of the system'. The MPs emphasised 'the need for a strong and effective parliamentary dimension to the WTO' and declared that parliamentarians 'have a duty to provide effective oversight of international trade negotiations, ensuring their transparency and fairness'.

Discussion

In the presentation on the development of the WTO's parliamentary dimension I have focused on two elements: the parliamentary dimension as such and the subject-matters that the parliamentarians have been concerned with. With the adoption of the Rules of Procedure in 2004 and their amendments in 2008 we may say that a

---

13. Annual 2011 Session of the Parliamentary Conference on the WTO. Outcome Document. Adopted by consensus on 22 March 2011. Online. Available: http://www.ipu.org/splz-e/trade11/outcome.pdf (accessed 22 June 2013).

first phase in the institutionalisation of the WTO's parliamentary dimension was completed. The Rules of Procedure state that the parliamentary conference should 'meet at least once a year'. However, the fact that no parliamentary conferences were held in 2007, 2009 and 2010, indicates that the institutionalisation of this parliamentary dimension is rather weak.

Bearing Crum and Fossum's discussion in mind, we see that the WTO's parliamentary dimension is far from a federal system. The WTO has a long way to go before the (unlikely) creation of a WTO-Parliament directly elected by the citizens of the member states, which was suggested in one of the scenarios (presented by Nogales (2006)) for the WTO in 2016. The present parliamentary dimension of the WTO has more features that resemble a loosely linked network. However, the concept of a network or a parliamentary field based on horizontal relationships between equal partners does not fully capture the character of the parliamentary dimension of the WTO. In relation to the Organisation, parliamentary actors are involved at three levels: the national, regional and (almost) global levels. The Parliamentary Conference is organised by the IPU and the EP and includes delegations designated by the Parliamentary Assembly of the Council of Europe, the CPA and the *Assemblée parlementaire de la Francophonie* together with members of the national parliaments of WTO member states. Furthermore, the 2011 conference in Geneva included observers from the ACP-EU Joint Parliamentary Assembly, the Andean Parliament, the EFTA Parliamentary Committee, the Inter-Parliamentary Assembly of the Eurasian Economic Community, the Nordic Council, and the Parliamentary Assembly of the Black Sea Economic Cooperation. Consequently, the parliamentary dimension of the WTO has developed beyond the horizontal parliamentary field towards a multilevel parliamentary field. But in contrast to the EU's multilevel parliamentary field, the WTO lacks a supranational parliamentary body that is directly elected by the citizens. This serves to underline the far weaker parliamentary dimension of the WTO, a point which is further underlined by the multilevel parliamentary field also including parties and interest organisations (Crum and Fossum 2012; introductory chapter of this volume). One may argue that such intermediaries are not included in the parliamentary dimension of the WTO. However, parliamentary panels are organised at the WTO Public Forum, an event which 'regularly attracts over 1,500 representatives from civil society, academia, business, the media, governments, parliamentarians and inter-governmental organizations'.[14] Nevertheless, it remains to be seen what type of institution the parliamentary dimension of the WTO may become.

It is first and foremost the parliamentarians themselves who have advocated that they should have a role to play in the WTO. The WTO itself has not been a driving force in the development of the parliamentary dimension and the parliamentary conference is still not fully integrated into the WTO. However, for its own reasons the WTO has gradually become more interested in the parliamentary dimension.

---

14. Online. Available: http://www.wto.org/english/forums_e/public_forum_e/public_forum_e.htm (date 22 June 2013).

After the turmoil at the Ministerial Conference in Seattle in 1999, the WTO became more aware of the need for transparency, legitimacy and better communications with civil society. Parliamentarians, as elected representatives of the people, may serve as a link between the WTO and the civil societies of the member states and thus legitimise the objectives of the WTO. Or, as the so-called Sutherland Report[15] on institutional challenges to the WTO puts it, 'legitimacy is central to the effective development of the WTO as a force for good in the world, and national parliaments are the key mechanism to secure that legitimacy' (Sutherland *et al.* 2004).

The declarations from the parliamentary conferences have revealed that a variety of parliamentary roles and functions have been accentuated in relation to the WTO, including transparency and oversight, training and capacity building, and the articulation of various interests. Gradually, the parliamentarians have engaged more strongly in the subject matters of WTO negotiations, their possible consequences for other policies, and the need to balance different interests and concerns. Issues such as domestic support to agriculture, animal welfare, rural development, public services, medicines and public health, and climate change have been included in the declarations. Such issues illustrate that international and domestic affairs interfere with each other and that the boundary between domestic and international politics and policies is crumbling. In order to meet this development and strengthen their role and influence, the parliamentarians apply not only the 'constitutionally correct' go-through-government strategy, but also bypass-government and go-through-the-WTO strategies.

Questions for further research and reflection

As we have seen, the first phase in the process of institutionalising the WTO's parliamentary dimension has been completed but the role to be played by parliamentarians in relation to WTO negotiations is not fully developed. A number of questions for further research – and reflection among parliamentarians as well as in the WTO – may be raised.

National interests and two-level games

A variety of domestic interests and actors are involved in the process of establishing negotiating positions and defining national interests. One of the most important roles of national parliaments in democratic systems in general is to prioritise and balance conflicting political interests. However, the significance of national parliaments in this process depends, among other things, on the strength of parliament *vis-à-vis* the executive. This calls for comparative analyses of variations (across countries and across time) showing how parliaments are involved in these processes. Such

---

15. The full name of this report is: The Future of the WTO. Addressing institutional challenges in the new millennium. Report by the Consultative Board to the Director-General Supachai Panitchpakdi.

analyses could include topics such as formal decision-making by parliaments, informal consultations between parliaments and governments, the organisational structures (e.g. parliamentary committees) established in order to handle such processes, and the influence exerted by various domestic interest groups.

An important aspect of two-level games is the interaction between the games played at the national and international levels respectively. National governments may use compromises and 'necessary' concessions to be given in international negotiations as a means to persuade domestic interest groups and opposition parties in parliament to agree to domestic policies that they would otherwise not accept, while government negotiators may use constraints imposed on the government by domestic interest group and parties as a playing card in the WTO negotiations. The occurrence of, and variations with regard to, such games and strategies are important topics for further analysis.

Go-through- or bypass-government strategies?

Executive-legislative relations may have an impact on the strategies chosen by national parliaments in their efforts to influence WTO negotiations. The 'constitutionally correct' go-through-government option is most applicable when the government is responsive to parliament and consequently we would expect strong parliaments to exert their influence primarily through the government, while relatively weak parliaments are expected to be more inclined to choose the bypass-government strategy. The engagement of the EP in the organisation of the parliamentary conferences on the WTO (together with the IPU) could be interpreted in a similar way. The EP has been rather week compared to the European executive, the Commission, which negotiates on behalf of the members of the EU. To some degree the parliamentary dimension of the WTO may represent a 'bypass-Commission' option for the EP.

In the case of minority governments, and to some degree also coalition governments, we would expect parliaments to be relatively strong and to employ the go-through-government strategy. In presidential systems and parliamentary systems with strong majority governments, we would expect the legislatures to have limited influence on the domestic arena and consequently to be more inclined to implement a bypass-government strategy in the international arena. The guidelines for relations between governments and parliaments that were adopted at the WTO conference in 2008 illustrate that parliamentarians may even apply a 'go-through-the-WTO' strategy in order to influence their national governments. Further research in this context should aim to make clear how parliamentarians' choices of strategies are in fact related to executive-legislative relations.

Clearly, a certain amount of resources and capacity are necessary for parliaments to be able to apply the bypass-government or go-through-the-WTO strategies and engage at the international level. Important questions for research and reflection in this context include: How do variations in the resources of national parliaments affect their participation in the parliamentary dimension of the WTO? And what can be done in order to increase parliamentary capacity in general as well as in developing countries in particular?

Influence or legitimise?

The development of the WTO's parliamentary dimension has mainly been a process of institutionalising a role to be played by parliamentarians. Gradually the attention of the parliamentary conferences has changed and declarations have focused more on the content or subject-matters of the WTO negotiations. However, one may indeed question the real influence exerted by the parliamentarians on the negotiations. The parliamentarians' influence seems limited so far, but more thorough analyses should be conducted in order to see how this develops.

It seems premature at present, but from a longer perspective one may ask whether a stronger involvement of national parliamentarians will change the balance of power among WTO members. According to Zahrnt (2008), delegates at the national missions at the WTO agreed that 'the greater average participation of parliaments tended to decrease their countries' readiness to open up their markets'. One of the reasons for this may be that parliamentarians have narrower constituencies and more specific interests than the executive bodies. Consequently, parliamentarians 'enlist support for their specific protectionist needs by endorsing the claims for protection by other parliamentarians'. However, the impression given by the declarations from the parliamentary conferences on the WTO is not particularly protectionist. The MPs have stressed the need to reach an agreement on trade liberalisation, noticing that the interests of developing countries and non-trade concerns should be taken into account.

The rather liberal positions on international trade expressed by the parliamentarians may seem surprising. At this stage one can only speculate on the reasons. The parliamentarians are searching for a role to play and advocate the need for a parliamentary dimension of the WTO. They seek to win acceptance from the WTO and may thus be reluctant to confront the aim of liberalising world trade. Furthermore, so far the parliamentarians have not been confronted with the challenging task of making necessary trade-offs, giving up negotiating positions and compromising the important interests of their respective countries. The fairly liberal consensus reached so far at the parliamentary conferences on the WTO may be put to a more severe test if and when the negotiations move closer towards the intended 'single undertaking'. More research is needed on the parliamentarians and their views, not only on the delegates at the national (government appointed) missions at the WTO.

The WTO itself has not been the driving force behind the development of the parliamentary dimension. Perhaps somewhat reluctantly, the WTO has accepted that national parliamentarians should have a role to play in relation to the negotiations in the intergovernmental organisation. However, the role that the WTO wishes parliamentarians to play may seem to be somewhat different from the ones I have discussed above. To put it bluntly, the WTO may consider the parliamentary dimension to be a possible tool for the legitimisation of the WTO and trade liberalisation, and we may ask whether the parliamentary dimension of the organisation will become a channel for parliamentarians to exert influence on the WTO, or simply an instrument for the WTO to co-opt the parliamentarians and legitimise its activities?

Concluding remarks

The World Trade Organization has become one of the most important international organisations in the world and we have seen how a *parliamentary* dimension has been added to this intergovernmental organisation. I have described the steps that have been taken in order to institutionalise a parliamentary dimension of the WTO, and how the parliamentarians have increased the attention paid to the substantive content of the negotiations. We have seen that this development can be explained by the intertwinement of international and domestic affairs, theoretical perspectives on national interests and two-level games, executive-legislative relations, and go-through- or bypass-government strategies in order to influence the WTO. The latter has been supplemented with a go-through-the-WTO strategy carried out in order to strengthen the influence of parliamentarians on national governments.

I have raised a number of questions related to the process of prioritising and balancing various national interests, the relationships between games played at the national and international levels respectively, executive-legislative relations and parliamentary strategies, and the role of parliamentarians with regard to exerting influence on or legitimising the WTO. The list of topics is definitely not comprehensive, but it illustrates the need for research and reflection, among parliamentarians and in the WTO itself, on representative democracy and the role of national parliamentarians in an intergovernmental organisation such as the WTO.

Important steps have been taken towards the institutionalisation of a parliamentary dimension of the WTO, but there is still more to be done. It remains to be seen what impact national parliamentarians can have on WTO negotiations, and what type of institution the parliamentary dimension of the WTO will become.

part v. democratic implications

chapter fourteen | the European Union: parliamentary wasteland or parliamentary field?

Christopher Lord

Introduction

It is one thing to believe that EU institutions should be subject to parliamentary control. It is another to determine how any parliamentary control should best be realised. Given that parliamentary control of Union decisions can plainly be allocated either to the EP or to national parliaments, it is perhaps surprising that little attempt has been made to derive some principled standards for discussing and deciding how such an allocation should be made. The aim of this chapter is to propose a standard that follows from core attributes of democratic legitimacy, together with a real world understanding of how parliamentary politics delivers those core attributes.

My starting point is with the following remark that Ben Crum and John Erik Fossum make in the introduction to this book:

> Rather than assuming these parliamentary institutions to be organised in a single hierarchical structure, the institutions in the field are connected by their shared function of representing people's interests in EU decision-making and the role perceptions and interactions that come with that.

Taking this remark in conjunction with other contributions Crum and Fossum have made to the concept of a parliamentary field (2009, 2012), I have three initial thoughts which I will attempt to elaborate a little further during the course of the chapter.

First, whatever the differences in their powers, capabilities, resources or interest in EU matters, whatever the cynicism or sincerity of their members, and whatever the rivalries and jealousies between parliaments at the national and European levels, there just are certain normative roles that parliaments usually need to perform if they are to contribute to democratic legitimacy.

Second, the concept of 'a European parliamentary field' may be preferable, for example, to that of a 'European Union political system'. The concept of a 'field' is, arguably, less likely than that of a 'system' to be taken as implying that parliaments at either level should have a prescribed place. To the extent that it is open to variety and variability, as well as reasonable disagreement on how parliamentary powers should be distributed between the two levels, the notion of a parliamentary field allows for debate about the normative qualities and practical consequences of available alternatives without assuming any particular solution in advance.

Yet, third, for all the openness and flexibility of the concept of a field, we cannot expect to be able to recognise the parliamentariness of any 'European parliamentary field' without the help of a standard that owes at least something to reasons for valuing parliamentary politics in the first place. I develop this argument in opposition to Pierre Bourdieu's own view of how legitimacy relates to the concept of a 'political field'. The chapter proceeds as follows. To demonstrate the importance of developing a standard for evaluating the contributions of the European and national parliaments to democratic legitimacy, the second section identifies five ways in which any democratic deficit in European integration can also be understood as a parliamentary deficit. The third section proposes a standard. The fourth illustrates its application. The fifth concludes.

Twin deficits? Five ways in which the democratic deficit may be a parliamentary deficit

Insufficient parliamentary control over EU decisions is the original sin of the democratic deficit. Those who first coined the term believed that wherever the Union exercises powers with less parliamentary participation or supervision than its member states, any transfer of powers from the national to the European level necessarily entails some democratic loss or deficit (Karlsson 2001). If we assume that direct democracy is impossible in mass systems save as an occasional dietary supplement and that it is, therefore, only through representatives that citizens can control, as equals, the making, amendment and administration of their own laws, then there are at least five possible grounds for arguing that any democratic deficit suffered by the Union is essentially a parliamentary deficit.

First, the delegation of legislative powers from national parliaments to the Council of Ministers can be seen as a parliamentary deficit in the *making* of laws. As Joseph Weiler remarks, the Council effectively allows the executive branch of each national government to 'reconstitute' itself as part of a multi-state legislature for the purposes of making Union law (1997). This increases the legislative powers of executive-based actors at the expense of elected legislators. Another difficulty is that the Council primarily associates national governments together for the purposes of intergovernmental bargaining and pooling technical expertise, not for those of meeting procedural requirements that may be needed for citizens to see themselves as authoring their own laws through representatives, such as transparency, and public justification of each decision that contributes to legislation. Since it is questionable how far the Council has the normative qualities of a legislature, it may be more accurate to describe the Union as only semi-parliamentary (Magnette 1999) than it is to suggest it resembles a fully parliamentary legislature organised into two chambers.

Second, a parliamentary deficit can be identified in arrangements for the *amendment* of Union laws. The Union's consensus system favours the *status quo* over alternatives to it. Just a handful of veto holders can often resist change and hold everyone else to policies that have become deeply unwelcome to them. They can conceivably even do this against the will of several parliamentary majorities, both in the EP and in a majority of national parliaments (Scharpf 2009; Lord 2011).

Third, a parliamentary deficit can likewise be identified in the *administration* of Union laws. What Deidre Curtin and Morten Egeberg term the EU's 'new executive order' (2008) - agencies, comitology committees, expert committees and so on - arguably, rests on a proliferation of administrative executive practices away from hierarchal forms of administration that can, in turn, be held accountable to politically appointed executive actors and, through them, to representative bodies and the voters.

Cutting across the foregoing parliamentary deficits is a fourth ground. Even where the European or national parliaments have acquired powers over the making, amendment or administration of Union policy and law, it is questionable how well citizens are linked to the use of those powers through electoral and party systems.

Here I will make an assumption that is core to the overall argument of the chapter. I said earlier that I wanted to propose a standard of parliamentary politics that follows from core attributes of democratic legitimacy, together with a real world understanding of how parliamentary politics deliver those attributes. My real world assumption is that any one parliament can only contribute to democratic legitimacy in so far as it operates as just one element within a wider field of parliamentary politics in which elections, parties, parliamentary deliberation, and parliamentary powers over the making and administration of legislation *all* need to combine together to ensure democratic legitimacy.

That, in turn, implies two conditions that I term 'encompassing' and 'infrastructural'. The encompassing condition requires that the powers of parliaments should allow publics to exercise public control wherever they want across the whole range of public decision-making. As John Stuart Mill put it: 'it is an open question what actual functions...shall be directly and personally discharged by the representative body [...] provided the functions are such as to secure to the representative body the control of everything in the last resort' (1972 [1861]). The infrastructural condition follows from the requirement that citizens should, in effect, be able to exercise parliamentary powers through their representatives. In practice this requires that parliaments should be part of an infrastructure of elections, parties and communications media that provides competition, choice and information.

Together, these requirements suggest a fourth way in which the Union may suffer from a democratic deficit that is also a parliamentary deficit. It may not be enough for the EP and national parliaments to have powers on Union issues, if those powers do not encompass all Union decisions, and, if parties and elections do not structure voter choice around Union decisions.

The four parliamentary deficits identified so far are, arguably, structural to the extent they relate to a feature of the Union that is unlikely to change any time soon: namely, its dependence on the enforcement structures of its member states. That, in turn, requires the Union to practice a form of 'executive federalism' (Dann 2003) in which decisions depend on the consensus and continuous involvement of those specialist parts of national public administrations that are responsible for the implementation of Union policy, even if that implies technocratic decision-making, confidentiality instead of transparency (Naurin 2007), and restricted room for the contestation and politicisation that would probably be needed to link voters to policies through a more competitive form of parliamentary politics (Bartolini 2005).

Yet even this understates the problem. A further structural feature of the Union is the autonomy of its law. Although space does not permit the development of the point here, this implies a fifth parliamentary deficit. As Fritz Scharpf has put it, it is unusually difficult by the normal standards of parliamentary democracy for elected legislatures to overturn judge-made law in the case of the EU (2009).

All five parliamentary deficits in European integration can be understood as part of a wider crisis of parliamentarism in modern democratic politics. It is often claimed that the *internal* coherence of even well-established parliamentary systems is increasingly challenged by shortcomings in how well elections, party competition, parliamentary deliberation and parliamentary powers over legislation and its execution all fit together to allow citizens to exercise public control as equals (Rosanvallon 2008). To the extent, moreover, that law, administration and finance are more adaptive than parliamentary politics to globalisation and Europeanisation, systems of parliamentary representation may also have lost some of their *external* power and autonomy in relation to those other systems they need to be able to regulate if they are to be the primary means by which 'individuals determine the terms of their living together as equals' (Bohman 2007).

Yet, nothing that has been said so far is uncontested: neither the claim that the EU is in democratic deficit at all (Moravcsik 2002; Majone 2005), nor the assumption that any democratic deficit it does suffer is at base a parliamentary deficit. Focussing only on the latter, one obvious objection is that the notion of a democratic deficit that is also a parliamentary deficit is simply out-of-date. Since the term democratic deficit was originally coined, the EP and national parliaments have gained powers on Union issues. Some believe this has even begun to create the necessary conditions for party and electoral politics to play a greater role in structuring voter choice, competition and control around Union questions. Thus, Hix *et al* (2007) argue that the party groups in the EP are now cohesive enough for party responsible government in the European arena. In other words, members of the EP vote the party-line often enough for European parties to be held responsible for their records in outgoing parliaments and their programmes for incoming parliaments. That, in turn, removes at least one possible obstacle to the more widespread contestation of European elections on European issues.

A more conceptual objection to the claim that the Union suffers from twin parliamentary and democratic deficits might be that the Union just is not the kind of polity that can, or needs to be, a parliamentary democracy. Assume, for example, that all the following conditions need to be satisfied if a parliamentary system is to deliver democratic legitimacy: a) freedoms of speech and association; b) free and fair parliamentary elections; c) appointment of the legislature and leading executive positions by popular vote; d) a form of political competition that offers voters choices relevant to the control of the political system; e) a civil society in which all groups have equal opportunity to organise to influence the polity; f) a public sphere in which all opinions have equal access to public debate; and g) a defined *demos* or, in other words, agreement on who should have votes and voice in the making of decisions binding on all.

Yet, it may be difficult to satisfy all these conditions simultaneously without certain attributes of statehood. The capacity of the state to concentrate power, resources and legal enforcement has been useful in all kinds of ways to democracy: in ensuring that the decisions of democratic majorities are carried out; in guaranteeing rights needed for democracy; in drawing the boundaries of defined political communities; in motivating voters and elites to participate in democratic competition for the control of an entity which can manifestly affect their needs and values (Lord and Harris 2006). Thus it is possible to doubt whether a non-state polity such as the Union can repeat a similar trick, at least on its own, and without heavy dependence on the infrastructures of member state democracies (Scharpf 1999).

Of course, all this assumes that the Union needs to be a parliamentary democracy, as opposed to a more presidential (Bogdanor 1986), direct (Abromeit 1998) or post-parliamentary (De Schutter and Lebessis 2001) form of democracy, or just a system in which publics voluntarily trade-off democratic control against the inconvenience of associating together at the European level as a single democratic people (Majone 2005). Space does not permit examination of these counter-suggestions to parliamentary control of the Union. It is enough for the purposes of this chapter to make the fairly obvious point that a debate – between those who allege all kinds of parliamentary deficits against the Union and those who believe that it neither can nor needs to be a parliamentary system – would benefit from greater clarification of the role of parliamentary politics in liberal democratic legitimacy. Few if any of the contributions to the debate attempt to make standards of parliamentary legitimacy as explicit as I hope to do in the next section.

Fields and legitimacy

What is involved in making standards of legitimacy explicit? Broadly, studies of legitimacy fall into two rival camps. According to one point of view, political power is largely self-legitimating. Legitimacy is therefore best studied by investigating the legitimation claims the powerful themselves make. According to a very different point of view, legitimacy has to begin with the person whose obedience is required and not with the person who requires it. Thus, Jürgen Habermas argues that legitimacy takes the form of 'political obligations' citizens 'put themselves under' through the propositional logic of their own 'moral claims' (Habermas 1996).

In fact, one of the most engaging statements of the view that concepts of legitimacy are largely created by power-holders themselves is provided by Pierre Bourdieu. Given that Bourdieu also did much to advance the notion that social relations are best understood as less than fully systematised fields of roles and resources, it might be thought that to talk of parliamentary 'fields' also requires accepting his view that it is power-holders who mainly set standards of parliamentary legitimacy. However, in what follows I want to argue the contrary case that a pragmatic view of legitimacy – in which its meaning is shaped by ordinary practice and language that no one dominates – is actually the more compatible with Bourdieu's concept of a field and the assumptions that lie behind it.

Bourdieu believed that modern societies are best understood as a number of intersecting fields: political, bureaucratic, commercial, legal and cultural (Benson and Neveu 2005). He argued that each of those fields is distinguished from all the others by distinct forms of competition for those forms of capital or resources that are needed to achieve its own standards of success. However, fields are not just arenas of competition. This is because each field defines what is valued, and why, in its own way. Each, therefore, has its own 'rules of the game, standards of practice and criteria of validity' (Hallin and Mancini 2004) that presuppose shared, or at least overlapping, beliefs between their participants. As Bourdieu puts it,

> the most irreducible adversaries have it in common that they accept a certain number of presuppositions that are constitutive of the very functioning of the field [...] There is a kind of fundamental complicity between the members of a field [in which] conflicts have the effect of concealing the very principles of those conflicts.

(Bourdieu 2005)

Each field varies in the autonomy with which it can sustain its own forms of competition and standards of validity in relation to the other fields that intersect it. Bourdieu has, accordingly, been described as 'following Weber and Durkheim in portraying modernity as a process of differentiation into a series of semi-autonomous spheres of action' (Benson and Neveu 2005). It is significant, however, that he wrote of 'fields' and not 'systems'. This was, in turn, related to his rejection of social theories that assume high levels of rationality in human behaviour, whether rationality of 'consciousness' or 'calculation' (Bourdieu 1994). He scorned the rationality of calculation assumed by rational choice and he rejected the rationality of consciousness involved in Kantian assumptions that individuals can 'consciously' construct their own social worlds out of laws they feel they can give themselves in light of their own moral beliefs. Instead, he argued that '[s]ocial agents construct the world through cognitive structures' that are not even 'forms of consciousness but *dispositions of the body*'. The world is thus one of scarcely rationalised habits or routines that are too 'arbitrary' (Bourdieu 1994) to be described as systems at the collective level or as rational behaviour at the individual level.

Yet in spite of his rejection of systemic views of social life, the political field had a special place in Bourdieu's thought. He argued that the state concentrated different forms of capital – varying from the means of physical coercion to softer forms of 'economic, informational and symbolic' domination – in a way that allowed it to regulate other fields (Bourdieu 1994). Central to Bourdieu's understanding of how that process works was his claim that Weber's definition of a state should be changed from an entity that 'successfully claims a monopoly of physical violence' to one that secures a 'monopoly of physical *and symbolic* violence' (Bourdieu 1994). The following passages explain what he meant by a monopoly of symbolic violence and why he regarded it as a defining attribute of states:

> In order to understand the power of the state – the particular symbolic efficacy it wields – [...] one must overcome the opposition between a physicalist vision of the social world that conceives of social relations as relations of physical force and a cybernetic or semiological vision which portrays them as relations of meaning or relations of communication [...] the state has the ability to impose and inculcate, within a given territorial expanse [...] identical or similar cognitive and evaluative structures [...] through the framing it imposes upon practices.

> (Bourdieu 1994)

> one of the major powers of the state is to produce and impose categories of thought that we spontaneously apply to all things of the social world – including the state itself.

> (Bourdieu 1977, 1991)

This understanding of the political field, and of the role of state within it, yielded a distinctive view of political legitimacy. Bourdieu shared the view that the ability of political authority to justify itself is amongst the most significant challenges faced by political order. For example, he argued that 'No power can be exercised in its brutality in an arbitrary manner [...] It must dissimulate itself, cloak itself, justify itself for what it is' (Wacquant 1993). Yet, as is suggested by this association of 'dissimulation' with 'justification', Bourdieu also believed that the challenge of legitimation is so easily met that it usually approaches a non-problem. As he put it, 'the fundamental question of political philosophy' consists of

> a problem that is not really posed as such in ordinary existence: the problem of legitimacy. Indeed, essentially, what is problematic is that the established order is *not* problematic [...] the question of the legitimacy of the state, and of the order it institutes, does not arise except in crisis situations.

> (Wacquant 1991).

Thus, for the most part, political order is self-validating and self-legitimating: 'state injunctions owe their obviousness, and thus their potency, to the fact that the state has imposed the very cognitive structures through which it is perceived' .

> (Wacquant 1991)

In sum, then, Bourdieu counsels us to look at the genesis of legitimacy claims, and, in particular, at the role of the powerful – those who are able to combine the manipulation of meaning and expectations with all the other resources to be found in the political field – in generating the tests by which the exercise of political power is itself judged. He further argues that we should neither over-estimate the coherence of legitimation claims, nor under-estimate their arbitrariness, nor under-estimate the self-deception invested in them, nor under-estimate the complicity of the dominated in their own domination.

Still, I believe that Bourdieu's concept of legitimacy is in tension with his concept of fields. Note that he can only make the claim that power-holders create their own legitimacy by assuming that the political field functions as a kind of master field that can impose categories of thought on others. At this point, the reader might be forgiven for suspecting that the notion of a field is in danger of collapsing back into the concept of a system.

Indeed, a very different view of legitimacy to that endorsed by Bourdieu may actually be more compatible with his view of social reality as consisting of a series of fields that overlap in relations of varying, but rarely complete, domination. Here, it is important to note that Bourdieu claimed to take his view of society from Wittgenstein's linguistic philosophy – hence, his criticism (above) of those who understand 'social relations as relations of physical force' rather than 'relations of meaning or relations of communication'.

Others, however, have used Wittgenstein's 'pragmatic' philosophy of meaning to reach a quite different understanding to Bourdieu's regarding how those aspects of social reality that rest on shared meaning – of which assumptions about the legitimacy of political power must be a foremost example – are established and tested in everyday language and social practice (see especially Searle 2010). No one need monopolise, control, or even fully understand such processes, *contra* Bourdieu's view that power-holders largely create their own legitimacy. Moreover, even the powerful will face at least two constraints in attempting to develop concepts of legitimacy aimed at achieving what Habermas terms 'social integration' through the 'binding forces of an intersubjectively shared language' (Habermas 1996). The first is any constraint involved in establishing mutual understanding, and the second, simple standards of consistency and non-contradiction. As the pragmatic philosopher Robert Brandom has put it: we can only make claims and get them accepted by others as a shared meaning if we are also prepared to commit to all that follows from that claim, to warrant that we are entitled to the claim, and to accept responsibility for repairing any inconsistencies between that one claim, and every other belief we endorse (Brandom 2008).

Indeed, it is precisely for reasons such as these that, far from following Bourdieu in assuming that the powerful can 'impose their own categories of thought', leading political philosophers have sought to develop accounts of legitimacy from an analysis of what even power-holders must accept if they are to endorse the simplest presuppositions of liberal societies without falling into contradictions. If liberal societies really do hold that individuals are assumed to be morally autonomous – or, in other words, free to judge for themselves what is good and right – then they are presumably also committed only to coerce their citizens in ways those citizens can regard as right (Rawls 1993; Habermas 1996). If, however, citizens are to be in a position to make that judgement, they need to be able to control the making, amendment and administration of the laws by which they are, themselves, bound. Thus, citizens of liberal societies must, in a sense, be able to author the laws by which they are coerced. Moreover, they need to be able to control their laws as equals if each person is to be of equal moral worth, and if there is not to be an element of rule of some of the people by others of the people (Estlund 2008). On top of that, it is each individual who is assumed to be free and equal. Therefore, any individual whose 'views are set aside' (*see* especially Mill 1972 [1861]) has a right to a justification that the laws have been made in ways that commit her too (Forst 2007). Thus, to summarise, liberal democratic legitimacy requires: public control; with b) political equality; and c) individual rights to justification (c.f. Beetham 1994; Weale 1999; Bohman 2007). It is by that standard that I propose we should evaluate whether parliaments contribute to liberal-democratic legitimacy. Likewise, it is by that standard that decisions should be made on how to allocate powers between different representative bodies that can perform the normative role of parliaments.

The parliamentary field as a distribution of legitimation roles between the European and national parliaments

Given the idea of democratic legitimacy with which I concluded the last section and the real world assumptions I made in Section Two, I propose the following test of how far parliamentary politics contribute to democratic legitimacy: how well do elections, parties, parliamentary deliberations and parliamentary powers over the making and administration of law combine in ways that allow citizens to exercise public control with political equality and individual rights to justification. In this section, I illustrate how that standard might be applied. I cannot stress too strongly that it really is just an illustration. The evaluation that follows does not, and cannot, claim to be either comprehensive or definitive.

The European Parliament

The EP's powers can be briefly summarised as follows. In a polity whose main business is rule-making, the EP co-decides an estimated 90 per cent of new legislation through a procedure that gives it both veto powers and agenda-setting opportunities to propose amendments to the other institutions (Tsebelis 2006). It also has powers over the administration, and not just the making, of Union laws in so far as it co-decides annual budgets; it has some scrutiny rights over comitology committees and EU agencies; and it can veto the appointment of the President and College of European Commissioners, as well as dismiss the College by a double majority. How far does all this deliver public control with political equality and individual rights to justification?

Justification

In research with Dionysia Tamvaki (Lord and Tamvaki forthcoming), I have used the Discourse Quality Index (DQI) developed by Jürg Steiner and others (2004) to test how far plenary debates in the EP meet various standards of justification.

We found that the overall level of justification is high in comparison with similar studies of national parliaments. We further found that debates cover the different kinds of justification that are needed if law-making is to be justified in terms of rights and values, as well as interests.[1] Moreover, parliamentary debates at the European level do seem to encourage representatives to justify their claims by appealing to European, as opposed to purely national, conceptions of the common good. Yet, in one respect the EP scores poorly in comparison to other parliaments studied by the DQI: representatives are less likely to be cross-examined on their justifications, which cannot, therefore, be said to undergo 'trial by debate' (Manin 1997). Beyond the evidence of the DQI it is also, of course, questionable how far the deliberations of the EP count as public justifications in the sense of being noticed by the public itself.

Political Equality

Consider two possible equalities: equal representation of individual persons and equal representation of whole democratic peoples. Strictly speaking, the EP achieves neither. The ratio of representatives to individuals is twelve times higher in the smallest (Malta) than the largest member state (Germany). Yet the EP is hardly like the US Senate in giving each state equal representation regardless of its size. Maybe it is neither surprising nor worrying that representation in the EP is not based on just one of the two equalities to the exclusion of the other. Even, however, if a case can be made for giving at least some weight to both equalities in the allocation of EP seats, it would presumably be desirable that any rule for trading the two inequalities off against one another – such as degressive proportionality - should be consistently applied. Yet it is unclear whether present arrangements satisfy even that basic requirement (Lord and Pollak 2012).

Public Control

Notwithstanding the description of the EP's powers at the beginning of this section, it is still possible to argue that those powers do not confer sufficient control over the making and administration of Union laws on elected representatives. Some legislation is still not covered by co-decision, and, in the view of some, it is a defect that the EP can only veto, and not constitute the political leadership of the Commission, which, of course, forms the main administrative authority at Union level. It also remains to be seen whether new arrangements for the scrutiny of comitology are sufficient to remove the Parliament's long established complaint that much of the detail of legislation is only filled in at the implementation stage with the result that poorly controlled rule-making by administrators substitutes for forms of law-making that are controlled by elected parliamentarians. As the Parliament puts it in one report, 'the supposed implementation of policy often actually constitutes the development and establishment of policy' (European Parliament 1998).

---

1. For the importance of this see Habermas 1996: 159–161.

However, as seen above, the main difficulty may lie less in the nature of the EP's powers than in how far the quality of its electoral link allows publics indirect control over the exercise of the Parliament's powers. In so far as they remain 'second-order', it is questionable how far European elections function as either *ex ante* or *ex post* mechanisms of public control. They neither amount to evaluations of rival programmes for forthcoming EPs nor appraisals of the relative performance of parties in outgoing EPs.

Now, I am well aware that Herman Schmitt and Jacques Thomassen (2000) have argued that there is at least one sense in which the EP is representative, in spite of second-order elections, namely, in the high correlation between MEPs' policy preferences and those of their voters. Still, it seems doubtful whether voters really can exercise adequate public control without making active and informed judgements of the political system in which representative office is held, or without a structure of political competition which allows them to pass judgement on how well power-holders have – or are likely to – exercise their powers in the political system in question. It follows from the often-convergent nature of political competition that large numbers of voters will frequently feel that more than one group of representatives is equidistant from their preferences. A sensible basis for choosing might then be to judge who is more likely to deliver. Yet, judging the relative credibility of commitments made by would-be representatives is likely to require understanding that is specific to the polity in which power is exercised: maybe information about past performance; maybe an ability to form predictions about which groups of representatives are most likely to be strategically positioned to get their way in the coming legislative term.

National parliaments

The powers of national parliaments over Union decisions can be understood with the help of two closely related distinctions. On the one hand the powers of national parliaments over initial delegations of authority to Union institutions can be distinguished from their continuing powers over everyday decision-making. On the other, the powers of national parliaments over the behaviour of their own governments in Union institutions can be distinguished from any indirect power they can secure over the overall process of Union decision-making.

To some degree, the powers of national parliaments are now defined through the Treaties and thus by common agreement of member states. At Amsterdam, national parliaments acquired the right to receive documents six weeks before they were decided by the Council; at Lisbon, they acquired a power – through the Early Warning Mechanism – to challenge Union proposals on the grounds of subsidiarity (Cooper 2006). However, a full list of the factors that govern the power of any one national parliament on Union matters would probably have to include at least the following: a) its role in the process by which its own member state ratifies changes to the EU Treaties; b) its ability to scrutinise subsequent decisions made under the Treaties; c) the extent to which the national parliament in question is 'executive-dominated' by its own government; d) the pay-offs to its members of spending time on the scrutiny of EU decisions; e) constraints that the EU's political system puts on all national parliaments; and f) the energy and cunning with which its members respond to a)-e). Although this list implies that national parliaments vary in how powerful they are on Union matters, a few general themes permit a common evaluation of how far their participation in Union decisions can secure public control with political equality and justification.

Justification and political equality

As far as justification is concerned, national parliaments are probably more likely to debate national points of view than they are to contribute to a European public sphere in which the views of all those who are bound by Union policies and laws can potentially be justified in relation to all other opinions. With regard to equality, on the other hand, national parliaments are structurally unequal in their powers over their own governments, which are, in turn, unequal in their weight in the Union's political system. Yet, it is, of course, possible to question how far justification and political equality should be considered matters of common concern at the Union level. Inequalities of influence and national parliamentary deliberations that take little account of views from other member states may just be considered a price that we pay for continuing to govern ourselves in more or less distinct national political communities. However, from another point of view, it may be hard to justify zero concern either for the negative externalities that might follow from only having to justify decisions to co-nationals (Joerges 2006) or for inequalities in how well national parliaments can represent the views of their publics on Union matters. Some responsibility for justification and equality across member states, it might be argued, follows from combining at the European level to make common policies from which there are no easy exit options, and from which consequences follow for the life chances of individuals, not just the fortunes of states.

Control?

A further difficulty is that national parliaments may only provide individual, and not collective, control of all those who contribute to Union decisions. Of course, holding governments individually responsible for their participation in Union decisions is a necessary condition for democratic control, since member states have both decision rights and a primary role in the implementation of Union policies. However, individual control of individual governments by individual national parliaments is unlikely to be a sufficient condition for two reasons.

First, the control of individual decision-makers can never add up to a fully adequate system of public control where, as Weber famously put it, there is a problem of many hands. Where outcomes are conditioned less by individual behaviours than by the ways in which individual actions combine, forms of individual accountability are likely to be both too strong and too weak: too strong to the extent that there may be substantial injustice in holding individual actors responsible at all (March and Olsen 1995); too weak to the extent that individual responsibility could create perverse incentives. For example, national parliaments and publics will share in any incentives member states have to impose negative externalities on others, to free ride on the stabilising efforts of others, or to behave in morally hazardous ways. Thus, confining public control of Union decisions to individual national parliaments may only make these behaviours more likely.

Second, even powerful domestic institutions in powerful member states may feel constrained in how far they can control policy coordination at the European level. Wolfgang Wagner provides a striking example, albeit one involving NATO rather than the EU, and the German Constitutional Court rather than a national parliament.

> By a narrow margin of 5:3 votes the Federal Constitutional Court (FCC) endorsed the government's decision to have the Bundeswehr participate in the AWACS mission over Bosnia. Concerns about alliance solidarity and reliability played a decisive role in the judgement. The court noted that the Bundeswehr made up 30 per cent of the AWACS personnel. As a consequence the withdrawal of German soldiers at the very moment of this mission would endanger the no-fly zone over Bosnia. Furthermore, *'allies and neighbours would inevitably lose trust in German policy, the resulting damage would be irreparable'*.
>
> (Wagner 2006b)

Factors that might sometimes deter national parliaments from unilateral opposition plausibly include concerns about a) the overall credibility of cooperation at the EU level; b) the reputation of their own country as a reliable partner; c) patterns of reciprocity; and d) the bargaining costs of re-opening agreements to cooperate which have been negotiated with difficulty (*see also* Thym 2006).

Conclusion: Have we found a parliamentary field?

This chapter has argued that the 'parliamentariness' of any European parliamentary field is best evaluated by a standard of how well parliaments at the European and national levels deliver public control with political equality and individual rights to justification. It has also provided an illustration of how that standard might be used to evaluate the participation of the EP and national parliaments in Union matters.

However, a standard should, ideally, not just be an evaluative tool. Rather, it should also help us make decisions of institutional design. So, I conclude with two brief reflections on how far a standard of public control with political equality and public justification might help with two of the most important questions in the institutional design of any European parliamentary field, namely, a) the allocation, and b) the coordination of parliamentary powers across the two levels.

My first thought is that a standard of public control with political equality and public justification can, to some degree, operate independently of any intrinsic normative preferences for allocating parliamentary powers to national or European levels. Consider the example of someone who believes that all political power should be subject to strong parliamentary control and, yet, national *demoi* and their representatives are the only possible source of EU legitimacy. Would such a person have good reason to support delegating substantial powers to the EP? I think the answer is 'yes'. Keith Krehbiel has shown that modern parliaments are influential in proportion to their ability to overcome asymmetries of information that favour the very expert and executive bodies they need to monitor (Krehbiel 1991). To the extent that the knowledge and capabilities needed to monitor Union matters are to some degree specific to the European arena, national parliaments will incur opportunity costs in attempting to monitor both domestic and Union matters (Lord 2004). Time and resources spent on following Union decisions over their sometimes long and complex policy cycles may be time and resources not spent on domestic scrutiny. Thus, if it could be shown that the EP could, in some sense, be understood as 'standing in' for national parliaments (perhaps because it reproduces the same left-right cleavage at the European level or because its members are under the ultimate control of national parties), or that it could at least allow national parliaments to save time and avoid distraction from domestic scrutiny by relying to some degree on information gathered by the EP where they need to form views on EU matters, a case could be made for weighting any allocation of parliamentary powers over Union ones, significantly towards the EP, even from a point of view that understands continued control of delegations of power by national parliaments as essential to the legitimacy of the Union. I take it that Erik Oddvar Eriksen and John Erik Fossum (2007) had something along these lines in mind in the concept of delegated democracy they developed for the RECON project (Eriksen and Fossum 2007).

My second thought is that a standard of public control with political equality and public justification helps us understand why the following may be three quite distinct *desiderata*: the aggregate level of parliamentary participation in Union decision-making; the allocation of parliamentary powers over Union decisions between the European and national parliaments; and the extent of any coordination between the European and national levels. It is, for instance, possible to support extensive parliamentary control of the Union as well as a division of labour between the EP and national parliaments designed to maximise that control, whilst being cautious about coordination between parliaments at the two levels (Kiiver 2007).

Consider the following argument from the democratic deficit debate: whilst there are many reasons for believing that it is hard to institutionalise the popular sovereignty of democratic majorities at the European level, the Union is, arguably, even better suited than the political systems of many of its member states to the delivery of the protective and constitutional benefits of democratic rule (Mény 2002). Precisely because it is not an integrated polity, its decisions are often exposed to a remarkably high number of veto points. Even under relatively unfavourable conditions, multiple veto points could work to reduce the risk of arbitrary and unjustified decisions. Given a high level of executive domination of parliaments across most member states that is, none the less, neither complete, unconditional nor constant, requiring Union decisions to run the gauntlet of scrutiny by several parliaments could introduce a margin of uncertainty into arrangements for accountability. That could be helpful. Decision makers may be more likely to anticipate from the outset how their decisions can be justified against all possible lines of criticism where they do not have too much advance information about the ways in which they are likely to be challenged and by whom (Chambers 2004). Thus, it might be a mistake for interparliamentary coordination to be so close that it acts as a substitute for the individual judgement of different parliaments in ways that reduce the uncertainty and diversity of challenges.

The possibility that coordination between parliaments at the European, national and regional levels might take more or less desirable forms when measured against core standards (such as public control, political equality and justification) underlines the importance of researching the different forms that coordination does, can and should take. Research into a European parliamentary field is essential. It must continue.

chapter fifteen | conclusion: towards a *democratic* multilevel parliamentary field?*

Ben Crum and John Erik Fossum

Introduction

The chapters in this volume provide a rich and nuanced picture of the manner in which interparliamentary coordination unfolds in the multilevel European context, and beyond. They clearly demonstrate that the internationalisation of politics has not left parliaments unaffected. All kinds of institutions have been developed to enable parliamentarians to stay closely attuned to international and supranational decision-making, and in particular, to allow them to inform themselves and to coordinate their actions with other representative actors in the international political system. Parliamentarians have become more dynamic; they engage in international parliamentary assemblies; some also opt to pursue a political career at the supranational level, in the EP. Even if much of the evidence confirms the impression that parliamentary arrangements lag behind the internationalisation of politics and the executive powers that are directly involved in it (Slaughter 2004), there has clearly been a wide range of parliamentary responses. This book thus confirms our main assertion, as presented in the introductory chapter, that there is more coordination than the formal arrangements, if considered in isolation, would suggest. The question that we focus on in this concluding chapter is what this entails for our understanding of representative politics in the EU, and beyond.

We start by identifying and discussing some of the general patterns that emerge from the analyses in the substantive chapters, with a view to shedding further light on the broader, more systemic, nature of interparliamentary relations. That discussion frames the responses to the empirical questions we presented in the introductory chapter, pertaining to: what shape interparliamentary relations take; what motivates parliamentarians to engage in interparliamentary relations; and what effects such relations have on the power of parliamentarians - in relation to executive actors, among themselves, and in society in general. Second, we draw on these empirical insights to clarify the broader implications of these patterns for the practice and theory of democracy. Here, the normative question is whether new forms of interparliamentary coordination allow for the sustainability of parliamentary democracy under conditions of internationalisation, the fragmentation of political sovereignty, and the proliferation of multilevel politics.

---

* We thank Eric Miklin for useful comments on this chapter.

The shape of interparliamentary coordination in Europe and beyond

In the introductory chapter, we underlined that interparliamentary coordination can proceed along two different tracks. First, interparliamentary coordination can occur through the establishment of a supranational parliament that is directly elected by the citizens and that is also linked in with national parliaments. We have referred to this as a distinct supranational track of interparliamentary coordination. An important reason for listing this as a system of interparliamentary coordination is that the supranational parliament is connected with the national parliaments. The other track referred to efforts to reinforce the ability of national parliaments to address international politics through the development of closer relations across borders. The former represents the development of a vertical structure, whereas the latter relies more on horizontal patterns of interaction and contact (across member state parliaments but also linking them to the EP). The chapters in the book testify to significant developments along both tracks in the EU, and some developments along the second track beyond the EU (with the book providing examples from NATO, the WTO and the now defunct WEU).

With regard to the EU, the chapters show that these developments add up to a qualitative change: in Europe, parliaments are increasingly oriented to one another; each is becoming an intrinsic part of the others' operating environment; and the patterns of representation linking state and society in each member state also open up and take on a more horizontal logic in the sense of interacting with and coordinating actions across the member states' representative structures. The ensuing structure is more than, and different from, a network, and takes on the shape of a multilevel parliamentary field. As Pollak and Slominski (Chapter Nine) note, 'A total of forty chambers with around 9,500 Members of Parliament is a force to reckon with'. At the same time, it must be underlined that this structure lacks a determinate pattern and is less hierarchical than the two-channelled systems of representation that mark federal states.

The EU, and the interparliamentary engagement that it incorporates, is unprecedented in several important respects. The first is that the EU has given rise to the only directly elected supranational parliament in the world, the EP. Its role has been gradually strengthened, over time, through successive treaty amendments. This development has been widely studied and commented upon already (e.g. Rittberger 2005). Hence, rather than simply focusing on this first track of interparliamentary coordination, the main thrust of this book has been to shed light on the second track of interparliamentary coordination and the important coexistence and interweaving of the second track with the first track in today's EU.

The contributions to the book testify to the sheer density of this pattern of interparliamentary coordination; and that forms a second distinctive feature of the EU. That density stems from the coexistence of the two tracks and the broader structure of decision making in the EU. The permanent European institutions that continuously produce new legislation make up a structure that clearly induces such interparliamentary coordination. While national governments remain key players, the internal logic of the Council of Ministers renders individual parliamentary efforts to hold 'their' executive officials accountable deficient. This situation not only gives parliaments reasons to coordinate with one another; it also effectively brings them into one another's operating environments. As the EU integration process is one of merging (more than separating out) different levels of governance, it situates the EP in a complex pattern of cooperation and competition with national parliaments. The EU's general style of decision making further contributes to the intensity of interparliamentary relations, based as it is on comprehensive patterns of sounding-out and consensus-seeking.

As the chapters in this book have shown, interparliamentary relations can take many different forms and operate across a broad range of institutional structures. Traditionally, institutionalised interparliamentary platforms have offered the most obvious arrangements for parliamentarians to mobilise collectively. Which platform is chosen depends on the policy area. For defence matters, the NATO-PA is the obvious venue (Wagner *et al.*, Chapter Seven). For other issues, such as police cooperation and Europol (Garibay, Chapter Six), parliamentarians may turn to COSAC. Also in coordinating institutional practices like the scrutiny of EU affairs (Buzogány, Chapter Two) and the use of the EWM (Knutelská, Chapter Three), COSAC plays a useful role. When it comes to EU legislation, some of these platform functions may actually be fulfilled by the EP (Crum and Miklin, Chapter Five), especially if it initiates interparliamentary meetings. However, the fact that the EP constitutes a separate, supranational institution and the fact that its interests need not automatically align with those of national parliaments, do not always make it a trusted partner.

Not only has the range of interparliamentary platforms steadily expanded, it is complemented with a wide array of more bilateral arrangements. Furthermore, the book has also brought to light the numerous, and increasing, forms of informal contact and interaction among individual parliamentarians and political parties (Crum and Miklin, Chapter Five; Shemer-Kunz, Chapter Ten; Beauvallet and Michon, Chapter Eleven).

As we should expect from an organisational field (cf. Powell and DiMaggio 1991), the EU's multilevel parliamentary field encourages patterns of mutual learning, emulation, and transfer of ideas and policy models. Two important examples are the establishment of EACs in all EU member states and the diffusion of scrutiny systems across the EU's member states. As Buzogány underlines in Chapter Two, the lack of an explicit European template meant that parliaments adapted scrutiny models to suit their own more specific needs and specific mode of organisation. Indeed, as all these different arrangements link parliaments together, it is important to underline that there is very little coercion: parliaments in this system consider themselves as, and operate as, relatively autonomous actors. Actual interparliamentary engagement to a very large extent hinges on the voluntary engagement of parliamentarians. For them, interparliamentary arrangements are important devices for information generation and exchange.

The third distinctive feature of the EU refers to how collective parliamentary influence has come to be institutionalised in the decision-making process. Specifically, such institutionalisation has been realised through the EWM and the Commission's Barroso Initiative (*see*, in particular, Cooper, Chapter Four;

Ruiz de Garibay, Chapter Six; Wagner *et al.,* Chapter Seven; and Pollak and Slominski, Chapter Nine). As they provide a means of exercising direct influence at the EU level, these arrangements provide a whole new set of incentives for national parliaments to engage in interparliamentary relations. The use of these new institutions has also been actively stimulated by the subsidiarity test runs organised by COSAC and by the introduction of the IPEX facility (Knutelská, Chapter Three). Importantly, then, these arrangements do not just give parliaments direct access to the international level without going through their governments, they also induce parliaments to act as a collective.

Admittedly, two-and-a-half years after the Lisbon Treaty came into force, the results of the EWM and the Barroso Initiative must be treated with due caution. In 2011, national parliaments filed sixty-four subsidiarity warnings and 622 opinions under the Barroso Initiative (European Commission 2012; cf. Cooper, Chapter Four). As these contributions varied a lot in their object and substance, they might be considered to be of little effect and as having merely raised the noise level in an already very complex decision-making system. However, in May 2012, for the first time, parliaments reached the required threshold for a 'yellow card' on the proposed Regulation on the Right to Strike ('Monti II'). The Commission has subsequently withdrawn this proposal, demonstrating that the EWM can have decisional effects. In fact, if one considers the practical challenges that national parliaments face, such as the strict time limits and the problems of translation (Knutelská, Chapter Three; Pollak and Slominski, Chapter Nine), these results are already greater than some more sceptical observers had expected (Raunio 2010). What is more, the success of the EWM is not necessarily best measured by the number of times that it is invoked. If the mechanism were to be activated too often, it would come to impose a major brake on the EU legislative process (Pollak and Slominski, Chapter Nine). It would furthermore indicate a failure on the side of the European Commission to internalise the principle of subsidiarity and to anticipate the criticism of national parliaments.

Ultimately, the EWM requires a 'responsible' usage that should increase the sensitivity of the Commission and the governments towards parliaments' concerns about EU legislation, but where parliaments only turn to its actual activation as a last resort. In that respect, as Buzogány (Chapter Two) suggests: 'the main value added [of the EWM] might be of a rather indirect nature', namely in awakening national parliaments to their role in EU decision-making (cf. Crum 2005).

As Knutelská (Chapter Three) asserts, the EWM and the Barroso Initiative have led to 'an emerging shared role perception' among the EU's national parliaments; and Cooper (Chapter Four) even suggests that the Early Warning Mechanism has effectively turned them into a collective entity, 'a virtual third chamber'. The actual experiences so far give reason to nuance this claim somewhat, since far from all of the EU's national parliaments are equally keen to manifest themselves as a virtual third chamber, and even those that do engage do not necessarily operate in the same direction. Still, the level of mutual awareness and interaction has gone up significantly and this does affect the operation of the EU political system as a whole.

The EWM has a particularly notable effect on the relationship between national parliaments and the EP. On first sight, the specific focus that the EWM places on subsidiarity risks antagonising both, as national parliaments are led to focus in particular on subsidiarity concerns and hence to mobilise against integration, whereas the EP is inclined to favour pan-EU solutions (cf. Cooper, Chapter Four). To the extent, however, that parliaments are able to transcend a narrow concern with subsidiarity, the EWM has the potential to spur broader forms of interparliamentary deliberation. In such processes of interparliamentary deliberation, the EP can serve as a central node (a 'clearinghouse of arguments', as Crum and Miklin put it in Chapter Five) as it operates as a permanent institution at the supranational level with distinctive deliberative traits (Lord, Chapter Fourteen). Indeed, the permanent exchange of views through the interparliamentary field fits very well with the general character of the EU as an inclusive and consensus-seeking political system.

More generally, the increasing role of national parliaments in EU affairs has forced the EP and the national parliaments to reconsider the ways in which they relate to each other. Traditionally, the EP has been sceptical of giving the national parliaments any standing in EU decision-making as it feared that it might undermine its own claim to be the main repository of democratic legitimacy in the EU. Such a sense of competition typically comes to the fore in Daniel Ruiz de Garibay's account of the failure to establish a joint supervisory committee for Europol (Garibay, Chapter Six). However, in recent years the EP has become more active in fostering interparliamentary engagement. This applies, above all, to policy areas that retain a strong national dimension, like the field of foreign and defence policy (Wagner, Chapter Twelve). In response to the Euro crisis, we see similar developments in financial and macro-economic affairs (Benz, Chapter Eight).

Also, national parliaments need not be naturally inclined to cooperate across jurisdictions. As Chris Lord (Chapter Fourteen) reminds us, national parliaments may well regard the EP as part of the 'Brussels complex' rather than recognising it as a natural partner. What is more, there is also no reason to assume that the interests of national parliaments will necessarily cohere. On the contrary, on many issues with distributive implications (like the EU budget) they will likely compete with one another.

Still, looking at the field as a whole, there are few EU policy areas that fall exclusively under the control of either the national parliaments or the EP. Hence, they have to take account of each other's engagement and, depending on the issue at hand, can adjust the division of tasks between them. For instance, when it comes to EU military missions, national parliaments scrutinise their governments' decision to join an EU mission. However, once a mission is under way the EP takes on a more active, monitoring role (cf. Wagner *et al.,* Chapter Seven). Similarly when it comes to EU legislation on the single market, national parliaments' primary task concerns the monitoring of the principle of subsidiarity, an issue that is unlikely to be picked up by the EP (Cooper, Chapter Four). However, when it comes to more substantive and, particularly, distributive concerns, the EP enters centre stage, not only as EU legislator but also as a liaison to the national parliaments and parties. This versatility in the form of coordination and division of tasks is one of the distinguishing traits of the parliamentary field and sets it apart from a fully integrated and institutionalised parliamentary (multi-chamber) system.

Thus, given the patterns of interaction and interweaving, one may start to envisage Europe's parliaments operating as a coherent force, collaborating towards common aims, and seeking to reinforce one another in doing so. However, that is still far from the pattern that emanates from the studies in this book. For now, the system of interparliamentary relations is not only complex and inchoate, but also quite uneven, across members and policy-areas. Also, the position of the EP remains ambiguous as it has approximated to, but is still not, a fully fledged parliament. The very notion of a 'field' indicates that coherence is far from assured and that collective force may well fail to manifest itself if there is no coordination among its components or if they operate at cross-purposes. It can be added that to the extent that parliaments fail to coordinate their actions, it becomes all the more attractive for governments to use internationalisation as a means to fend off scrutiny.

In the introductory chapter we presented two additional sets of empirical questions besides establishing what forms of interparliamentary relations are actually maintained: what motivates these contacts and what effects do they bring about? The findings on the forms of interparliamentary relations in the EU give credence to the claim that they form part of a multilevel parliamentary field. That, in turn, leads us to consider how this might affect actors' motivations to engage in such relations and what specific effects this structure of relations actually has for EU decision-making.

Motivations and patterns of interparliamentary interaction

The multilevel parliamentary field in the EU shapes, and is shaped by, actors' motivations. These motivations can be captured by contrasting the general norm of parliamentary rule with the more mundane stimuli that drive parliamentarians' day-to-day behaviour in order to capture the extent to which the field actually affects parliamentarians' motivations. We do so in this section through considering some of the concrete examples that the various chapters have provided. These illustrations in turn help to elucidate how the field is structured, how it operates, and who it involves. That will further expose its frailty but will also show how it contributes to condition and shape actors' motivations and behaviour.

In general, the establishment of interparliamentary arrangements in the EU and beyond is legitimated by reference to the norm of parliamentary rule. This norm is at the heart of modern representative democracy and holds that parliament represents the people as political equals and that, hence, all 'publicly-made decisions' (Lord, Chapter Fourteen) are to be subject to parliamentary control. This is notable because, for a long time, this norm of parliamentary rule was considered not to apply to the international realm. The systematic internationalisation of politics has changed that. In effect, the recognition of the appropriateness of the norm of parliamentary rule is at the heart of the concern with the EU's democratic deficit (Lord, Chapter Fourteen; Eriksen and Fossum 2012), and motivates the steps taken to provide the WTO with a parliamentary dimension (Rommetvedt, Chapter Thirteen). Having said that, it is also clear that the mere insertion of (inter) parliamentary arrangements in international politics does not suffice to secure the norm of parliamentary rule. In particular, as these arrangements do not come with explicit prescriptions for exactly what is expected from them and how they relate to the established parliamentary bodies, they provide parliamentarians with few concrete recommendations on how, precisely, they should relate to interparliamentary coordination. However, rather than setting the norm of parliamentary rule aside in international politics, political and academic concern is now shifting to how it can be reconstructed under these changed conditions.

This changing context has several important implications, which the chapters in this book have brought forth. One is that governments engaging in international politics are under pressure to explain how (and who) they can compensate for the loss of parliamentary control at the national level. The general lack of institutional arrangements and systems of accountability at the international level means that governments' responses are likely to be half-hearted and may take different forms. In fact, internationalising decision power may be a way for governments to escape from the constraints of parliamentary control (Putnam 1988; Koenig-Archibugi 2004; Wagner, Chapter Twelve). Responses vary. One typical response is to simply underline the importance of parliamentary control and to call upon the national parliaments to engage as much as possible, with the option of coordinating with their peers abroad. At the other extreme, governments may turn to the establishment of a supranational parliament, as they did with the EP.

In practice, the EU has pursued both tracks simultaneously, with renewed vigour since the Treaty of Lisbon. The problem that, given its distinctive structure, is particularly felt in the EU, is that there is no clearly defined template for how parliamentary actors should behave in order to best ensure the norm of parliamentary sovereignty. This entails that whereas the field induces interparliamentary interaction, there is no uniform or unified logic of parliamentary sovereign rule to commit parliamentarians to fully exploiting the interparliamentary arrangements that are provided for them.

Despite the concerns about the ineffectiveness of parliamentary rule at the international level, it is hardly a surprise that, in practice, for most parliamentarians their primary focus remains their own institution and not necessarily the broader multilevel setting in which it has come to be embedded. Behaviour within parliaments is dominated by party politics and, more specifically, by more mundane questions, such as whether one's party is part of the governing coalition or of the opposition (Pollak and Slominski, Chapter Nine; Shemer-Kunz, Chapter Ten; Beauvallet and Michon, Chapter Eleven). Eventually, it is also the party that decides whether one will be put on the list again for the next election, whether one is allowed to rise through the ranks, or whether other candidates are nominated in one's place (cf. Hix 2002). Against that background, engagement in interparliamentary relations beyond one's parliament (and beyond one's constituency) may well appear as a distraction.

The heart of (national) parliaments' engagement with international and European affairs is formed by the scrutiny of their governments' involvement (Buzogány, Chapter Two) which is obviously integral to their day-to-day tasks. However, much of that scrutiny is likely to be rather unrewarding because of the well-known two-level logic of international negotiations (Putnam 1988): one can try to bind one's own government, but in the end the international decision will be determined through its interaction with other governments that are beyond one's control. In that sense, the chances of parliamentary success are small - in any case, smaller than in any direct engagement on domestic issues.

However, as noted, an important merit of maintaining interparliamentary relations is that it allows parliamentarians access to information without having to go through their government. Ideally this information can be used to increase the leverage of the parliament over the government. Wagner *et al.* (Chapter Seven) provide the telling example of Dutch MP Maarten Haverkamp who drew on experiences in other EU countries to challenge his Minister's claim that the stationing of armed forces on ships passing Somalia was not a feasible option. However, as far as we can see, such examples are still rare. In most cases the use of the information one acquires through interparliamentary relations is more indirect: parliamentarians establish new contacts that may be of possible future use; they get insights into the policy preoccupations of other states; and they get access to international officials and sites that one has no direct access to from one's own institution (Wagner, Chapter Twelve; Wagner *et al.,* Chapter Seven; Rommetvedt, Chapter Thirteen).

This book has also shown that parliamentarians can have interests in interparliamentary relations that go well beyond information gathering. Maintaining interparliamentary relations may, for instance, be a source of standing among one's peers. This is particularly the case if one is active in domains like foreign policy, defence or EU affairs. Interparliamentary relations are much less likely in other, more exclusively domestic, areas, where at least the notion of parliamentary sovereignty still retains the appearance of staying intact. The implication is that only a sub-set of parliamentarians engage in interparliamentary affairs, which is likely to be rather unrepresentative of the whole and already biased towards international affairs and an internationalist orientation (Beauvallet and Michon, Chapter Eleven).

Moreover, the chapters by Shemer-Kunz (Ten) and by Beauvallet and Michon (Eleven) reveal that the multilevel parliamentary field actually opens up new career prospects for parliamentarians. In their chapter, Beauvallet and Michon show how the EP provides female politicians with a means of acquiring political experience to catch up with men who often enjoy privileged access at the national level. Women's experience in the EP and the networks they develop there, in turn, help them to gain access to national politics later on. Shemer-Kunz (Chapter Ten) shows how a similar logic can apply to whole parties. A newcomer at the national level, the French Greens, used its easier access to the EP as a 'back door' to consolidate its presence in national politics.

The motivations for MEPs to engage in interparliamentary relations reflect the EP's distinctive role in the EU's multilevel parliamentary field. On the one hand, and in line with the widely held notion that the EP is a worthy carrier of the norm of parliamentary rule, a clear majority of MEPs have for a long time aspired for the EP to become the linchpin of the EU's democratic legitimacy. In that light, national parliaments easily appear as undesirable competitors, and it has often resisted granting them an effective platform in EU affairs (Garibay, Chapter Six). On the other hand, many MEPs hold a strong interest in their national parliament, possibly also because they have been a member of it in the past, or aspire to become one, in the future.

While Article 10 of the EU Treaty of Lisbon may have forced upon the EP the fact that it will have to allow national parliaments to operate as a second channel of EU democratic legitimacy, its interest in engaging with them has been reduced again by the increasing submersion of the EP into the inner dynamics of EU decision-making (Pollak and Slominski, Chapter Nine). The EP has responded to the extension of its legislative powers – powers it has been granted under the treaties – by turning itself into a 'working parliament' whose members become heavily specialised and engage closely and early on with the Council and the Commission to leave their mark on EU legislation. This strong orientation towards legislation risks coming at the expense of more external and representative functions that the EP may exercise.

To sum up, then, the focus on the structure of motivation has shown that the field in overall terms offers relatively weak inducements for parliamentarians to enter into comprehensive and resource demanding forms of interparliamentary interaction. However, as the scrutiny of governments' engagement in international affairs becomes an ever more important task for parliaments, the potential value of interparliamentary engagement increases. This is even more the case to the extent that the emergence of a new level of supranational representation affects parliamentarians' career patterns. These developments may induce parliamentarians to exploit the institutions that are established for interparliamentary engagement and thus contribute to the reconstitution of the norm of parliamentary rule at the international level. A closer look at what our contributors have said on when and how the arrangements are used and who benefits from them will shed additional light on the emerging structure.

Who uses interparliamentary relations and who benefits?

As the preceding analysis underlines, the use of interparliamentary arrangements has, first of all, to come out of the individual parliaments. The different chapters have also highlighted the great diversity among parliaments in terms of the powers they enjoy (e.g. Wagner *et al.*, Chapter Seven), their internal organisation (Buzogány, Chapter Two), their composition (e.g. Crum and Miklin, Chapter Five), and the interests they pursue (e.g. Benz, Chapter Eight). When it comes to European or international issues that do not lie immediately within their purview, parliaments are often slow to pick them up. They may well need to be stirred into action by interest group engagement or by signals from foreign counterparts (Crum and Miklin, Chapter Five). However, once they do so, and recognise the international dimension to the issue, they are likely to turn to interparliamentary arrangements.

Many of the preceding findings suggest that interparliamentary relations serve as 'a weapon of the weak'. This is an obvious field effect and relates to the general notion that while strong, established actors can get by with the resources they command, weak actors benefit disproportionately from regulated interaction, insofar as the regulations are symmetrical and not explicitly set up to subdue the weak, of course. In that light, interparliamentary relations appear as a means of emancipation through which weaker political actors strengthen their position in relation to stronger ones. This logic may work at different levels. First of all, it can be seen at the level of the relationship of parliaments with executives, where executives essentially control the international game (Putnam 1988) and parliaments use interparliamentary relations to catch up with them. Second, it can be seen in the relations among parliaments, where weaker parliaments may learn from stronger ones. Finally, the logic of emancipation can be discerned within parliaments where interparliamentary relations are more likely to be employed by the opposition than by the government coalition, as the latter already has privileged access to government information (Wagner *et al.,* Chapter Seven; Crum and Miklin, Chapter Five). In parallel to that, the active alignment of different parliamentary levels may be of particular importance for small parties, as Shemer-Kunz (Chapter Ten) indicates. Also Beauvallet and Michon's analysis (Chapter Eleven) shows that moving beyond the national parliament may be a means of emancipation.

Notably, within the complex multilevel field structure, it is far from self-evident which parliament is strong and which one is weak; different measures of strength may even contradict each other. Thus, a parliament in a prominent state may enjoy less formal powers *vis-à-vis* its government and still have greater leverage over the field as a whole in comparison to a parliament that enjoys much more formal power but does so in a smaller and more marginal state. The spread of scrutiny measures (Buzogány, Chapter Two) shows that the field can contribute to even out power differentials between executives and legislatures within member states, but the effectiveness of this copying process hinges on these measures being put to effective use, which is far from always the case.

At the same time, given the still rather voluntaristic nature of the field, we should expect it to have a limited effect on what constitutes a weak and what constitutes a strong parliament; in other words, the deciding factors here will still be state-internal factors. Typically, Pollak and Slominski (Chapter Nine) show that, for a long time, the Austrian Parliament counted as a strong parliament in terms of the formal powers at its disposal while in its actual relations with the government it was remarkably weak. Another aspect is that a parliament may enjoy considerable standing because of the strength of the country it represents, even if, as a parliament, its powers are comparatively limited. *Vice versa* some parliaments may be very powerful over their governments, while this may be of limited interest given their country's rather marginal impact. Ultimately, in practice, the added value of many interparliamentary relations hinges on the involvement of some strong parliaments; if they are just an exclusive gathering of weak parliaments no one is likely to benefit much in the overall scheme of things.

The most consistent indications that particularly weak parliaments take an interest in interparliamentary relations come from the non-EU case studies. Wagner (Chapter Twelve) finds his hypothesis confirmed: members of weak parliaments, in the sense that they have no veto power over military missions, are more likely to attend the NATO-PA than their colleagues from strong parliaments. Similarly, in the context of the WTO, Rommetvedt (Chapter Thirteen) suggests that strong parliaments will exercise their influence directly through their government, while weak parliaments are more likely to link up with other parliaments and thus to bypass their government.

Within the EU, the patterns seem rather mixed and interparliamentary relations clearly benefit from the involvement of (some of the) stronger parliaments. Thus, Knutelská (Chapter Three) finds that both (some) strong (most notably the French Senate) and weak parliaments file information on IPEX, although the information from strong parliaments is probably the most sought after. For the Barroso Initiative, whereby the Commission directly invites questions and opinions from national parliaments, the Portuguese Parliament – clearly not the strongest EU parliament – is the most fervent user, followed by the Italian Senate and the Czech Senate (Commission 2012). However, turning to the 'hard' powers of the EWM, stronger parliaments – like the Swedish Parliament, the Parliamentary Chambers of the UK, and the Polish Senate and *Sejm* – come to the fore (Commission 2012).

When we move to the level of parties, the evidence that interparliamentary cooperation is a weapon (particularly) of the weak is more mixed. Certainly, there is some evidence that opposition parties turn to interparliamentary relations to compensate for their secondary role in national politics (cf. Wagner *et al.,* Chapter Seven). By working via colleagues in other parliaments or at the international level, they may get access to information, and even influence, that they do not have access to at the national level. At the same time however, we find that big and well-established parties and party groups are particularly well-positioned to reap the benefits from interparliamentary cooperation because they control prominent positions at the different levels and have the facilities to maximise the connections between them. Particularly notable is, for instance, the extent to which the German CDU and SPD factions are not only key players in the EP itself but are also very active in connecting to their home parties and the rest of Europe (e.g. Crum and Miklin, Chapter Five). Another reason why established parties in the political centre are often ahead in interparliamentary coordination is that they tend to be positively disposed towards European and other international initiatives. For more extremist parties that are more sceptical of European integration, transnational engagement comes less naturally and is less likely to be succesful. Thus, we saw on various occasions that the leftist GUE/NGL found itself outside of the political mainstream and hence was not able to make its force felt in interparliamentary coordination (Crum and Miklin, Chapter Five; Wagner *et al.,* Chapter Seven).

Still, there is one way in which the multilevel parliamentary field is particularly conducive to smaller parties, and that is in offering them an alternative road to power when the national road is particularly hard to travel. This is the analysis that Shemer-Kunz provides of the French Greens, who have better election results in

European elections than in national ones and where the EP essentially serves as a stepping stone to the national political arena. Kunz (drawing on Hix and Lord 1997) also points to the (earlier) case of the French Front National that only rose to prominence in national politics after having made its breakthrough in the 1984 European elections. Similarly, one may wonder whether the Liberal Democrats would ever have made it into the British Government without the EP as a 'training ground'.

Finally, we should note the way that the present Euro crisis appears to affect different parliaments in different ways. As Benz demonstrates (Chapter Eight), the Euro crisis actually risks contributing to a bifurcation of European parliaments. On the one hand, in countries that are not able to stabilise their budgetary position by themselves, parliaments are effectively undermined. In these countries, policies are imposed by international creditors, and technocratic governments are brought into office to implement them (Benz, Chapter Eight; Schmidt 2011). On the other hand, however, parliaments in creditor countries have in some cases been able to strengthen their position as they strictly monitor their government's involvement in the stabilisation efforts. What is more, these stronger parliaments even maintain bilateral relations with one another instead of turning to the usual pan-European platforms (Benz, Chapter Eight). This applies particularly in Germany (but to a lesser extent also to countries like France, Finland and the Netherlands), where the *Bundestag* also knows its constitutional position is protected by the Federal Constitutional Court. Notably, however, the concern of the Federal Constitutional Court to protect parliamentary democracy is limited to its national borders and does not include the fall-out from German and European measures on the parliamentary powers in other European states.

Ensuring political control under conditions of equality and public deliberation

This book has given support to our contention, as set out in the introductory chapter, that the notion of the multilevel parliamentary field is a useful heuristic for understanding the nature of the EU's representative structure: national and European parliaments have become enmeshed in a single system of multilevel governance.[1] As we also noted in the Introduction, this development offers no ready assurance that the ensuing arrangement will be or will remain democratic; the democratic quality of this arrangement must be established with reference to the question of whether it can comply with the relevant democratic requirements.

---

1. We would like to reaffirm that we do not think of the multilevel parliamentary field as a political field in the Bourdieuian sense (as Lord also warns against in his chapter). Arguably, though, a case can be made to regard the European integration process as a whole as a political field in the Bourdieuian sense since, in many respects, it emerges as a self-perpetuating elite project that operates by its own standards and is largely insensitive to external normative challenges. In such an account the parliamentary field would figure as an effective, rather than symbolic, antidote as it provides manifold, disconnected access points into the system, both from the national and the European level.

To what extent, if at all, can a multilevel parliamentary field, as a structure made up of interacting parliaments, live up to 'parliamentary democracy' as a doctrine? To address this question we can follow Chris Lord (Chapter Fourteen) in taking the essence of parliamentary democracy to be defined by three elements:[2]

(a) public control with;

(b) political equality, and;

(c) individual rights to justification (i.e. deliberation).

In short: can the multilevel parliamentary field ensure public control with political equality and offer proper justification to all involved?

This question in turn has two facets. One pertains to whether the existing structure in the EU can fulfil these requirements *in practice*. The other pertains to whether the notion of a fully-fledged multilevel parliamentary field (with fully developed parliamentary systems at both of the two main levels: the member state, and the EU) may be able to fulfil these democratic requirements *in principle*. This second question requires explicit attention to theory: how much of a 'field' effect of horizontal patterns of interaction and imbricated constituencies can a modern system of representative democracy accommodate? In answering this question, much will ride on whether it is possible to forge a system of deliberation that can deliver an adequate form of deliberative accountability (cf. Mansbridge 2003) and is capable of ensuring public control with political equality. In an internationalising world, this is an essential challenge for democratic theory. It can usefully be addressed through drawing on the notion of a 'deliberative system' (Parkinson and Mansbridge 2012). This approach shares with ours the focus on capturing systemic features and holds normative promise precisely because it is bent on understanding how the various carriers of a 'talk-based approach to political conflict and problem-solving'[3] work together to form a democratic whole. From a normative perspective the challenge is to establish whether or the extent to which a multilevel parliamentary field can foster such systemic deliberative qualities, and if so, which systemic configuration offers the greatest prospects.

Given the substance of the preceding chapters, our focus here is on the first, more practical and situated, question. Still, our findings may have bearings on the second facet, as they may indeed bring mechanisms of accommodation to light that have not been recognised in the theoretical debate so far.

Thus, taking up the first facet, we focus on the system in place in the EU and assess the EU in relation to the democratic requirements, not so much as ideal requirements but from a more comparative perspective, that is, in relation to how they are addressed in modern democratic states. There is no doubt, as the chapters

---

2. Notably, these three elements run as good as parallel with the three parliamentary tasks distinguished by Cooper (Chapter Four): legislation, representation and deliberation (cf. also Rommetvedt, Chapter Thirteen).

3. Parkinson and Mansbridge 2012: 4.

in this book also explicate in various ways, that the EU's multilevel parliamentary field falls well short of the ideal requirements, as set out above, and arguably also of what is the case in many national democratic systems (even if the quality of national systems varies considerably). However, this need not imply that the EU's parliamentary field is bound to be precluded from living up to these requirements, in manners comparable to states. Indeed, on each of the three aspects our analyses give some inklings of how the field may come to bolster the EU's democratic credentials.

Arguably, the aspect on which the multilevel parliamentary field appears most evolved is *deliberation*. Certainly, the field is home to few, if any, fully integrated political debates. However, the parliaments, which can be understood as 'strong publics' (Fraser 1992; Eriksen and Fossum 2002), figure as eminent sites for political deliberation, and their dispersion throughout the Union serves as a guarantee for diversity and inclusion. At the same time, even if these debates are not systematically integrated, we have considerable evidence of mutual observation and debates getting linked on important political points (Buzogány, Chapter Two; Knutelská, Chapter Three; Crum and Miklin, Chapter Five). This means that the field represents an external check on each parliament in the system; we can think of this as providing an additional structure of justification where parliaments must increasingly justify their actions to one another.

In that sense, parliaments are far from closed off from one another; they are inherently porous and open to insights and demands for justifications from other sites. Such linkages are reinforced by the new institutional facilities of the EWM and IPEX. Yet, we should note that most parliaments remain rather centred on their respective domestic political logics and that so far there are no signs of parliaments genuinely internalising a pan-European perspective that also takes full account of the concerns expressed by other parliaments (Lord, Chapter Fourteen; cf. Savage and Weale 2009). Indeed, in times of crisis, like the present, it is rather that there are signs of parliaments disassociating themselves from others, and focusing their interactions on a few, similar-minded ones (cf. Benz, Chapter Eight).

A fundamental question is whether parliaments, through the parliamentary field, effectively *control* public decision-making in the EU. Are parliaments sovereign, still? There is obviously much reason to be concerned on this point. At various instances throughout this book it has been pointed out that the pooling of power by governments compromises parliamentary control. Far from all EU decisions are properly covered by parliamentary powers, and not all issues on which governments have given up their veto have come within the purview of the EP (cf. Lord, Chapter Fourteen; Eriksen and Fossum 2012). Further, in EU politics, legislation has become increasingly abstract whereas much of the actual specification of the decisions is delegated to the implementation process, which is at best only partially open to the scrutiny of parliamentary representatives. What is more, the exercise of authority in the complex system of the EU is prone to the problem of 'many hands' where everyone and, hence, no one, can be held accountable for a certain decision (Lord, Chapter Fourteen). At the same time, turning to parliaments themselves, we have seen on various occasions that their engagement is prone to collective action problems and that, hence, they may well fail to effectively mobilise. In addition, there are good reasons to doubt whether the parliamentarians involved in the multilevel field are effectively and adequately linked to voter preferences on EU affairs (Lord, Chapter Fourteen). And yet, despite all these reservations, we find that parliaments do make a difference in EU decision-making and that they do so on important issues and in a way that responds to popular concerns. This was certainly the case with the EP's amendment – with the implicit support of many national parliamentarians – of the Services Directive (Crum and Miklin, Chapter Five). Much also suggests that this equally applies to the successful invocation of the EWM on the proposed Regulation on the right to strike.

Finally, can adequate representation in terms of *political equality* be ensured in the multilevel parliamentary field? The studies in this book give credence to Chris Lord's (Chapter Fourteen) point that the EU's multilevel parliamentary field essentially lacks the necessary infrastructure to turn it into an effective parliamentary system, with elections, parties, deliberation and powers all working harmoniously together. Basically, the EU parliamentary field risks operating as a formal decision-making routine without being embedded in a proper ecology that connects it to its public – in fact, it does not even have a single, integrated public (constituency). What is more, we did see that some actors and some parliaments clearly have much more leverage in the field than others that may actually not even matter much to the rest. Moreover, these inequalities are becoming amplified as a result of the present crisis (Benz, Chapter Eight).

Yet, at the same time, it is important to note the difference between the EU and an established democratic state: the latter can rely on an explicit and detailed normative script, whereas the former cannot, and is still very much an entity in the making with obvious experimental traits. In that sense we can think of the multilevel parliamentary field not only as a structure for fostering deliberation in representation, but as part of a larger process of deliberation over representation[4] where constituencies essentially inter-penetrate one another: who should represent whom, in what sense, and at what level? The main normative potential of the EU's multilevel parliamentary field is that it forms an intrinsic element in the working out of these questions.

Ultimately, the limited capacity of the field to ensure political equality may be somewhat compensated for by its distinctively porous and inclusive character, and the fact that it tends to operate through consultation and consensus-seeking rather than by simply overruling minority positions. It contains procedures to accommodate objections, and even if an objection is sidetracked in one parliament, there are openings for it to be picked up in another. So even if the field cannot ensure political equality in a strict sense (irrespective of the problematic issue of what exactly political equality would require in a political system of citizens *and* states), it does ensure all actors that are part of it a kind of minimum opportunity of access.

---

4.   For more on this distinction *see* Fossum (2013).

From this perspective, the field's diverse and fragmented nature actually holds a specific virtue: it provides new and marginal actors with inroads to challenge exclusivist tendencies that have become entrenched in the established domestic systems. As we have underlined at various points, interparliamentary relations are often a weapon of the weak; by drawing on the resources of other parliaments they are able to emancipate themselves in their own, domestic setting. This applies to opposition parties, to new parties more generally, particularly where they face significant electoral thresholds (like the Greens in France) (Shemer-Kunz, Chapter Ten), and to female politicians, as Beauvallet and Michon suggest (Chapter Eleven). Thus, even if national parliaments remain essentially autonomous entities, the field provides for 'feedback effects' from European politics back into national politics that affect individual parties but, by implication, also party systems as a whole (Shemer-Kunz, Chapter Ten; referring also to Mair 2006).

The analysis has shown that there remain many challenges for the field to improve its democratic credentials. The important question is to establish which direction of field development – loose transnational versus tight supranational – will be most beneficial in democratic terms. This study has suggested that a crucial virtue of the present structure lies in its fragmented and quite voluntaristic nature. While respecting the autonomy of each parliamentary institution involved, the field stimulates deliberation and justificatory processes across polities. In that sense, the field serves more as a vehicle for ensuring or reinforcing external checks or 'soft' controls on internal processes than as a tightly knit system of institutionalised coordination. Ultimately, however, the question is whether more institutionalised coordination is desirable to increase its overall effectiveness or whether this will require such incursions into the autonomy of the individual parliaments that it will only amplify democratic problems. That, in turn, encourages us to direct our future attention to the deliberative systems approach.

Concluding reflections

This book has shown that the particular development of two tracks of interparliamentary coordination that we find in Europe combine to make up a distinctive structure that can be characterised as a multilevel parliamentary field. The density of these relations among parliaments varies but that is precisely what sets this looser structure apart from the kind of system of representation we find in federal states. As the contributions to this book provide a snapshot image of the EU's multilevel parliamentary field, they highlight the following features:

- National parliaments remain (mostly) autonomous actors that have considerable room to operate according to their own logic; in that sense their character and identity are not eradicated by their forming part of a field;
- it follows that the EU's multilevel parliamentary field is uneven throughout: there is great diversity in terms of forms of coordination and divisions of tasks;

- a hallmark of the field is deliberation, in many locations; it takes place both vertically, between national and supranational institutions, and, increasingly, horizontally, across the representative structures, where each connects a particular political system with its society;

- there are occasional instances where parliaments are able to exert collective power/control;

- tensions and competition are, so to speak, inherent to the nature of the field;

- political equality is not institutionally ensured and there are notable inequalities;

- the field is inclusive: the diverse and fragmented character opens space for contestation and demands for justification. As such, it can serve as an important democratic corrective to local (national) imbalances and as a site for learning.

The studies in this book bring out the merits of working from a holistic perspective to capture representative politics in the EU and beyond. At the same time, we underline that the picture we provide here is only a snapshot (a full-scale examination of the field requires far more research and documentation).[5]

From these studies it is readily apparent that a multilevel parliamentary field akin to that of the EU cannot be transposed to other international organisations without fundamentally restructuring them. In particular, the EU stands apart because of the distinct combination of the two tracks of interparliamentary coordination that it provides for; obtaining this level of coordination requires the institutionalisation of a supranational system of parliamentary representation.

Yet, this book also shows that many of the interparliamentary arrangements that make up the second, horizontal, track are by no means exclusive to the EU. Outside the EU there are different, *ad hoc* as well as more institutionalised, forums and meeting-places where parliamentarians come together, exchange ideas and information, and coordinate their work. At this point in time, the globe is spanned by an extensive web of interparliamentary platforms that connect parliamentarians and that reaches far beyond Europe (Kissling 2011). The NATO-PA and the Parliamentary Conference of the WTO, as discussed in Chapters Twelve and Thirteen, are just two examples of such platforms.

In fact, the operation of the EU multilevel parliamentary field is not necessarily confined to the borders of the EU but can be seen to stretch well beyond it (Wagner *et al.,* Chapter Seven; Rommetvedt, Chapter Thirteen). Note, for instance, the prominent role that the EP (together with the IPU and national parliamentarians) plays in the WTO Parliamentary Conference; the ensuing structure takes on certain field attributes with different parliamentary platforms (like the IPU) nested within one another, while at the same time operating side by side with their constituting members (most notably national parliaments) (Rommetvedt, Chapter Thirteen).

---

5. This would require the careful consideration of each structure of representation that links each political system with its society and all the links across these.

While these dynamics certainly respond to calls for increased legitimation from within the different international organisations, the chapters in this book testify to the central role of the EU in driving these processes (as Rommetvedt's chapter on the WTO also bears out). Of course, such a role is perfectly in line with the EU's commitment to the promotion of democratic practices, as is, for instance, evidenced in the democratic requirements for EU membership and in its relations with affiliated countries in general.

The general picture that emerges from this study is that the internationalisation of politics drives parliaments to become linked together across borders as well as through the vertical structures of representation that link each political system to 'its' society. In the EU this process has reached a rather advanced stage: within it, parliaments have become enmeshed in a broad, multilevel structure of political authority that none of them can control on their own, but which all of them bestow with some modicum of legitimacy. Our explorations fall short of giving a determinate answer to the question of *whether* a fully-fledged field can live up to democratic requirements. The insights they provide in interparliamentary relations do, however, make clear that there is an important middle ground for the parliamentary control of international politics between, on the one hand, isolated national parliaments losing control and, on the other hand, the establishment of a supranational parliamentary order. Thus, it seems to us that further analysis of the possible forms that these field configurations can take is needed, together with a systematic assessment of their democratic credentials which recognises both their contribution to democratising international politics as well as their likely ramifications for domestic democracy.

| bibliography

Abromeit, H. (2008) *Democracy in Europe, Legitimising Politics in a Non-State Polity,* Oxford: Berghahn Books.

Achin, C. (*et al.*) (2007) *Sexes, genre et politique,* Paris: Economica.

Advisory Council on International Affairs (2010) *Piraterijbestrijding op Zee. Een Herrijking van Publieke en Private Verantwoordelijkheden,* Den Haag.

Ágh, A. (2006) *Magyarország az Európai Unióban,* Budapest: Századvég.

Andersen, S. S. and Burns, T. (1996) 'The European Union and the erosion of parliamentary democracy: A study of post-parliamentary governance', in Svein S. Andersen and Kjell A. Eliassen (eds) *The European Union: How Democratic Is It?,* London: Sage, 227–52.

Andeweg, R. B. and Nijzink, L. (1995) 'Beyond the two-body image: Relations between Ministers and MPs', in H. Döring (ed.) *Parliaments and Majority Rule in Western Europe,* Frankfurt: Campus, 152–78.

Anghel, S., Born, H., Dowling, H. and Fuior, T. (2008) 'National parliamentary oversight of ESDP missions', in D. Peters, W. Wagner and N. Deitelhoff (eds) *The Parliamentary Control of European Security Policy,* RECON Report No. 6, Oslo: ARENA, 51–76.

Auel, K. and Benz, A. (2005) 'The politics of adaptation: The Europeanisation of national parliamentary systems', *The Journal of Legislative Studies,* 11(3): 372–93.

—— (eds) (2006) *The Europeanisation of Parliamentary Democracy,* London: Routledge.

Austrian Chamber of Labour (2005) 'Stellungnahme der Bundesarbeiterkammer zum Vorschlag für eine Richtlinie über Dienstleistungen im Binnenmarkt', Vienna: Austrian Chamber of Labour.

Austrian National Council (2010) 'Reasoned Opinion,' Vienna, 15 September 2010.

Barbé, E. and Herranz-Surrallés, A. (2008) 'The power and practice of the European Parliament in security policies', in D. Peters, W. Wagner and N. Deitelhoff (eds) *The Parliamentary Control of European Security Policy,* RECON Report No. 6, Oslo: ARENA, 77–105.

Barents, R. (2010) 'The Court of Justice after the Treaty of Lisbon', *Common Market Law Review,* 47: 709–28.

Barnea, S. and Rahat, G. (2011) '"Out with the old, in with the New": What constitutes a new party?', *Party Politics,* 17 (3): 303–20.

Barrett, G. (2008) *National Parliaments and the European Union: The constitutional challenge for the Oireachtas and other member state legislatures,* Dublin: Clarus Press.

Bartolini, S. (2005) *Restructuring Europe: Centre formation, system building and political structuring between the nation state and the European Union*, Oxford: Oxford University Press.

Beauvallet, W. (2007) *Profession: eurodéputé. Les élus français au Parlement européen et l'institutionnalisation d'une nouvelle figure politique et élective (1979–2004)*, unpublished thesis, Strasbourg University.

—— (2010) 'The European Parliament and the politicisation of the European space – the case of the two port packages', in J. Rowell and M. Mangenot (eds) *Reassessing Constructivism: A political sociology of the European Union*, Manchester: Manchester University Press, 164–81.

Beauvallet, W. and Michon, S. (2008) 'Les femmes au Parlement européen: effets du mode de scrutin, des stratégies et des ressources politiques. L'exemple de la délégation française', *Swiss Political Science Review*, 14: 663–90.

—— (2010) 'Professionalization and socialization of the Members of the European Parliament', *French Politics*, 8: 145–65.

Beer, S. H. (1990 [1966]) 'The British legislature and the problem of mobilizing consent', in P. Norton (ed.) *Legislatures*, Oxford: Oxford University Press.

Beetham, D. (ed.) (1994) *Defining and Measuring Democracy*, London: Sage/ ECPR.

Beisheim, M. and Brunnengräber, A. (2008) 'Das Parlament im Globalisierungsprozess. Ein Desiderat in der Parlamentarismus – und *Global governance*-Forschung', *Zeitschrift für Internationale Beziehungen,* 15 (1): 73–100.

Belgische Kamer van Volksvertegenwoordigers (2008) 'Integraal Verslag', Plenumsvergadering, 20 November, 36–7.

Bengtson, C. (2007) 'Interparliamentary cooperation within Europe', in J. O'Brennan and T. Raunio (eds) *National Parliaments within the Enlarged European Union*, Abingdon: Routledge, 46–63.

Benson, D. and Jordan, A. (2011) 'What have we learned from policy transfer research? Dolowitz and Marsh revisited', *Political Studies Review,* 9 (3): 366–78.

Benson, R. and Neveu, E. (2005) 'Field Theory as a work in progress' in R. Benson and E. Neveu (eds) *Bourdieu and the Journalistic Field*, Cambridge: Cambridge University Press, 1–28.

Benz, A. (2003) 'Compound representation in EU multi-level governance', in B. Kohler-Koch (ed.) *Linking EU and National Governance*, Oxford: Oxford University Press, 82–110.

—— (2004) 'Path-dependent institutions and strategic veto-players - National parliaments in the European Union', *West European Politics,* 29 (5): 875–900.

—— (2011) 'Linking multiple demoi. Interparliamentary relations in the EU', in J. M. Beneyto and I. Pernice (eds) *Europe's Constitutional Challenges in the Light of the Recent Case Law of National Constitutional Courts*, Baden-Baden: Nomos, 267–77.

Berg, P. and Schmitz, G. J. (2006) *Strengthening Parliamentary Oversight of International Trade Policies and Negotiations: Recent developments in Canada and internationally*, Parliamentary Information and Research Service, Library of Parliament. Online. Available at: http://www.parl.gc.ca/Content/LOP/ResearchPublications/prb0568-e.pdf (accessed 22 June 2013).

Bessette, J. M. (1994) *The Mild Voice of Reason: Deliberative Democracy and American National Government*, Chicago: University of Chicago Press.

Best, E. (2008) 'The Lisbon Treaty: A qualified advance for EU decision-making and governance?', *EIPASCOPE* 2008/1.

Best, H. and Cotta, M. (eds) (2004) *Parliamentary representatives in Europe 1848–2000*, Oxford: Oxford University Press.

Beyme, K. V. (1997) *Der Gesetzgeber. Der Bundestag als Entscheidungszentrum*, Opladen: VS Verlag für Sozialwissenschaften.

Birkinshaw, P. and Ashiagbor, D. (1996) 'National participation in community affairs: Democracy, the UK Parliament and the EU', *Common Market Law Review*, 33: 499–529.

Blichner, L. (2000) 'The anonymous hand of public reason: Interparliamentary discourse and the quest for legitimacy', in E. O. Eriksen and J. E. Fossum (eds) *Democracy in the European Union: Integration through deliberation*, London and New York: Routledge, 141–63.

Blondel, J. and Cotta, M. (eds) (2000) *The Nature of Party Government: A comparative European perspective*, London: Palgrave.

Blondel, J., Sinnott, R. and Svensson, P. (1997) 'Representation and voter participation', *European Journal of Political Research*, 32 (2): 243–72.

Bogdanor, V. (1986) 'The future of the European Community: Two models of democracy', *Government and Opposition*, 21 (2): 161–73.

Bohman, J. (2007) 'Democratizing the transnational polity, the European Union and the presuppositions of democracy', in E. O. Eriksen and J. E. Fossum (eds) *How to Reconstitute Democracy in Europe? Proceedings from the Recon Opening Conference*, Oslo: Recon/ARENA: 65–89.

Born, H. (2004) 'The use of force under international auspices: Strengthening parliamentary accountability', in H. Born and H. Hänggi (eds) *The 'Double Democratic Deficit': Parliamentary accountability and the use of force under international auspices*, Aldershot: Ashgate, 203–15.

Born, H. and Hänggi, H. (2005) *The Use of Force under International Auspices: Strengthening parliamentary accountability*, Policy Paper No. 7, Geneva: Geneva Centre for the Democratic Control of Armed Forces (DCAF).

Bourad, A. (2011) 'José Bové ou la candidature "collective" et "spontanée"', paper presented at the annual Congress of the French Association of Political Science, Strasbourg, September 2011.

Bourdieu, P. (1977) 'Sur le pouvoir symbolique', *Annales* 32 (3): 405–11.

—— (1981) 'La Représentation Politique', *Actes de la recherches en sciences sociales*, 36–7: 3–24.

—   (1984) *Distinction: A social critique of the judgment of taste*, trans. Richard Nice, Harvard: Harvard University Press.

—   (1991) *On Language and Symbolic Power*, Cambridge: Polity Press.

—   (1994) 'Rethinking the state: Genesis and structure of the bureaucratic field', *Sociological Theory*, 12 (1): 1–18.

—   (1998) *Practical Reason: On the Theory of Action*, Stanford: Stanford University Press.

—   (2005) 'The political field, the social field and the journalistic field' in R. Benson and E. Neveu (eds) *Bourdieu and the Journalistic Field*, Cambridge: Cambridge University Press, 29–47.

Bouwen, P. (2004) 'The logic of access to the European Parliament: Business lobbying in the Committee on Economic and Monetary Affairs', *Journal of Common Market Studies*, 42: 473–95.

Boy, D. (1999) 'Les Verts, Cohn-Bendit, l'environnement et l'Europe', *Revue française de science politique*, 49 (4): 676–86.

Brandom, R. (2008) *Between Saying and Doing: Towards an analytic pragmatism*, Oxford: Oxford University Press.

Brok, E. and Gresch, N. (2004) 'Untitled contribution', in N. Gnesotto (ed.) *The Security and Defence Policy of the European Union: The first five years (1999–2004)*, Paris: Institute for Security Studies.

Bryder, T. (1998) 'Party groups in the European Parliament and the changing recruitment patterns of MEPs', in D. Bell and C. Lord (eds) *Transnational Parties in the European Union*, Aldershot: Ashgate, 189–203.

Buzogány, A. (2012) 'True control or trompe-l'œil? Parliamentary scrutiny of EU policies in the Hungarian Parliament', in K. Arató, Z. Enyedi, and Á. Lux (eds) *Structures and Futures of Europe*, Budapest: Ad Librum, 129–53.

Buzogány, A. and Stuchlík, A. (2012) 'Subsidiarität und parlamentarische mitsprache: Nationale Legislativen nach Lissabon', *Zeitschrift für Parlamentsfragen*, 43 (2): 356–77.

BVerfG (2009) 'Decision of the German Federal Constitutional Court on the Treaty of Lisbon', 2 BvE 2/08 of 30 June 2009. Online. Available at: http://www.bverfg.de/entscheidungen/es20090630_2bve000208en.html (accessed 1 July 2013).

Carrubba, C. J. and Timpone, R. (2005) 'Explaining vote switching across first and second order elections: Evidence from Europe', *Comparative Political Studies*, 38 (3): 260–81.

Castiglione, D. and Warren, M. (2006) 'Rethinking Democratic Representation: Eight theoretical issues', paper prepared for delivery to 'Rethinking Democratic Representation', Centre for the Study of Democratic Institutions, University of British Columbia, 18–19 May.

Chambers, S. (2004) 'Behind closed doors: Publicity, secrecy, and the quality of deliberation', *The Journal of Political Philosophy*, 17 (4): 389–410.

Charlemagne, (2012) 'Elected, but how democratic?', *The Economist*, 17 March.

Checkel, J. T. (2005) 'International institutions and socialization in Europe: Introduction and framework', *International Organization*, 59 (4): 801–26.

Chutikul, K. (2003) *Options for a Parliamentary Dimension of the WTO*, Discussion paper presented to the Parliamentary Conference on the WTO, Geneva, 17–18 February 2003. Online. Available at: http://www.ipu.org/splz-e/trade03/2c.pdf (accessed 4 July 2013).

Cohen, A. (2013) 'The genesis of Europe: Competing elites and the emergence of a European field of power', in N. Kauppi and M. Rask Madsen (eds) *Transnational Power Elites: The new professionals of governance, law and security*, London: Routledge.

Cohen, J. and Sabel, C (1997) 'Directly-deliberative polyarchy', *European Law Journal*, 3(4): 313–42.

Coman, E. E. (2009) 'Reassessing the influence of party groups on individual Members of the European Parliament', *West European Politics,* 32 (6): 1099–117.

Common Market Law Review Editorial Comments (2009) 'European elections – Is the European Parliament important today?', *Common Market Law Review*, 46: 767–71.

Conference of Speakers of the European Union Parliaments (2004) 'Guidelines: Interparliamentary cooperation in the European Union'. Online. Available at: http://www.ipex.eu/IPEXL-WEB/euspeakers/getspeakers.do?id=082 dbcc5319ee5f60131ae26c80b043c (accessed 1 February 2012).

—— (2008) 'Guidelines for interparliamentary cooperation in the European Union'. Online. Available at: http://www.ipex.eu/IPEXL-WEB/euspeakers/getspeakers.do (accessed 1 February 2012).

—— (2010) 'The Stockholm Guidelines for the Conference of Speakers of EU Parliaments'. Online. Available at: http://www.ipex.eu/IPEXL-WEB/euspeakers/getspeakers.do (accessed 1 February 2012).

Cooper, I. (2006) 'The watchdogs of subsidiarity: National parliaments and the logic of arguing in the EU', *Journal of Common Market Studies*, 44 (2): 281–304.

—— (2012) 'A 'Virtual third chamber' for the European Union? National parliaments after the Treaty of Lisbon', *West European Politics*, 35 (3): 441–65.

Corbett R., Jacob, F. and Shackleton, M. (2000) *The European Parliament*, 4th edn, London: John Harper Publishing.

COSAC (2004a) 'Report on developments in European Union procedures and practices relevant to parliamentary scrutiny', XXXI Conference of Community and European Affairs Committees of Parliaments of the European Union, Dublin, 19–20 May.

—— (2004b) 'XXXII COSAC Conclusions', The Hague, 23 November. Online. Available at: http://www.cosac.eu/en/documents/contributions/ (accessed 1 February 2012).

—— (2005) 'Speech by Vice-President Wallström', COSAC Chairpersons' meeting, Luxembourg, 9 February. Online. Available at: http://www.cosac.eu/33-luxembourg-2005/meeting-of-the-chairpersons-of-cosac-8–9-february-2005–9-feb/ (accessed 4 July 2012).

— (2007) 'Eighth bi-annual report: Developments in European Union procedures and practices relevant to parliamentary scrutiny', XXXVIII Conference of Community and European Affairs Committees of Parliaments of the European Union, Estoril, 14–15 October.

— (2008) 'Conclusions adopted by the XL COSAC meeting', Paris, 3–4 November.

— (2009a) 'Eleventh bi-annual report on EU practices and procedures', Prague, May.

— (2009b) 'Replies for the EU parliaments to COSAC's eleventh bi-annual report', Prague, May.

— (2009c) 'Twelfth bi-annual report on EU practices and procedures', Stockholm, October.

— (2009d) 'Report on the results of the subsidiarity check on the proposal for a Council framework decision on the right to interpretation and to translation in criminal proceedings', Stockholm, 5–6 October. Online. Available at: http://oide.sejm.gov.pl/oide/en/images/files/international/cosac_report_subs_2009_338_en.pdf (accessed 1 July 2013).

— (2010a) 'Thirteenth bi-annual report on EU practices and procedures' Madrid, May.

— (2010b) 'Replies from the EU parliaments to the questionnaire for the thirteenth bi-annual report', Madrid, May.

— (2010c) 'Fourteenth bi-annual report on EU practices and procedures', Brussels, October.

— (2011a) 'Fifteenth bi-annual report on developments in the European Union procedures and practices relevant in parliamentary scrutiny – Appendix', Budapest, May 2011. Online. Available at: http://www.cosac.eu/en/documents/biannual/ (accessed 8 April 2012).

— (2011b) 'Sixteenth bi-annual report on EU practices and procedures', Warsaw, October. Online. Available at: http://www.cosac.eu/en/documents/biannual/ (accessed 9 April 2012).

Costa, O. (2001) *Le Parlement européen, assemblée délibérante*, Bruxelles: Ed. de l'Université de Bruxelles.

Costello, R. and Thomson, R. (2011) 'The nexus of bicameralism: Rapporteurs' impact on decision outcomes in the European Union', *European Union Politics,* 12 (3): 337–57.

Council of the European Union (2006a) 'Europol: The way forward towards more efficiency and accountability – draft Council conclusions', 8234/1/066, April.

— (2006b) 'Friends of the Presidency's report to the future of Europol', 9184/1/06, 19 May.

— (2006c) 'Draft Council conclusions on the future of Europol', 9670/1/06, 30 May.

— (2009) 'Council decision of 6 April 2009, Establishing the European Police Office (Europol)', 2009/371/JHA, *Official Journal of the European Union,* 15 May.

CPA Study Group (2002) *Report of a CPA Study Group on Parliament and the International Trading System*, Saint Lucia: Commonwealth Parliamentary Association. Online. Available at: http://www.agora-parl.org/node/291 (accessed 22 June 2013).

Crespy, A. and Schmidt, V. (2012) 'The Clash of the Titans/The White Knight and the Iron Lady: France, Germany and the simultaneous double game of EMU reform', paper presented at the ECSA-Canada ninth biennial conference 'Europe in an Age of Austerity: Integration, Disintegration, or Stagnation?', Ottawa, 27–28 April.

Crum, B. (2005) 'Tailoring representative democracy to the European Union: does the European constitution reduce the democratic deficit?', *European Law Journal*, 11 (4): 452–67.

— (2012) *Learning from the EU Constitutional Treaty: Democratic constitutionalization beyond the nation-state*, Abingdon: Routledge.

Crum, B. and Fossum, J. E. (2009) 'The multilevel parliamentary field: a framework for theorizing representative democracy in the EU', *European Political Science Review*, 1 (2): 249–71.

— (2012) 'A democratic backbone for international organisations: The multilevel parliamentary field', in T. Evas, U. Liebert and C. Lord (eds) *Multilayered Representation in the European Union: Parliaments, courts and the public sphere*, Baden-Baden: Nomos, 91–105.

Curtice, J. (1989) 'The 1989 European elections: Protest or green tide?', *Electoral Studies*, 8 (3): 217–30.

Curtin, D. (2009) *Executive Power of the European Union: Law, practices and the living constitution*, Oxford: Oxford University Press.

Curtin, D. and Egeberg, M. (2008a) 'Towards a new executive order in Europe?', Special issue of *West European Politics*, 31 (4).

— (2008b) 'Tradition and innovation: Europe's accumulated executive order', *West European Politics*, 31 (4): 639–61.

Cygan, A. (2001) *National parliaments in an integrated Europe: an Anglo-German perspective*, The Hague: Kluwer Law International.

Czech Chamber of Deputies (2010) '20th Resolution of the Committee for European Affairs', Prague, 7 October.

Damgaard, E. (1994) 'The strong parliaments of Scandinavia', in G. W. Copeland and S. C. Patterson (eds) *Parliaments in the Modern World*, Ann Arbour, MI: The University of Michigan Press, 85–103.

— (2003) *Folkets styre. Magt og ansvar i dansk politik,* Århus: Aarhus Universitetsforlag.

Damgaard, E. and Jensen, H. (2005) 'Europeanisation of executive-legislative relations: Nordic perspectives', *The Journal of Legislative Studies*, 11 (3): 394–411.

Dann, P. (2003) 'European Parliament and executive federalism: Appraising a parliament in a semi-parliamentary democracy', *European Law Journal*, 9 (5): 549–74.

de Lassalle, M. (2005) 'Nationalisation des élections européennes', in Y. Deloye (ed.) *Dictionnaire des élections européennes*, Paris, Economica, 474–8.

de Puig, L. M. (2008) *International Parliaments*, Strasbourg: Council of Europe Publishing.

Deschouwer, K. (2000) *The European Multi-level Party Systems: Towards a framework for analysis*, European Forum Series, EUI Working papers, RSC 2000/47.

—— (2003) 'Political parties in multi-layered systems', *European Urban and Regional Studies*, 10 (3): 213–26.

De Schutter, O., Lebessis, N. and Paterson, J. (eds) (2001) *Governance in the European Union*, Brussels: European Commission.

Deutscher Bundestag (2010) 'Delegation des Verteidigungsausschusses zu Gesprächen nach Montenegro, Kosovo und Dschibuti', press release 12 February. Online. Available at: http://www.bundestag.de/presse/ pressemitteilungen/2010/pm_1002122.html (accessed 1 June 2011).

De Wilde, P. (2012) *Why the Early Warning Mechanism does not alleviate the Democratic Deficit*, OPAL Online Paper No. 6/2012, Maastricht.

Deutscher Gewerkschaftsbund Bundesvorstand (2005) *EU-Richtlinie 'Dienstleistungen im Binnenmarkt'. Konfliktfelder aus Sicht des DGB*, Berlin.

Dieterich, S., Hummel, H. and Marschall, S. (2010) *Parliamentary War Powers: A survey of 25 European Parliaments*, DCAF Occasional Paper No. 21, Geneva: Geneva Centre for the Democratic Control of the Armed Forces (DCAF).

Dijkstra, H. (2011) *The Role of the Council Secretariat and the European Commission in EU Foreign Policy*, PhD Thesis, Universiteit Maastricht.

DiMaggio, P. J. (1988) 'Interest and agency in institutional theory', in L. G. Zucker (ed.) *Institutional Patterns and Organizations*, Cambridge, MA: Ballinger, 3–21.

DiMaggio, P. J. and Powell, W. W. (1983) 'The iron cage revisited: Institutional isomorphism and collective rationality', *American Sociological Review*, 48 (2): 147–60.

Dimitrakopoulos, D. G. (2001) 'Incrementalism and path dependence: European integration and institutional change in national parliaments', *Journal of Common Market Studies*, 39 (3):405–22.

Dolowitz, D. and Marsh, D. (1996) 'Who learns what from whom: A review of the policy transfer literature', *Political Studies*, 44 (2): 343–57.

Dorn, N. (2012) 'Render unto Caesar: EU financial market regulation meets political accountability', *Journal of European Integration* 34 (3): 205–21.

Dougan, M. (2008) 'The Treaty of Lisbon 2007: Winning minds, not hearts', *Common Market Law Review* 45 (3): 617–703.

Dutch Parliament (ed.) (2002) *From Europol to Parlopol: interparliamentary conference on democratic control of Europol*, Amsterdam: Boom.

EELV-PS (2011) '2012–2017 : socialistes et écologistes, ensemble pour combattre la crise et bâtir un autre modèle de vivre ensemble', November. Online. Available at: http://eelv.fr/wp-content/uploads/2011/11/texte_complet_daccord_EELV-PS1.pdf (accessed 20 December 2011).

Ehrhart, H. G. and Petretto, K. (2012) *The EU and Somalia. Counter-piracy and the question of a comprehensive approach*, Study for the Greens/ European Free Alliance, Hamburg.

Eiselt, I., Pollak, J. and Slominski, P. (2007) 'Codifying temporary stability? The role of interinstitutional agreements in budgetary politics', *European Law Journal*, 13 (1): 75–91.

Elias, N. (1991) *The Society of Individuals*, Oxford: Blackwell.

EPP (2009) 'Relations with national parliaments', EPP Group in the European Parliament, Brussels, 12 November.

Eppler, A. (2012) 'Vertikal und horizontal, bi- und multinational: Interparlamentarische Beziehungen in EU-Angelegenheiten', in G. Abels and A. Eppler (eds) *Auf dem Weg zum Mehrebenenparlamentarismus*, Baden-Baden: Nomos, 297–314.

Eriksen, E. O. (2000) 'Deliberative supranationalism in the EU', in E. O. Eriksen and J. E. Fossum (eds) *Democracy in the European Union: Integration through deliberation?*, London: Routledge, 42–64.

— (2006) *Deliberation and the problem of democratic legitimacy in the EU: Are working agreements the most that can be expected?*, ARENA Working paper 08/2006, Oslo: ARENA. Online. Available at: http:// www.arena.uio.no/publications/working-papers2006/papers/wp06_08. pdf (accessed 13 July 2012).

— (2009) *The Unfinished Democratization of Europe*, Oxford: Oxford University Press.

Eriksen, E. O. and Fossum, J. E. (2000) *Democracy in the European Union: Integration through deliberation?*, London and New York, NY: Routledge.

— (2002) 'Democracy through strong publics in the European Union?', *Journal of Common Market Studies*, 40 (3): 401–24.

— (2007) *Europe in Transformation: How to reconstitute democracy?*, RECON Online Working Paper 2007/01 Oslo: ARENA.

— (2012) 'Representation through deliberation – The European case', *Constellations*, 19 (2): 325–39.

Estlund, D. (2008) *Democratic Authority*, Princeton, NJ: Princeton University Press.

EU NAVFOR Website. Online. Available at: http://www.eunavfor.eu/about-us/ mission/ (accessed 11 July 2012).

European Commission (2002) 'Communication to the European Parliament and the Council – Democratic control over Europol', COM (2002) 95.

— (2006) '2005 Annual Report on the relations with the national parliaments, report from the Commission', SEC/2006/0350. Online. Available at: http://ec.europa.eu/dgs/secretariat_general/relations/relations_other/npo/ index_en.htm (accessed 2 February 2012).

—   (2007) '2006 Annual Report on relations between the Commission and national parliaments', SP(2007)2202/04. Online. Available at: http:// ec.europa.eu/dgs/secretariat_general/relations/relations_other/npo/docs/ sp%282006%292202.pdf (accessed 2 February 2012).

—   (2009a) '2008 Annual Report on relations between the European Commission and national parliaments', COM(2009)343. Online. Available at: http://eur-lex.europa.eu/LexUriServ/LexUriServ. do?uri=COM:2009:0343:FIN:EN:PDF (accessed 2 February 2012).

—   (2009b) 'Practical arrangements for the operation of the subsidiarity control mechanism under Protocol No. 2 of the Treaty of Lisbon: letter of President Barroso and Vice-president Wallström of 1 December 2009'. Online. Available at: http://ec.europa.eu/dgs/secretariat_general/ relations/relations_other/npo/index_en.htm (accessed 1 February 2012).

—   (2010) '2009 Annual Report on relations between the European Commission and national parliaments', COM(2010)291. Online. Available at: http://eur-lex.europa.eu/LexUriServ/LexUriServ. do?uri=COM:2010:0291:FIN:EN:PDF (accessed 2 February 2012).

—   (2011a) '2010 Annual Report on relations between the European Commission and national parliaments', COM(2011)345. Online. Available at: http://ec.europa.eu/dgs/secretariat_general/relations/ relations_other/npo/docs/ar_2010_en.pdf (accessed 2 February 2012).

—   (2011b) 'Commission reply to Opinions concerning subsidiarity received from national parliaments on the proposal for a Directive on the Conditions of Entry and Residence of Third-Country Nationals for the Purposes of Seasonal Employment (COM (2010) 379)', Brussels, 21 January.

—   (2012) '2011 Annual Report on relations between the European Commission and national parliaments', COM 375 final, Brussels, 10 July.

European Convention (2002) 'Final report of Working Group IV on the role of national parliaments'. Online. Available at: http://register.consilium. europa.eu/pdf/en/02/cv00/cv00353.en02.pdf (accessed 1 February 2012).

European Parliament (1998) 'Report on the moderation of procedures for the exercise of implementing powers – Comitology', Brussels: European Parliament.

—   (1999) 'Recommendation to the Council on Europol: reinforcing parliamentary controls and extending powers', A4–0064/1999, Brussels: European Parliament.

—   (2000) 'Report on the initiative from the Portuguese Republic with a view to the adoption of a Council Act on the drawing up on the basis of Article 43(1) of the Convention on the Establishment of a European Police Office and of a Protocol amending Article 2 and the Appendix to that Convention (A5–0312/2000)', Rapporteur: A. Karamanou, [2000/0809(CNS)] Brussels: European Parliament.

—   (2002a) 'European Parliament resolution on relations between the European Parliament and the national parliaments in European integration (2001/2023/(INI))', P5_TA(2002)0058, Brussels: European Parliament. Online. Available at: http://www.europarl.europa.eu/RegData/seance_pleniere/textes_adoptes/definitif/2002/02–07/0058/P5_TA%282002%290058_EN.pdf (accessed 4 July 2012).

— (2002b) 'Resolution on the initiative of the Kingdom of Belgium and the Kingdom of Spain with a view to adopting a Council Act drawing up a Protocol amending the Convention on the establishment of a European Police Office', A5–5455/2002, Brussels: European Parliament.

— (2008a) '12. Sea piracy (debate)', CRE-23/09/2008–12. Brussels: European Parliament. Online. Available at: http://www.europarl.europa.eu/sides/getDoc.do?pubRef=-//EP//TEXT+CRE+20080923+ITEM-012+DOC+XML+V0//EN (accessed 13 July 2012).

— (2008b) 'Resolution of 23 October 2008 on piracy at sea' P6_TA(2008)0519. Brussels: European Parliament.

— (2009a) 'European Parliament resolution of 7 May 2009 on the development of the relations between the European Parliament and national parliaments under the Treaty of Lisbon', P6_TA(2009)0388. Brussels: European Parliament. Online. Available at: http://www.europarl.europa.eu/RegData/seance_pleniere/textes_adoptes/definitif/2009/05–07/0388/P6_TA%282009%290388_EN.pdf (accessed 4 July 2012).

— (2009b) 'European Parliament resolution of 25 November 2009 on the communication from the Commission to the European Parliament and the Council – An area of freedom, security and justice serving the citizen – Stockholm Programme', P6_TA(2009)0090. Brussels: European Parliament.

— (2009c) 'Resolution of 15 January 2009 on the situation in the Horn of Africa', P6_TA(2009)0026. Brussels: European Parliament.

— (2009d) 'Resolution of 26 November 2009 on a political solution to the problem of piracy off the Somali coast', P7_TA(2009)0099. Brussels: European Parliament.

— (2010) 'External Action Service: EP's budgetary powers guarantee parliamentary oversight'. Brussels: European Parliament. Online. Available at: http://www.europarl.europa.eu/news/public/story_page/030-76948-176-06-26-903-20100625STO76828-2010-25-06-2010/default_en.htm (accessed 1 July 2013).

— (2011) 'Report on the European semester for economic policy coordination (2011/2071(INI)', A7–0384/2011, 15 November. Brussels: European Parliament. Online. Available at: http://www.europarl.europa.eu/sides/getDoc.do?pubRef=-//EP//NONSGML+REPORT+A7-2011-0384+0+DOC+PDF+V0//EN (accessed 1 July 2013).

Evans, P., Jacobson, H. and Putnam, R. (eds) (1993) *Double-Edged Diplomacy: International bargaining and domestic politics*, Berkeley, CA: University of California Press.

Fabbrini, S. (2008) *Compound Democracies: Why the United States and Europe are becoming similar*, Oxford: Oxford University Press.

Falk, R. and Strauss, A. (2001) 'Toward Global Parliament', *Foreign Affairs*, 80 (1): 212–20.

Fasone, C. (2011) 'Interparliamentary cooperation and democratic representation in the European Union', in S. Kröger and D. Friedrich (eds) *The Challenge of Democratic Representation in the European Union*, Houndmills, Basingstoke and New York, NY: Palgrave Macmillan, 41–58.

Faucher-King, F. (2005) 'Ecologie', in Y. Déloye (ed.) *Dictionnaire des élections européennes*, Paris, Economica, 184–8.

Favell, A. and Guiraudon, V. (2011) (eds) *The Sociology of the European Union*, London: Palgrave.

Fitzmaurice, J. (1996) 'National parliamentary control of EU policy in the three new member states', *West European Politics*, 19 (1): 88–96.

Flockhart, T. (2004) '"Masters and novices": Socialization and social learning through the NATO Parliamentary Assembly', *International Relations*, 18 (3): 361–80.

Forst, R. (2007) *Das Recht auf Rechtfertigung. Elemente einer konstruktivistischen Theorie der Gerechtigkeit*, Frankfurt am Main: Suhrkamp.

Fossum, J. E. (2013) 'A New Representation-Deliberation Interface?', paper presented at the EUSA Thirteenth Biennial Conference, Baltimore (MD), 9-11 May.

Fossum, J. E. and Crum, B. (2012) 'The EU polity and its pattern of representation', in E. O. Eriksen and J. E. Fossum (eds) *Rethinking Democracy and the European Union*, London: Routledge, 74–92.

Fox, R. (2012) 'Europe, democracy and the economic crisis: Is it time to reconstitute the "Assises"?', *Parliamentary Affairs*, 65 (2): 463–69.

Fraga, A. (2005) 'After the Convention: The future role of national parliaments in the European Union (and the day after nothing will happen)', *The Journal of Legislative Studies*, 11 (3–4): 490–507.

Frankel, J. (1970) *National Interest*, London: Macmillan.

Franzoi Dri, C. (2008) 'The Mercosur Parliament: Democracy and integration on European patterns?', paper prepared for the 3rd GARNET Annual Conference 'Mapping Integration and Regionalism in a Global World', Bordeaux, September.

Fraser, N. (1992) 'Rethinking the public sphere: A contribution to the critique of actually existing democracy', in C. Calhoun (ed.) *Habermas and the Public Sphere*, Cambridge, MA: MIT Press, 109–42.

—— (2008) *Scales of Justice*, Cambridge: Polity Press.

Freedman, J. (2002) 'Women in the European Parliament', *Parliamentary Affairs*, 55: 179–88.

Georgakakis, D. (2004) 'Was it really just "poor communication"? Lessons from the Santer Commission's resignation', in A. Smith (ed.) *Politics and the European Commission: Actors, interdependence, legitimacy*, London: Routledge, 119–33.

— (2008) 'La sociologie historique et politique de l'Union européenne: Un point de vue d'ensemble et quelques contrepoints', *Politique européenne*, 25: 53–85.

— (2009) 'The historical and political sociology of the European Union: A uniquely French methodological approach?', *French Politics*, 7: 437–55.

Georgakakis, D. and Weisbein, J. (2010) 'From above and from below: A political sociology of European actors', *Comparative European Politics*, 8: 93–109.

Goetz, K. H. and Meyer-Sahling, J. H. (2008) 'The Europeanisation of national political systems: Parliaments and executives', *Living Reviews in European Governance* 3 (2). Online. Available at: http://www.livingreviews.org/lreg-2008-2 (accessed 1 July 2013).

Grevi, G. (2009) 'ESDP Institutions', in G. Grevi, D. Helly and R. Keohane (eds) *European Security and Defence Policy: The first 10 years (1999–2009)*, Chaillot Papers, Paris: European Union Institute for Security Studies, 19–67.

Habegger, B. (2010) 'Democratic accountability of international organizations: Parliamentary control within the Council of Europe and the OSCE and the prospects for the United Nations', *Cooperation and Conflict*, 45 (2): 186–204.

Habermas, J. (1996) *Between Facts and Norms*, Cambridge, MA: MIT Press.

— (1998) *Die postnationale Konstellation*, Frankfurt am Main: Suhrkamp.

Hallin, D. and Mancini, P. (2004) *Comparing Media Systems: Three models of media and politics*, Cambridge: Cambridge University Press.

Hänggi, H. (2004) 'The use of force under international auspices: Parliamentary accountability and "Democratic Deficits"', in H. Born and H. Hänggi (eds) *The 'Double Democratic Deficit': Parliamentary accountability and the use of force under international auspices*, Aldershot: Ashgate, 3–16.

Hansen, T. B. and Scholl, B. (2002) 'Europeanization and domestic parliamentary adaptation – A comparative analysis of the Bundestag and the House of Commons', *European Integration online Papers (EIoP)*, 6 (15). Online. Available at: http://eiop.or.at/eiop/texte/2002–015a.htm (accessed 16 October 2011).

Haroche, P. (2009) *L'Union européenne au milieu du gué*, Paris: Economica.

Hegeland, H. and Neuhold, C. (2002) 'Parliamentary participation in EU affairs in Austria, Finland and Sweden: Newcomers with different approaches', *European Integration online Papers (EIoP)*, 6 (10): 1–16.

Helly, D. (2009) 'EU Navfor Somalia', in G. Grevi, D. Helly and R. Keohane (eds) *European Security and Defence Policy: The first 10 years (1999–2009)*, Chaillot Papers, Paris: European Union Institute for Security Studies, 391–402.

Herranz-Surrallés, A. (2010) *Background Paper on the Involvement of the Spanish Parliament in the Atalanta Operation*, July, unpublished manuscript.

—— (2011) *The Contested 'Parlamentarisation' of EU Foreign and Security Policy: The role of the European Parliament after the Treaty of Lisbon*, PRIF Report No. 104, Frankfurt am Main: Peace Research Institute Frankfurt.

Hilger, M. (2008) 'An insider's view: perspectives for interparliamentary cooperation on European security policy', in D. Peters, W. Wagner and N. Deitelhoff (eds) *The Parliamentary Control of European Security Policy*, RECON Report No. 6, Oslo: ARENA, 133–44.

Hix, S. (2002) 'Parliamentary behavior with two principals: Preferences, parties, and voting in the European Parliament', *American Journal of Political Science*, 46 (3): 688–98.

—— (2006) 'Why the EU needs (Left-Right) Politics? Policy reform and accountability are impossible without it', Notre Europe, Policy Paper No. 19, 1–28. Online. Available at: http://www.notre-europe.eu/media/policypaper19-en.pdf?pdf=ok (accessed 4 July 2013).

Hix, S. and Lord, C. (1997) *Political Parties in the European Union*, New York, NY: St. Martin's Press.

Hix, S. and Marsh, M. (2007) 'Punishment or protest? Understanding European Parliament elections', *The Journal of Politics*, 69 (2): 495–510.

Hix, S., Noury, A. G. and Roland, G. (2007) *Democratic Politics in the European Parliament*, Cambridge: Cambridge University Press.

Hix, S. and Raunio, T. (2000) 'Backbenchers learn to fight back: European integration and parliamentary government', *West European Politics*, 23 (4): 142–68.

Hobolt, S. B., Spoon J. J. and Tilley J. (2008) 'A vote against Europe? Explaining defection at the 1999 and 2004 European Parliament elections', *British Journal of Political Science*, 39 (1): 93–115.

Hoetjes, B. J .S. (2001) 'The Parliament of the Netherlands and the European Union: early starter, slow mover', in A. Maurer and W. Wessels (eds) *National Parliaments on their Ways to Europe: Losers or latecomers*, Baden-Baden: Nomos, 337–58.

Holzhacker, R. (2005) 'The Power of opposition parliamentary party groups in European scrutiny', *Journal of Legislative Studies*, 11 (3/4): 428–45.

Hooghe, L. and Marks, G. (2001) *Multi-level Governance and European Integration*, Oxford: Rowman & Littlefield.

House of Commons (2008) 'Subsidiarity, national parliaments and the Lisbon Treaty'. Online. Available at: http://www.publications.parliament.uk/pa/cm200708/cmselect/cmeuleg/563/563.pdf (accesssed 4 July 2013).

—— (2010) 'Letter to the Commission', London, 13 October.

House of Commons Foreign Affairs Committee (2011) 'Future interparliamentary scrutiny of EU foreign, defence and security policy', London: Stationary Office, 12 January.

House of Lords (2008) 'EUROPOL: Coordinating the fight against serious and organised crimes', 29th Report, Session 2007–08.

—   (2010) 'Subsidiarity assessment: Admission of third-country nationals as seasonal workers', London, 13 October.

Houses of Oireachtas (2010) 'Oireachtas National Parliament Office'. Online. Available at: http://www.oireachtas.ie/viewdoc.asp?fn=/documents/committees30thdail/j-EuropeanAffairs/OirParlOffice/document1.htm (accessed 4 July 2013).

Hrbek, R. (2011) 'The role of national parliaments in the EU', in H. J. Blanke and S. Mangiameli (eds) *The European Union after Lisbon: Constitutional basis, economic order and external action*, Heidelberg: Springer Verlag, 129–57.

Hveem, H. (1998) 'Globalisering – retorikk og realiteter', *Samtiden*, 5/6: 36–46.

IPEX (2006) 'IPEX – a presentation', Fact Sheet Nr. 1, January.'. Online. Available at: http://www.ipex.eu/IPEXL-WEB/about/guidelines.do (accessed 5 July 2013).

Janowski, C. A. (2005) *Die nationalen Parlamente und ihre Europa-Gremien*, Baden-Baden: Nomos.

Jensen, T. and Winzen, T. (2012) 'Legislative negotiations in the European Parliament', *European Union Politics*, 13 (1): 118–49.

Jérôme, V. (2011) 'Mécanismes d'investiture et principe de légitimité chez Les Verts/Europe Ecologie: Du partisan au médiatique?', paper presented at the annual Congress of the French Association of Political Science, Strasbourg, September.

Joerges, C. (2000) '"Gutes Regieren" im Binnenmarkt', in C. Joerges and J. Falke (eds) *Das Ausschußwesen der Europäischen Union. Praxis der Risikoregulierung im Binnenmarkt und ihre rechtliche Verfassung*, Baden-Baden: Nomos, 349–81.

—   (2002) '"Deliberative supranationalism" - Two defences', *European Law Journal*, 8: 133–51.

—   (2006) 'Deliberative political processes revisited: What have we learned about the legitimacy of supranational decision-making?', *Journal of Common Market Studies*, 4 (4): 779–802.

Joerges, C. and Neyer, J. (1997) 'Transforming strategic interaction into deliberative problem-solving: European comitology in the foodstuffs sector', *Journal of European Public Policy*, 4 (4): 609–25.

Joint Study [Joint Study CEPS, EGMONT and EPC] (2007) 'The Treaty of Lisbon: Implementing the institutional innovations', Brussels, November. Online. Available at: http://www.ceps.eu/files/book/1554.pdf (accessed 4 July 2013).

Jun, U. and Kuper, E. (1997) 'Die parlamentarische Versammlung der Westeuropäischen Union: Neuanfang oder Auflösung?', in U. Jun and E. Kuper (eds) *Nationales Interesse und integrative Politik in transnationalen parlamentarischen Versammlungen*, Opladen: Leske & Budrich, 149–76.

Jungar, A. C. (2010) 'The choice of parliamentary EU scrutiny mechanisms in the new member states', in B. Jacobsson (ed.) *The European Union and the Baltic States: Changing forms of governance*, New York: Routledge: 121–43.

Karlsson, C. (2001) *Democracy, Legitimacy and the European Union*, Uppsala: Acta Universitatis Upsaliensis.

Katz, R. and Mair, P. (1995) 'Changing models of party organization and party democracy: The emergence of the Cartel Party', *Party Politics*, 1 (1): 5–28.

Kauppi, N. (1999) 'Power or subjection? French women politicians in the European Parliament', *The European Journal of Women's Studies*, 6: 329–40.

— (2005) *Democracy, social resources and political power in the European Union*, Manchester: Manchester University Press.

Kietz, D. and Maurer, A. (2007) 'The European Parliament in treaty reform: Predefining IGC's through interinstitutional agreements', *European Law Journal*, 13 (1): 20–46.

Kiiver, P. (2006a) *National and Regional Parliaments in the European Constitutional Order*, Groningen: Europa Law Publishing.

— (2006b) *The National Parliaments in the European Union: A critical view on EU constitution-building*, The Hague: Kluwer Law International.

— (2007) 'European scrutiny in national parliaments: Individual efforts in the collective interest', in J. O'Brennan and T. Raunio (eds) *National Parliaments within the Enlarged European Union*, Abingdon: Routledge, 66–78.

— (2008) 'The Treaty of Lisbon, the national parliaments and the principle of subsidiarity', *Maastricht Journal of European and Comparative Law*, 15: 77–83.

King, A. (1976) 'Modes of executive-legislative relations: Great Britain, France, and West Germany', *Legislative Studies Quarterly*, 1 (1): 11–36.

Kissling, C. (2011) *The Legal and Political Status of International Parliamentary Institutions*, Background Paper No. 4, Berlin: Committee for a Democratic UN, January.

Kitschelt, H. (1986) 'Political opportunity structure and political protest: anti-nuclear movements in four democracies', *British Journal of Political Science*, 16 (1): 58–95.

Knutelská, V. (2011a) 'National Parliaments as new actors in the decision-making process at the European level', *Journal of Contemporary European Research*, 7 (3): 327–44.

— (2011b) 'Working practices winning out over formal rules: Parliamentary scrutiny of EU matters in the Czech Republic, Poland and Slovakia', *Perspectives on European Politics and Society*, 12 (3): 320–39.

Koenig-Archibugi, M. (2004) 'International governance as a new *raison d'état*? The case of the EU Common and Security Policy', *European Journal of International Relations*, 10 (2): 147–88.

Konstadinides, T. (2009) *Division of Powers in European Union Law: The delimitation of internal competences between the EU and the member states*, Alphen aan den Rijn: Kluwer.

Koopmans, R. and Erbe, J. (2004) 'Towards a European public sphere? Vertical and horizontal dimensions of Europeanized political communication', *Innovation: The European Journal of Social Science Research*, 17 (2): 97–118.

Kraft-Kasack, C. (2008) 'Transnational parliamentary assemblies: A remedy against the democratic deficit of international governance?', *West European Politics*, 31 (3): 534–57.

Krehbiel, K. (1991) *Information and Legislative Organisation*, Ann Arbor, MI: University of Michigan Press.

Kropp, S. (2010) 'German parliamentary party groups in Europeanised policymaking - Awakening from the sleep? Institutions and Heuristics as MPs' resources', *German Politics*, 19 (2): 123–47.

Kurtán, S. (2002) 'A "bécsi modell". Az osztrák parlament és az EU-csatlakozás', *Politikatudományi Szemle*, (3–4): 71–100.

Ladrech, R. (2007) 'National political parties and European governance: The consequences of "missing in action"', *West European Politics,* 30 (5): 946–60.

—   (2010), *Europeanization and National Politics*, London: Palgrave.

Langhelle, O. (ed. forthcoming) *International Trade Negotiations and Domestic Politics*, Abingdon: Routledge.

Larhant, M. (2005) *La coopération interparlementaire dans l'UE*, Policy Paper No. 16, Paris: Notre Europe Etudes & Recherches.

Latvian Parliament (2010) 'Letter to the Commission', Riga, 14 October.

Lazowski, A. (2006) 'The Polish Parliament and EU affairs', in J. O'Brennan and T. Raunio (eds) *National Parliaments within the Enlarged European Union*, Abingdon: Routledge, 204–19.

Leinen, J. (2010) 'Das Europäische Parlament und der Vertrag von Lissabon', in O. Leiße (ed.) *Die Europäische Union nach dem Vertrag von Lissabon*, Wiesbaden: VS Verlag für Sozialwissenschaften, 97–113.

Lieb, J. and Maurer, A. (2009) *Der Vertrag von Lissabon. Kurzkommentar*, 3rd edn, Diskussionspapier, Berlin: Stiftung Wissenschaft und Politik, April.

Lindberg, B. (2008) 'Are political parties controlling legislative decision-making in the European Parliament? The case of the Services Directive', *Journal of European Public Policy*, 15 (8): 1184–204.

Lodge, J. (1996) 'The European Parliament', in S. Andersen and K. Eliassen (eds) *The European Union: How democratic is it?*, London: Sage, 187–214.

Lord, C. (2004) *A Democratic Audit of the European Union*, Basingstoke: Palgrave.

—   (2011) 'Polecats, lions and foxes: Coasian bargaining theory and attempts to legitimate the Union as a constrained form of political power', *European Political Science Review,* 3 (1): 83–102.

Lord, C. and Harris, E. (2006) *Democracy in the New Europe,* Basingstoke: Palgrave Macmillan.

Lord, C. and Pollak, J. (2010) 'Representation and accountability: Communicating tubes?', *West European Politics,* 33 (5): 968–88.

—   (2012) 'Unequal representation: A comment on the ruling by the German Constitutional Court on the Lisbon Treaty', in T. Evas, U. Liebert and C. Lord (eds) *Multilayered Representation in the European Union: Parliaments, courts and the public sphere*, Baden-Baden: Nomos, 59–72.

Lord, C. and Tamvaki, D. (2012) 'The politics of justification? Applying the 'Discourse Quality Index' to the study of the European Parliament', *European Political Science Review*, 5 (1): 27–54.

Louis, J-V. (2008) 'The Lisbon Treaty: The Irish "No": National parliaments and the principle of subsidiarity – Legal options and practical limits', *European Constitutional Law Review*, 4 (3): 429–52.

Magnette, P. (1999) 'L'Union Européenne, Un régime semi-parlementaire', in P. Delwit, J. M. De Waele and P. Magnette (eds) *À quoi sert le Parlement européen?*, Bruxelles: Éditions Complexe.

Magone, J. (2007) 'The Southern European pattern of parliamentary scrutiny of EU legislation: Emulating the French model', in R. Holzhacker and E. Albaek (eds) *Democratic Governance and European Integration: Linking societal and state processes of democracy*, Cheltenham: Edgar Elgar, 229–48.

Mair, P. (2006) 'Party system change', in R. Katz and W. Crotty (eds) *Handbook of Party Politics*, Thousand Oaks, CA: Sage, 64–74.

—   'Political opposition and the European Union', *Government and Opposition*, 42 (1): 1–17.

Majone, G. (1996) 'The European Commission as Regulator' in G. Majone (ed.). *Regulating Europe*, London: Routledge, 61–79.

—   (2005) *Dilemmas of European Integration: The ambiguities and pitfalls of integration by stealth*, Oxford: Oxford University Press.

Manin, B. (1997) *The Principles of Representative Democracy*, Cambridge: Cambridge University Press.

Manning, B. (1977) 'The congress, the executive and intermestic affairs: Three proposals', *Foreign Affairs*, 55: 306–24.

Mansbridge, J. (2003) 'Rethinking representation', *American Political Science Review*, 97 (4): 515–27.

—   (2009) 'A "Selection Model" of political representation', *Journal of Political Philosophy*, 17 (4): 369–98.

March, J. G. and Olsen, J. P. (1989) *Rediscovering Institutions: The organizational basis of politics*, New York, NY: Free Press.

—   (1995) *Democratic Governance*, New York, NY: Free Press.

Mardell, M. (2006) 'Europe diary: Services Directive', *BBC News*, 14–16 February. Online. Available at: http://news.bbc.co.uk/2/hi/europe/4710578.stm (accessed 4 July 2013).

Marrel, G. and Payre, R. (2006) 'Des carrières au Parlement européen. Longévité des eurodéputés et institutionnalisation de l'arène parlementaire', *Politique européenne*, No.18: 69–104.

Marschall, S. (2005) *Transnationale Repräsentation in parlementarischen Versammlungen. Demokratie und Parlamentarismus jenseits des Nationalstaates,* Baden-Baden: Nomos.

— (2008) 'Transnational parliamentary assemblies and European security policy', in D. Peters, W. Wagner and N. Deitelhoff (eds) *The Parliamentary Control of European Security Policy,* RECON Report No. 6, Oslo: ARENA, 109–32.

Marsh, M. (1998) 'Testing the second-order election model after four European elections', *British Journal of Political Science,* 28 (4): 591–607.

Matarazzo, R. and Leone, J. (2011) 'Sleeping Beauty awakes: The Italian Parliament and the EU after the Lisbon Treaty', *The International Spectator,.* 46 (3): 129–44.

Mather, J. (2001) 'The European Parliament: A model of representative democracy?', *West European Politics,* 24 (1): 181–201.

Mattelaer, A. (2010) 'The CSDP mission planning process of the European Union: Innovations and shortfalls', in S. Vanhoonacker, H. Dijkstra and H. Maurer (eds) *Understanding the Role of Bureaucracy in the European Security and Defence Policy, European Integration online Papers (EIoP),* Special Issue, 1 (14): 1–18.

Mattson, I. and Strøm, K. (1995) 'Parliamentary committees', in H. Döring (ed.) *Parliaments and Majority Rule in Western Europe,* Frankfurt: Campus, 249–307.

Maurer, A. (2001) 'National parliaments after Amsterdam: Adaptation, re-calibration and Europeanisation by process', paper for the Working Group Meeting, XXIV COSAC, 8/9 April.

— (2002) *Parlamentarische Demokratie in der Europäischen Union. Der Beitrag des Europäischen Parlaments und der nationalen Parlamente,* Baden-Baden: Nomos.

— (2003) *Der Entwurf für Teil I der Verfassung zur Gründung der Europäischen Union,* Stiftung Wissenschaft und Politik, Berlin.

— (2008a) 'The European Parliament after Lisbon: Policy-making and control', paper presented to the Federal Trust Workshop: 'The European Parliament in an enlarged European Union: Beyond the Lisbon Treaty', 25 April, London. Online. Available at: http://www.eu-consent.net/ library/deliverables/D19.pdf (accessed 4 July 2013).

— (2008b) 'National parliaments in the architecture of Europe after the Constitutional Treaty', in G. Barrett (ed.) *National Parliaments and the European Union: The constitutional challenge for the Oireachtas and other member state legislatures,* Dublin: Clarus Press.

— (2009a) 'Mehrebenendemokratie und Mehrebenenparlamentarismus: Das Europäische Parlament und die nationalen Parlamente nach Lissabon', in S. Kadelbach (ed.) *Europäische Integration und parlamentarische Demokratie,* Baden-Baden: Nomos, 19–74.

— (2009b) 'European Parliament – Council-Commission relations in the field of the EU's External Relations and Common Foreign and Security Policy', Note, EP-DOC 2009/08/02/INTA-EXPO-INPO.

Maurer, A., Kietz, D. and Völkel, C. (2005) 'Interinstitutional agreements in the CFSP: Parliamentarisation through the backdoor', *European Foreign Affairs Review,* 10 (2): 175–95.

Maurer, A., Parkes, R. and Wagner, M. (2009) 'Explaining group membership in the European Parliament: The British Conservatives and the movement for European reform', *Journal of European Public Policy*, 15 (2): 246–62.

Maurer, A. and Wessels, W. (eds) (2001) *National Parliaments on their ways to Europe: Losers or latecomers?*, Baden-Baden: Nomos.

Mayer, N. and Perrineau, P. (1992) *Les comportements politiques*, Paris: Armand Colin.

Mény, Y. (2002) 'De la Démocratie en Europe: Old concepts, new challenges', *Journal of Common Market Studies*, 41 (1): 1–13.

Mérand, F. and Saurugger, S. (2010) 'Does European integration theory need sociology?', *Comparative European Politics*, 8 (1): 1–18.

Miklin, E. (2008) *Nationales Interesse oder individuelle Ideologie? Die Rolle des Links-Rechts-Schemas im EU-Ministerrat am Beispiel der Dienstleistungsrichtlinie*, unpublished thesis, Universität Wien.

—— (2009) 'Government positions on the EU Services Directive in the Council: National interests or individual ideological preferences?', *West European Politics*, 32 (5): 943–62.

Mill, J. S. (1972 [1861]) *Utilitarianism, On Liberty, and Considerations on Representative Government*, London: Dent.

Milner, H. V. (1997) *Interests, Institutions and Information: Domestic politics and international relations*, Princeton, NJ: Princeton University Press.

Monar, J. (2011) 'Justice and Home Affairs', *Journal of Common Market Studies*, 49 (Annual Review): 145–64.

Moravcsik, A. (1994) *Why European Community Strengthens the State: Domestic politics and international institutions*, Center for European Studies Working Paper, Series 52. Cambridge (Mass.), MA: Center for European Studies. Online. Available at: http://www.princeton.edu/~amoravcs/library/strengthen.pdf (accessed 18 July 2011).

—— (2002) 'In defence of the "Democratic Deficit": Reassessing legitimacy in the European Union', *Journal of Common Market Studies*, 40 (4): 603–24.

NATO Parliamentary Assembly (2009) 'The growing threat of piracy to regional and global security', 169 CDS 09 E rev. 1.

—— (2010) 'Maritime security: NATO and EU roles and co-ordination', 207 CDS 10 E bis.

Naurin, D. (2007) *Deliberation Behind Closed Doors: Transparency and lobbying in the European Union*, Colchester: ECPR Press.

Navarro, J. (2010) 'The creation and transformation of regional parliamentary assemblies: Lessons from the Pan-African Parliament', *The Journal of Legislative Studies*, 16 (2): 195–214.

Neuhold, C. and de Ruiter, R. (2010) 'Out of REACH? Parliamentary control of EU affairs in the Netherlands and the UK', *The Journal of Legislative Studies*, 16 (1): 57–72.

Neunreither, K. (1994) 'The democratic deficit of the European Union: Towards closer cooperation between the European Parliament and the national parliaments', *Government and Opposition*, 29 (3): 299–314.

— (2005) 'The European Parliament and national parliaments: conflict or cooperation?' *The Journal of Legislative Studies*, 11 (3–4): 466–489.

Newman, M. (1996) *Democracy, Sovereignty and the European Union*, London: C. Hurst.

Niesen, P. (2008) 'Deliberation ohne Demokratie? Zur Konstruktion von Legitimität jenseits des Nationalstaats', in R. Kreide and A. Niederberger (eds) *Transnationale Verrechtlichung. Nationale Demokratien im Kontext globaler Politik*, Frankfurt: Campus Verlag, 240–59.

Norris, P. (1999) 'Recruitment into the European Parliament', in R. Katz and B. Wessels (eds) *The European Parliament, National Parliaments, and European Integration*, New York, NY: Oxford University Press, 86–102.

Norris, P. and Franklin, M. (1997) 'Social representation', *European Journal of Political Research*, 32: 185–210.

Norton, P. (ed.) (1990) *Legislatures*, Oxford: Oxford University Press.

— (1993) *Does Parliament Matter?*, New York, NY: Prentice Hall.

— (1995) 'Conclusion: Addressing the democratic deficit', *The Journal of Legislative Studies*, 1 (3): 177–93.

O'Brennan, J. and Raunio, T. (eds) (2007a) *National Parliaments within the Enlarged European Union: From 'victims' of integration to competitive actors?*, Abingdon: Routledge.

— (2007b) 'Introduction: Deparliamentarization and European integration', in J. O'Brennan and T. Raunio (eds) *National Parliaments within the Enlarged European Union*, Abingdon: Routledge: 1–26.

Olsen, J. P. (1983) *Organized Democracy: Political Institutions in a Welfare State – the case of Norway*, Oslo: Universitetsforlaget.

Olson, D. M. and Ilonszki, G. (2011) 'Two decades of divergent post-Communist parliamentary development', *The Journal of Legislative Studies*, 17 (2): 234–55.

Packenham, R. A. (1990 [1970]) 'Legislatures and political development', in P. Norton (ed.) *Legislatures*, Oxford: Oxford University Press.

Pahre, R. (1997) 'Endogenous domestic institutions in two-level games and parliamentary oversight of the European Union', *Journal of Conflict Resolution*, 41 (1): 147–74.

Papadopoulos, Y. (2007) 'Problems of democratic accountability in network and multilevel governance', *European Law Journal*, 13(4): 469–86.

Pedersen, O. K. (2002) *EU i forvaltningen*, København: Jurist- og Økonomforbundets Forlag.

Peters, B. G. and J. Pierre (2004) 'Multi-level governance and democracy: A Faustian bargain?', in I. Bache and M. Flinders (eds) *Multi-level Governance*, Oxford: Oxford University Press, 75–89.

Peters, D. and Wagner, W. (2011) 'Between military efficiency and democratic legitimacy: Mapping parliamentary war powers in contemporary democracies', *Parliamentary Affairs*, 64 (1): 175–92.

Peters, D., Wagner, W. and Deitelhoff, N. (2008) 'Parliaments and European security policy: Mapping the parliamentary field', in D. Peters, W. Wagner and N. Deitelhoff (eds) *The Parliamentary Control of European Security Policy*, RECON Report No. 6, Oslo: ARENA, 3–27.

Peters, D., Wagner, W. and Glahn, C. (2011) *Parliamentary control of military missions: The case of the EU NAVFOR Atalanta*, RECON Online Working Paper 2011/24, Oslo: ARENA.

Piris, J-C. (2010) *The Lisbon Treaty: A legal and political analysis*, Cambridge: Cambridge University Press.

Pitkin, H. (1967) *The Concept of Representation*, Berkeley, CA: University of California Press.

Pítrova, L. and Coxová, M. (2007) 'Parliamentary control of EU decision-making in the Czech Republic', in O. Tans, C. Zoethout and J. Peters (eds) *National parliaments and European democracy. A bottom-up approach to European constitutionalism*, Groningen: Europa Law Publishing, 205–23.

Pogge, T. (2002) 'Self-constituting constituencies to enhance freedom, equality and participation in democratic procedures', *Theoria*, 49: 26–54.

Poguntke, T., Aylott, N., Carter, E., Ladrech, R. and Luther, K. R. (eds) (2007) *The Europeanization of National Political Parties: Power and organisational adaptation*, New York, NY: Routledge.

Poguntke, T. and Webb, P. (2005) *The Presidentialization of Politics: A comparative study of modern democracies*, Oxford: Oxford University Press.

Pollak, J. and Slominski, P. (2003) 'Influencing EU politics? The case of the Austrian Parliament', *Journal of Common Market Studies*, 41(4): 707–29.

— (2009) 'Zwischen De- und Reparlamentarisierung – Der österreichische Nationalrat und seine Mitwirkungsrechte in EU-Angelegenheiten', *Österreichische Zeitschrift für Politikwissenschaft*, 38 (2): 193–212.

Powell, W. and DiMaggio, P. (eds) (1991) *The New Institutionalism in Organizational Analysis,* Chicago, IL: University of Chicago Press.

Putnam, R. D. (1988) 'Diplomacy and domestic politics: the logic of two-level games', *International Organization*, 42 (3): 427–60.

Raunio, T. (2005) 'Holding governments accountable in European affairs: Explaining cross-national variation', *The Journal of Legislative Studies*, 11 (4): 319–42.

— (2007) 'National Legislatures in the EU Constitutional Treaty,' in J. O'Brennan and T. Raunio (eds) *National Parliaments within the Enlarged European Union*, Abingdon: Routledge.

— (2009) 'National parliaments and European integration: What we know and agenda for future research', *The Journal of Legislative Studies,* 15 (4): 317–34.

— (2010) *Destined for irrelevance? Subsidiarity control by national parliaments*, Europe Working Paper 36/2010, Madrid: Real Instituto Elcano.

—   (2011) 'The gatekeepers of European integration? The functions of national parliaments in the EU political system', *Journal of European Integration*, 33 (3): 303–21.

Raunio, T. and Hix, S. (2000) 'Backbenchers learn to fight back: European integration and parliamentary government', *West European Politics*, 23 (4): 142–68.

Rawls, J. (1993) *Political Liberalism*, New York, NY: Columbia University Press.

Rehfeld, A. (2005) *The Concept of Constituency: Political representation, democratic legitimacy and institutional design*, Cambridge: Cambridge University Press.

—   (2009) 'Representation rethought: On trustees, delegates, and gyroscopes in the study of political representation and democracy', *American Political Science Review*, 103 (2): 214–30.

Reif, K. (1984) 'National elections cycles and European elections', *Electoral Studies*, 3 (3): 244–55.

Reif, K. and Schmitt, H. (1980) 'Nine second-order national elections: A conceptual framework for the analysis of European election results', *European Journal of Political Research*, 8: 3–44.

Risse, T. (2000) 'Let's argue! Communicative action in world politics', *International Organization*, 54 (1): 1–39.

Risse, T. and van de Steeg, M. (2003), 'An emerging European public sphere? Empirical evidence and theoretical clarifications', paper presented at the international conference on 'The Europeanization of Public Spheres? Political Mobilisation, Public Communication, and the European Union', Berlin, 20–22 June.

Rittberger, B. (2005) *Building Europe's Parliament: Democratic representation beyond the nation-state*, Oxford: Oxford University Press.

—   (2006) '"No integration without representation!" European integration, parliamentary democracy, and two forgotten communities', *Journal of European Public Policy*, 13 (8): 1211–29.

Rizzuto, F. (2004) 'European integration and the French Parliament: From ineffectual watchdog to constitutional rehabilitation and an enhanced political role', *The Journal of Legislative Studies*, 10 (1): 123–49.

Rometsch, D. and Wessels, W. (1996) 'Conclusion: European Union and national institutions', in D. Rometsch and W. Wessels (eds) *The European Union and Member States: Towards institutional fusion?*, Manchester: Manchester University Press, 328–65.

Rommetvedt, H. (2003) *The Rise of the Norwegian Parliament*, London/Portland, OR: Frank Cass.

Rommetvedt, H., Zajc, D. and Langhelle, O. (2009) 'The internationalisation of national parliaments: The Norwegian *Storting* and the Slovene *Državni zbor*', *Politics in Central Europe*, 5 (1): 55–85.

Rosanvallon, P. (2008) *La Légitimité Démocratique: Impartialité, reflexivité, proximité*, Paris: Seuil.

Saalfeld, T. (2005) 'Deliberate delegation or abdication? Government backbenchers, ministers and European Union legislation', *The Journal of Legislative Studies*, 11 (3): 343–71.

Šabič, Z. (2008) 'Building democratic and responsible global governance: The role of international parliamentary institutions', *Parliamentary Affairs*, 61 (2): 255–71.

— (2010) 'Parliamentarians as international actors: Members of the US Congress and international parliamentary institutions', paper presented at the meeting of the International Studies Association in New Orleans, 17–20 February.

Sahlin-Andersson, K. (1996) 'Imitating by editing success: The construction of organizational fields and identities', in B. Czarniawska and G. Sevón, (eds) *Translating Organizational Change*, Berlin: De Gruyter, 69–92.

Sainteny, G. (1987) 'Les dirigeants écologistes et le champ politique', *Revue française de science politique*, 37 (1): 21–32.

— (1997) *Les Verts*, Paris: Presses Universitaires de France.

— (2000) *L'introuvable écologisme français*, Paris: Presses Universitaires de France.

Saurugger, S. (2008) 'Une sociologie de l'intégration européenne?', *Politique européenne*, 25: 5–22.

Savage, D. and Weale, A. (2009) 'Political representation and the normative logic of two-level games', *European Political Science Review*, 1 (1): 63–81.

Saward, M. (2006) 'The representative claim', *Contemporary Political Theory*, 5 (2): 297–318.

— (2010) *The Representative Claim*, Oxford: Oxford University Press.

Scarrow, S. E. (1997) 'Political career paths and the European Parliament', *Legislative Studies Quarterly*, 22: 253–62.

Scharpf, F. (1988) 'The Joint decision trap: Lessons from German federalism and European integration', *Public Administration*, 66 (3): 239–78.

— (1999) *Governing in Europe: Effective and democratic?*, Oxford: Oxford University Press.

— (2009) 'Legitimacy in the multilevel European polity', *European Political Science Review*, 1 (2): 173–204.

Schelling, T. C. (1973) *The Strategy of Conflict*, London, Oxford and New York, NY: Oxford University Press.

Schmidt, V. (2006) *Democracy in Europe. The EU and national polities*, Oxford: Oxford University Press.

— (2011) 'Can technocratic government be democratic?', *Telos*. Online. Available at: http://www.telos-eu.com/en/european-politics/can-technocratic-government-be-democratic.html (accessed 1 July 2013).

Schmitt, H. and Thomassen, J. (2000) 'Dynamic representation: The case of European integration', *European Union Politics*, 1 (3): 340–63.

Searle, J. (2010) *The Making of the Social World: The structure of human civilization*, Oxford: Oxford University Press.

Šefčovič, M. (2010) 'The new role of national parliaments under the Lisbon Treaty', Speech at the Real Instituto Elcano, Madrid, 22 October.

Seiler, D.-L. (2005) 'Partis politiques européens', in Y. Déloye (ed.) *Dictionnaire des élections européennes*, Paris: Economica, 536–42.

SER (2005) *Advisory Report. The directive on services in the internal market*, Advice No. 05/07, The Hague.

Shackleton, M. (2000) 'The politics of codecision', *Journal of Common Market Studies*, 38: 325–42.

Shemer-Kunz, Y. (2010) *Au-delà des élections nationales de second ordre: Les Verts français et les élections européennes de 2009*, unpublished Master's thesis, University of Strasbourg.

Slagter, T. H. (2009) 'National parliaments and the ECJ: A view from the Bundestag', *Journal of Common Market Studies*, 47 (1): 175–97.

Slaughter, A.-M. (2004) *A New World Order*, Princeton, NJ: Princeton University Press.

Sonnicksen, J. (2010) 'Die demokratischen Grundsätze', in A. Marchetti and C. Demesmay (eds) *Der Vertrag von Lissabon. Analyse und Bewertung*, Baden-Baden: Nomos, 143–60.

Sørensen, E. (2011) *Enhancing democracy through inter-demos governance networks*, Working Paper No. 51, Zürich: National Centre of Competence in Research (NCCR): 'Challenges to Democracy in the 21st Century'. Online. Available at: http://www.nccr-democracy.uzh.ch/publikationen/workingpaper/wp51 (accessed 17 August 2012).

Sprungk, C. (2010) 'Ever more or ever better scrutiny? Analysing the conditions of effective national parliamentary involvement in EU affairs', *European Integration online Papers (EIoP)*, 14(2).

Steiner, J., Bächtiger, A., Spörndli, M. and Steenbergen, M. (2004) *Deliberative Politics in Action: Analyzing parliamentary discourse*, Cambridge: Cambridge University Press.

Sutherland, P. *et al.* (2004) *The Future of the WTO: Addressing institutional challenges in the new millennium.* Report by the Consultative Board to the Director-General Supachai Panitcpakdi, Geneva: World Trade Organization. Online. Available at: http://www.wto.org/english/thewto_e/10anniv_e/future_wto_e.pdf (accessed 4 July 2013).

Szalay, K. (2005) *Scrutiny of EU Affairs in the National Parliaments of the New Member States*, Budapest: Magyar Országgyülés Európai Ügyek Bizottsága.

Tans, O., Zoethout, C. and Peters, J. (eds) (2007) *National Parliaments and European democracy: A bottom-up approach to European constitutionalism*, Groningen: Europa Law Publishing.

TCO/LO (2004) 'Proposed amendments to the Directive on Services', Stockholm: TCO/LO.

TEU (2008) 'Consolidated versions of the Treaty on European Union and the Treaty on the Functioning of the European Union', *Official Journal of the European Union*, 2008/C 115/01, 9 May.

Thym, D. (2006) 'Beyond Parliament's reach? The role of the European Parliament in the Common Foreign and Security Policy', *European Foreign Affairs Review*, 11 (1): 109–27.

Töller, A. E. (2010) 'Measuring and comparing the Europeanisation of national legislation: A research note', *Journal of Common Market Studies*, 48 (2): 417–44.

Trubowitz, P. (1998) *Defining the National Interest: Conflict and change in American foreign policy*, Chicago, IL: University of Chicago Press.

Tsebelis, G. (2006) 'The European Convention and the Rome and Brussels IGCs: a veto player's analysis' in T. König and S. Hug (eds) *Policy-making Processes and the European Constitution. A comparative study of member states and accession countries*, Abingdon: Routledge.

Urbinati, N. and Warren, M. (2008) 'The concept of representation in contemporary democratic theory', *Annual Review of Political Science*, 11: 387–412.

Vallance E. and Davies, E. (1986) *Women of Europe: Women MEPs and equality policy*, Cambridge: Cambridge University Press.

van den Burg, I. and Knottnerus, R. (2005) *De Bolkesteinbubble. Het Voorstel voor een Europese Dienstenrichtlijn: een omstreden erfenis,* Nederlandse Delegatie van de Sociaal-Democratische Fractie in het Europees Parlement/PvdA-Eurodelegatie, 03–2005.

van Eekelen, W. (2004) 'Decision-making in the Atlantic Alliance and its parliamentary dimension', in H. Born and H. Hänggi (eds) *The 'Double Democratic Deficit': Parliamentary accountability and the use of force under international auspices*, Aldershot: Ashgate, 111–30.

van Kessel, S. (2006) *Responsiveness to European Policy at the Domestic Level*, unpublished MSc thesis, Vrije Universiteit Amsterdam.

van Kessel, S. and Pelkmans, J. (2007) *Encapsulating Services in the 'polder': Processing the Bolkestein Directive in Dutch Politics*, The Hague: WRR Web publication No. 31. Online. Available at: http://www.wrr.nl/fileadmin/nl/publicaties/PDF-webpublicaties/Encapsulating_services_in_the_polder.pdf (accessed 4 July 2013).

Vauchez, A. (2008) 'Droit et politique', in C. Belot, P. Magnette and S. Saurugger (eds) *Science politique de l'Europe*, Paris: Economica: 53–80.

Verzichelli L. and Edinger, M. (2005) 'A critical juncture? The 2004 European elections and the making of a supranational elite', *The Journal of Legislative Studies,* 11: 254–74.

von Ondarza, N. (2010) 'Die Auflösung der WEU als Chance', SWP-Aktuell 61, Berlin: Stiftung Wissenschaft und Politik.

Wacquant, L. (1993) 'From ruling class to field of power: An interview with Pierre Bourdieu on La Noblesse d'État', *Theory, Culture and Society*, 10 (1): 19–44.

Wagner, A.-C. (1998) *Les nouvelles élites de la mondialisation, une immigration dorée en France*, Paris: PUF.

Wagner, W. (2006a) 'The democratic control of military power Europe', *Journal of European Public Policy*, 13(2): 200–16.

—— (2006b) *Parliamentary Control of Military Missions: Accounting for pluralism*, DCAF Occasional Paper No. 12, Geneva: Centre for the Democratic Control of Armed Forces (DCAF).

— (2010) *Die Demokratische Kontrolle Internationalisierter Sicherheitspolitik. Demokratiedefizite bei Militäreinsätzen und in der europäischen Politik innerer Sicherheit*, Baden-Baden: Nomos.

Wagner, W., Peters, D. and Glahn, C. (2010) *Parliamentary War Powers around the World, 1989–2004: A New Dataset*, DCAF Occasional Paper No. 22, Geneva: Geneva Center for the Democratic Control of Armed Forces (DCAF).

WBI (2001) *Governance: A participatory, action-oriented program*, World Bank Institute. Online. Available at: http://info.worldbank.org/etools/docs/library/205639/fy02_brief.pdf (accessed 4 July 2013).

Weale, A. (1999) *Democracy*, London: Macmillan.

Weber, A. (2009) 'EU naval operation in the Gulf of Aden (EU NAVFOR Atalanta): Problem unsolved, piracy increasing, causes remain', in M. Asseburg and R. Kempin (eds) *The EU as a Strategic Actor in the Realm of Security and Defence? A systematic assessment of ESDP missions and operations*, SWP-Studie RP 14, Berlin: Stiftung Wissenschaft und Politik, 70–83.

Weber, M. (1959) *Le savant et le politique*, Paris: Plon.

Weiler, J. (1997) 'Legitimacy and democracy of Union governance' in G. Edwards and A. Pijpers (eds) *The Politics of European Union Treaty Reform*, London: Pinter, 249–87.

Weiler, J., Haltern, U. and Mayer, F. C. (1995) 'European democracy and its critique', *West European Politics*, 18 (3): 4–39.

Wendler, F. (2012) 'Debating the European debt crisis', paper presented at the ECSA-Canada ninth biennial conference 'Europe in an Age of Austerity: Integration, Disintegration, or Stagnation?', Ottawa, 27–28 April.

Wessels, W. and Diedrichs, U. (1997) 'A new kind of legitimacy for a new kind of parliament: The evolution of the European Parliament', *European Integration online Papers (EIoP)*, 1 (6): 1–15.

Westlake, M. (1995) 'The European Parliament, the national parliaments and the 1996 intergovernmental conference', *Political Quarterly*, 66 (1): 59–73.

Wheare, K. (1967) *Legislatures*, Oxford: Oxford University Press.

Wincott, D. (1998) 'Does the European Union pervert democracy? Questions on democracy in new constitutionalist thought on the future of Europe', *European Law Journal*, 4 (4): 411–28.

Wolf, K. D. (1999) 'The new raison d'état as a problem for democracy in world society', *European Journal of International Relations*, 5 (3): 333–63.

Zahrnt, V. (2008) 'Domestic constituents and the formulation of WTO negotiating positions: what the delegates say', *World Trade Review*, 7 (2): 393–421.

Zehnpfund, O. and Rhomberg, A. (2009) *Parlamentarische Mitwirkung in Angelegenheiten der Europäischen Union in Dänemark, Frankreich, Österreich, Polen, Tschechien und im Vereinigten Königreich*, Berlin: Deutscher Bundestag.

Zilber, T. B. (2002) 'Institutionalization as an interplay between actions, meanings, and actors: The case of a rape crisis center in Israel', *Academy of Management Journal*, 45 (1): 234–54.

Zimmer, M. (2009) *Piraterie vor Somalia. Staatsverfall, Kriegsökonomie und die internationale Gemeinschaft*, HSFK-Standpunkt Nr. 6/2009, Frankfurt: Hessische Stiftung Friedens und Konfliktforschung.

Zimmermann, A. and Favell, A. (2011) 'Governmentality, political field or public sphere? Theoretical alternatives in the political sociology of the EU', *European Journal of Social Theory,* 14 (4): 489–515.

Zralá, M. (2005) 'Parliamentary scrutiny in the Czech Republic after accession to the European Union', in J. Dieringer, E. Györi, and A. Maurer (eds) *Europäische Entscheidungen Kontrollieren*, Dresden: Thelen, 181–7.

| list of interviewees

Interview number	Interviewee	Date	Place
Interview 1	Staff member CDU/CSU group, *Bundestag*	30.05.2006	Berlin
Interview 2	Member of SPD group, *Bundestag*	31.05.2006	Berlin
Interview 3	Member Left Party group, *Riksdagen*	15.11.2006	Stockholm
Interview 4	Member of Swedish Government and Social Democratic Party	16.11.2006	Stockholm
Interview 5	Member of SPÖ group, *Nationalrat*	07.07.2006	Vienna
Interview 6	Member of the ÖVP group, *Nationalrat*	12.06.2006	Vienna
Interview 7	Member of Green Party group, *Nationalrat*	31.05.2007	Vienna
Interview 8	Member of the Austrian Government	31.06.2007	Vienna
Interview 9	Green local official	16.04.2009	Strasbourg
Interview 10	MEP (France, Greens)	25.03.2009	Strasbourg
Interview 11	MEP (France, Greens)	02.05.2009	by telephone
Interview 12	Green local official	20.03.2009	Strasbourg
Interview 13	MP (France, Greens)	18.04.2009	Strasbourg
Interview 14	Green local official	19.03.2009	Strasbourg
Interview 15	MEP (France, Greens)	09.03.2010	Strasbourg
Interview 16	Campaign staff	16.11.2009	Strasbourg
Interview 17	Mr. Ed Lock, Representative of the House of Lords	01.01.2010	by telephone
Interview 18	Mr. Peter Juul Larsen, Representative of the Danish Parliament	October 2010	Brussels
Interview 19	Mr. Emilio De Capitani, Head of Unit LIBE Committee Secretariat	October 2010	Brussels
Interview 20	Lord Bowness, Member of the House of Lords European Affairs Committee	October 2010	London
Interview 21	Ms. Sophia In 't Veld MEP, Vice-Chair EP LIBE Committee	October 2010	by telephone
Interview 22	Mr. Díaz de Mera MEP, Member of the LIBE Committee	October 2010	Brussels
Interview 23	Ms. Beatrice Gianani, Representative of the Italian Senate	October 2010	Brussels
Interview 24	Ms. Loreta Raulinaitytè, Permanent Member COSAC Secretariat	October 2010	Brussels

| index